Regulation through Revelation

Information provision is increasingly being used as a regulatory tool. The U.S. Environmental Protection Agency's Toxics Release Inventory (TRI) program requires facilities that handle threshold amounts of specific chemicals to report yearly their releases and transfers of these toxic substances. The TRI data have become the yardstick by which regulators, investors, environmental organizations, and local community groups measure company environmental performance. This book tells the story of the TRI from its origin and implementation to its revision and retrenchment. The mix of case study and quantitative analysis shows how the TRI operates and how the information provided affects decisions in both the public and private sectors. The lessons drawn about the operation of information provision programs should be of interest to multiple audiences. They include analysts who care about environmental policy, researchers and policymakers interested in the use of information as a regulatory instrument, and students in political science, economics, public policy, and law interested in how regulations are actually made, enforced, and evaluated.

James T. Hamilton is Charles S. Sydnor Professor of Public Policy at Duke University, where he has taught since 1991, as well as a professor of economics and political science there. Professor Hamilton has written or coauthored six books, including *All the News That's Fit to Sell: How the Market Transforms Information into News* (2004). For his accomplishments in teaching and research, he has received awards such as the David N. Kershaw Award from the Association for Public Policy Analysis and Management (2001), the Kennedy School of Government's Goldsmith Book Prize from the Shorenstein Center (1999), and Trinity College's (Duke) Distinguished Teaching Award (1993). Professor Hamilton's scholarly publications reflect his interests in the economics of regulation, public choice/political economy, environmental policy, and the media.

Regulation through Revelation

The Origin, Politics, and Impacts of the
Toxics Release Inventory Program

JAMES T. HAMILTON

Duke University

CAMBRIDGE
UNIVERSITY PRESS

CAMBRIDGE UNIVERSITY PRESS
Cambridge, New York, Melbourne, Madrid, Cape Town, Singapore, São Paulo

Cambridge University Press
40 West 20th Street, New York, NY 10011-4211, USA

www.cambridge.org
Information on this title: www.cambridge.org/9780521855303

First published 2005

Printed in the United States of America

A catalog record for this publication is available from the British Library.

Library of Congress Cataloging in Publication Data

Hamilton, James, 1961–
Regulation through revelation : the origin, politics, and impacts of the Toxics Release
Inventory Program / James T. Hamilton.
p.   cm.
Includes bibliographical references and index.
ISBN 0-521-85530-6 (hardcover)
1. Toxics Release Inventory Program (U.S.)   2. Pollution – Government policy – United
States.   3. Hazardous wastes – Government policy – United States.   4. Environmental
policy – United States.   I. Title.
HC110.P55H36   2005
363.73′0973 – dc22   2005010717

ISBN-13   978-0-521-85530-3 hardback
ISBN-10   0-521-85530-6 hardback

For Jamie, a revelation in his own right

Contents

Acknowledgments

The operation of the Toxics Release Inventory shows how freely information can circulate in the Internet age. Analyzing this information provision program, however, could not be done for free. I would not have been able to write this book without the generous support of a Fellowship in Environmental Regulatory Implementation provided by Resources for the Future, a fellowship program funded by a grant from the Andrew W. Mellon Foundation. Suggestions from Scott Parris and Simina Calin of Cambridge University Press and advice from anonymous reviewers helped improve the manuscript. I also benefited greatly from discussions about information provision in environmental policy with Steven Balla, Cary Coglianese, Scott de Marchi, Dan Esty, Archon Fung, Shanti Gamper-Rabindran, Ted Gayer, Mary Graham, Howard Kunreuther, Francis Lynn, Molly Macauley, Paul Portney, David Roe, Peter Sand, Christopher Schroeder, David Spence, Mark Stephan, Kip Viscusi, David Weil, and Jonathan Wiener. John Brehm and I coauthored the work on detection-controlled estimation described in Chapter 3, and I valued his ready willingness when he taught at Duke to discuss statistical issues. I learned a great deal from policymakers, environmentalists, and industry officials who offered their perspectives on the TRI, including Maria Doa, John Dombrowski, Thomas Marvin, Paul Orum, Cody Rice, and Sam Sasnett. I appreciate very much the permission of the following journals to publish parts of research that appeared in previous publications: *American Journal of Political Science, Economic Inquiry, Journal of Environmental Economics and Management*, and *Journal of Risk and Uncertainty*. I am grateful for the expert research assistance of Kim Krzywy and Amy McKay. This book is dedicated to my son, Jamie, who generates and shares information with great glee.

Introduction

Searching for the real-life impacts of an environmental regulation can be hard. Industrial plants don't have signs on them that say, "Warning: (Costly) Environmental Regulations at Work." Neighborhood yards don't have placards that say, "Another (Statistical) Case of Cancer Avoided Here." Yet if a regulation improves environmental protection, plant decisions and neighborhood environments change. The overall impact of environmental policies consists of the aggregation of effects of particular regulations in particular places.

Consider the effects of one regulation – the U.S. Environmental Protection Agency's Toxics Release Inventory (TRI) program – in one place – Baton Rouge, Louisiana. Under the Emergency Planning and Community Right-to-Know Act of 1986, plants (primarily in manufacturing) with ten or more employees that produce or use quantities of toxic chemicals above a threshold must file reports with the EPA. For each of the nearly 650 chemicals covered in the TRI, a facility annually submits a report if it meets a chemical's reporting threshold. The TRI form tracks a plant's releases and transfers of a chemical broken down by where the toxic ends up: air, land, underground injection, surface water, public sewage, or off-site transfer (primarily to storage or disposal facilities). The form also contains information on facility management of production-related wastes and tracks pollution prevention activities at the site. Since the first release of TRI data in 1989 covering 1987 toxics data, the TRI has become a prime measure of a plant's or company's environmental performance. In the 1987 figures, Louisiana ranked third in the nation (behind California and Texas) in total TRI releases and transfers. The state's large number of chemical plants helped land six Louisiana parishes on the list

1

of top 25 counties in the nation with the largest sum of TRI releases and transfers, including the parish of East Baton Rouge.[1] If the operation of the TRI influences the releases of toxics, Baton Rouge may be a likely place to look for impacts.

For the 2001 reporting year, the 22 plants in East Baton Rouge that submitted TRI forms generated 9.8 million pounds of environmental releases and the 16 facilities in West Baton Rouge reported more than 900,000 pounds.[2] The Baton Rouge TRI forms chronicle the release of a range of chemicals, including hydrochloric acid, styrene, propylene, and nickel compounds. The facilities reporting are as diverse as the substances they emit. Edo Specialty Plastics (15,500 pounds of on-site releases; plastic pipe industry) is a yellow warehouse-style building just down the road from the Country Club of Louisiana, a development of half-million-dollar homes, and the estate of televangelist Jimmy Swaggart.[3] Westside Galvanizing Services (2,002 pounds of on-site releases, 946,653 pounds of total waste managed; metal coating and allied services industry) is a cluster of buildings at the end of a private drive. Heat and smoke are visible in the plant's large manufacturing shed, and noise marks the production process. Nearby neighbors include the West Baton Rouge Correctional Facility, a burned-out sugarcane field, and an ExxonMobil gas plant. Intercontinental Terminals (4,600 pounds of on-site releases, 334,200 pounds of waste managed; chemicals and allied products industry) is right next to the levee. The mix of huge stacks and pipes frames a view of the state capitol dome visible in the distance. Capitol Steel Inc (nickel compounds released; fabricated structural metal industry) is a cramped site of welding, noise, and truck traffic. The plant is on a busy street populated by deteriorating houses, small businesses with bars on the windows, and shops advertising participation in the WIC (Women, Infants, and Children) and Food Stamps poverty programs.

Although the TRI form requires a plant to list on-site and off-site releases of toxics and to provide the name and number of a public contact, nothing requires facilities to respond to questions about what goes on inside the plants. Of the Baton Rouge TRI plants I reached, just five public or technical contacts responded to questions, and only on the condition that I not reveal their names and employers.[4] A clear sample bias emerged, given that the facilities with the largest TRI figures refused to respond to questions. At the five plants where contacts were willing to talk about the TRI, most had one person responsible for filling out the forms. The time required ranged from a facility were a person spent one day to compile a single TRI form to a plant with ten forms filed, which took approximately 80 hours to complete. One facility sent data to an environmental consultant in another state to complete the report. Complaints about the TRI from those filling out the forms included the thresholds that triggered reporting and the incomplete guidance provided on lead reporting. When asked about the efficacy of the reporting requirements, they said the data had initially shocked managers when it first came out, that it allowed managers to follow what was going on at plants, and that Louisiana's Department of Environmental Quality did focus on lowering the states's TRI figures. As relatively small reporters, however, they said they received little public contact about their emissions. As one filer put it, "There are many bigger fish to fry in Louisiana."

At least three groups have used the TRI data extensively in Louisiana – environmental activists, regulators, and academics. Wilma Subra, a chemist living in New Iberia, Louisiana, won a MacArthur Fellowship for her work in helping communities deal with the impact of hazardous chemicals. Describing her work with TRI data, she notes:

I have used TRI in my work with citizens all over the world. I use the data to track trends in the releases and transfers. I also use the data to compare accidental releases and upset conditions. Where toxic monitoring of ambient air is performed, I use TRI to be sure the correct chemicals are being monitored. I teach the community members the importance of the TRI and how to use it. The EPA has performed mobile monitoring in fenceline communities. I use TRI to identify which facilities are releasing the chemicals detected. . . . The data has been one of the most important sources of information that has caused the facilities to change their behavior. After all it is self reported and the facilities must stand behind what the data represents.[5]

The state Department of Environmental Quality (DEQ) uses the data to monitor facility performance. Commenting on the TRI's impact, Delecia Lafrance of the DEQ observes:

As indicated in the decreasing trends over time since the inception of the TRI program, facilities have significantly reduced releases and become more aware of their annual release totals. By disclosing TRI information to the public, industries are more accountable to citizens and the environment. The public accessibility of TRI data has encouraged facilities to look at process alternatives, chemical substitutions, and alternative technology that generate less waste and/or decrease releases.[6]

Paul Templet, a professor at Louisiana State University, uses TRI data to write about environmental policy. Analyzing the operation of the TRI, he concludes:

I believe it has changed the local plants behavior both directly and indirectly. Directly by exposing the levels of releases causing plants to reduce releases. Indirectly, because people like me use it to point out how my state compares to others and publish the results. I was also Secretary of the Louisiana Dept. of Env. Quality and used the data to compile lists of the largest dischargers and to call for reductions. I also used it to condition the facility's tax subsidies.[7]

Writers for the Baton Rouge daily newspaper, *The Advocate*, also use the TRI in environmental coverage. A 2003 story in *The Advocate* triggered by the release of the 2001 TRI data quoted plant officials talking about their efforts to reduce releases. Overall, Louisiana TRI releases dropped from 154.5 million pounds in 2000 to 123 million pounds in 2001, prompting Mary Lee Orr of the Louisiana Environmental Action Network to observe, "I think that governments and industry are not only realizing that lost product [e.g., chemicals lost as pollution] is bad for business, it's bad for the community and bad for workers."[8] Mark Schleifstein, a staff writer for *The Times-Picayune* in New Orleans, frequently uses the TRI data in industry stories. Asked to comment on the impact of the data, he replied:

A back of envelope estimate is that the first years of the list caused about $5 billion in investment in chemical plants in Louisiana for "debottlenecking" and other process changes aimed at reducing emissions. A company owning several fertilizer plants spent $70 million reconstructing its waste piles to reduce its numbers. Shell Oil developed a recycling method for hydrochloric acid to drop its injection well numbers. At many chemical plants we visited for the 1989 series, executives told us that the key critics of their numbers were their boardrooms. Typical response when numbers came out, said several execs, was "Let me get this straight. You're allowing x million pounds of product go up in the air? water? underground?" Louisiana Department of Environmental Quality has had varied response to the data, depending on which governor has been in office. All have been aimed at publicizing the numbers and pointing out where they've fallen. During a four-year stretch under Gov. Buddy Roemer (88–92), the agency was more aggressive and used TRI as a tool to jawbone companies into more rapid emissions reductions. Louisiana Environmental Action Network, umbrella group representing more than 100 enviro orgs across the state, has used TRI data from time to time to target specific industries, types of waste disposal, etc. Ditto Greenpeace.[9]

When asked how well the TRI has worked, Schleifstein replied:

Based on the experience in Louisiana, it's been extremely successful. Emissions have dropped by 82 percent since 1987, although they've been pretty much level since 1995. Pretty good for a program that simply requires the publication of numbers.

Focusing on a single area, Baton Rouge, shows how the TRI affects people. For those filling out the forms at reporting facilities, the TRI's requirements can mean a day or week of their lives each year. For a small set of environmental activists or regulators, the TRI can help them achieve the goals of their careers – pollution prevention and reduction. If the scrutiny generated by the TRI results in fewer emissions of air carcinogens or lower releases of toxics into waterways, the TRI can (for a set of people who may never realize it) improve human health. This approach to analyzing the TRI misses a key set of questions, however – where did the TRI come from? How has it operated and changed over time?

This book answers those questions by telling the story of the TRI as a regulatory program. The creation of an information provision program may appear an unlikely event, given that the policy imposes costs concentrated on industries likely to oppose the measure and creates benefits diffused among a public unlikely to lobby actively for its creation. The chemical plant accident in Bhopal, India, in December 1984, however, generated public scrutiny of toxics use and production and emboldened a set of political entrepreneurs in the House and Senate to insert a reporting provision in a broader hazardous waste bill. The Emergency Planning and Community Right-to-Know Act of 1986 (EPCRA) established the initial set of chemicals, industries, and facilities that would have to provide the EPA with yearly reports on their toxic releases and transfers. The legislation also marked the first time that Congress required an agency to create a publicly accessible electronic database, which later become known as the Toxics Release Inventory. The first TRI figures, capturing toxics information from 1987, were released in 1989 with great fanfare. More than 19,000 facilities had submitted more than 74,000 reporting forms, which detailed 22.5 billion pounds of releases and transfers for the 320-plus chemicals then listed on the TRI.[10] The ensuing attention led companies to pledge reductions, environmentalists to use the data to press for change, and regulators to point to the TRI as evidence for the power of information. During the 1990s, the TRI expanded to include more chemicals and industries. By reporting year 2001, close to 25,000 facilities were submitting TRI forms, which by now contained data on releases and on the management of production-related waste. For the set of chemicals and industries continuously tracked from 1988 to 2001, total releases and transfers had dropped 54.5%.

The analysis in the book roughly follows a regulatory time line: votes to set up the program, early implementation of information provision, revisions to the program, assessments of the impact of the TRI, and broader lessons to be learned about regulatory implementation from the operation of the TRI. I use a wide range of methods in the book, including a statistical analysis of roll-call votes, a stock market event study, a detection-controlled estimation model of regulatory noncompliance, and qualitative analyses of the legislative, administrative, and judicial actions that defined the TRI. A common theme unites these analyses – the impact of information provision about pollution quantities depends strongly on the distribution of other types of information. The initial legislative votes to set up the TRI were influenced by the lack of information voters have about technical amendment votes in Congress. Firm compliance with the TRI in the early years of the program turned on another type of information, the knowledge that the program even existed and imposed reporting requirements. Company incentives to reduce pollutants depended on the degree that environmental information circulated to investors, who in turn bought/sold company shares depending on the release of TRI information. Attempts to reduce the impact of the program were unsuccessful when Republicans led a high-profile fight in Congress to reform risk regulation. But later attempts to scale back the program's reach were successful because they involved less-visible regulatory actions. Finally, concerns about the use of information by terrorists caused the government to reduce the availability of chemical release information. Overall, the evolution of the TRI shows how the presence or absence of information aside from the TRI figures affected the impact of the TRI data.

Chapter 1 shows that information provision as a policy tool generated opposition from its inception. The amendment adding toxics reporting to the Superfund reauthorization bill passed in the House in December 1985 by a vote of 212 to 211. The greater the amount of toxic releases and transfers in the congressional district that would be tracked in TRI, the more likely the legislator was to oppose the provision of information about pollution. The eventual text of EPCRA, which President Reagan signed in October 1986, specifically defined who would have to report and also outlined administrative procedures that would allow interest groups to petition the EPA to add or delete chemicals from reporting requirements. Chapter 2 describes the rulemaking that led to crafting of the TRI reporting form, which was published in February 1988. Firms had until July 1, 1988, to submit their reports on toxics releases and transfers in 1987. The EPA quickly fashioned a reporting program and collection mechanism, so that on June 19, 1989, the EPA was able to release the national TRI figures. The analysis in Chapter 2 shows that the information was news to at least two sets of people, investors and reporters. The release of the TRI data generated drops in stock market value for some of the reporting firms, though this was less likely for companies already known to have significant pollution problems. Reporters were also less likely to write about a firm's TRI releases if the company was in a pollution-intensive industry or had a track record of involvement at Superfund sites.

Chapter 3 chronicles the early years (1987–1992) of the TRI's operation. Two complaints about the initial TRI were that nearly a third of those who should have filed may not have submitted forms and that the scrutiny generated by the program focused on pounds of pollutants rather than risks. In Chapter 3, I analyze TRI nonreporting in Minnesota, which in 1991 launched an extensive program to find facilities that should have submitted 1990 TRI forms. The results show that a plant's failure to file a TRI form relates more to ignorance about reporting requirements than to evasion of the regulation. Though Minnesota added a substantial number of facilities to the TRI through its enforcement program, these facilities turned out to be relatively small polluters, so overall TRI totals for the state did not greatly increase. To explore the impact of risk on firms' toxic emissions, I examine reported changes at the plant level of the release of carcinogens into the air between 1988 and 1991. Controlling for the quantity of air toxics released in 1988, I find that plants whose emissions generated higher numbers of expected cancer cases did reduce their emissions more between 1988 and 1991. The nature of the community bearing the pollution risk also affected firm decisions. The higher the voter turnout in the area, a proxy for residents' likelihood of collective action, the greater the reductions in a plant's release of air carcinogens.[11]

Discussing the operation of "the TRI program" is a misnomer, because the scope and implementation of the TRI have changed frequently over time. In Chapter 4, I show how the reporting requirements and their impacts have shifted in reaction to EPA's formal rulemaking process, congressional activity, presidential politics, court decisions, and informal agency activity. Interest groups were able to use the administrative procedures spelled out in EPCRA to petition the EPA to add and delete chemicals from the TRI list. The course of the TRI changed even more with changes in policymakers. Under President Clinton, the EPA added 286 chemicals to the reporting list and required seven more industries to file reports. When Republicans gained control of the House and Senate in 1995, they tried (unsuccessfully) to reduce the scope of TRI reporting through regulatory reform proposals that never made it into law. Under President George W. Bush, the EPA shifted attention to ways to reduce the reporting burdens associated with the TRI. Throughout the program, the EPA also used informal actions, such as the creation of the 33/50 voluntary pollution program or creation of software that combined TRI data with risk measures, to focus attention on particular industry segments or facilities.

A common set of factors may influence the operation of regulatory programs: public opinion, media coverage, enforcement policy, and office politics. Chapter 5 explores these factors in the evolution of the TRI. The high level of public interest in toxics that helped generate EPCRA dissipated over time, even as the regulatory program it created lived on. Media coverage in the popular press focused on political battles, such as the 1995 attempts to pass regulatory reform legislation or the 1996 election year focus on the TRI in speeches by President Clinton. The trade press continued to cover the TRI when it fell out of public view, in part because rulemakings continued to generate disputes in the regulatory community. With the election of George W. Bush and Republican control of Congress, the direction of TRI policy changed. Budgets shrank, inspections dropped, and the focus of agency policy became how to reduce the reporting burden. Actions by the Office of Management and Budget (OMB) particularly directed the EPA's attention to lessening the costs to industry of reporting. The budget for the TRI program dropped 39% from FY 1997 to FY 2004. The agency was able to maintain operations in part through changes in technology, such as the development of the TRI-ME reporting software and development of the Internet-accessible Central Data Exchange for firms to submit their reports. These actions lowered costs to filers and reduced the transaction costs of data processing for the agency.

The academic research summarized in Chapter 6 demonstrates that the TRI changed decisions and debates. Quantitative studies show that the toxics information brought news to investors, reporters, and residents. Case studies reveal how the TRI alerted some managers to environmental releases they did not previously know about and led many to undertake actions to reduce their TRI figures. Environmentalists used the data to develop national reports, pressure firms for reductions, and press legislators for changes in environmental policy. Regulators used the data to target particular industries, firms, and plants for scrutiny and enforcement actions. The impact of the TRI on decisions made at a plant appeared to vary with the nature of the surrounding community, the characteristics of the parent company, the environmental laws in the state, and the enforcement of traditional command and control regulations. The existence of the TRI, coupled with advances in geographic information systems (GIS) technology, helped fuel environmental equity debates about the distribution of pollution exposure across demographic groups. The operation of the TRI also demonstrated the feasibility of using information provision as an environmental policy tool and encouraged the development in other countries of Pollutant Release and Transfer Registers (PRTRs).

Though the TRI requires plants to report their releases and transfers of toxic chemicals, much of what goes on inside these facilities remains unknown. What are the costs of producing the TRI data? What resources go into the changes in production process or pollution control aimed at reducing TRI figures? How accurate are firm estimates of releases? What fraction of reported reductions in TRI emissions are due to information provision versus other factors, such as variations in production or the enforcement of command and control regulations? Answering these questions would better establish the costs of the program and the chain of causation between information provision and altered decisionmaking. Though current research on the TRI shows the benefits of new information generated by the reporting requirements, more information and analysis are needed in the future to understand the net benefits of the program.

Chapter 7 concludes with lessons from the regulatory implementation of the TRI and lessons for regulatory implementation in other environmental programs. From many perspectives, the operation of the TRI is a successful story of policy innovation. The EPA was able to set up within a short period of time the first publicly accessible electronic database mandated by Congress. The TRI did provide individuals in the private and public sectors with new information about toxics. People did learn, their actions did change, and debates were altered by the existence of the TRI. The development of the Internet and diffusion of computers have both lowered the costs of reporting in the program and raised its benefits by raising accessibility.

The operation of a single regulatory program cannot define the overall success or failure of particular approaches to environmental regulation. Yet the story of the TRI does offer a series of lessons that may serve as hypotheses to be tested with other environmental policies. These lessons include the following. Perceived flaws in regulation emerge more from politics than from lack of foresight. The impact of regulations on the ground varies with changes in who occupies the White House and Congress. Administrative procedures, and judicial review, do allow interest groups another shot at influencing the course of regulatory policy. Ideas spread. Information provision can work. Intermediaries lower the costs to the public of public information. The impact of information is not uniform. Regulators learn over time. The following chapters illustrate these lessons through the story of the TRI.

ONE

Legislating an Incomplete Contract

Environmental regulations follow a long paper trail. They start life as a proposed bill in Congress, travel through committee hearings, generate floor debates, and emerge as a final bill passed by the House and Senate and signed by the President. The exact wording of the regulations comes later in a public rulemaking process, though the actual meaning and impact of the rules may depend on future court cases, agency guidance documents, and enforcement decisions by regulators. For the Toxics Release Inventory program, the path from law to regulation runs through an unlikely spot – the Union Carbide plant in Bhopal, India. On the night of December 2–3, 1984, a leak at the chemical plant generated clouds of methyl isocyanate that killed more than 2,000 people. Worldwide media attention generated debates over how to prevent such accidents and exposures. By the end of December 1984, four subcommittees in the U.S. House of Representatives were investigating Bhopal. In 1985, multiple bills were introduced to provide residents with information about what chemicals were used by plants in their neighborhoods.[1] Speakers frequently referred to Bhopal during debate, generating 82 references to the incident in the *Congressional Record* in 1985–1986. In 1986, Congress finally passed the Emergency Planning and Community Right-to-Know Act (EPCRA), whose implementation gave rise to the regulatory program known as the Toxics Release Inventory program. In this chapter, I examine how theories of regulation help explain the politics behind the passage of EPCRA, the design of its legislative language, and the rationales for mandating information provision about pollution.

The political economy of EPCRA demonstrates the impact of information on delegated decisionmaking. Environmental regulations, like other forms of government rules, depend on a series of delegated decisions. Voters delegate to Congress members the power to write laws that control pollution, though the likely ignorance of voters about the activities of their representatives may influence the degree to which Congress members respond to their constituents. Congress members delegate decisions over the exact wording of environmental regulations to agencies, in which hidden actions by regulators and hidden information may allow bureaucrats to pursue their own agendas. Information provision programs such as the TRI delegate the generation and reporting of information to firms, though the latitude involved in estimating pollution figures leaves companies discretion in developing their toxic emission reports. The origin, implementation, and overall impact of the TRI ultimately depend on how information is distributed among voters, policymakers, firms, and interest groups. This chapter analyzes how voter information affected the passage of EPCRA, how concerns about delegated decisionmaking were reflected in the text of the legislation, and theories of how and why the TRI might work (though these theories were not a significant part of the debate over the creation of the program).

Choosing Instruments to Control Pollution

Governments may choose from a wide variety of policy instruments to control pollution, including tax and subsidy schemes, marketable permits, information provision programs, liability systems with well-defined property rights, and command and control selection of emission standards or technologies. Economists throughout the 1980s devoted significant effort to modeling the relative merits of these instruments. The question of why politicians would prefer one manner of controlling pollution over another also attracted attention, starting with Buchanan and Tullock's (1975) positive theory of externality control, in which polluters find direct regulatory controls on emissions more profitable than pollution taxes. Theories of instrument selection have been developed in which politicians choose policies based on the relative costs and benefits to shareholders, workers, and environmentalists; are affected by the constraints imposed by political institutions; and are driven to select the most efficient policy instrument to achieve a given level of redistribution.[2] There have been few empirical tests, however, of what drives instrument selection in environmental policy.

There is a large empirical literature devoted to explaining the level of support for environmental programs in Congress. Most articles focus on the degree that a legislator's stand on a given environmental bill can be explained by narrow district interests (generally the material interests of constituents) or by ideology (either constituents' or the member's own policy preferences). Studies of voting on environmental legislation by Ackerman and Hassler (1981), Crandall (1983), Pashigian (1985), and Yandle (1989) offer evidence that legislators' actions are in part explained by the district- or state-level impacts of proposed legislation on their constituents. Kalt and Zupan (1984) find that, controlling for constituents' material self-interest in proposed strip mining legislation, the ideology of constituents and the personal ideologies of their representatives influence voting on this aspect of environmental preservation. As Grier (1993) demonstrates, debate over the general role of legislator-specific ideology in voting continues. In studying votes in the House and Senate on the proposed size of the Superfund during debate over the program's renewal, Hird (1993, p. 333) concludes that "congressional voting on Superfund is found to represent legislator's environmental and liberal ideologies as much as (if not more than) narrowly-defined self-interest." He links the importance of ideology to voting on Superfund in part to the bill's symbolic environmental appeal.

In environmental legislation, the final impact of a bill on industry and the environment often depends on issues resolved through technical amendments. Downs's theory (1957) of rational ignorance holds that citizens do not seek out detailed information on public policy because their votes individually have such a small probability of affecting political outcomes. Arnold (1990) notes the additional complication that constituents often face difficulties in linking up congressional actions with real-world outcomes. Both theories predict that Congress members may be less constrained by general constituent interests on amendment votes because these votes are less likely than final legislative votes to be covered in the media. As Denzau and Munger (1986) and Grier and Munger (1991) note, groups with specific interests, such as affected industries, may find it less costly to persuade a Congress member to vote their way on a measure if the representative's constituents are supportive or indifferent to the measure. In the case of technical amendments, affected parties may be more influential than on highly visible votes because the lack of media coverage translates into a lower probability that the vote will become a major campaign issue in future elections. This implies that voting on the instruments to control pollution will be driven in part by the specific district-level costs and benefits of these measures, whereas voting on the final passage of a bill will be more driven by general constituent interests.

The law (EPCRA) that created the Toxics Release Inventory program actually passed as part of Superfund reform legislation in 1986. In this chapter, I use votes from the debate in the U.S. House of Representatives in 1985 over the reauthorization of the Superfund program to answer two related questions that emerge from theories of rational political ignorance: what factors influence politicians' support for different instruments to control pollution, and how do the interests that Congress members take into account vary with the anticipated degree of scrutiny of their actions? Superfund voting offers a natural test of hypotheses about what drives the selection of policy instruments in environmental programs, for during the debate over reauthorization House members were presented with votes on amendments that explicitly asked them to adopt particular instruments. House members were given the chance to vote for Coasian policies relating to the provision of information about toxic emissions by polluting facilities and the ability of facility neighbors to sue in federal courts for personal injuries arising from toxic exposure. Representatives were also given the Pigouvian option of levying a targeted tax on chemical and petroleum producers to fund the program or of relying on a broader-based tax to fund the program.[3]

Analysis of the votes on these amendments and final authorization also reveals a set of legislators who voted against the environmental position on all amendments and yet voted for the final bill. Because the amendment to provide toxic release information was voted on twice, the data also provide information on legislators who change positions after more attention is focused on a particular issue. These votes thus allow one to explore how legislator positions vary with the degree of scrutiny anticipated for a vote.

The results indicate that legislator votes on policy instruments to control pollution are affected by the district-level incidence of the costs and benefits of these particular measures. These factors are less important in passage of the final bill, a symbolic vote influenced more strongly by the broader electoral constituency of a representative. In making contributions to Congress members, the PACs representing the affected chemical and petroleum industries appear to contribute more on the basis of a legislator's stand on contested technical amendments than on a representative's general environmental position or vote on the final passage of the bill. This provides further evidence of the role that business interests may play in the selection of instruments to control pollution.

Legislating Superfund

The original "Superfund" legislation passed in 1980 established a $1.6 billion fund to clean up contaminated hazardous waste sites. Debate over the program's reauthorization continued throughout 1984 and 1985 as legislators tried to address a number of questions. How large should the cleanup fund be? Who should pay for the cleanups? How many sites should be cleaned up, and how quickly? Should victims be able to sue for damages? In December 1985, the House voted on a series of Superfund amendments on whether to adopt particular instruments to control pollution. Two of the instruments, liability for toxic torts and targeted taxes on chemicals, affected both the cleanup of past waste and firm incentives for future waste handling. The third policy, information provision about pollution levels, created incentives to deter the future generation of waste.

The notion of requiring plants to report their toxic emissions to the public proved so controversial that it generated two votes. On December 5, 1985, the House passed by 183 to 166 an amendment by Rep. Bob Edgar (D-Pa.) that required facilities to make public their releases of substances suspected of causing cancer, birth defects, and other chronic health problems. This tightened the public reporting provision already in the bill, which required companies to report releases of acutely toxic substances. Because the vote occurred at 11 PM, when many members were absent, the amendment's opponents hoped that the more stringent reporting requirements could be killed through another vote. In subsequent days, there was significant lobbying by industry groups and the EPA against the expanded reporting provisions and activity by environmentalists who stressed the benefits of providing residents with information on polluting facilities. Edgar's right-to-know amendment survived another vote on December 10, 1985, by a margin of 212 to 211.

House members faced the opportunity to strengthen the incentives for firms to handle wastes properly in the future in a proposal offered by Rep. Barney Frank (D-Mass.). Frank's amendment would have given citizens the right to use federal courts to sue companies for damages and injuries arising from the release of toxic substances. Though many states allowed such toxic tort suits, this amendment permitted individuals to bypass obstacles to bringing these suits in state courts by explicitly allowing suits in federal courts for injuries and damages discovered after the passage of the bill. Although environmental groups supported this expansion of the liability system, insurance companies, polluters, and the Reagan administration opposed it. The measure failed by a vote on December 10 of 162 to 261.

The House also faced the choice of how to fund the Superfund program. The initial fund depended on a tax on oil and chemical feedstocks estimated at $1.38 billion, with the rest of the $1.6 billion fund coming from general revenues. The Ways and Means Committee reported an amendment to the reauthorization bill that would have raised $4.5 billion from a new broad tax, $1.5 billion from a chemical tax, $1 billion from a petroleum tax, $1.6 billion from a tax on hazardous waste disposal, $180 million from general revenues, and money from other sources for a total of $10 billion in funding. Rep. Thomas Downey (D-N.Y.) offered an amendment that depended on raising $10 billion in funding through higher taxes targeted at polluters: $3.1 billion from petroleum, $2.1 billion from chemicals, $2 billion from a tax on hazardous waste disposal, $1.6 billion from general revenues, and the remaining funds from other sources. Votes on funding were structured so that if the Downey amendment failed, the Ways and Means amendment would have won by default, thereby providing House members with the opportunity to adopt a broad tax without explicitly voting for it. Downey put together a coalition for his targeted tax that included environmentalists and nonpetrochemical businesses to counter the lobbying efforts of oil and chemical firms. The Downey amendment was adopted by a vote of 220 to 206.

After a series of votes on these and other amendments, the House passed the Superfund reauthorization bill on December 10, 1985, by a vote of 391 to 33. Disagreements among House and Senate conferees kept both chambers from voting on the final version of the bill for many months. The revised conference version of the bill cleared the House by a vote of 386 to 27 on October 8, 1986, and was signed into law by President Reagan, despite earlier threats of a pocket veto.[4]

The amendments examined in the Superfund reauthorization debate allow one to ask the question, controlling for a legislator's support for environmental programs, of what influences the selection of specific policy instruments.[5] The factors that determine a legislator's vote on policy instruments may differ from those that influence her position on support for the bill overall, in part because of the rational ignorance of constituents about the details of legislation and the legislative process noted by Downs (1957) and Denzau and Munger (1986). Votes on instrument selection generally come through amendments whose technical details are unlikely to generate much media attention in a legislator's district. As Arnold (1990) points out, a legislator may take into account the potential preferences voters in a district might have if they became informed about the details of the amendment because the possibility exists that a challenger or an interest group may raise the issue in a future campaign. The relative ignorance of constituents about the details of amendment votes, however, means that the interests of those particularly affected by the amendment may be more important in the legislator's vote on policy instruments. A vote on final passage of a bill may be more likely to attract attention in the broader electorate, however, so that the impact of general constituents' preferences will be increased relative to that of the parties who influence the legislator on the amendment votes.[6]

A representative may consider at least three separate sets of parties when considering how to vote. When voting on final passage of the bill, the legislator may be most concerned with how his broad electoral constituency may view the bill. Their preferences will also be a constraint in voting on technical amendments, but the legislator here will be more likely to consider the interests of particular parties in the district that are helped or hurt by these policy instruments. The influence of particular parties affected by policy instruments may be more important on technical amendments because they are more likely to monitor behavior on these measures and because it is the technical amendments that may settle the details that have a significant impact on these groups. The preferences of the contributors inside and outside the district may also influence the representative on amendments that are not highly visible to other constituents.

The assertion that voting on final passage will involve different incentives than voting on amendments depends in part on the assumption that amendment votes receive less media coverage. For the Superfund votes, this is clearly the case. If one examines articles on Superfund that appear in the Lexis general interest publication file within ten days before or after a vote, there were in these windows surrounding votes 31 articles for the amendment votes on December 5, 1985, 42 articles for the passage of the full bill on December 10, 1985, and 63 articles in the window surrounding the final Superfund authorization vote on October 8, 1986.[7] In terms of the flow of information in general publications, the final passage in 1986 garnered nearly twice the coverage of the amendment votes. There was a different pattern within the specialized publications read by business and environmental lobbyists. In three Bureau of National Affairs publications that track environmental policy developments for professionals, coverage of the technical amendments (30 articles in these publications in windows surrounding amendment votes) was nearly as large as coverage surrounding the final passage (35 articles). Thus for the general public, articles about final passage greatly outnumber voting on technical amendments, whereas in publications for the regulatory community, coverage of both types of votes is about equal.[8]

According to this model of the impact of constituent information on congressional voting, a legislator will consider the preferences of her broad electoral constituency when casting the vote on final passage of the Superfund reauthorization because the measure will be viewed as symbolic of (and even synonymous with) support for the environment. One measure of constituent ideology included in the models is the percentage of the vote for Reagan in the 1984 elections, because the more conservative the electorate in the district, the more it may pay for a legislator to take an antienvironmental stand on issues. The degree to which a legislator exhibits support for environmental issues in general will also influence her vote on a highly publicized issue such as Superfund reauthorization. The legislator's League of Conservation Voters scorecard captures her "brand name" identification with environmentalism, though whether the member casts these votes because of her constituents' ideology or her own ideology is left open to interpretation here. Environmental group membership per 1,000 residents in the state is also included to reflect the ideology of voters in a district, because it measures the relative number of people who place enough of a use, existence, or bequest value on the environment to join these groups. Party is also included to control for a legislator's broader ideology.

On the final vote on passage of the bill, one would thus expect a legislator to take into account the preferences of the broad electorate in her district. The more conservative a member's district, the lower a member's general support for environmental programs. The lower membership rates in environmental groups in the state, the less likely the member would be to vote for Superfund passage. Republicans would also be expected to be less likely to vote for the bill. Representatives with more sites listed or proposed for the National Priorities List of sites qualifying for cleanup funds would also be more likely to vote for final passage, because the listing of sites would create attentive publics in the affected communities.

These forces also influence a legislator's vote on policy instruments to control pollution. In voting on amendments, however, the concentration of the costs and benefits of particular instruments to control pollution will also determine which groups directly affected by the legislation will influence voting on instrument selection.

The district-level costs and benefits of the pollution instruments varied by amendment. Consider the Edgar amendment, which required facilities to report their releases and transfers of chemicals with acute and chronic effects. Proponents argued that information provision by itself could serve as an instrument to control pollution because firms would reduce emissions to avoid public and regulator scrutiny generated by the public reporting of their pollution figures in the Toxics Release Inventory

(TRI). This amendment imposed costs on polluters in terms of gathering data, reporting information to the EPA, and reducing emissions because of the pressure generated by greater public scrutiny.[9] The more pollution in the district, the higher the expected costs for manufacturers and hence the more likely they would be to lobby legislators. Representatives from more polluted districts might be less likely to vote for disclosure because of the cost imposed on industry. Note that disclosure could also lead to risk reductions for residents in polluted districts because information provision could lead to reduced emissions and transfers. Because costs to polluters are concentrated (there were an average of 53 facilities per congressional district that would end up reporting under the TRI in 1987) and the benefits are dispersed across the residents of the district, one might expect that higher toxic emissions in a district would make a representative less likely to support the creation of the Toxics Release Inventory.

Some residents of the district might be more likely to identify with the benefits of the TRI, such as neighbors around Superfund National Priorities List (NPL) sites (where uncertainty about chemical exposures often exists) or communities surrounding the facilities of companies or other entities in the district listed as potentially responsible parties (PRPs) at Superfund sites.[10] The greater the number of these types of neighborhoods in a district, the more likely a legislator might vote for information provision by polluters.

Likely winners and losers in a district were also identifiable for the amendment by Rep. Frank that would allow individuals injured by hazardous substances to sue in federal courts. The higher the amount of current pollution generated in a district, the less likely a representative might be to vote for provisions that would raise the costs for industry of handling hazardous waste. The higher the number of NPL sites or firms or other entities listed as PRPs in a district, the greater the potential that some district residents would be concerned about personal injury suits arising from hazardous waste handling. For the third instrument considered, a tax targeted at petroleum, chemical feedstocks, and hazardous waste disposal, the higher the toxic pollution generated in the district, the more likely that firms in the area would be affected adversely by the proposal and hence the less likely the representative would be to vote for the targeted tax.

Hazardous waste sites with significant levels of contamination are placed by the EPA on the National Priorities List, which qualifies a site for the expenditure of federal remediation funds. Although there were 2 sites per congressional district listed by the EPA as final or proposed NPL sites in 1986, there were 57 sites per district in the EPA's Superfund tracking database (called CERCLIS) that did not meet this criterion. The overwhelming majority of these non-NPL sites had been investigated by the EPA, which had decided the sites did not merit inclusion on the list of sites qualifying for remediation funds. Some non-NPL sites were sites waiting in the evaluation pipeline, so they might eventually be listed as final sites. The number of non-NPL sites is included as a separate variable in the voting models. One might expect that the greater the number of non-NPL sites, the less likely a representative would be to vote for an amendment or final passage. On amendment voting, representatives might favor polluter interests over communities threatened by pollution at non-NPL sites because those exposed to these risks might not be as energized as constituents around NPL sites. Evidence from Kohlhase (1991) indicates that actual listing on the NPL does change reactions to hazardous waste sites, as indicated by the creation of a premium for houses farther from the site once it is listed on the NPL. On voting on the full bill, representatives might be less likely to vote for the Superfund if a greater number of non-NPL sites is a measure of the relative importance of polluters to employment in the district. Because there were 57 non-NPL sites versus 2 NPL sites per district, non-NPL sites may thus serve as a better proxy for general polluter interests in a district, whereas NPL sites reflect the number of communities highly attentive to risks from hazardous waste sites.

Petroleum and chemical firms faced higher costs under each of the policy instruments considered. They would be likely to generate pollution to report under the TRI, likely to be involved in suits involving personal injury from hazardous waste generation and disposal, and likely to pay significant fees under the targeted tax provisions. If one views the contributions of PACs from these firms as indicators that the companies believe the representative is sympathetic toward the interests of these firms, then higher PAC contributions from these firms should indicate that the legislator will be less likely to vote for policy instruments that impose higher costs on these industries. The coefficients on contributions do not capture the influence of contributions per se. Contributions are interpreted here as an indicator of the degree of support for the interests of oil and gas firms, which may arise from a number of reasons: a legislator's desire to represent oil and gas interests in the district, a representative's willingness to trade access or support for contributions, or a legislator's agreement on policy grounds with the position of the industry.[11]

Comparisons across voting on the amendments and final authorization (i.e., the 12/10/85 authorization vote) also will yield insights into which interests legislators are responsive to in their selection of policy instruments. Although there was a core group of legislators who voted against all three amendments, nearly all of them voted in favor of the final authorization. Among those who voted against the environmentalists' position on all amendments, one would expect those representatives to vote for the final bill and thereby demonstrate symbolic support for the environment if they came from more liberal districts or had a general "brand name" for environmentalism.

Differences in voting between the first vote on the Edgar TRI amendment, which took place at 11 PM on December 5, 1985, when not all representatives were present, and the second vote on the Edgar amendment five days later also provide evidence on how voting may differ with additional scrutiny. In the five-day interim between votes, a significant amount of lobbying took place in which parties potentially affected by the information provision legislation contacted legislators and made their concerns known. Legislators who switched positions between the first and second votes should thus be expected to make their decisions in part based on the interests of the parties affected by the costs of the additional reporting requirements.

This model of policy instrument selection predicts that interest groups should be more interested in legislator votes on amendments, in which significant dollar values are at stake and legislators face fewer constraints from district scrutiny, and less interested in legislator votes on the final authorization, in which the outcome is a foregone conclusion and the symbolic nature of the vote is important in conveying information to constituents. This would predict that if interest group contributions for the 1986 election cycle were examined, voting on the 1985 amendments should result in higher contributions for legislators, whereas voting on the reauthorization should have no impact on contribution patterns. This effect should be true controlling for whether the legislator was on the Ways and Means Committee or the Energy and Commerce Committee, two committees important to the drafting of the legislation. Because committee power matters to interest groups, representatives on these committees should be expected to garner higher PAC contributions from the oil and chemical industries.[12] The model of 1986 contributions also controls for a representative's general environmental record (1986 LCV scorecard). To isolate the marginal impacts of particular votes on contributions, I include 1984 PAC contributions from the relevant group of PACs (and whether the representative was an incumbent in 1984) so that one can examine, controlling for a legislator's general environmental record and past levels of industry support, how voting on particular measures influences 1986 contributions.

The limitations of these tests should be acknowledged. Votes on both amendments and final passage may involve strategic voting, such as log-rolling, in which Congress members trade support in one area for support in another.[13] Many important issues that affected the costs of Superfund cleanups never came to a vote in amendment form, such as the require-ment that the EPA give preference to permanent remedies in site cleanups and that site managers use environmental standards from state environ-mental programs if they were stricter than federal requirements. Many of these issues were resolved in committee rather than on the floor. Thus the absence of influence on amendment voting does not mean a particular interest did not influence a member's overall legislative effort, it simply may mean that the influence is not captured through the measure of floor votes.[14] One may also question whether these votes relate only to instru-ment selection, because in the liability and toxics reporting votes, the decision was structured as yes/no rather than a selection among different instruments. In addition, there is not a great deal of variation to explain in the vote on the full Superfund bill because the regression sample con-tains 389 members voting in favor and only 33 voting against. Though the results should be interpreted with these caveats, overall, the votes offer a good test of theories of instrument selection and rational ignorance.

The district-level incidence of the policy instruments considered during the Superfund debate is captured primarily through four variables: the total toxic releases and transfers in the district in 1987, the total number of final and proposed sites in the district on the National Priorities List, the total number of non-NPL sites in the district listed in EPA's database of hazardous waste sites (CERCLIS), and a count of the companies and other entities in the district listed by the EPA as a potentially responsi-ble party (PRP) at Superfund sites. Because each of these variables may relate to the magnitude of pollution in the district, they reflect the differ-ences across districts in both the relative costs of making waste cleanups or control more costly and the relative benefits to district residents of reduced risks from pollution. Thus the expected signs on these variables will vary depending on whether one believes more pollution in the district will lead a representative to be less likely to favor controls (i.e., the mem-ber is responsive to industry concerns) or more likely to favor controls (i.e., the member is responsive to environmental concerns).[15]

For each congressional district, total toxic releases to the air, land, and water and total off-site transfers to publicly owned treatment works and to off-site treatment and disposal facilities were calculated from the 1987 TRI data.[16] Facility zip codes were used to match the manufacturing plants reporting their pollution levels under the TRI program to congressional districts. A list of potentially responsible parties at Superfund sites was also matched through zip codes to congressional districts. The number of firms and other entities in the district listed as PRPs at Superfund sites represents a measure of potential interest by companies and other district organizations (e.g., local governments) in the liabilities arising from the program. Because PRPs also generate hazardous waste, however, their numbers can provide an additional variable measuring the risks posed by hazardous waste in the district (from residents' perspectives) and district interests in the costs of regulating future waste generation.[17] The total number of final and proposed sites on the National Priorities List, which are the sites that qualify for large expenditures of federal cleanup funds, measures the potential number of areas in the district concerned about the cleanup of past waste contamination.[18] The number of non-NPL sites per district may reflect the importance of polluting industries in the district and (for sites that have not been evaluated yet) the potential for even greater liability under Superfund. These two site measures have different expected signs because NPL communities should be more highly attuned to the risks of Superfund sites (which would lead representatives to vote in favor of more stringent pollution control), whereas residents surrounding non-NPL sites may be less cognizant of the program (which would lea. representatives to favor polluter interests rather than environmental concerns).

Support for environmentalism among constituents in a district is measured by statewide membership per 1,000 residents in the Sierra Club, Greenpeace, and the National Wildlife Federation. This captures people with use values for the environment as well as existence and bequest motives. The percentage vote for Reagan in the district in 1984 is used to capture constituents' ideology, on the belief that the more conservative the district residents, the higher the vote for Reagan in the 1984 election.

The 1986 League of Conservation Voters (LCV) scores for legislators' environmental votes in 1985 and 1986 are also included in the analysis (though votes relating to Superfund were removed from these totals). A legislator's scorecard on votes across a wide range of environmental issues may represent a number of influences: an attempt to represent the ideologies of constituents (who may be pro- or antienvironment); a reflection of the legislator's own ideological preferences, distinct from that of constituents; or an attempt to represent the economic interests of district constituents or "electoral constituents" such as campaign contributors.[19] This analysis does not attempt to disentangle the sources of a legislator's overall environmental voting record and the degree of slack in the principal-agent relationship between representatives and voters. Rather, the LCV scorecard here is used to control for the general level of environmentalism exhibited in the voting of a representative, so that one can ask the question, given a general level of support for environmental programs, what drives preferences over the types of instruments used to implement environmental programs. Party is also used as a measure of a legislator's general ideology, though again, the question is left open as to whether a representative's party affiliation represents the member's true preferences or simply represents brand-name signaling to constituents.

PAC contributions from 1984 and 1986 are also included in the analysis. The figures from 1984 are contributions reported to the Federal Election Commission by companies whose primary business was in the petroleum or chemical industry. The 1986 PAC data are broken down into three groups: contributions from the 11 companies estimated to pay 70% of the pre-1986 Superfund feedstock tax; companies whose primary business was in the petroleum or chemical industry; and companies whose primary or secondary business was in these industries.[20] In the regressions that include the 1984 PAC data, the coefficients on contributions are not meant to reflect the impact of money on voting decisions. PACs may give contributions to legislators who would support their positions without contributions in order to aid their reelection or to alter the positions of legislators. I am, rather, using the PAC funds to measure the degree that a legislator is generally sympathetic toward the interests of oil and chemical firms. The "elect friendly legislators" strategy would suggest a positive relationship between PAC contributions and general support for oil and chemical interests, whereas the "influence legislators" strategy would suggest a nonlinear relationship in which PAC contributions are highest for the median legislator in terms of support for oil and gas interests (a nonlinear relationship that is in part captured by the squared term for PAC contributions). The model of 1986 PAC contributions explores whether votes on technical amendments were rewarded more than votes on the final passage of the bill or positions on general environmental issues.

Analyzing the Amendment Votes

Rational voter ignorance about the details of policies implies that different factors should influence voting on technical amendments versus final passage of a bill. Because votes on amendments are less likely to receive coverage in the press and many voters may be less likely to have preferences over some of the issues involved, representatives will be more likely to consider the particular incidence within their districts and support from contributors in deciding which instruments to use to control pollution. In the final passage of the bill, however, the ideological interests of the broader electoral constituency will be more likely to influence a representative's vote because the decision is more likely to be covered in the media and viewed as a measure of support for the environment. The results in Tables 1.1 through 1.4 support these hypotheses.

Table 1.1 confirms that, controlling for legislators' general levels of support for environmentalism, representatives faced with the selection of different policy instruments to control pollution made their decisions in part based on the relative costs and benefits to their geographic and electoral constituencies. In the final vote on reauthorization of the Superfund, factors related to the ideology of the general electorate in a district and the interests of particular voters (as distinct from firms) in the district were the only variables that were statistically significant. The more liberal the voters in the district, and the stronger a legislator's general support for environmental programs, the more likely the representative was to vote for final passage of the bill. The vote was symbolic in the sense that constituents were likely to see it as an indicator of support for the environment. For nearly all legislators in the regression sample (389 of 422), it paid to register support for the final reauthorization. The greater the number of NPL sites, the more likely a representative was to vote for final passage, which may indicate a response to the communities likely to be highly attuned to the program. More non-NPL sites translated into a lower probability of voting for final passage, which could indicate a greater number of constituents associated with polluting industries in a district.[21] The variables associated with the firm-level incidence of the bill's benefits and costs, such as the amount of toxic releases and number of district PRPs, were not statistically significant. PAC contributions from the chemical and petroleum firms were not statistically significant, consistent with the theory that these firms would be more likely to care about the resolution of technical amendments than symbolic positions on a final bill destined to pass.

Table 1.1. *Determinants of Congressional Voting on Superfund Revisions, 1985*

Variable	Toxics Release Inventory (12/10/85)	Injury Liability	Targeted Tax	Superfund Reauthorization
Intercept	−.25	1.81	.16	9.91***
	(1.51)	(1.44)	(1.09)	(3.09)
Toxic releases and	−9.15e-9***	−8.16e-9**	−5.65e-9*	3.87e-10
transfers (lbs)	(3.7e-9)	(3.88e-9)	(3.15e-9)	(9e-10)
NPL final or	.12**	.03	.05	.33**
proposed sites	(.06)	(.06)	(.05)	(.16)
Non-NPL CERCLIS	.001	−.004	−.005	−.01**
sites (#)	(.004)	(.004)	(.003)	(.006)
Potentially	.002	.01***	.003	.002
responsible	(.005)	(.005)	(.004)	(.01)
parties (#)				
1984 PAC $ from	−.0002**	−.0003***	−.0002**	−2.21e-6
chemical and	(.0001)	(.0001)	(.00009)	(.0002)
petroleum firms				
1984 PAC ^{2} from	1.19e-8	1.45e-8*	4.06e-9	7.24e-9
chemical and	(7.3e-9)	(7.54e-9)	(6.94e-9)	(1.82e-9)
petroleum firms				
1984 vote for	−.07***	−.09***	−.03**	−.16***
Reagan (%)	(.02)	(.02)	(.01)	(.04)
Environmental group	.23***	.14***	.21***	.13
membership	(.06)	(.05)	(.05)	(.08)
(statewide, per				
1,000)				
1986 League of	.03***	.02***	.02***	.05***
Conservation	(.007)	(.007)	(.006)	(.02)
Voters score				
Democrat	1.67***	1.11***	−.23	.51
	(.39)	(.39)	(.33)	(.70)
Yes/No votes	211/210	161/260	220/204	389/33
LR test (chi-square)	269.66	239.04	136.70	89.68

Note: Dependent variable in the logit = 1 if the House member voted in favor of the measure. Standard errors are in parentheses. ***Statistically significant at .01 level; **significant at .05 level; *significant at .10 level.

In voting on amendments dealing with information provision, torts, and targeted taxes, representatives did take into account the ideologies of the general electorate in their districts. The vote for Reagan in the district, environmental group membership, and League of Conservation Voters scorecards were all statistically significant in explaining whether a legislator favored a particular instrument to control pollution. In voting on the instrument amendments, however, the incidence of benefits and costs in the district and among contributors became important determinants of support for particular instruments. The greater the amount of toxic releases and transfers in the district, the more likely the legislator was to oppose the provision of information about pollution. This is consistent with a representative taking into account the interests of polluters (who may be few in number and thus more easily mobilized) in the district over the interests of the many residents in the district potentially put at risk by the emissions of the firms. Most residents affected by the TRI releases may be unaware of their effects and thus unlikely to connect a vote on the amendment with toxic exposures. In districts with more Superfund NPL sites, however, residents surrounding these areas may be more likely to be concerned about information about hazards. This may explain why legislators were more likely to vote in favor of the release of the pollution data the higher the number of NPL sites in their districts.

On the Frank amendment to allow personal injury suits in federal courts for future exposure to hazardous substances, legislators again voted on this policy instrument in part based on its district-level incidence. The more toxic pollution generated in the district, the less likely a representative was to vote in favor of the measure. The greater the number of potentially responsible parties in the district, the more likely a legislator was to favor making the tort system easier to use. Because PRPs are often firms or entities that still generate hazardous waste, districts with more PRPs may be ones in which there are many neighborhoods concerned about injury from exposure to waste. This concentration of the benefits of the bill into a recognizable group may help explain why legislators from these districts were more likely to support using the tort system to control future pollution.

The higher the amount of toxic waste produced in a district, the less likely the representative was to vote for a tax targeted at petroleum, chemical feedstocks, and hazardous waste disposal. The larger the contributions in the 1984 elections from PACs of firms primarily in the oil and chemical industries, the less likely a legislator was to vote for a tax targeted at these industries. Higher contributions were also associated with lower support for the toxic tort and information provision amendments. These results indicate the more a legislator supported the interests of oil and gas firms, the less likely he was to favor any pollution control instrument here.[22]

In the regression sample, there were 133 representatives who voted against all three amendments. Yet 102 of these legislators ended up voting for final passage of the bill. Table 1.2 confirms that among legislators who voted against the environment on all three amendments, those with more liberal constituents were more likely to vote for the environmental position on the final authorization vote. Representatives from districts with more NPL sites were more likely to vote for the final bill. This underscores the importance of using the final vote to signal support for the environment to a legislators' broad constituency if that constituency tends to be liberal and to residents surrounding NPL sites.[23] If one simply looked at legislators who voted for the final authorization as "environmentalists," however, one would miss the gradations in support evident across the votes on policy instruments. Among those who voted yes on authorization, representatives who voted against the environmental position on all three amendments were more likely to come from districts with higher pollution, more conservative constituencies, and lower environmental group membership, and were more likely to be sympathetic to the interests of oil and gas contributors. Conversely, those legislators who voted for the environment on all three amendments also differed in terms of their district characteristics. They represented more liberal constituents, came from areas with more environmental group members per capita, were less likely to represent the interests of oil and gas contributors, were more likely to be Democrats, and were more likely to support general environmental measures.

Table 1.3 offers estimates of the impact of additional scrutiny on the behavior of legislators. After the TRI passed in an initial vote, opponents of the bill organized an intensive lobbying campaign against the information provision measure. Table 1.3 reveals how the additional scrutiny changed voting patterns on the bill. On the initial vote on the bill, the district-level incidence variables were not statistically significant. Legislators were more likely to favor information provision the more liberal their constituents, the higher their support for environmental measures in general, the greater the environmental group membership in their area, and the lower their support for oil and gas interests (as evidenced by lower contribution levels). After the lobbying campaign intensified scrutiny of legislators' positions on this issue, however, Table 1.1 indicates that in the second vote on December 10, 1985, the district-level incidence of the policy instrument also became a statistically significant factor in legislators' decisions. The greater the amount of toxins released in a district, the less likely representatives were to favor the collection and release of pollution information. The more Superfund NPL sites in the district, the more likely the representative was to favor the dissemination of information about pollution. Additional lobbying by interest groups

Table 1.2. *Determinants of the Difference between Legislators' Votes on Superfund Amendments and Their Votes on Reauthorization*

Variable	Among Those Who Voted No on All 3 Amendments, Voted Yes on Reauthorization?	Among Those Who Voted Yes on Reauthorization, Voted No on All 3 Amendments?	Among Those Who Voted Yes on Reauthorization, Voted Yes on All 3 Amendments?
Intercept	7.93**	−4.14**	−2.58**
	(3.37)	(1.82)	(1.30)
Toxic releases and	7.46e-10	1.07e-8***	−7.79e-9
transfers (lbs)	(1.44e-9)	(3.70e-9)	(5.03e-9)
NPL final or	.27*	−.11	−0.1
proposed sites (#)	(.16)	(.08)	(.07)
Non-NPL CERCLIS	−.01*	.003	−.0001
sites (#)	(.007)	(.004)	(.004)
Potentially	−.001	−.0005	.0007
responsible	(.01)	(.006)	(.005)
parties (#)			
1984 PAC $ from	.00003	.0003**	−.0003**
chemical and	(.0003)	(.0001)	(.0001)
petroleum firms			
1984 PAC ^{2} from	7.08e-9	−9.72e-9	9.74e-9
chemical and	(2.06e-8)	(8.10e-9)	(1.35e-8)
petroleum firms			
1984 vote for	−.12***	.09***	−.05***
Reagan (%)	(.04)	(.02)	(.01)
Environmental	.10	−.16***	.36***
group membership	(.08)	(.06)	(.06)
(statewide,			
per 1,000)			
1986 League of	.03	−.05***	.02***
Conservation	(.02)	(.009)	(.007)
Voters score			
Democrat	.68	.01	1.17***
	(.82)	(.43)	(.44)
Yes/No votes	102/31	102/287	117/272
LR test (chi-square)	32.35	174.28	189.45

Note: Dependent variable in the logit = 1 if the statement was true for the House member (i.e., yes = 1). Standard errors are in parentheses. ***Statistically significant at .01 level; **significant at .05 level; *significant at .10 level.

Table 1.3. *The Impact of Additional Scrutiny on Congressional Voting on the Toxics Release Inventory*

Variable	First Toxics Release Inventory Vote (12/5/85)	Among Those Who Voted Yes on the First TRI, Voted Yes on the Second TRI Vote?	Among Those Who Voted No on the First TRI, Voted Yes on the Second TRI Vote?
Intercept	.33	1.66	4.22
	(1.74)	(2.80)	(4.78)
Toxic releases and	−5.42e-9	−1.68e-8***	−1.06e-8
transfers (lbs)	(3.50e-9)	(6.66e-9)	(7.55e-9)
NPL final or	.05	−.02	.36*
proposed sites (#)	(.07)	(.18)	(.20)
Non-NPL CERCLIS	.00009	.01	−.03*
sites (#)	(.005)	(.01)	(.02)
Potentially	.006	−.004	.01
responsible	(.006)	(.01)	(.01)
parties (#)			
1984 PAC $ from	.0003***	−.0005***	.0003
chemical and	(.0001)	(.0003)	(.0003)
petroleum firms			
1984 PAC ^{2} from	1.13e-8	1.28e-8	−4.08e-9
chemical and	(8.28e-9)	(2.51e-8)	(1.46e-8)
petroleum firms			
1984 vote for Reagan	−.07***	−.01	−.15**
(%)	(.02)	(.03)	(.07)
Environmental group	.21***	.43***	−.18
membership	(.07)	(.14)	(.15)
(statewide, per			
1,000)			
1986 League of	.04***	.009	.03
Conservation	(.008)	(.02)	(.03)
Voters score			
Democrat	1.50***	−1.73	2.27*
	(.43)	(1.35)	(1.34)
Yes/No votes	183/165	164/17	12/151
LR test (chi-square)	231.05	40.29	34.97

Note: Dependent variable in the logit = 1 if the House member voted in favor of the measure. Standard errors are in parentheses. ***Statistically significant at .01 level; **significant at .05 level; *significant at .10 level.

and the potentially heightened interest of affected parties in the district caused legislators to take the district-level incidence of pollution into account.

Table 1.3 analyzes what led some legislators to change their position across the two votes. Among those who voted yes on the initial TRI vote, legislators were more likely to vote yes on the second vote on the amendment the lower the pollution level in the district and the higher the environmental group membership in the area. Representatives more sympathetic to the interests of chemical and oil firms were less likely to vote yes on the second TRI vote. Among those who voted against the TRI originally, representatives were more likely to vote yes on the second vote the greater the number of NPL sites in the district and the more liberal the constituents. They were less likely to vote yes the greater the number of non-NPL sites in the district. These patterns are consistent with a story in which additional lobbying and scrutiny led legislators from districts where residents were concerned about hazardous waste contamination or where constituents were generally liberal to find it in their interests to change their votes.

Table 1.4 explores the contribution patterns of PACs in more depth. If the vote on the Superfund reauthorization were viewed as largely symbolic, then one would not expect PACs to penalize legislators who voted for the bill. Votes on the policy instruments, however, would be worth more to firms because these votes involved specific amendments potentially worth billions of dollars to the industry and the detailed nature of the amendments left representatives some freedom to consider interests beyond those of the general electorate. The close votes on some of the amendments also mean that additional support by a representative would be more highly valued on these measures. If PACs in 1986 were attempting to elect legislators who had supported their interests in the past (or rewarding legislators who had voted their way on important issues), Table 1.4 indicates in part which votes were important in defining support for the industry. The specifications include the amount of PAC money contributed to the candidate in 1984 as a control for the general level of support by the industry for the candidate.[24] Three different aggregations of PACs are examined: PACs of the 11 chemical and petroleum firms estimated to bear 70% of the Superfund taxes (contributed in total an average of $2,040 per representative); PACs with chemical and petroleum businesses ($3,458 per representative); and PACs with primary or secondary interests in chemical and petroleum industries ($6,406 mean). Different samples are examined because the Superfund votes may mean relatively

Table 1.4. *Tobit Models of 1986 PAC Contributions*

Variable	11 Chemical and Petroleum Firm PACs	Chemical and Petroleum PACs, Primary Business	Chemical and Petroleum PACs, Primary or Secondary Business
Intercept	2760***	1060*	3682***
	(568)	(641)	(1090)
Voted for Toxics Release	−557*	−625	−1012
Inventory	(332)	(407)	(650)
Voted for injury liability	−332	385	283
	(330)	(313)	(635)
Voted for targeted tax	−1104***	−954***	−2098***
	(315)	(288)	(500)
Voted for Superfund	−35	381	530
reauthorization	(425)	(544)	(868)
Energy and Commerce	914***	1621***	2415***
Committee member	(364)	(471)	(754)
Ways and Means	1051***	2936***	3876***
Committee member	(400)	(501)	(798)
1986 League of	−7	−.4	−2
Conservation Voters	(6)	(7)	(11)
score			
Democrat	−314	169	60
	(301)	(369)	(601)
Incumbent in 1984	−1343***	−686	−1397***
	(356)	(436)	(696)
1984 PAC \$ from relevant	.7***	.8***	.7***
PACs	(.1)	(.1)	(.1)
Number of observations	379	379	379
Log likelihood	−2612	−3125	−3446

Note: Dependent variable is total PAC contributions (\$) to a House member from a given set of PACs for the 1986 election cycle. Standard errors are in parentheses. ***Statistically significant at .01 level; **significant at .05 level; *significant at .10 level.

more to the 11 companies bearing the majority of the taxes than to companies that have only a secondary interest in Superfund.

The vote on the reauthorization did not have a statistically significant impact on the amount of money received by a House member. For the 11 companies that paid 70% of the Superfund taxes under the original financing system, the vote on the targeted tax was central to defining support for the industry. A legislator who voted for the targeted tax (which entailed additional taxes of \$3.1 billion on petroleum, \$2.1 billion on chemicals, and $2 billion from a tax on hazardous waste disposal) received nearly $1,100 less in contributions from these firms. This is more than half the mean contribution per representative from these companies. These firms were also likely targets of the TRI reporting requirements. A legislator who voted for the TRI received nearly $560 less from these firms. Firms with primary or secondary interests in the chemical and petroleum industries were also likely to contribute less to a legislator who voted for the targeted tax. Contributions from these interests dropped by about a third for representatives who voted for the targeted tax.

The chemical and oil PACs gave much more to legislators on the committees relevant to chemical regulation and taxation, the Ways and Means Committee and the Energy and Commerce Committee. This is consistent with a pattern of giving to maintain access to legislators with a greater ability to influence the content of legislation, giving more to support legislators whose efforts have an important impact on industry legislation, or simply buying legislator effort in committee. For the oil and chemical PACs as a whole, the general environmental position of a legislator was not important in determining the amount of PAC money contributed. The League of Conservation Voters scorecard was not statistically significant in the contributions equations. Overall, these PACs gave support to legislators based on their performance on votes of interest to the industry and their legislative power on committees, not based on their general environmental stands or votes on symbolic issues.

The results indicate that the theory of rational political ignorance can help explain legislator preferences for policy instruments to control pollution. Controlling for a legislator's general support for environmental programs, a representative was likely to vote for specific policy instruments such as targeted taxes, toxic tort reform, or the Toxics Release Inventory in part based on the concentration of costs and benefits from these policies in his or her district. Legislators from districts with more toxic emissions faced a dilemma in trading off support within their districts, for the proposed policies often would increase the costs of polluting industries but reduce the risks to residents from exposure to hazardous chemicals. Perhaps because the costs to polluters were concentrated among a group likely to take action whereas the benefits of general toxics use reduction would be dispersed among constituents, legislators generally voted against environmental restrictions as toxic emissions increased in a district. As the number of NPL sites increased in a district, however, representatives were more likely to vote in favor of pollution control instruments. This shift toward the interests of those bearing pollution risks may be because residents around NPL sites were more likely to be attentive to legislator actions.

A comparison of legislator positions on Superfund reauthorization versus voting on the technical amendments also points out the importance of allowing models of legislators' decision processes to vary depending on the type of vote analyzed. The vote in the House on Superfund reauthorization was symbolic in the sense that constituents were more likely to see it covered in the press and could use it as an indicator of support for environmental programs in general. For this vote, legislator decisions were based on the ideology of constituents and the representative and the interests of attentive voters, such as those surrounding NPL sites. The variables relating to the district-level incidence of the program, such as toxic emissions and the number of PRPs, had no explanatory power, which could lead one to conclude that voting on Superfund largely depended on ideology. In votes on policy instruments, however, the lower likelihood that these votes would be examined by most constituents and the significant interests at stake for polluters and some residents within the district and contributors within and outside the district meant that legislators took these interests into account. PAC contributions in 1986 confirm that legislators were rewarded for their positions on amendments rather than positions on final authorization or general environmental positions. To find the narrow interests that influence legislator behavior on a highly visible environmental program such as Superfund, one may have to look at voting on more narrow questions about policy instruments in which the local incidence of costs and benefits is clear but monitoring by a representative's broader electorate is less likely.

Legislation as Contract

The core requirement of the Emergency Planning and Community Right-to-Know Act of 1986 (EPCRA) can be summarized in one sentence: plants must provide the public with information about their releases and transfers of toxic chemicals. The two-year process of devising the legislative language of EPCRA demonstrates how crafting a statute is like writing a complex, contentious, and ultimately incomplete contract. Recent scholarship in political science and law uses theories of contract and institutional design to explain how Congress members strategically choose both the text of a bill and the rulemaking procedures that will help define the regulations arising from the legislation.[25] Congress members may at times prefer to leave legislation vague if it is costly to negotiate the specifics of a bill, if constituents today do not know exactly what they would prefer in the future as regulations are written to implement the bill, or if this allows representatives to shift the blame for controversial decisions to agencies. The key insight of the McNollgast (1987, 1989) research is that representatives can use the administrative procedures implementing a bill as instruments of political control. The general administrative procedures that govern rulemaking allow for interested parties to participate as regulations are drafted through the notice and comment process (described more fully in Chapter 2). The particular rulemaking procedures written into a bill can also influence the outcome of regulatory decisions by setting up processes that allow a rule to be changed, stacking the deck to favor particular constituents in rulemaking, and setting up explicit mechanisms to monitor agency behavior. In drafting a legislative text, representatives thus face questions about whether to use specific versus general language and how to design the rulemaking process, choices that in part depend on the degree that they trust the agency.

In the House of Representatives, multiple community right-to-know proposals circulated in 1985 in the wake of Bhopal. By 1986, at least 23 states had community right-to-know (RTK) laws, which were often an outgrowth of earlier efforts to enact worker right-to-know laws to mandate the provision of hazard information within facilities.[26] Some chemical industry representatives voiced support for a national community RTK program, fearing the compliance costs associated with adapting to many different state programs.[27] Debates in hearings and on the floor of the House centered on questions such as whether a national program would preempt tougher state reporting requirements, thresholds for chemical use that would trigger reporting, and the list of chemicals to be covered.[28] The debate on December 5, 1985, over the Edgar amendment to add chemicals with chronic health effects to the TRI highlighted many of the concerns of some representatives with the design of the reporting program. These included what the EPA would do if it had flexibility to choose among 60,000 chemicals to require reporting, how many facilities would have to report if thresholds were set too low, the prospect for individuals to be overwhelmed with information about releases and transfers and the likelihood they would misinterpret chemical hazards, and the costs to the EPA of implementing the program. EPA officials expressed opposition to some versions of the right-to-know proposals, in part because of concern about transaction costs and the possibility that the data would be confusing to the public.[29] The language in the House bill that passed on December 10, 1985, ultimately gave great discretion to the EPA Administrator. The text gave the agency head the power to set reporting thresholds, and directed the Administrator to assemble a list of chemicals (including those with acute and chronic health effects) that facilities would have to report. In case the Administrator lagged in implementation, however, the House bill set up a default chemical list if the agency had not announced its list within 24 months of the law's enactment.

Debate in the Senate in 1985 on the community RTK provisions demonstrated a concern with the paperwork burdens on small businesses and an appreciation for the difficulties associated with defining the set of chemicals covered by reporting.[30] Reporting requirements in the version of the Superfund bill passed by the Senate in September 1985 used specific language to limit the scope of the program. Reporting was limited to firms in particular industries. Thresholds of chemical use that triggered coverage were spelled out in the legislation. The initial program was designed to generate chemical release reports in 1987, 1990, and 1993. For the reporting to continue beyond that, Congress would have to take additional action. The bill gave the President, the agent the Senate version delegated authority to, the power to establish the list of chemicals that met the criteria of human health effects (acute or chronic) or environmental effects discussed in the bill. The differences in language between the House and Senate were ultimately resolved in a conference committee bill, which was passed by both chambers and signed by President Reagan on October 17, 1986.

The final text of the toxic reporting requirements emerged from the conference committee as Title 3 of the Superfund Amendments and Reauthorization Act, the Emergency Planning and Community Right-to-Know Act of 1986. The bill used specific language to define who had to report, created administrative procedures to allow for the expansion or contraction of the program, stacked the deck in favor of increasing the set of chemicals covered, and set up monitoring mechanisms to increase the likelihood that the EPA Administrator would adhere to the provisions laid out in the bill. Section 313 of the bill used clear language to designate who had to report their toxic releases.[31] Plants with ten or more full-time employees in the manufacturing Standard Industrial Classification (SIC) code industries that manufactured, processed, or otherwise used specific chemicals in amounts above a threshold had to file reports with the EPA on their toxic releases and transfers. The chemicals covered initially by reporting where those on a list printed in report by the Senate Committee on Environment and Public Works.[32] The thresholds were explicitly stated in the legislative text. Use of a toxic chemical in amounts of 10,000 or more pounds per year triggered reporting. Manufacturing or processing a chemical on the list in amounts of 75,000 or more pounds in 1987, 50,000 pounds in 1988, or 25,000 pounds in 1989 or later years would require a plant to report. The legislative text specified particular items that plants had to report in the forms, including facility name and location, a certification by a senior management official that the data were complete and accurate, and the annual quantity of the chemical entering different environmental media.

The legislative text grants the EPA Administrator discretion to add or delete SIC codes for the set of reporting plants and to add particular plants to the reporting program. The Administrator can by rulemaking add a chemical to the TRI list if he or she believes evidence indicates the substance may cause "significant adverse acute human health effects at concentration levels that are reasonably likely to exist beyond facility site boundaries as a result of continuous, or frequently recurring, releases," may cause cancer or chronic health effects, or may cause significant damage to the environment because of its toxicity or tendency to persist and accumulate in the environment. The Administrator can add a substance to the list if any of these requirements are met, or delete a chemical if there is not "sufficient evidence" to establish any of these criteria. The legislation explicitly limits the ability of the Administrator to expand reporting by noting that chemicals added on the Administrator's initiative on the basis of potential environmental damage can constitute "no more than 25 percent of the total chemicals on the list." The Administrator can also alter the thresholds that trigger TRI reporting, as long as the revised thresholds still "obtain reporting on a substantial majority of total releases of the chemical."

The legislative language sets up administrative procedures to allow parties to modify which chemicals are covered, consistent with the McNollgast prediction that Congress members will fashion administrative procedures to facilitate participation by interested parties in rulemakings. Any person can petition the Administrator to add or delete a chemical based on evidence of acute or long-term human health effects. The Administrator then has 180 days to start a rulemaking on the procedure or to publish an explanation of why the petition is not granted. Governors can petition the EPA to add or delete a chemical based on the two human health criteria (acute or long-term health effects) or the environmental damage criteria. Deckstacking is evident in the way that petitions to add chemicals by a governor are privileged. If the governor petitions to delete a chemical, the motion is treated in the same way as that of any other person. If the governor asks the Administrator to add a chemical to reporting, the chemical is added to the list within 180 days of the petition unless the Administrator starts a rulemaking to add the chemical or publishes an explanation of why the substance does not meet the criteria spelled out in the legislation.

The legislation gives the Administrator some discretion to reduce the frequency of reporting, but the conditions under which this can happen reduce the probability that the Administrator would be able to do this. The law states that the frequency of reporting can be modified, but cannot be increased beyond annual reporting. To decrease reporting frequency, the Administrator has to determine the extent to which TRI data have been used by many parties and the degree that the information is available elsewhere. The frequency modification would have to be done through a rulemaking, and would require the Administrator to inform Congress of intent to initiate the rulemaking and then wait at least 12 months. This delay would allow Congress to pass legislation or take other actions to reverse the agency's efforts to reduce reporting. The legislative language explicitly invites the courts to engage in judicial review of the Administrator's actions on reporting frequency, because it notes that in a review of the frequency rulemaking, "a court may hold unlawful and set aside agency action, findings, and conclusions found to be unsupported by substantial evidence." Finally, the text notes that any modification of reporting frequency could not begin until 1993 at the earliest. The combination of requirements here thus make it difficult for the Administrator to reduce the frequency of TRI reporting.

The language sets up at least three sources for monitoring the agency's implementation of the toxics reporting. The bill requires the Comptroller General to produce a report no later than June 30, 1991, that would include analysis of how the EPA made the TRI data available to the public, the extent that the data were used by federal and state agencies and by the public, and options for improving the program. The legislation requires the EPA Administrator to arrange for the National Academy of Sciences to do a study within five years on the "value of mass balance analysis in determining the accuracy of information on toxic chemical releases" and on the implications of using this approach in national toxic reporting. This study would thus focus debate on the desirability of expanding reporting to require the reporting of more detailed information on plant use of toxic chemicals. The legislation allows citizens to bring civil suits against facilities for failing to file TRI reports. Citizens can also bring suits against the Administrator for failure to respond to addition/deletion petitions within 180 days, to publish the reporting form to be used for TRI reporting, or to establish a computerized database to make the information available to the public.

Specific language in the bill steered the agency toward quick and open implementation of the program. The text required the agency to publish a "uniform toxic chemical release form for facilities" by June 1, 1987. If the form had not been published by then, the legislation required plants to send in their information via letters, an option that would impose significant processing costs on the EPA. The bill stresses that the data are to be made widely available, stating that "release forms required under this section are intended to provide information to the Federal, State, and local governments and the public, including citizens of communities surrounding covered facilities." EPCRA was the first bill to require an agency to create a computerized database to make information available to the public. The language specifically required the Administrator to "make these data accessible by computer telecommunication and other means to any person on a cost reimbursable basis." The bill established civil penalties of up to $25,000 for each violation of a reporting requirement by a facility, with each day of violation defined as a separate violation. The language of the bill created a loophole in reporting, however, for it did not specify the degree that the release estimates had to be accurate. The text stated that the plant could use "readily available data (including monitoring data) collected pursuant to other provisions of law, or, where such data are not readily available, reasonable estimates of the amounts involved." The language specifically states that new efforts to collect better data are not required, noting "nothing in this section requires the monitoring or measurement of quantities, concentration, or frequency of any toxic chemical released into the environment beyond that monitoring and measurement required under other provisions of law or regulation."

Rationales for the TRI

The congressional debate over EPCRA did not feature extended discussions of what market failures are addressed by government provision of information or whether the benefits of the TRI would balance out its costs.[33] Arguments for the bill focused on the intrinsic value people place on knowing about community hazards and stressed that individuals had a right to know about potential pollution exposures. Those opposed to the bill focused on the costs, especially for small businesses, of assembling and reporting the information. Left unexamined was the question of why government would need to require plants to produce information on their toxic releases and transfers. The information about a given facility's pollution emissions fits the economist's definition of a public good. There is no rivalry in consumption of the good, meaning that one person can learn what a plant's pollution levels are without preventing another person from learning this too. The consumption of the knowledge does not lessen its availability for others. Pollution data is also subject to nonexclusion, which means that a person can consume the data without necessarily having to pay for its creation. Once the word gets out that a firm is generating a given level of pollution, for example, more people can learn about this even if they did not pay for the creation of this knowledge. Public goods such as information may be underprovided in the marketplace, because once pollution figures are established, they can circulate freely. A person might have little incentive to invest in the creation of pollution data if the figures could not be kept private and circulated only to those willing to pay. Correcting the underprovision of a public good by requiring companies to calculate and release their pollution figures is one argument for why the TRI could correct a potential market failure.

Many stakeholders have ended up using the TRI data: firms, regulators, neighbors, interest groups, and investors. Yet from an individual perspective, none of these groups had the incentives to compile the TRI figures prior to the passage of the right-to-know legislation. Plant managers did not collect data on many toxic releases and transfers for internal use. Because the release of many toxic chemicals is legal, regulations did not force firms to internalize their externalities, and hence managers did not always need to track emissions that were legal. Creating internal information on pollution might backfire if a company were sued down the road by a plant's neighbors and data were used to establish liability. This is the specter that continues to discourage voluntary pollution audits. Information on pollution releases could provide outsiders with data to reverse engineer production processes, which would lead firms to treat some pollution data as trade secrets rather than information to be shared widely. Failure to track pollution could be evidence of inefficiency within a firm. In some cases, waste reduction might benefit the environment and reduce overall firm costs. The failure to track pollution, however, might keep managers outside the plant from recognizing the potential gains to be realized through pollution reduction.[34] Finally, the significant transaction costs of creating the data are a significant deterrent to their collection. In its initial rulemaking, the EPA estimated that each TRI form took 32 hours to complete. Plants faced an average estimated cost of $13,000 the first time they filled out TRI forms and $9,000 in subsequent years.[35] Because the benefits of knowing their pollution levels were questionable and the costs very tangible, firms prior to the TRI did not devote significant resources to monitoring and tracking their toxic releases and transfers.

The logic of collective action kept the neighbors of a plant from devoting many resources to tracking the pollution of nearby plants.[36] The Coase Theorem (1960) implies that in a world without transaction costs, if facilities have the right to release toxics, then residents will costlessly negotiate with them and pay the firms to reduce emissions until the cost of reducing pollution by an additional pound equals the amount individuals are willing to pay the firm to reduce. Yet in the real world, there are transaction costs to negotiating with plants and coordinating activities. Neighborhoods could try and force plants to reduce their emissions, but this may require collective actions such as campaigns to lobby regulators or representatives, court cases, or boycotts. Even if an individual values the environment a great deal, the likelihood that his or her activity will be decisive in the collective political activity means that most individuals will not take actions to stop a firm's pollution. Some residents may act, particularly if they place an ideological value on taking a stand and gain utility purely from engaging in politics. Most will remain inactive, however, because for each person, the costs of political activity would be greater than the expected benefits.

The media often play a watchdog role in protecting the interests of residents and consumers, but the logic of collective action again generates the result that reporters were unlikely to track and chart pollution outcomes. Reporters faced few incentives to dig out the details of plant toxic releases prior to EPCRA. Most readers would choose to remain rationally ignorant about the details of facility operations, because their possession of this knowledge would generate few benefits in terms of an ability to force plants to reduce their pollution. Simply put, when individuals face low incentives to be politically active, this means they have few incentives to gather the information necessary for collective action. Even if journalists were interested in toxic emissions, the ability of facilities to shield their activities from observation and to guard pollution data as trade secrets that are part of the production process would have made it very costly prior to the creation of the TRI for reporters to assemble pollution information.[37]

Local, state, and federal regulators have an interest in firm emission levels, but without legislation, they would have a hard time requiring plants to devote resources to generating data and would face claims of trade secrets if they tried to get plants to reveal their pollution figures. Investors have an interest in knowing a firm's pollution patterns because they may be predictive of future environmental liabilities or regulatory fines. The significant transaction costs of assembling these data, compounded by the likely lack of cooperation from plants, would make it hard for stockholders or their agents to gather release data.

The passage of EPCRA changed the calculus of stakeholders concerned about pollution. Firms with toxic releases and transfers were now faced with public reporting requirements. If they did not collect and submit the data, they faced the prospect of EPA civil penalties. The opportunity cost of assembling the data for those outside the firm was reduced to the time spent accessing the EPA database and analyzing the information stored there. The existence and spread of the TRI data allowed regulators to target their enforcement efforts, policymakers to fashion new legislation, reporters to write about company pollution levels, the stock market to reward and punish firms based on their emissions, environmentalists to focus attention on persistent polluters, and plant neighbors to press for reductions in exposure. In debate over EPCRA, the discussion did not focus on how the dissemination would work. The assumption appeared to be that if the database were built, then the public would come to use it. In the following chapters, I explore how the TRI was initially set up and the first reactions to the data by investors, reporters, and regulators.

Conclusions

The reporting requirements of the TRI impose concentrated costs on industries and create dispersed benefits for individuals who enjoy cleaner air and water. This distribution of costs and benefits at first makes it appear unlikely that community right-to-know legislation would ever pass, for firms would be much more likely than individuals to overcome the problems of collective action and lobby representatives on the bill. This chapter shows, however, the chain of events that ultimately resulted in the development of the EPA's Toxics Release Inventory program. The Bhopal accident in 1984 focused public attention on the potential for chemical accidents and highlighted the lack of understanding about the releases and transfers of toxic substances. Political entrepreneurs in Congress, especially Rep. Edgar and Sen. Stafford, offered proposals during the Superfund reauthorization process to capitalize on interest in broadening information about pollution available to the public.[38]

The two votes in the House on Edgar's amendment to include in the reporting system chemicals with chronic effects show how legislators' votes varied with likely scrutiny in their district. In the first vote on the

Edgar TRI amendment, the greater the amount of toxic pollution released in the district, the less likely the representative was to vote for reporting. Representatives were more likely to be responsive to polluters (who were employers and potential contributors) in their districts than to the probable beneficiaries of cleaner air, who were unorganized and unlikely to connect cleaner environments with votes on a technical amendment. The more Superfund NPL sites in the district, a measure of likely concerned citizens in the area, the more likely the legislator voted for the collection and dissemination of information. In the second vote on the TRI, the additional lobbying by interest groups and potentially heightened interest of affected parties caused some representatives to switch their votes. Among those who voted yes initially, legislators were more likely to vote yes again the lower the pollution level in the district and the higher the environmental group membership in the area. Among those who voted against the first TRI proposal, representatives were more likely to switch and vote yes on the second vote where residents were concerned about hazardous waste contamination and where constituents were generally liberal.

In addition to affecting passage of EPCRA, the distribution of political attention and information affected the design of the reporting program. The bill's final language set forth many specific requirements to define the TRI's operation. Because EPA officials openly opposed expanded versions of chemical emissions reporting, the use of detailed language to constrain agency discretion makes sense in the McNollgast framework. If statutory language had delegated broad choices to EPA, especially an EPA with a reputation during the Reagan administration for lax environmental enforcement, legislators might expect the agency to choose the narrowest reporting options to lower the expected costs on industry.[39] By specifying the industries, chemicals, and reporting thresholds for the emissions inventory, EPCRA constrained the ability of EPA to limit the program's scope. The administrative procedures set forth in the text also favored expansion of the program, especially in privileging the ability of governors to trigger the consideration of additional chemicals for reporting. The requirement for a GAO evaluation report and the establishment of the right of citizens to bring civil suits against firms for failure to report and to bring suits against the Administrator for the failure to implement the program ensured scrutiny for the EPA's operation of the TRI. After EPCRA passed in 1986, the agency quickly instituted the next step in the development of the reporting requirements, the administrative rulemaking described in the next chapter.

Table A1.1. *Descriptive Statistics*

Variable	N	Mean	Standard Deviation	Minimum	Maximum
District characteristics					
Toxic releases and transfers (lbs)	435	48,325,647	260,506,370	18,308	5.2e9
NPL final and proposed sites	435	2.0	2.5	0	18
Non-NPL sites	435	55.6	39.0	0	275
Potentially responsible parties (#)	435	26	31	0	201
Vote for Reagan, 1984 (%)	435	58.3	12.1	5.0	83.0
Environmental group membership (statewide, per 1,000)	435	8.7	3.1	2.5	20.2
Legislator characteristics					
1984 PAC contributions from chemical and petroleum firms ($)	432	3,375	3,450	0	18,950
1986 PAC contributions from 11 chemical and petroleum firms ($)	392	2,040	2,818	0	17,250
1986 PAC contributions from chemical and petroleum firms, primary business ($)	392	3,458	3,376	0	22,600
1986 PAC contributions from chemical and petroleum firms, primary or secondary business ($)	392	6,406	6,475	0	34,100
League of Conservation Voters score, 1986	434	49.8	25.0	0	94
Legislator dummies					
Democrat	435	.58	.49	0	1
Incumbent in 1984	435	.89	.32	0	1
Energy and Commerce Committee member	435	.10	.30	0	1
Ways and Means Committee member	435	.08	.28	0	1

(*continued*)

Table A1.1 (*continued*)

Variable	N	Mean	Standard Deviation	Minimum	Maximum
Voted for Toxics Release Inventory, first vote	349	.52	.50	0	1
Voted for Toxics Release Inventory, second vote	423	.50	.50	0	1
Voted for injury liability	423	.38	.49	0	1
Voted for targeted tax	426	.52	.50	0	1
Voted for Superfund reauthorization	424	.92	.27	0	1

TWO

Defining Terms

Rulemaking and the Initial TRI Data Release

Although books and songs have been written about how a bill becomes a law, fewer tales surround the process of rulemaking. This chapter analyzes the generation of the first set of regulations defining the Toxics Release Inventory from three different perspectives. I first examine the notice and comment rulemaking process that produced the TRI reporting form. Next I explore how the activities of regulators, Congress members, industry officials, environmentalists, and journalists affected the implementation of the reporting program in 1988 and 1989. During the legislative debate over the TRI, many claims were made about whether the information collected would really be new or news. In the final section of the chapter, I conduct a stock market event analysis and examine patterns of newspaper coverage to see the extent that the first release of TRI data in 1989 was news to two sets of observers: investors and journalists.

Defining the Form

On October 17, 1986, when President Reagan signed the Emergency Planning and Community Right-To-Know Act as part of the Superfund reauthorization bill, the resulting law (Public Law 99-499) contained explicit implementation deadlines. The EPA had until June 1, 1987, to issue a reporting form, and firms had until July 1, 1988, to fill out their TRI reports listing their 1987 emissions and deliver the data to the EPA and state governments. The Administrative Procedure Act (APA) contains the road map for how the regulations defining the reporting requirements would be written. Under the notice-and-comment rulemaking process defined by the APA, the agency first publishes a proposed rule in the *Federal Register* and invites comments on its requirements. After interested parties provide the agency with written input, the EPA issues the text of the final rule through publication in the *Federal Register*. If the agency fails to consider and reply to substantive comments in announcing the final rule, parties can sue the agency for "arbitrary and capricious" action and attempt to block the regulation. Legal scholars praise the notice-and-comment process for embodying process values such as public participation, fairness, and openness. Political economists, such as the McNollgast scholars, are more likely to view the rulemaking process as an instrument of political control.[1] In this interpretation, the rules that govern rulemaking are valued by legislators because they can affect the substance of what emerges from agency decisionmaking.

Given that EPA officials had opposed expansive right-to-know provisions during the congressional debate over the TRI and that the EPA under President Reagan in general had a reputation for putting cost considerations ahead of environmental protection, it is not surprising that the text of EPCRA spelled out in detail many of the reporting requirements rather than delegating discretion to the agency.[2] The Democratic and moderate Republican legislators who championed the RTK provisions had agreed on language that specified the initial list of reporting industries, the thresholds for chemical manufacture or use that triggered report filing, and the particular chemicals and compounds originally covered. To define exactly what information the EPA would require in the TRI reports, however, the agency needed to engage in notice-and-comment rulemaking. On January 8 and 9, 1987, the EPA convened a pre-proposal meeting on the TRI that attracted more than 100 participants. Regulators also met with company officials and public interest group representatives as they sketched out and informally circulated reporting proposals. The comments received at these meetings and other outside submissions became part of the rulemaking docket record. On June 4, 1987, the agency issued the proposed rule governing the TRI in the *Federal Register*.[3] Because of the initial suggestions received in the informal process initiated by the EPA, the agency was already reacting to comments in issuing the proposed rule.

In the text of the proposed rulemaking, the EPA responds to suggestions for both expanding and contracting the reporting requirements and seeks explicit feedback in areas where the text of the legislation leaves leeway. The agency proposed to require a facility to provide a number of data elements not mentioned in the EPCRA legislation. Commenters suggested requiring a plant to list the parent company name, which the

EPA noted would be helpful for "comparative analysis of industry activities." The proposed rule called for a plant to provide the parent company name and the Dun and Bradstreet identifier numbers for the company and the facility. The EPA proposed that the form list a facility's water permit number under the National Pollutant Discharge Elimination System (NPDES), information that states and public interest groups indicated would make it easier to link the TRI with other plant-level pollution data. The EPA also proposed that plants identify the off-site locations where toxic wastes were shipped, stating that "this information will give users of the data an important indication of the relative level of responsibility for the ultimate disposition of the chemical in the environment." Implicitly balancing the benefits of information with costs, the agency noted that the information on plant ownership, NPDES number, and off-site shipment destination should all be readily available for facility employees. On questions that would reduce the amount of information provided, the agency asked for comments on whether it should expand the reporting exemption to remove more small businesses (with the Small Business Administration suggesting a 50-employee threshold before facility reporting would be required) and on whether quantities should be reported in detail or in ranges. The EPA noted that asking for TRI reports in ranges rather than quantity estimates might be problematic because "neither the statute nor the legislative history of section 313 provides for reporting emissions data as a range." The agency also proposed an optional section on the TRI form that would give information on waste minimization actions and production levels at the facility. The proposed rule noted that filling out the section would be "optional because actions that reduce releases could in some cases reveal trade secret information and because the statute does not specifically request information on reductions in releases." Though commentators had suggested expanding the reporting beyond manufacturing industries to include federal facilities and commercial waste treatment plants, the EPA did not propose covering facilities outside the Standard Industrial Classification code industries 20 through 39.

The EPA published the final rule on toxic release reporting on February 16, 1988, after receiving more than 100 written comments on the proposed version, holding three open meetings on the regulations, and meeting with interested parties.[4] The regulations did not deviate from the requirements set forth in the language of EPCRA. As required in the text of the bill, the EPA's regulations required a facility to file a TRI report if it was in the manufacturing SIC codes, had ten or more full-time employees, manufactured or processed a chemical above a threshold (75,000 pounds in 1987, 50,000 pounds in 1988, or 25,000 pounds in 1989 or later) or otherwise used more than 10,000 pounds of a chemical if it was one of 329 chemicals listed in the Senate Environment and Public Works Committee Print No. 99-169. Part of the final rule filled in technical details, such as how to define whether a plant has ten or more employees. The EPA indicated that because a full-time employee on average would work 2,000 hours per year, a facility would be covered if it had at least 20,000 employee hours worked per year. Parts of the rule required facilities to report information not directly mentioned in the bill's language, which meant the EPA had chosen to expand the data gathering. In other parts of the rule, however, the agency made decisions that represented a compromise between the wider revelation of information favored by public interest groups and the narrower interpretation of EPCRA pushed by industry.

Acting on suggestions from commenters, the EPA's final TRI form required facilities to report their latitude and longitude. The agency noted the "primary reason for asking for this information is its importance for geographic information systems. These computer-based systems enable EPA and other organizations to model exposures resulting from chemical releases and produce graphic representations of such exposures." Plants had to provide the name of a technical representative who could answer questions about the reports from the EPA or state governments and a public contact who would deal with broader inquiries. The final form retained questions about where a plant sent waste for off-site treatment and disposal. The agency noted:

Most industry commenters objected to the reporting of off-site waste transfers for several reasons. First, commenters stated that such information is not required by statute, was not intended by Congress, and is duplicative because of RCRA reporting requirements for hazardous waste. The strongest objection, however, was that the off-site chemical transfers do not constitute "a release into the environment" by the reporting facility and should not be reported as such on the form.

Despite these objections, the agency retained the wider reporting interpretation. The agency noted that the conference report on the bill "states that reportable releases shall also include releases 'to waste treatment and storage facilities.'" Because off-site transfers may be a substantial proportion of the chemical wastes for some plants, the agency explained that leaving this information out "could be misleading to the public."

Overall, the agency appeared to favor expanding reporting where the costs of generating the information would be low for the facility and the potential benefits to the public would be high in terms of getting a fuller profile of plant pollution.[5]

The text of EPCRA indicated that the form would "include an appropriate certification, signed by a senior official with management responsibility for the person or persons completing the report, regarding the accuracy and completeness of the report."[6] The legislation also indicated that if monitoring data are not available, then "reasonable estimates of the amounts involved" could be used on the forms. In writing the rules to flesh out these requirements, the EPA received comments about the degree of responsibility assumed by the senior manager and the degree of accuracy in reporting. For both questions, the EPA adopted a compromise interpretation that held industry to standards consistent with the legislative text but did not push the reporting as far as possible. In the proposed rule, the agency wanted the senior official certifying the TRI forms to indicate they were "true, accurate, and complete based upon his or her personal examination of the completed forms." This represented a quandary in part because the legislation allowed estimates, opening up the question of how accurate an estimate had to be. The agency modified the language on the reporting form in the final rule, so that the senior manager had to sign a certification saying:

I hereby certify that I have reviewed the attached documents and, to the best of my knowledge and belief, that the submitted information is true and complete and that the amounts and values in this report are accurate based on reasonable estimates using data available to the preparers of this report.

The EPA decided in general against using range reporting for quantities or requiring a particular degree of precision in quantity reporting. Instead, the agency chose a middle path of "requiring that estimates of releases and transfers of toxics to off-site locations be expressed as a figure rounded to a degree of accuracy no greater than two significant digits." For the first three years of reporting, the EPA would allow releases of less than 1,000 pounds to be reported as a range.

In addition to the APA, there are other rules governing rulemaking that affected the TRI final rulemaking. Executive Order 12291 required agencies to do a Regulatory Impact Analysis (RIA) for major rules, those defined in part as having an economic impact of at least $100 million. The creation of an RIA was one way to require regulators to focus on the costs imposed by potential regulations. The RIA created for the Toxics Release Inventory generated the agency's best estimate for the scope of the regulation, indicating that 31,800 facilities would file an average of ten reports per plant at a cost of $12,898 per plant the first year and $8,300 to $9,100 per plant in the following years. The agency envisioned compliance costs for industry to be $527 million in the first year of reporting and $299 million in the second year (in which costs are lower because of learning and investments made in the first year). EPA costs were estimated to range from $7.7 million to $26.4 million per year. These numbers provided a benchmark for later complaints about the level of compliance with TRI reporting, because they allowed legislators and public interest groups to compare actual levels of TRI reports with these projected levels of reporting.

To comply with the Regulatory Flexibility Act, the EPA also analyzed in the TRI rulemaking how small businesses in particular might be affected by reporting requirements. The Small Business Administration filed comments suggesting ways to exempt more small facilities, arguing that the emissions from these plants might not be a significant proportion of all releases and that reporting costs would represent a particular burden for smaller entities. The EPA decided not to exempt "larger" small businesses and retained the threshold specified in the legislation that exempted facilities with less than ten full-time employees. The agency did create for three years the option for facilities to report releases and transfers of a chemical of less than 1,000 pounds as a range. The agency indicated that small businesses might particularly benefit from this because they lacked the technical monitoring capacity of larger firms. As a final cross-cutting measure, the information collection required in the rule was reviewed by the Office of Management and Budget under the Paperwork Reduction Act.

After the TRI form was published in February 1988, many questions remained about whether industries would be able to comply in time and how the agency would deal with the large amount of information coming in from reporting facilities.

Generating the First Reports

The EPA had limited time and resources to implement the collection and release of the first version of the Toxics Release Inventory. From the start, the program was criticized for the type of data collected, the accuracy of the estimates, the relative lack of enforcement, and ease of public access to the data. Charles Elkins, head of the Office of Toxic Substances, declared:

There was tremendous cynicism within the agency because the data was so shallow in terms of what they were used to dealing with. In their eyes, TRI data is an inch deep and a mile wide. It doesn't give enough information on why the releases occurred, for example, or what's behind the numbers.[7]

Company officials wanted the EPA to add information about health effects to the TRI to make it clear that not all exposures were hazardous, but Elkins rejected that approach. He indicated:

I told the chemical industry, "I'm not going to solve your problems. Don't count on me to protect you from the public reactions."[8]

When Congress passed EPCRA, it did not provide additional funding to the EPA for implementing the program, so for 1987, the agency used $16 million in Superfund money to run the Title III program.[9] J. Winston Porter, the EPA assistant administrator for solid waste and emergency response, indicated that larger plants would comply with the program because they had the knowledge and expertise and were fearful of liability. He noted that smaller companies would be more difficult to engage in compliance. The limited funds left for enforcement led him to conclude that EPCRA would initially be a program essentially of voluntary compliance.[10] Describing the strategy to focus on the filing rather than the accuracy of reports, an agency official noted in 1989:

We have concentrated most of our enforcement thus far on ensuring that the people who are supposed to report in fact did report. That's where we focus the bulk of our enforcement activities thus far rather than go onsite. The TRI data is an estimate. It's not a precise measurement, so an onsite inspection might not in fact be particularly effective in terms of compliance.[11]

The agency planned to release the data to the public in many forms: reports, microfiche, CD-ROM, and computer tapes. Requests for information could be filled by the EPA's Title III Reporting Center. Individuals could also look up information at federal repository libraries and some county libraries. To make the data electronically available, the agency chose to make the information accessible via the National Library of Medicine's Toxnet. The NLM was chosen in part because user rates were relatively low ($18 to $25 per hour) and because it provided access to health and toxicity data.[12] In the pre-Internet era, however, some individuals challenged how easy the NLM was to use. As Senate staffer Ronald Outen, who had championed public access, put it:

It's hard for Joe Public to hop on his Apple, dialup, and get information. What we had wanted was something where you could ask simple questions like, "Who are the emitters of Benzene in our zip code?" and "How do the emissions of Refinery A and Refinery B compare?" We find here that it is difficult to use [Toxnet].[13]

The EPA released the national TRI database and first annual report (*The Toxics-Release Inventory: A National Perspective*) in June 1989. The text of the report demonstrated the pains the agency took to qualify interpretations of the data. The 74,152 reports filed by 19,278 facilities resulted in an estimate of 22.5 billion pounds of TRI releases and transfers in 1987. The agency pointed out, however, that a single facility accounted for 5.2 billion pounds in releases of sodium sulfate, which was eventually delisted because of lack of evidence on significant toxicity. When sodium sulfate was dropped from the calculations, national TRI totals were 10.4 billion pounds of toxic releases and transfers. On the second page of the national report, the EPA acknowledged the limits of the data:

TRI release data reveal the amounts of TRI chemicals that are annually and routinely discharged into the environment.... These data do not, however, directly gauge the amounts of chemicals to which humans or the environment are *exposed*, nor do they measure the *risks* posed by TRI chemicals. Many factors combine to determine how much of a risk, if any, is imposed by particular releases and transfers of TRI chemicals.... Nor are the releases necessarily an indication of violations of environmental laws; many EPA and State programs permit some releases of toxic chemicals under controlled or properly managed conditions that prevent or minimize risks.[14]

The national report also stressed that the data reported in the TRI were not necessarily accurate, noting:

TRI only requires facilities to report data that are already known or reasonably ascertainable to them. It does not require companies to measure or otherwise verify the data they submit. Thus, much of the quantitative data reported were estimated with unknown accuracy. In addition, some reporting facilities misunderstood the intent of the form or made mistakes in reporting. Because this is the first year of reporting under TRI, it is reasonable to suppose that the quality of the reported data will improve in subsequent years as facilities gain more experience.[15]

The report analyzed TRI releases by state, industry, media, and county. Individual companies and facilities were not highlighted, except for the listing of 28 facilities that had filed 40 forms claiming trade secrets (which accounted for .01% of releases and transfers). The EPA Administrator William K. Reilly praised the data as a "breakthrough that will facilitate citizen involvement in assessing the risks of toxic chemicals and developing community strategies to prevent pollution."[16] He criticized those who failed to file their TRI reports, noting:

These companies have a legal responsibility to provide the data.... We will not allow non-reporting companies to thwart the right of citizens to find out which toxic chemicals are being released into their communities."[17]

As the EPA designed the TRI program, Congress members had oversight hearings to focus attention on implementation issues that concerned them. Sen. Frank Lautenberg (D-N.J.), a chief proponent of EPCRA, held the first oversight hearing on the law in May 1988. At the hearing, another of the measure's original supporters, Rep. James Florio (D-N.J.), testified:

I am not convinced that the EPA has set aside the proper resources to enforce this law and ensure compliance. In its fiscal 1989 budget request, EPA said it needs only three fulltime people in Washington office and eight in regional offices to work on enforcement over the next two years. It is inconceivable that 11 people will be able to enforce the law on 30,000 facilities nationwide.[18]

Senator Lautenberg also chastised the agency for failing to push for greater funding:

One thing we do need is a commitment from EPA to ask for the resources. Even if you don't get them, at least have your consciences clear that you have asked for them, that you have stated the case, that you have argued the benefits and argued the value.... You fought your case from the EPA's standpoint, and we fought ours from the Senate and the Congressional standpoint. But we came to an agreement, a bill that was signed by the President of the United States. Now, you have an obligation to enforce that law.[19]

Once facilities had filed their 1987 TRI forms (which were due by July 1, 1988), agency officials were back on Capitol Hill testifying at oversight hearings in spring 1989. EPA Administrator Reilly estimated that 25% of plants that should have submitted 1987 TRI forms did not file. The limited inspection resources meant that as of May 1988, only 39 enforcement cases had been brought. Seeing the glass as half full, an EPA official testified:

First of all, this was the first year of the reporting and we got 75 percent and I think we're surprised that we got that high. My sense is that as the inventory becomes more familiar to companies and they are more aware of who is covered, that they in fact are covered, that you will see compliance in fact go up. Additionally, as we bring fines against companies who don't comply, that usually serves to encourage the noncompliers to step forward.[20]

Representative Luken replied, "That may be, but fining 25 companies out of a possible 9,000 violators might not scare too many people." Senator Lautenberg described the EPA's enforcement strategy of taking action after incidents occurred as "explosion first, ask questions later."[21] By the time the 1987 data were released in June 1989, the EPA had brought enforcement actions against 85 firms for failing to comply with EPCRA reporting and issued 1,500 notices of noncompliance.[22] This included $1.65 million in fines announced against 42 firms the same week that the TRI data were first released, a move that attracted attention to enhanced enforcement at a time when people were first learning about the program in the media.

Corporate responses to the challenge of generating and filing the first TRI reports varied. Officials at some larger companies, which were more likely to have environmental compliance expertise and more likely to face scrutiny, publicized their TRI efforts. On June 30, 1988, the day before the first TRI reports were due at the EPA, the CEO of Monsanto promised to reduce the firm's worldwide releases of toxic air emissions by 90% over a four-year period.[23] DuPont spent an estimated $2 million to develop the company's first TRI reports, devoting more than 20 man-years to create the TRI figures for the chemicals and specialties section of the firm and designing a computer system to facilitate reporting.[24] Describing the process of assembling information for the first TRI deadline, a Dow official noted "every time you go through a reevaluation like getting the data for the first time for 313, it focuses a little bit different attention, and we found a few areas that needed more work than we had been emphasizing for that particular area."[25] Noting how the information generated caused senior officials to learn new data about their plants, an EPA official concluded:

The first year's worth of information was more of a CEO's right-to-know.... A lot of CEOs had never seen the yearly figures of how much was being wasted, emitted, or disposed of.[26]

This process of higher-ups learning more about pollution and taking action was envisioned in the design of the TRI. As Senate staffer Outen put it:

We surmised that a lot of CEOs historically viewed emissions from their plants as a problem to be dealt with by the compliance department.... They had never taken ownership of emissions.[27]

Chemical companies were better prepared to develop TRI reports in part because of the industry's earlier development of chemical awareness and communication programs instituted after the Bhopal incident.[28] Firms in other industries, however, were less prepared for and in some cases unaware of the new reporting regulations. Teresa Pugh, the environmental quality director for the National Association of Manufacturers, noted in March 1988 that small firms in particular lacked the environmental quality or government relations employees who could make them aware of the program and help them comply. Even after education workshops and other efforts had been made, she noted, "We've had a tough time getting companies to understand they must comply with the law.... most companies still don't have any concept of what this law means."[29]

Although EPCRA supporters were eager for the release of the first data, the new reporting requirements were not met with universal support in industry. A column published in *Chemical Week* summarized many objections expressed to the program:

Clearly – or so it seems to me – Title III of SARA (Superfund Amendments and Reauthorization Act of 1986), aka the Emergency Planning and Community Right-to-Know Act of 1986, is an overreaction by the U.S. Congress to Bhopal. Just a glance at its encyclopedic requirements tells you that it is classic bureaucratic overkill. It will tell people much more than they need to know or, in most cases, ever wanted to know. It will likely scare some folks needlessly, when they first see all those chemical names and numbers. It will probably be a bonanza, for a while, for environmental activists and weirdos, who sometimes seem to be interchangeable. And it may well expose some trade secrets.[30]

A frequent objection expressed by corporate officials was that individuals would equate toxic emissions with toxic outcomes because the reports lacked information on likely exposures and health effects. Glynn Young, manager of environmental and community relations at Monsanto, said the large emission figures would "sound scary to the public" and urged more efforts to provide context for the figures.[31] The president of the Synthetic Organic Chemical Manufacturers Association predicted "there is likely to be a public panic" if there were not more explanations offered about toxic releases.[32] Charles DiBona, president of the American Petroleum Institute, declared:

The important question in all this is the extent to which there is public exposure to these materials. We have no reason to believe that people are exposed to the releases we will be reporting to a degree endangering their health.... [Without context information] it could become quite terrifying to the public. That's what is worrying us.[33]

Environmentalists remained active throughout the implementation process for the TRI. As the EPA began to design the TRI, approximately a dozen public interest groups came together to form the Working Group on Community Right-to-Know to monitor the agency's actions.[34] Interest group representatives testified and provided submissions at the oversight hearings held in the House and Senate. Gerald Poje of the National Wildlife Federation, for example, warned at the May 1989 Senate hearing of access problems with the agency's database:

People with computer expertise, with knowledge of the TRI data, with knowledge about how it should look, who have done reports themselves analyzing the data, are having a tremendous amount of difficulty extracting this information through this test system at the National Library of Medicine.[35]

Poje also served as a media source in articles about the program. Praising the TRI in a *Washington Post* article in June 1989, he asserted, "It's an absolutely revolutionary concept for the federal government to collect data and make it available to the general public in computer-usable form."[36]

Environmental groups made the TRI data more accessible to the public by conducting studies that were easily apprehensible. The Natural Resources Defense Council obtained an early version of the TRI database from the EPA in April 1989. This allowed them to analyze the information so that when the EPA released the TRI data on June 19, 1989, the NRDC was able to release its own report on the same day entitled *A Who's Who of American Toxic Air Polluters: A Guide to More than 1500 Factories in 46 States Emitting Cancer-Causing Chemicals*. The report examined releases of 11 cancer-causing TRI chemicals and developed lists such as the top 125 largest emitters into the air of particular carcinogens. The report used the language feared by opponents of the TRI, because the NRDC was much more willing than the EPA to link emissions to risks:

Toxic air emissions take an annual toll of thousands of cases of cancers and other illnesses. Many of the 328 pollutants subject to the inventory requirements can kill or injure immediately if released in great enough quantity. Others can cause death or serious illness after years of exposure to even low concentrations. Still others contaminate major ecosystems like the Great Lakes and the Chesapeake Bay. Some chemicals on the list attack the earth's protective ozone shield. Other compounds are photochemically reactive, and combine with nitrogen oxides in the lower atmosphere to cause health-damaging ozone smog at ground level.[37]

By highlighting specific factories and their emissions, the NRDC report generated stories in local newspapers about emissions at local plants. In one of these articles, Deborah A. Sheiman, who helped write the report, declared the data showed, "Industries are using the sky as a garbage dump to dispose of hundreds of millions of pounds of unregulated cancer-causing chemicals."[38] Charles Elkins, director of the EPA Office of Toxic Substances, later praised the NRDC's efforts, declaring, "they are doing exactly what the Congress and the EPA wanted the public to do."[39]

Although companies submitted their reports on 1987 releases and transfers to the EPA by July 1, 1988, the agency's collection of 1987 TRI data did not become publicly available until 1989. In March 1989, Rep. Henry Waxman released data on TRI totals by industry. In mid-April, the EPA released summary data by state.[40] On June 19, 1989, the agency released the national TRI data that allowed individuals to find information about specific facilities. Industry trade journals wrote about the data. Local newspapers wrote stories about the releases of local firms, such as the *St. Louis Post-Dispatch* story entitled "Monsanto on List of Possible Cancer-Causing Pollution."[41] The most in-depth media assessment of the TRI came from a series in *USA Today*, which bought its own set of TRI data tapes from the EPA to analyze. When EPCRA had been debated, opponents talked about how the TRI information might scare residents near polluting facilities. The language of the *USA Today* articles did focus on risks and fears, which is not surprising given the demand for entertainment even in hard news coverage. The *USA Today* report was entitled "The Chemicals Next Door: A First Peek 'behind the Plant Gates.'" The article began:

"People always ask you, 'Being surrounded by refineries, are you scared?'" says Marilyn Davis, 35. "Yes. We are."[42]

The paper went on to use dramatic language to describe the results of their TRI analysis:

USA Today's three-month investigation and analysis of EPA's Toxic Release Inventory found an unexpected volume of chemicals in many not-so-obvious places. In 1987, a whopping 7 billion pounds of toxic chemicals – a veritable witches' brew of poisons – were pumped into the air, land, and water by 19,278 factories.[43]

The paper personalizes the data by interviewing neighbors surrounding facilities, company officials, and environmental activists. The reporters are careful not to claim that exposure to TRI emissions can definitively be linked to illness. They rather use the words of people bearing the risks and exposures to summarize the uncertainty, noting that for a resident near an oil storage tank farm:

She suspects friends' allergies are aggravated by the pollution but, like most here, says no one offers real answers. "You know people who have cancer, but you don't know where it comes from," she says.[44]

Although the initial release of TRI data generated scrutiny in policy circles and articles in some newspapers, the question remains of how much of the information was treated as new. The following section explores this by examining in detail the reaction of investors and journalists to the June 1989 TRI data release.

Pollution as News

Stock market event studies are premised on the assumption that the stock market operates efficiently in terms of reflecting current information and expectations. The general approach in event studies is to estimate the relationship between a firm's return and the market return over a time period prior to the event studied. This market model is used to generate a predicted return for each firm based on the performance of the market. If the market receives "new" (i.e., unexpected) information about a firm, the company's stock price may move positively or negatively depending on the import of the information. The prediction error for a firm, the difference between the normal return predicted by the market model for the company and the company's actual return on a given day, is used as a measure of the abnormal returns attributed to the release of new information about the company. A growing number of works have used the event study methodology to examine the relationship between firm financial performance and the costs of environmental laws.[45]

The event study methodology is ideally suited for examining the impact of the release of the Toxics Release Inventory data, for the main focus of the community right-to-know law that set up the TRI is information provision. Unlike other regulatory actions in which the release of information is incidental to the program, the TRI is designed to affect firm behavior by having information serve as a regulatory tool. Pollution figures reported in the TRI provide "news" to the financial community to the extent that the data diverge from expectations about a firm's pollution patterns. Data on emissions and off-site transfers can affect analysts' estimates of many different types of environmental costs: cleanup costs in dealing with hazardous waste sites under the Resource Conservation and Recovery Act (RCRA) and Superfund, transaction costs arising from litigation over pollution liability, pollution control and abatement expenditures, and penalties and fines from enforcement actions. Higher-than-expected levels of pollution emissions can thus lead to upward revision of projections of these environmental costs. High TRI figures may lead to higher costs of operation because the figures invite stricter scrutiny by regulators, environmentalists, and facility neighbors. High pollution figures may also result in loss of reputation and goodwill.

In this section, I test the extent to which the TRI data provided "news" to investors by examining whether their release generated abnormal returns associated with changes in expectations of pollution costs. Among the many different versions of the event study methodology, I chose to follow the model developed by Dodd and Warner (1983). Abnormal daily returns were calculated for June 19, 1989 (day 0 in the event study, the date of the initial public release of the TRI data), for firms traded on the New York or American Stock Exchange that had valid stock price and TRI information. A cross-section model of the determinants of the dollar value of the stock price reaction to the release of the TRI data was also estimated. Logistic analysis of whether a firm's TRI figures were mentioned in newspaper coverage was used to explore the degree that the release of the data was treated as "news" by journalists.

Studying the reaction of investors and journalists to news about corporate pollution records provided in the TRI involved collecting information on emissions, stock prices, and media coverage. Company pollution totals for 1987 were calculated primarily from TRI data released by the EPA in 1989.[46] Several things should be noted about the compilation of the corporate TRI figures. The first is the level at which data are reported. Under the provisions of EPCRA, manufacturing facilities (defined by SIC codes 20–39) with ten or more employees that manufacture or process quantities above a certain threshold of toxic substances on a list (at the time) of more than 300 chemicals had to file a separate form for each chemical detailing its release. For each chemical, the facility submitted a form listing releases to the environment broken down by emission pathways: air, land, underground injection, surface water, public sewage, and off-site transfer (primarily to storage or disposal facilities). When the 1987 data were made public on June 19, 1989, the format of the data meant that pollution figures at the facility level rather than companywide totals were emphasized. The TRI data, however, contain information on facility name and parent company ownership, so media coverage often linked particular facilities with their parent companies. A report released by the

Natural Resources Defense Council on June 19, 1989, focused attention on a particular subset of the TRI data: facilities with the largest air emissions of certain carcinogenic TRI chemicals. This report also listed facility names that associated emissions with corporate owners.[47]

Additional characteristics of the TRI data are that they are self-reported by companies and are maintained by the EPA as "running totals." Under EPCRA, firms are free to calculate their emissions using different methodologies, including mass-balance calculations, engineering studies, and direct monitoring. Investor reactions to the data in part may depend on beliefs about the relative accuracy of these figures.[48] The TRI data are maintained by the EPA as a continuously revised file, so figures for 1987 pollution totals change as companies submit revisions or new reports. The version of the TRI data used in this study dates from July 1989. Though the data may contain flaws that were later eliminated, it is this earlier data that journalists and investors were reacting to in 1989.

TRI data on facility chemical releases were aggregated to the company level for publicly traded firms in the following manner. TRI reporting forms contain an entry for the facility to report the Dun and Bradstreet (D & B) number of its parent company. These parent numbers were extracted and matched by Dun and Bradstreet with the stock ticker symbol of the parent company used on the New York, American, or other stock exchanges. Many facilities were still left without a ticker symbol after this process, in part because some TRI records lacked D & B numbers and in part because some of the plants were privately held rather than owned by public companies. Facilities that were not matched by Dun and Bradstreet were checked manually against industrial directories to determine the ultimate corporate ownership of the plant (a process often aided by the facility's name and address listing in the TRI).[49] Additional facilities were assigned stock ticker symbols through this process. Privately held facilities were not aggregated by company but rather were added into a single category of "private facilities." Company-level pollution totals for publicly traded firms were derived by totaling TRI figures by the stock ticker symbol associated with the reporting facilities.

Responses to the release of the TRI data in 1989 in part depended on the extent this information on firm pollution figures provided new information. Permit reporting requirements in other EPA regulatory programs, previous judicial cases arising with pollution liability, and SIC codes of facilities associated with a company (e.g., whether a firm owns multiple plants involved in chemical production, SIC code 28) were indicators of potential pollution patterns available before the TRI data were released.

I have chosen to proxy a firm's historical pollution record in part by calculating for the publicly traded firms in the sample the number of Superfund sites where the company had been identified as a potentially responsible party (PRP) as of 1989 (PRPs can be held jointly and severally liable for cleanup costs at hazardous waste sites). This calculation was done by searching the address list of PRPs notified by the EPA (obtained under the Freedom of Information Act) and counting the number of times firms in the sample appeared on the list. Information on facility ownership from the summations of pollution data was used to attempt to trace out the corporate linkages between firms, but no further attempt was made to investigate ownership relationships. The number of Superfund sites per company is thus an approximation of the firm's actual exposure to liability under this program. It is the relative exposure that is important here, however, because this number is used to indicate information available prior to the TRI data about the degree that a firm was involved in pollution-intensive activities.

As another way to measure the prior perceptions about the pollution patterns of firms, I created a set of dummy variables for the industries in which companies operated. Dun and Bradstreet company listings provide SIC code information on the primary line of business for each firm. Dummy variables were created for firms with two-digit SIC codes in the top five industries with the highest TRI releases and transfers for 1987, which were (in descending order of releases and transfers) chemicals, paper, primary metals, petroleum, and textiles. Pollution-intensive activities are a significant part of these companies, a fact that investors were apprised of before the TRI data releases. A separate dummy variable was also constructed if the firm's primary line of business was not in these five industries but was in manufacturing, which again would be an indicator of potential pollution. Additional company-level variables compiled primarily from Dun and Bradstreet data included firm sales (in millions) and employment for 1988. These variables were included in part to test for reputation effects (e.g., Do firms with higher sales face greater penalties in terms of loss of goodwill because of pollution?) and economies of scale in pollution control (e.g., Do investors believe there will be economies of scale in handling pollution problems in larger firms?).

Data on stock prices came from the Center for Research in Security Prices (CRSP). The stock ticker symbols from the TRI facilities were matched against the CRSP daily stock price information for the New York and American stock exchanges (OTC firms were dropped from this part of the analysis). Firms with TRI data and stock data were included in the sample if there were complete stock return data for January through June 1989. Data from January 3, 1989, to May 24, 1989 (the first 100 trading days of the year), were used to estimate the market model for each firm. Fourteen companies were excluded because they had confounding events, identified through the *Wall Street Journal*, during the time period surrounding the event that could have significantly affected their returns for reasons other than the release of the TRI data.

Figures on media coverage of company releases under the TRI program were calculated by searching the Lexis database and *Wall Street Journal* index for calendar year 1989 for articles containing TRI information. For each TRI company mentioned in publications covered by these databases, the number of articles containing references to the firm's TRI pollution figures were totaled. Company names were then matched with stock ticker symbols so that patterns of media coverage for publicly traded firms could be analyzed.

Pollution and Ownership

Investors in publicly traded companies may be concerned about pollution levels for a number of reasons: the cost of future liabilities arising from pollution cases, regulatory compliance costs associated with emission reductions, and loss of goodwill connected with high pollution figures. Although concern about these factors may create incentives for firms to reduce their toxic releases, an initial question arises about how important publicly traded (as contrasted with privately held) firms are in the generation of pollution. Table 2.1 provides a lower bound estimate of the fraction of pollution generated by publicly traded firms. Approximately 73% of the 22.5 billion pounds of toxic releases and transfers reported in the 1987 TRI data came from companies traded on stock exchanges. This figure on pollution by publicly held companies is a lower bound estimate because facilities that could not be classified from information in the TRI data, Dun and Bradstreet files, and other industrial directories were by default placed in the private firm category. A total of 893 different publicly traded companies were linked with facilities reporting TRI data; these firms accounted for 43% of the facilities reporting and 48% of the forms submitted for 1987 (each form represents pollution figures for a particular chemical at a given facility).[50] Although nearly three quarters of all pollutants tracked by the TRI are from publicly traded companies, these firms accounted for only 46% of the TRI wastes shipped off-site to storage and disposal facilities. This is consistent with the hypothesis that

Table 2.1. *The Estimated Distribution of Pollution by Type of Company Ownership, 1987*

	Public Firms	% from Public Firms	Private Firms	% from Private Firms
Air (M lbs.)	1,592	59.9	1,066	40.1
Land (M lbs.)	1,898	77.3	556	22.7
Underground (M lbs.)	2,618	81.1	611	18.9
Off-site (M lbs.)	1,178	46.1	1,375	53.9
Surface water (M lbs.)	8,068	83.8	1,558	16.2
Public sewage (M lbs.)	999	51.9	926	48.1
Total releases/transfers (M lbs.)	16,354	72.9	6,093	27.1
Facilities (#)	5,424	42.7	7,276	57.3
Submissions (#)	35,252	47.6	38,742	52.4
Companies (#)	893			
	NYSE or AMEX, Matched Firms	Publicly Traded, Not Matched Firms	Over-the-Counter Firms	Confounding-Events Firms
Air (M lbs.)	1,458	58	77	20
Land (M lbs.)	1,850	32	16	.3
Underground (M lbs.)	2,575	4	38	0
Off-site (M lbs.)	1,029	80	69	12
Surface water (M lbs.)	7,901	64	103	1
Public sewage (M lbs.)	864	98	37	32
Total transfers/releases (M lbs.)	15,678	337	339	66
Facilities (#)	4,340	442	640	121
Submissions (#)	29,715	2,509	3,024	707
Companies (#)	450	179	262	14

AMEX, American Stock Exchange; M, million; NYSE, New York Stock Exchange.

publicly traded companies may be more likely to deal with wastes on-site because of potential economies of scale. Private firms' facilities may be smaller, however, so that waste streams may not be sufficient for on-site treatment, and hence these firms may account for proportionately more off-site disposal of toxins.

Of the 893 publicly traded firms identified as owning facilities reporting TRI data, 436 made it into the regression sample used to estimate stock price reactions. As Table 2.1 reveals, the 450 publicly traded firms from the New York and American stock exchanges that had complete CRSP stock price data (referred to as the "matched" companies) accounted for the vast majority of the pollution from publicly held companies. These 450 firms reported TRI releases or transfers of 15.7 billion pounds, out of a total of 16.4 billion emitted by public firms overall. Firms dropped from the sample because they did not have complete CRSP stock return data (179 companies) or were traded over the counter (262 firms) together accounted for only a fraction of the pollution from public companies. Confounding events such as merger announcements around the event window caused 14 New York or American exchange companies to be dropped from the regression sample, leaving a total of 436 publicly traded companies to be analyzed. The model of investors' reactions to the TRI focuses on these publicly held companies.

Table 2.2 contains a summary of the descriptive statistics for these 436 publicly held companies. The average firm had ten facilities that submitted TRI forms to the EPA. Each company filed close to 67 TRI forms, each of which represents the use or production of a listed chemical at one of its facilities. Firms were listed in 1989 as potentially responsible parties at an average of four Superfund sites, with the number of sites with liability ranging from 0 to 56 for these companies. Firm size varied substantially: sales in millions of dollars (1988) averaged $4,010 and ranged from $15 to $101,000. More than three quarters of the firms listed a primary line of business in manufacturing industries, with the greatest concentration (12%) in the chemical industry.

Media Coverage of Toxic Emissions

In the print sources catalogued by Lexis (plus the *Wall Street Journal*), stories about pollution using information from the TRI mentioned 134 companies in 1989. Though coverage of the TRI data was spread throughout the year after its release by the EPA, 40% of the firms that did receive coverage were first referred to in articles on June 19 or 20, 1989. Approximately 63% of the references to particular facilities or companies were to plants owned by publicly held corporations, consistent with the estimate that 73% of the total TRI releases and transfers were generated by these types of companies. Of the 893 publicly traded companies whose emissions are totaled in Table 2.1, only 58 received media coverage relating to their TRI releases in 1989. This coverage was further concentrated on companies on the main exchanges: 56 of the 629 firms on the New York or American exchanges reporting TRI releases were mentioned in print coverage, versus stories about only 2 of the 262 firms traded over the counter that had TRI releases.

Table 2.2. *Firm Descriptive Statistics (N = 436)*

Variable	Mean	Standard Deviation	Minimum	Maximum
Continuous variables:				
Abnormal return on day 0 ($)	−4,055,675	69,901,452	−5.349e-8	5.664e-8
TRI air (lbs.)	3,298,156	8,477,991	0	77,028,940
TRI land (lbs.)	4,243,364	47,866,685	0	9.716e-8
TRI underground (lbs.)	5,906,814	76,516,770	0	1.531e-9
TRI off-site (lbs.)	2,332,537	6,157,186	0	46,130,750
TRI surface water (lbs.)	18,118,475	1.820e-8	0	3.714e-9
TRI public sewage (lbs.)	1,908,315	6,618,038	0	68,223,748
TRI facilities (#)	10	14	1	111
TRI submissions (#)	67	116	1	171
Previous articles (#)	951	2,515	1	35,316
Sales ($M)	3,994	9,320	15	101,000
Employees (#)	27,725	58,161	350	817,000
Superfund sites (#)	4	7	0	56
Dummy variables:				
Media coverage of TRI Releases in 1989	.12	.32	0	1
Media coverage of TRI Releases on Day 0	.03	.18	0	1
Chemicals industry	.12	.32	0	1
Paper industry	.04	.19	0	1
Primary metals industry	.05	.21	0	1
Petroleum industry	.03	.16	0	1
Textiles industry	.01	.11	0	1
Other manufacturing industries	.53	.50	0	1

M, million.

The low levels of coverage of TRI releases in the print sources catalogued by Lexis are consistent with the economic theory of information provision developed by Anthony Downs (1957). According to Downs, people desire information for entertainment, consumption decisions, production activities, and political actions. Because it is rational for most individuals to free ride on participation in public policy, individuals will remain rationally ignorant about information that could help them make decisions about political issues such as environmental policy. This in turn may mean that journalists have reduced incentives to provide information such as detailed accounts of pollution patterns because their readers will choose to remain ignorant about such details. The coverage of the environment that does emerge may be aimed at satisfying the entertainment demand of readers (e.g., human interest coverage of pollution), informing those with a strong ideological interest in the environment, or providing information to those whose production activities are affected by environmental policies (e.g., corporate officers, environmentalists, lawyers). Because the publications catalogued in the Lexis data file searched are general interest publications, it is not surprising that only a fraction of the firms reporting TRI releases received coverage relating to their pollution totals.

Table 2.3 explores the determinants of why some companies' TRI releases were treated by journalists as "news" whereas other firms' filings received no media coverage in the newspapers and periodicals indexed by Lexis or in the *Wall Street Journal*. Of the 450 firms reporting TRI releases that had useable stock price data from the New York or American exchange, 50 received media coverage mentioning their TRI releases during 1989. Though these firms accounted for only 11% of the companies in the publicly traded firms in the regression sample, their TRI data accounted for approximately 29% of the facilities, 38% of the submission forms, and 71% of the total emissions and transfers among these 450 publicly traded firms. Thus for this sample of firms on the New York or American exchange, the media did focus on firms accounting for a large fraction of the pollution. Table 2.3 contains the results of logistic regressions examining the factors that influenced whether the emissions figures submitted to the EPA by a company's plants were used by the press in stories about pollution. Though three different specifications are presented (one focusing only on the pollution subtotals reported in the TRI data, another adding more information on pollution patterns and general company characteristics, and a third incorporating a measure of previous media coverage), the results are similar across the specifications, so attention will be focused on the full specification, (3).

Among the different pollution pathways contained in the TRI data, air pollution releases, land releases, underground injections, and waste shipped off-site to treatment or disposal facilities attracted the attention of journalists. The higher the reported levels of these pollution pathways,

Table 2.3. *Determinants of Media Coverage of TRI Releases*

	(1)	(2)	(3)
Constant	−3.281***	−3.597***	−3.535***
	(.263)	(.524)	(.523)
Air (lbs.)	1.320e-7***	1.212e-7***	1.150e-7***
	(2.991e-8)	(4.465e-8)	(4.548e-8)
Land (lbs.)	1.337e-8	2.516e-8**	2.449e-8***
	(1.065e-8)	(1.236e-8)	(1.241e-8)
Underground (lbs.)	2.243e-8**	3.017e-8**	2.960e-8**
	(1.031e-8)	(1.452e-8)	(1.457e-8)
Off-site (lbs.)	1.153e-7***	1.183e-7***	1.188e-7***
	(3.025e-8)	(4.440e-8)	(4.448e-8)
Surface water (lbs.)	−7.330e-9*	−1.060e-8**	−1.040e-8**
	(4.032e-9)	(5.131e-9)	(5.143e-9)
Public sewage (lbs.)	2.449e-8	2.416e-8	2.353e-8
	(2.734e-8)	(3.361e-8)	(3.375e-8)
Facilities (#)		−.086**	−.079**
		(.036)	(.037)
Submissions (#)		.021***	.020***
		(.007)	(.007)
Sales ($M)		−.00006	−.00007
		(.00005)	(.00005)
Employees (#)		.000017**	.000014*
		(7.597e-6)	(8.739e-6)
Superfund sites (#)		−.087*	−.080*
		(.048)	(.049)
Chemicals		−2.566**	−2.634**
		(1.150)	(1.166)
Paper		1.717**	1.693**
		(.862)	(.855)
Primary metals		−4.801**	−4.804**
		(2.401)	(2.429)
Petroleum		−.084	−.107
		(1.408)	(1.376)
Textiles		1.745	1.730
		(1.231)	(1.229)
Other manufacturing		−.247	−.339
		(.581)	(.590)
Previous articles (#)			.0001
			(.0001)
Log likelihood	−98.0	−77.0	−76.5
Number of observations	436	436	436

Note: Dependent variable in logistic regression equals 1 if there was an article about the company's TRI releases in 1989. Of the 436 companies in the regression sample, 50 had media coverage. Standard errors are in parentheses.
***Statistically significant at the .01 level; **statistically significant at the .05 level; *statistically significant at the .10 level.
M, million.

the more likely the firm's TRI figures were mentioned by journalists in stories about pollution. This effect was strongest for air releases and off-site shipments. The TRI air numbers may have attracted attention for many reasons. The Natural Resources Defense Council released a report on the day that the EPA made the TRI data public that focused on air emissions, a report that generated press stories on the TRI releases. Air pollution figures may also have attracted attention because of the upcoming debate over amendments to the Clean Air Act or because threats from this pollution pathway are seen to be of more interest to readers concerned about pollution. Shipments of waste off-site by facilities to treatment or disposal centers may have generated coverage because of the controversies surrounding interstate waste trade shipments or the "not-in-my-backyard" (NIMBY) siting battles associated with disposal facilities. Probability of coverage decreased with the size of water releases, which may be because these emissions were deemed less newsworthy because they were perceived by journalists to be less hazardous or because they were previously known through information from clean water programs.

Holding emission levels constant, the more facilities a company's emissions are spread over, the less likely it will be mentioned in media coverage. This indicates that for a given amount of pollution, reporters are more likely to write about emissions concentrated at a few facilities rather than emissions spread out over many plants. Because the data were reported at the facility level rather than the company level, it is not surprising that stories may have focused on the size of emissions by facility. In addition, the more submissions reported by the company, the greater the likelihood of coverage. Because each submission (Form R) represents the release of a particular chemical at a given facility, this indicates that the more that pollution is spread across a diverse number of chemicals, the greater the likelihood that it will generate coverage. Firms with more employees were also more likely to be covered, which may relate to journalists' incentives to cover stories of interest to a greater number of workers in their communities.

The degree that the TRI figures were perceived by journalists to be "news" may in part have depended on the previous amount of information available about a company's pollution patterns. For example, large releases by companies involved in production of pollution-intensive goods such as chemicals might be less newsworthy because readers already associated these firms with pollution. The industry dummy variables in Table 2.3 indicate that firms whose main line of business was the production of chemicals or primary metals were less likely to have their TRI releases written about by journalists. Firms in the paper industry were more likely to be written about, which may indicate that journalists found their releases to be higher than previously known.

The historical pollution record of a firm is also represented in Table 2.3 by the number of Superfund sites at which a firm had been identified as a potentially responsible party by the EPA in 1989. A company's involvement at such sites often generates publicity because of litigation, regulatory actions, and community responses to the potential contamination. The number of sites may also be seen as a general indicator of the degree that a firm was a generator of hazardous waste in the past. Table 2.3 shows that the larger the number of Superfund sites associated with a firm, the less likely its TRI figures were to be mentioned in news coverage. This is consistent with the hypothesis that in cases in which a firm's pollution patterns were previously known, journalists were less likely to write about the figures on toxic releases and transfers in the TRI.

Specification (3) also allows one to investigate whether TRI media coverage also followed general patterns of media coverage. Some firms, because of factors such as location near major media markets or involvement in particular industries, may be covered more closely by journalists; firms may also vary in the degree to which they seek coverage of their activities through public relations actions. These types of variations were reflected in a count for each firm of the total number of articles in Lexis that mentioned the firm from June 1988 to May 1989. Holding the pollution-specific variables constant, the greater the general tendency of a firm to receive coverage, the more likely its TRI figures were to receive coverage. This effect, however, was not statistically significant.

In sum, most of the publicly traded firms in the sample did not receive any coverage of their TRI releases in the print sources tracked here during 1989. Decisions by journalists to cover the releases of particular firms are consistent with hypotheses about what constitutes "news." The higher the air, land, and underground injection releases or off-site transfers, the greater the diversity in chemicals released, and the higher the number of employees of a firm, the more likely its TRI releases were noted in news coverage. The more its emissions were spread out across different facilities or the more previous information (such as line of business or Superfund exposure) indicated that it was involved in the generation of pollution, the less likely journalists were to treat a firm's TRI data as news.

Investor Reactions

Table 2.4 contains the estimations of abnormal returns for the companies reporting TRI releases calculated according to the event study

Table 2.4. *Abnormal Returns for Firms Reporting TRI Releases*

Window	All Firms	Firms with Media Coverage	Firms with Superfund Sites
−1	.00000767	−.000349	−.000504
	(.249)	(.446)	(−.169)
0	−.00284***	−.00348**	−.00373***
	(−3.841)	(−2.017)	(−3.602)
0–5	−.0120***	−.00931**	−.00958***
	(−6.029)	(−2.485)	(−3.634)
Number of observations	436	50	258

Note: Media coverage refers to firms (50) with media coverage in 1989 of TRI releases. Z-statistics are in parentheses. ***Statistically significant at the .01 level. **Statistically significant at the .05 level.

methodology. For day −1, the trading day before the TRI data were released on Monday, June 19, 1989, the average of the abnormal returns for companies on the New York or American exchange that had useable stock price information and reported TRI releases (N = 436) was not statistically significant. This indicates that the data were not being leaked to the market in the day before the official announcement by the EPA of the figures. On the day the information was released (day 0), the average abnormal return for these firms was negative and statistically significant (−.00284, Z statistic = −3.8). The negative returns were also statistically significant for several subsets of these firms. Companies whose TRI emissions received media coverage during 1989 (N = 50) had an average abnormal return of −.00348, whereas companies whose previous waste generation and handling had caused them to be listed as potentially responsible parties at Superfund sites (N = 258) had an average abnormal return of −.00373.[51]

These abnormal returns translate into large dollar losses for the firms resulting from the release of the TRI information. For the first day the TRI data were released (day 0), the abnormal return attributed to reaction to the TRI data translates into an average loss of $4.1 million in stock market value. Firms that eventually enjoyed media coverage of their releases experienced average abnormal returns of −$6.2 million on day 0. Firms with Superfund sites had average abnormal returns on day 0 of −$5.9 million.

These results indicate that the day the TRI data were officially released and articles appeared with information about facility emissions, companies with TRI emissions did experience negative, statistically significant abnormal returns. The magnitude of the abnormal return should not be confused with the estimated liabilities and compliance costs associated with a firm's toxic emissions (which would likely be much higher). These negative abnormal returns reflect the change in investor expectations about a firm's pollution costs brought about by the additional information provided by the TRI data.[52] To the extent that previous information on a firm's pollution record was available, it would already have been incorporated into the stock price. Because TRI information may continue to reach investors beyond day 0, Table 2.4 also examines a larger event window of days 0 through 5. Since media coverage mentioning specific firms extended beyond the initial release day, this larger window allows for a longer time period for the information to reach investors. The results indicate that over this extended time period, the average of the cumulative abnormal returns for firms reporting TRI releases is negative and statistically significant. The longer time period also raises a greater risk that confounding events exist for firms in the sample that have not been accounted for, so that the cross-sectional analysis of the abnormal returns will focus on the results for day 0.

Table 2.5 examines the determinants of the dollar value of abnormal returns to the TRI firms experienced on day 0. The dependent variable for each company is the dollar value of the day 0 abnormal return, calculated by multiplying the abnormal return by the price on day −1 and the number of shares outstanding.[53] The reported standard errors are corrected for heteroskedasticity using White standard errors. Two specifications are presented, one that focuses on the influence of the pollution subtotals and company characteristics on investor reactions and another that adds variables related to media coverage of the TRI data and industry characteristics.

None of the individual TRI pollution pathways was statistically significant in explaining the variation in the dollar value of abnormal returns. Investors may have not reacted to specific levels of TRI releases in part because when the 1987 data were released by the EPA, the figures were accompanied by caveats that release and transfer estimates could be difficult to interpret because they represented the first efforts by firms to estimate their releases.[54] Investors did react, however, to the number of TRI chemicals a firm reported handling at its facilities. For each additional TRI chemical a company submitted a report to the EPA on, the firm's stock value dropped $236,000. Investor reaction to the number of chemicals rather than the level of emissions may be because of greater

Table 2.5. *Cross-Section Analysis of the Abnormal Returns ($)*
on Day 0 of the TRI Data Release

Constant	−2,432,021	−10,831,358*
	(4,509,362)	(7,386,213)
Air (lbs.)	−.379	−.401
	(1.085)	(1.085)
Land (lbs.)	.009	.022
	(.036)	(.039)
Underground (lbs.)	.206	.223
	(.160)	(.185)
Off-site (lbs.)	.062	−.034
	(1.083)	(1.084)
Surface water (lbs.)	−.082	−.094
	(.062)	(.074)
Public sewage (lbs.)	.111	−.030
	(.542)	(.617)
Facilities (#)	126,748	71,362
	(1,183,721)	(1,184,714)
Submissions (#)	−223,520***	−236,460***
	(60,505)	(61,240)
Sales ($M)	1,903	2,168
	(2,384)	(2,405)
Employees (#)	−102	−103
	(340)	(340)
Superfund sites (#)	2,015,126*	1,908,891*
	(1,084,382)	(1,046,734)
Chemicals		15,227,832
		(14,679,288)
Paper		5,086,792
		(11,956,908)
Primary metals		16,922,357*
		(9,710,114)
Petroleum		15,175,060
		(17,696,669)
Textiles		4,090,127
		(8,263,985)
Other manufacturing		10,384,338
		(8,016,390)
Media coverage on day 0		30,823,148
		(25,025,569)
R^2	.075	.084
Observations (#)	436	436

Note: Dependent variable in the OLS regression is the dollar value of the estimated abnormal return on the first day the TRI data were made public (6/19/89). Standard errors in parentheses are corrected for heteroskedasticity. ***Statistically significant at the .01 level; *Statistically significant at the .10 level. M, million.

credibility given to information about whether a chemical was released compared with the information presented in 1989 on its actual release level. In addition, there may be a fixed cost associated with dealing with each chemical that is reflected in the estimated impact of reporting an additional TRI chemical.

Previous information about a company's pollution patterns, however, results in lower changes in stock values for a firm. With other pollution variables held constant, a company with an additional Superfund site had an increase in the dollar value of the abnormal return by nearly $1.9 million. This indicates that for a given amount of toxic releases and transfers revealed in the TRI, a company's drop in stock value is substantially reduced if investors previously had incorporated information about pollution (proxied for here by the number of Superfund sites the EPA had associated a company with) into expectations about the firm's performance. Firms in the primary metals industry experienced less of a negative abnormal return than others, which may be because investors already perceived these companies as polluters. Note that the dummy variable for whether the firm's TRI totals received media coverage on the first day the figures were released was not statistically significant.[55]

Conclusions

In its first formal year of operation in 1989, the Toxics Release Inventory (TRI) represented an innovative attempt by the EPA to use information as a regulatory tool. Descriptions of the program stressed how the data could be used by environmentalists, regulators, and corporate officials to monitor part of the pollution performance of companies. The results here show the extent that the TRI data first released by the EPA in June of 1989 were "news" to two sets of decisionmakers often overlooked in discussions of environmental programs: journalists and investors. The majority of publicly traded companies that reported TRI emission figures to the EPA did not receive media coverage in the general interest publications covered by Lexis. For some of these companies, however, journalists did find the TRI figures noteworthy and included them in stories about pollution. The higher the air emissions, the more land releases or underground injections, the greater the amount of waste shipped off-site, and the more chemical submissions reported by a firm, the more likely it was to receive coverage. The more dispersed its pollution was across facilities and the more information available about the company's pollution patterns prior to the TRI (proxied for by Superfund site exposure or primary line of business in polluting industries), the less likely journalists were to treat the firm's TRI releases as news.

The event study methodology is especially well suited for studying the impact of the TRI because the program's function is to provide new information. The results indicate that the TRI data did provide "news" to investors. For companies that reported TRI data to the EPA, the average abnormal return on the day this information was made public was negative and statistically significant. In terms of the dollar values of the abnormal returns, firms reporting TRI information lost on average $4.1 million in stock value on the first day the data were released. The greater the number of different chemical submissions reported by the firms, the larger the drop in stock value for the company. These effects were reduced, however, for firms on which investors had previous information about pollution patterns, such as companies with exposure at Superfund sites. The release of the TRI clearly provided new information to two communities: print journalists writing about pollution and investors concerned about the impact of pollution on financial performance. It remained to be seen how the information would be used by others, including the communities that contained facilities that generated TRI reports.

THREE

Spreading the Word in the Public and Private Sectors

The operation of the Toxics Release Inventory program in its early years (1987–1992) involved a cast of thousands – thousands of manufacturing firm employees who filled out thousands of forms describing chemical releases and transfers at thousands of plants. Although the TRI Form Rs provided a detailed picture of toxics emitted in a given community, if members of the public heard anything at all about the program, the news often came in the form of stories about national or state reports produced by the EPA or environmental groups. Reports based on the yearly release of TRI figures became a way for the EPA to chart the progress of the program and for interest groups to highlight both the dangers posed by chemical exposures and the shortcomings involved in the production or interpretation of the pollution data.

In September 1990 the EPA released the second annual TRI report, which contained the agency's analysis of 1988 TRI data. The headline to many was that total TRI releases and transfers had dropped from 7 billion pounds in 1987 to 6.2 billion pounds in 1988. In the first page of the report, however, the agency noted that the 11% decline in reported figures did not translate into an 11% reduction in actual emissions:

While some of the decrease in TRI totals is due to actual reductions in the quantity of wastes generated or disposed of, much of the apparent decline between 1987 and 1988 stems from "paper" changes, that is, from changes in how wastes were estimated or reported, rather than changes in waste generation practices. For instance, some recycled materials that were inadvertently reported in 1987 . . . were not reported in 1988. For the facilities reporting the 10 largest decreases, at least 66 percent of the reduction is due to paper changes in the data.[1]

The report noted that 50 of the approximately 20,000 plants reporting in 1988 accounted for more than one third of all TRI releases and transfers; a table listing these facilities focused attention on the largest TRI reporters. The concentrated nature of emissions underscored the difficulties in assessing trends across TRI facilities from changes in national totals. The report also noted that only 32% of TRI figures were calculated based on actual measurement of releases or transfers. On a pounds basis, 22% of TRI figures were estimated based on mass balance equations, 4% on emission factors, and the largest segment (37%) on "other" approaches such as engineering judgment. The report also contained information on the toxicity of the TRI chemicals and indicators of whether a given chemical was considered a carcinogen.

Throughout the 1990s, there was a two-year lag between companies' submission of TRI forms to the EPA and the agency's release of the data and publication of the annual report. The third TRI national report, which contained assessments of 1989 data, was released in September 1991. For the 1989 reporting year, 22,569 plants reported releases and transfers of 5.7 billion pounds, a drop of 11% from the previous year. The agency cautioned, however, that 59% of the total decreases in TRI figures were accounted for by changes at 127 plants. On a plant basis, "almost as many facilities showed increases in TRI amounts as showed decreases."[2] While continuing to list the top 50 facilities in terms of releases and transfers, the EPA also summed TRI figures across companies and reported the top ten parent companies: DuPont, Monsanto, American Cyanamid, BP, Renco Group, 3M, Vulcan Chemicals, General Motors, Eastman Kodak, and Phelps Dodge. The agency also noted that actual monitoring or measurement accounted for only 26% of the TRI figures reported. "Other" methods of estimation, including engineering calculations and best judgment, accounted for 45% of the TRI totals reported.

The sixth annual TRI report, which analyzed TRI submissions covering 1992, followed a familiar pattern of assessing aggregate trends, identifying large emitters, and providing cautions about data quality. The 23,630 plants that submitted TRI forms (81,016 in total) in 1992 generated a reported 3.2 billion in releases to air, water, land, or underground injection. This represented a decline of approximately 35% from 1988, the base year that the EPA adopted because of problems with the first year (1987) of reported data. Reported transfers of TRI chemicals to publicly owned treatment works and disposal/treatment centers dropped by 34%

between 1988 and 1992. The report again identified the top 50 plants and the top ten firms in terms of TRI releases: DuPont, Freeport-McMoran, American Cyanamid, Monsanto, Asarco, Renco Group, Vulcan Materials, Arcadian Fertilizer, Eastman Kodak, and BP. Because of provisions in the Pollution Prevention Act of 1990, TRI plants had to report as of 1991 information on chemical quantities involved (on- and off-site) in recycling and energy recovery. This meant that the 1992 report provided even more details on chemical waste management at reporting facilities. The EPA also acknowledged the persistent difficulty in determining what reductions in reported emissions actually represent. The agency did conduct a survey of 960 TRI facilities to examine the reasons for reported changes in TRI figures between 1989 and 1990.[3] In terms of the percentage of the quantity of reported TRI increases, 19% came from production changes, 7% from estimation method changes, 2% from source reduction, and 73% from "other factors." For reported decreases, 13% came from production changes, 5% from estimated methods changes, 20% from source reduction, and 62% from "other factors." As the 1992 report stressed, the origins and impacts of reported changes in TRI figures remained undefined.

Environmental groups produced studies in the early years of the TRI program that were more likely than the EPA national reports to focus on health effects and to direct attention to the total amounts of pollutants released by companies. In June 1990, the Citizens Fund released a summary of the 1988 TRI data in a report entitled *Poisons in Our Neighborhoods: Toxic Pollution in the United States*. The report listed for each state the top ten companies, facilities, counties, and zip codes by five different categories of TRI data: total toxic releases and transfers; total carcinogens, total pounds of chemicals thought to cause birth defects, total air releases, and total water releases. The environmental group's analysis of the TRI was much more explicit than the EPA reports in highlighting health risks (e.g., poisons, carcinogens) and in aggregating the data so that companies with high releases could be easily identified in local communities. In its 1991 report using 1989 TRI data entitled *Manufacturing Pollution: A Survey of the Nation's Toxic Polluters*, the Citizens Fund used the same five categories of TRI data to identify the top 50 plants and companies nationwide releasing particular types of toxics (e.g., carcinogens or those suspected of causing birth defects). To explore the meaning of reported reductions in TRI releases between 1989 and 1988, the environmental group contacted the 50 plants with the highest reductions and conducted interviews with officials at 45 of these facilities. The report found that:

The main reasons for reductions at these 45 facilities were changes in waste estimation techniques, reinterpretation of EPA's reporting requirements (almost always in a more favorable direction), lower levels of production, or other factors beyond the control of the facility, such as decreased runoff due to less rainfall.[4]

The survey of 45 plants did find 13 facilities where reductions in TRI figures came from actual measures taken to reduce the release of pollutants or use of toxic chemicals.

In its 1992 report about the 1990 TRI data, the Citizens Fund continued to focus attention on large polluters by publishing the identities of the top 100 companies and plants categorized by their releases of different types of TRI chemicals. In surveying the plants with the largest emission reductions between 1989 and 1990, the environmental group found "that a majority of the facilities surveyed acknowledged that these changes did not represent actual reductions, but were the results of changed EPA reporting requirements, or errors in the 1989 reports."[5] The Citizens Fund also generated a unique analysis to demonstrate the inequities involved in the distribution of TRI facilities. As the report notes:

Analyzing the toxic chemical releases for the 50 largest industrial toxic polluters by zipcode and comparing those releases to the releases in the zipcodes of the companies' chief executives, it was found that 230 times more toxic waste was emitted in the neighborhoods near the plants than in the communities of the chief officers of the companies.[6]

While environmental groups used the TRI data extensively to focus attention on large polluters and the potential health effects of their releases, the groups also pointed out the flaws with the information and the need to expand the program. In 1991, 16 environmental groups released a report produced by the Natural Resources Defense Council entitled *A Right to Know More*.[7] The study pointed out that the TRI only covered a small subset of chemicals and noted that there were more than 500 chemicals regulated under other environmental laws as toxic that were not subject to TRI reporting. Because the program only covered manufacturing facilities, many other polluting establishments were left out of toxic reporting requirements. Those identified as exempt from reporting included federal facilities, utilities, hazardous waste disposal plants, and oil and gas wells and pipelines. Finally, the study faulted the TRI for the type of data collected. The environmental groups, who ultimately wanted to reduce the aggregate use of toxics, wanted the EPA to collect more information on the chemicals used and stored at a facility. Although TRI figures tracked releases into the environment or amounts shipped off-site, the quantities of chemicals used on-site or incorporated into final products remained outside the reporting requirements.

Environmental groups also used TRI reports to chronicle success stories. A 1991 report by the Center for Policy Alternatives and the Working Group on Community Right-to-Know provided ten case studies of how the TRI data were used to pressure companies to reduce toxics use or emission. For example, the release of the TRI data catalyzed community activists in Northfield, Minnesota, to join with the Amalgamated Clothing and Textile Workers Union to pressure a Sheldahl Incorporated plant. In union contract negotiations, the company promised to reduce use and emissions of methylene chloride, a toxic listed as a probable carcinogen. The Atlantic States Legal Foundation used the citizen suit provision in EPCRA to file civil suits against companies that failed to file TRI forms. The environmental group negotiated settlements that included adoption of pollution prevention and toxic use reduction programs. The Massachusetts Public Interest Research Group used the TRI data on chemicals that destroy the ozone to convince Raytheon, the firm identified as the state's largest releaser of chemicals harming the ozone, to pledge to reduce their releases.

The reports discussed here are part of a large body of studies generated by TRI information. Research by Lynn and Kartez (1994) demonstrates that the release of the TRI data generated many reports in the early years of the program. They found 95 reports using TRI information released between 1987 and 1990, with public interest groups producing more than 60 of the studies and state agencies accounting for most of the rest. The public interest group reports were more likely to supplement the release data with information on health effects (64% of their reports contained this information versus 30% of state agency reports). Public interest group reports were also more likely to include information on ecological effects (mentioned in 37% of these reports) than were state agency studies (only 20% had information on ecological impacts).

In a separate survey of TRI users (N = 147), Lynn and Kartez note the disparate reactions of citizen groups, state agencies, and industry users to the information. Citizen groups rated state data diskettes for personal computers, printed data lists, and reports by intermediaries such as state governments and public interest groups as the most useful forms of TRI data. Industry respondents, in contrast, rated the National Library of Medicine's TOXNET databases as the most useful forms of TRI data. This

supports the General Accounting Office (GAO) study (1991) that found
"49% of total TRI access on NLM's TOXNET was by industry users and
25% by research scientists, rather than by citizens, citizen organizations,
or state agencies."[8] When asked whether lack of computer equipment
was an obstacle to using TRI information, 37% of public interest groups
reported this problem versus 20% of state agency or industry users. The
Lynn and Kartez survey also revealed how TRI data use varied by group.
As they note:

Of the various uses, the three most frequently reported by state 313 agencies are:
comparing TRI data to permits (64%), source reduction efforts (48%), and comparing emissions patterns at similar facilities (41%...). Among public interest
and environmental groups, the three most frequent uses include: directly pressuring facilities for change (85%), educating citizens (79%), and lobbying for policy
changes (75%). Among the limited industry sample, the most frequent uses are
for source reduction efforts (58%), educating citizens (53%), and developing
company profiles (53%).[9]

Citizen group and industry respondents often agreed on the overall
impacts of TRI data use. More than half the respondents in each of the
categories agreed that the release of the TRI led to source reduction
efforts at reporting plants, media coverage of the toxic releases, and the
prompting of industry-citizen meetings.

In its first years of operation, the TRI program also generated changes
in state laws. By 1991, more than 12 states had passed toxic use reduction legislation, with environmental groups linking the passage of some
of these laws to the scrutiny and debate arising from the TRI.[10] Though
31 states had right-to-know laws prior to the passage of EPCRA, many
changed their requirements to comply with the provisions of Title III.
EPCRA imposed multiple duties on the states, including the establishment of State Emergency Response Commissions. Under EPCRA, businesses must submit their TRI forms both to the EPA and a state agency
designated by the governor. States have a responsibility to make the
TRI information available to the public. A 1989 survey by the National
Governors Association found that of 47 responding states, at least 28 were
spending more than $200,000 per year to implement Title III of EPCRA.
The report found, however, that "few states...have established aggressive regulatory programs to ensure that facilities covered under Title III
submit complete and accurate data."[11] The NGA found that even the
well-developed state right-to-know programs had "fewer than two field
inspectors."[12]

Overall, the release of the TRI data in the early years of the program generated attention, action, and complaints about the nature of the data. Two concerns voiced included the degree to which the plants that should have been reporting under the program were actually filing the forms and the extent to which reporting facilities were focused on reducing pounds of pollutants rather than reducing the risks associated with their emissions. The next two sections explore the incentives involved in nonreporting and in emissions reductions in the early years of the TRI.

Noncompliance in TRI Reporting: Are Violators Ignorant, or Evasive, of the Law?

Both the EPA and the GAO estimate that about one third of the facilities that were required to report toxic emissions under the TRI program did not participate in its first years of operation (U.S. GAO 1991, p. 49). A substantial theoretical and empirical literature explains the economics and politics involved in regulatory compliance. A firm choosing to comply with a regulation trades off the marginal costs of compliance (e.g., resources devoted to changes in technologies or business practices to comply) with the marginal benefits of compliance.[13] In the literature on regulatory compliance, the marginal benefits of compliance often relate to the expected value of fines avoided, which in turn are a function of the probability of inspection, the likelihood a violation is found, and the magnitude of the penalty assessed. Research on regulators reveals that they may adopt a policy of police patrols or fire alarms in scheduling inspections (McCubbins and Schwartz 1984). The probability a facility is visited and intensity of enforcement may be driven both by the nature of the surrounding residents and the efforts of elected representatives in the area (Scholz and Wei 1986; Scholz 1991; Scholz, Twombly, and Headrick 1991). The frequency with which regulators venture out and the willingness to find violations may vary over time with responses to executive and legislative actions (Wood 1988, Wood and Waterman 1991, Waterman and Wood 1993). Facilities across different states may face regulators whose zeal for environmental policies varies with the importance of different industries to the state economies and the role environmentalists play in local politics (Lester and Bowman 1983, Wood 1992). A firm faced with decisions over generation of environmental externalities will incorporate the likelihood that residents in a local community will engage in political activities to oppose its pollution (Hamilton 1993).[14]

In our analysis of information provision programs, we consider a motive for noncompliance distinct from evasion: ignorance of regulatory requirements.[15] Although many regulatory programs involve regular on-site inspections, the initiative for compliance with self-reporting programs begins with a firm's action, which may in turn depend on whether the company knows that a particular information provision is required. Although the relationship between the EPA and a polluting facility is clearly a principal-agent structure, there is no explicit contract in the TRI program. Under typical contract arrangements, we would assume that a facility is aware of its reporting requirements and faces penalties if it fails to report. Here, failure to comply may be a result of ignorance or evasion. Studying compliance decisions with the TRI thus offers insight into the general relations among principals and agents, and the specific hazards involved in information provision programs.

The EPA and state regulators believe the early implementation of the TRI was hampered by substantial nonreporting, the failure of facilities subject to TRI reporting requirements to submit information to the EPA. A study for the EPA estimated that the compliance rate for firms subject to the TRI reporting was approximately 66% in the first year of the program (Abt Associates 1990).[16] In a 1992 survey of state officials dealing with TRI, 29 out of 44 states responding ranked identifying and reducing the number of TRI nonreporters as the most important priority for improving the program (Bureau of National Affairs 1993a). Although officials in 13 states in the survey indicated that they had statutory authority to take action against nonreporters, regulators in most states rely on the EPA to prosecute nonreporters. The EPA can levy fines of $25,000 per day for failure to file under EPCRA, though the agency rarely seeks the full amount of such fines. In actions taken against 37 manufacturers in June 1993 for failure to submit TRI forms, the agency sought an average of $75,000 in proposed fines per company, partly in an attempt to publicize the impending July 1 deadline for filing 1993 TRI figures (Bureau of National Affairs 1993b). The expected penalty facing a nonreporter, which is a function of the fines levied and the probability of being caught, remains low because of the low probability of being caught.[17]

Minnesota offers an ideal setting to examine the determinants of nonreporting, for in 1991, the state's Emergency Response Commission (ERC) conducted a project funded by the EPA to improve the quality of TRI data reported by facilities in the state (Minnesota Emergency Response Commission 1992). The study focused on determining which facilities that met the reporting requirements failed to submit 1990 TRI forms to the state. The Minnesota ERC identified suspected nonreporters using the following methodology. The EPA's National Enforcement Information Services Center (NEISC) provides states with data on plants potentially subject to EPCRA reporting. Minnesota received from the NEISC a list of approximately 3,400 facilities located in the state that had never reported TRI data, had ten or more employees, listed a SIC code in the manufacturing range (20–39), and had been assigned a number by the Dun and Bradstreet corporation (the database itself was derived from Dun and Bradstreet's facility information files). The Minnesota regulators pared the list down by excluding plants they felt were unlikely to exceed the 10,000-pound threshold for using TRI chemicals. This led them to exclude, for example, small printing facilities, machine shops, and metal fabricators. The remaining facilities formed the basis of a list of firms to be surveyed by the state.[18]

The ERC mailed out letters to more than 1,300 facilities that asked three questions: did the facility have ten or more full-time employees?; was the facility included in the manufacturing SIC codes (20–39)?; and did the plant use more than 10,000 pounds of any of the chemicals on an enclosed list of the substances subject to TRI reporting? Follow-up letters and phone calls were used so that less than 1% of the facilities failed to respond to the request for information. During this process, 14 facilities that had failed to report previously submitted TRI forms to the agency for 1990, which the ERC attributed to its outreach program. In total, the state received responses from 165 facilities that indicated they should have filed TRI reports for 1990. As of December 1, 1991, 142 of these firms had submitted Form Rs to the ERC. The remaining facilities were the subject of on-site investigations in 1992, in which ten of the 23 facilities were found to be subject to reporting. In an additional 25 inspections, the agency found five facilities that should have submitted TRI reports.

Among the 142 facilities that submitted 1990 forms in response to the agency's efforts, a plurality of the plants (63) were identified by surveying part of the list provided by the EPA's NEISC, the list derived from Dun and Bradstreet. Other sources of the names and addresses of nonreporters discovered by the survey were the Minnesota Directory of Manufacturers (37 facilities), the Section 312 reports (14), the hazardous waste inventory (7), the air quality inventory (6), and tips to the regulators (1). Fourteen facilities also came forward and identified themselves as nonreporters during the surveying process. The 142 previously nonreporting plants accounted for an additional 268 Form Rs for 1990, totaling 3.6 million in releases and transfers (fugitive and stack air each totaled about

1.4 million pounds from these facilities). The increase in the number of plants reporting over 1989 is significant, although the pollution from these nonreporters is a small fraction of total state releases and transfers. In 1989, a total of 481 facilities had submitted Form Rs in Minnesota, which totaled 81 million pounds of releases and transfers.[19]

Although facilities that ultimately submitted TRI forms were easily identified, the universe of plants that potentially might be covered by the TRI's reporting requirements is much broader. To create a sample of firms potentially subject to EPCRA reporting in 1990, we constructed an extract from Dun and Bradstreet data on Minnesota firms that contained information on any facilities that had ten or more employees and were in manufacturing industries (SIC codes 20–39). This resulted in a sample of 4,087 facilities with Dun and Bradstreet data on such variables as the number of employees at the facility, firm age, and total company sales.

Using the Dun and Bradstreet extract as the base of facilities potentially covered by the TRI, we linked the information from the Minnesota ERC to this data by using the Dun and Bradstreet numbers associated with facilities. This allowed us to divide our sample of plants potentially subject to TRI reporting into many subsamples: facilities subject to TRI reporting (identified through TRI filings) versus facilities not subject to filing (identified through the survey responses), facilities that complied with the law by reporting (those that filed on time) versus facilities that did not report but should have (identified from the ERC's survey and inspections), and facilities detected from the EPA's NEISC list of facilities versus those detected by surveying from other lists or from inspections.[20]

We analyze the Minnesota TRI data using a modified detection-controlled estimation model. Feinstein (1989, 1990) coins the term *detection-controlled estimation* (DCE) to refer to models in which identification of noncompliant cases is incomplete. In the simplest form, a DCE model is a two-stage system of equations, one governing compliance and a second describing detection conditional on noncompliance. The statistical – indeed, substantive – problem is that individuals who are not detected as noncompliers may be either compliers or undetected noncompliers. The basic DCE model comprises a useful point of departure for construction of our own modified detection-controlled estimation model. Our research problem is further compounded by the question of coverage: not all the facilities in our universe are covered by the Toxics Release Inventory, and as such, not all facilities have to file. Figure 3.1 demonstrates the three steps in our problem. The first question is one of coverage: does facility *i* fall under the jurisdiction of the Toxics Release

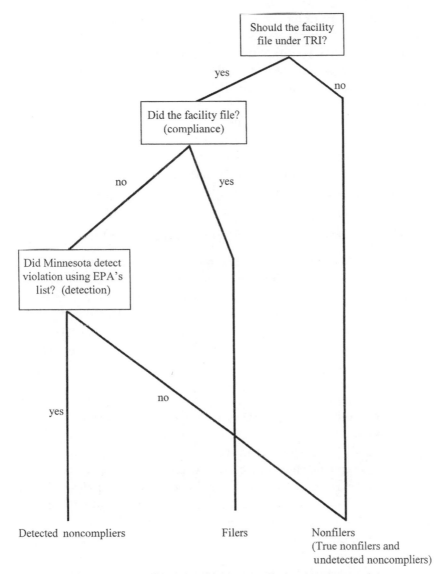

Figure 3.1. Modified detection-controlled estimation model.

Inventory? As long as the facility has ten or more employees, falls into the appropriate Standard Industrial Classifications, and produces at least 25,000 pounds or uses at least 10,000 pounds annually of certain listed toxins, that facility should file. If the facility should file, then the second question is one of compliance: does the facility file with the TRI?

Some facilities fail to file for reasons of evasion; other facilities fail to file for reasons of ignorance of the program. Finally, for facilities that fail to file with the TRI, the question becomes one of detection: conditional on eligibility for the program and failing to file, was the facility detected by the Minnesota regulators using the EPA's list of plants to target for inspection?

Our dependent variable falls into three categories. One category denotes whether a facility did not file (but was not detected using EPA methods as a noncomplier), a second category denotes facilities that did file, and a third category denotes facilities that did not file and were detected as noncompliers using the EPA's list.[21]

Coverage, Violation, and Detection Hypotheses

To estimate the detection-controlled model, we need to develop three separate models for a facility's probability of being covered by the TRI, of being in violation with TRI (conditional on violation), and of being detected by Minnesota regulators using the EPA list (conditional on violation). The first and third of these models are relatively technical models whose parameters are given by the details of the program. The second model – of propensity for violation – is the substantive core of this section.

We model coverage as a function of facility size and production processes. A facility in Minnesota should have filed a 1990 TRI report with the state Emergency Response Commission if it met three requirements: had ten or more employees, engaged in manufacturing activity (as defined by SIC codes 20–39), and manufactured at least 25,000 pounds or used at least 10,000 pounds annually of any substance on a list of more than 300 chemicals. To represent the set of facilities potentially covered by this reporting requirement, we examined the 1992 Minnesota Dun and Bradstreet files (which generally would contain 1991 values for many variables) for facilities that had at least ten employees and reported SIC codes ranging from 20 through 30.[22]

Because we cannot directly observe the chemical production or use at these facilities, we are left with the question of how to model the set of characteristics associated with chemical use or manufacture that make it likely that a plant will be covered by the TRI reporting requirements.

One of the TRI reporting thresholds is the number of employees at the facility. The number of employees also provides information about the scale of the production process at the site. If facilities with more employees produce more or make greater use of other inputs, such as the

TRI chemicals, then facilities with more employees should be more likely to be covered by TRI requirements. Facilities with toxic emissions may also be more likely to be regulated by the EPA under air pollution control programs, so those plants with air program permits should also be more likely to be covered under TRI. The plants listed in the EPA's Resource Conservation and Recovery Information System (RCRIS) database for Minnesota are generators of hazardous waste, transporters, treatment, storage, or disposal facilities, or sites investigated under the Resource Conservation and Recovery Act (RCRA) program but not found to be subject to its requirements (85 sites were investigated and found not to be subject or had missing data on whether they were subject to RCRA).[23] Because there is overlap between chemicals defined as hazardous under RCRA and the TRI chemicals, plants in the RCRIS database should be more likely to be subject to TRI reporting.[24] Finally, if the plant is a branch of a multiestablishment firm (versus a single, stand-alone facility or a headquarters facility) the plant may be less likely to be covered, because some outlets of multiestablishment firms may be less likely to have substantial manufacturing at each site (e.g., some sites could be related primarily to distribution).

Our second model describes whether a facility (that should file a TRI report) fails to file the form. The violation model builds, in part, on the theoretical and empirical literature on regulatory compliance. If non-compliance stems from calculated evasion, managers at a facility covered by TRI reporting trade off the marginal costs of compliance with the marginal benefits of compliance. At a minimum, the costs of filing TRI forms involve the time devoted to determining chemical use at the plant and estimating emissions and transfers.[25] The public scrutiny attracted by the data may also increase pressure from regulators or interest groups for the firm to engage in pollution reduction programs, entailing additional costs. The greater the number and amounts of chemicals at the facility, the larger the potential costs of filing and hence the more likely a facility may choose to evade. We proxy facility size with the log of plant employment, reasoning that the larger the facility, the greater the cost of compliance. If a facility is covered by RCRA, its production process may entail more TRI reporting and higher compliance costs, which would make the plant more likely to evade reporting. Controlling for whether a facility is in the RCRIS database, however, we believe that the smallest hazardous waste generators would be less likely to violate because the amount of chemicals they handle would make it less costly to comply with reporting compared with medium or large hazardous waste generators.

The marginal benefits to compliance include the avoidance of fines for nonreporting.[26] The expected value to a firm of avoided fines depends in part on the facility's estimated probability of inspection, the likelihood that a violation is assessed, and the penalty amount. Factors that increase these parameters would raise the expected benefits from compliance and thus lead to a lower probability of violation. Because communities with more politically active residents may be more likely to "pull the fire alarm," we include the percentage of the county adult population that voted in the 1988 presidential election in the belief that this would increase the likelihood of inspections. We also included the percentage of the county voters who voted in an environmental trust fund referendum in 1988, because these residents might also be more likely to pull the fire alarm to generate inspections. If there are fixed costs for regulators to travel to an area for inspections that can be spread across visits to plants, we believe that more manufacturing in a county (measured by number of manufacturing facilities) should be associated with a higher probability of inspection and thus lower violation probability. A regulator's willingness to impose costs on facilities may also vary with the impact on the community (as noted by Scholz, Twombly, and Headrick 1991, who found that OSHA penalties were lower in areas with higher unemployment, even though inspections in those areas were more frequent). The higher the unemployment level, the lower the expected fine for a given violation in the area.[27]

Additional factors that may indicate the propensity of a plant to evade reporting include data on the facility's past behavior. Total notices of violations, administrative action enforcements, and judicial actions in the hazardous waste, air, and water programs in 1990 and 1991 were summed for each facility. This count of past environmental violations was included in the model on the basis that the same factors that led a plant to violate one set of environmental laws might also lead it to evade TRI requirements. A dummy variable is also included for whether the Dun and Bradstreet database listed the facility's employment figure as the minimum of a range rather than an actual figure, on the belief that a facility that withheld information from a private organization about its operations would also be more likely to withhold data from the government.[28]

Although traditional models of regulatory compliance focus on evasion, we believe that ignorance of reporting requirements may also provide an explanation for the failure of covered firms to file TRI forms. Ignorance of the existence of the TRI program or uncertainty as to whether the facility was required to report its chemical releases may play an important role in explaining 1991 violations in Minnesota of the TRI for at least two reasons. First, as an information provision program, the TRI relies on the facility to take action to inform regulators that it is covered by submitting calculated pollution figures. Those unfamiliar with the law's reporting requirements may thus fail to submit their pollution data to the EPA and state regulators. Second, the TRI was still a relatively new program in 1991, so sufficient information about the operation of the program may not have reached all parties subject to 1990 reporting.

We model ignorance, in part, as a function of interaction with regulators in other programs. Facilities that are covered by other environmental regulatory programs, such as federal air, water, and Superfund programs, are more likely to interact with state or EPA regulators who would visit the facility or provide plant managers with information alerting them to the TRI. This degree of contact would be greater for larger polluters, such as those with major water discharge permits or air emission permits. The greater the coverage under other programs, the more likely the plant managers would be to know about the TRI's requirements. We also have counts for July 1990 to June 1992 on a county level of the number of presentations made by Minnesota regulators about pollution prevention opportunities for industry and the number of facilities visited by regulators at the companies' request to explore pollution prevention plans. The higher the number of these visits in the area, the less likely facilities would remain ignorant of the operation of the TRI's right-to-know reporting requirements.

Firm characteristics also contribute to a likelihood of ignorance. Larger firms, measured here by the log of company sales, may be more likely to have dedicated environmental staff who are responsible for learning about compliance requirements of environmental programs. Facilities that are owned by subsidiaries of other companies are also more likely to have available the advantages of environmental staff to draw upon.[29]

The third, detection, equation models whether the plant was detected by the Minnesota regulators following standard EPA procedures. Ordinarily, state regulators would use lists in targeting their inspections. Part of the list of facilities is provided by the federal EPA, a list ultimately derived from Dun and Bradstreet listings. The model thus captures characteristics of facilities likely to be detected as violating the TRI, if the regulators used the list of firms provided by the EPA. The Minnesota regulators did not survey all the firms on the list provided by the EPA, and added a substantial number of facilities from other sources to their survey. Whether a violator was detected using the EPA list is a function of several factors. Because the EPA chose the Dun and Bradstreet files as a source of potential TRI filers to be examined, detection relates to whether the facility was likely to be in the Dun and Bradstreet subset provided by the EPA. Second, the Minnesota regulators chose to survey only some facilities on this list, so detection also relates to whether the regulators believed the facility was likely to be using TRI chemicals and other factors that might spark regulator interest in a plant.

The older the firm, the more likely the regulator would be able to assess whether the facility was a likely violator and hence the more likely the regulator would be to include the plant on the list to be surveyed (which raises the probability of detection). The larger the number of site visits by regulators to explore pollution prevention opportunities at plants in a county, the more likely regulators would be familiar with facilities in a county and thus include them in the detection survey. Regulator attention might also be drawn by community concern for the environment. We measure this by the percentage of the county voters who voted on an environmental bond referendum in 1988. The higher the level of interest in environmental policy, the more likely regulators might be to include facilities in the area on the EPA list to be surveyed.

Identification of the detection-controlled estimation model requires at least one unique variable for each of the three equations. In the coverage model, we use whether the facility is a branch in order to identify coverage from violation and detection. A facility that is a branch of a multiestablishment firm is more likely to be engaged in nonmanufacturing activities (such as warehousing or administration) than a facility that is a stand-alone entity. Hence, this variable predicts whether manufacturing occurs at the site rather than whether the facility is likely to violate because of ignorance or evasion, or whether it would be detected using EPA methods. In the violation model, we have multiple variables that measure either ignorance or evasion but are not related to the specific method of detection nor to the likelihood that a plant is covered by the TRI reporting requirements. In the detection model, we include log of the age of the firm as a proxy for regulator familiarity. Whether manufacturing goes on at a facility is independent of the age of the firm. Further, older firms are no more likely to violate than younger firms, other things being equal.

Results

Table 3.1 contains the results of our modified detection-controlled estimation model of coverage, violation, and detection. Nearly all the variables in the coverage model, which relate to technology and production processes, had the expected sign and were statistically significant. The larger the log of the number of plant employees, the higher the probability that the facility was covered by TRI reporting requirements. This is consistent with the hypothesis that the plant is more likely to exceed the chemical use or manufacturing threshold that triggers reporting as the number of employees rises. We use the natural log of the number of employees under the assumption that the sensitivity of the likelihood of coverage should be greatest for facilities with relatively few employees.

Plants tracked in the EPA's hazardous waste database are also more likely to be covered by TRI reporting requirements, again indicating that similar production processes may give rise to regulation across these different environmental programs. Almost 40% of the facilities in our sample were tracked in the RCRA program's hazardous waste database. Controlling for whether the plant was regulated under RCRA, facilities that were in the EPA's air pollution database (2% of the Minnesota plants) were less likely to be covered, although this coefficient was not statistically significant. Finally, facilities that were branches were less likely to be covered under TRI. This negative coefficient is consistent with the notion that branches of multiestablishment firms may be involved in processes other than manufacturing or that the division of manufacturing across branches may mean that TRI reporting thresholds are not met at the branch level. Nearly a quarter of the facilities (23%) were branches of multiestablishment firms.

The estimates for the violation model support the ignorance hypothesis, and elements of the evasion hypothesis. We evaluate the evasion hypothesis by way of variables that should be associated with either the marginal costs or benefits of compliance, reflective of a calculated decision to evade scrutiny under TRI. Of the variables that we considered to be related to costs of compliance, only one was statistically significant at conventional levels. Whether the facility was a small hazardous waste generator was negatively related to its propensity to violate, and strongly so. Small generators under the hazardous waste program were less likely to violate TRI reporting requirements, consistent with our hypothesis that such facilities would have lower expected compliance costs relative

Table 3.1. *Modified Detection-Controlled Estimation Model of Coverage, Violation, and Detection in the Toxics Release Inventory, Minnesota Data*

Variable	Estimate	Standard Error
Coverage		
Constant	−2.91	.79
Log (number of employees at location)	.54	.17
Is facility in EPA air database?	.29	.51
Is facility a branch?	−.39	.17
Is facility in RCRA database?	1.03	.26
Violation		
Constant	4.48	.69
Log (number of employees at location)	.13	.16
Employees reported as minimum of range?	.07	.21
Log (sales volume)	−.25	.06
Is facility in EPA air database?	.77	.57
Is facility in RCRA database?	.16	.23
Is facility in SIC 32 industry?	.0005	.57
Is facility in EPA water database?	−.10	.13
Is facility in Superfund program database?	−.29	.30
Is facility a subsidiary?	−.44	.22
Major waste discharger?	−1.86	.74
Air pollution emissions >100 tons/year	−.005	.74
Small hazardous waste generator?	−1.09	.20
Medium hazardous waste generator?	.06	.69
Any enforcement actions?	.15	.64
Percent turnout in presidential election	.001	.001
Percent turnout on environmental trust fund	.002	.05
Unemployment in county	−2.04	5.19
Site visits by Minnesota regulators	.56	.58
County presentations by Minnesota regulators	−.93	.53
Number of manufacturing establishments in county, 1987	−.02	.64
Detection		
Constant	−1.09	.45
Is facility in RCRA database?	.28	.43
Percentage turnout on environmental trust fund	−.02	.41
Log (firm age)	.11	.09
Site visits by Minnesota regulators	1.15	.51

Note: Estimates are for modified detection-controlled estimation model of facility filing with the Toxics Release Inventory using probit link functions. $N = 4087$, $2 \times (L - L_0) = 732$.

to medium or large hazardous waste generators, and thus have less of an incentive to evade reporting.

Two other variables associated with the costs of compliance were of the right sign, but not statistically significant at conventional levels. We considered the size of the facility as measured by the number of employees at the location to be associated with the marginal costs of compliance. Conditional on coverage by the TRI program, facilities with more employees (and hence potentially greater compliance costs because of greater chemical use) were less likely to violate. The parameter estimate is only significant at the $p < .10$ for a one-tailed test. Facilities in the RCRA database were more likely to violate, although the RCRA coefficient is smaller than its standard error.

None of the variables associated with the marginal benefits of compliance was statistically significant at conventional levels, and some were not of a sign consistent with the general hypothesis. We identified variables as associated with the benefits of compliance largely in terms of the facilities' ability to avoid penalties. Two variables were related to the political activity in the county, with the underlying hypothesis that the greater the political activity, the more likely that citizens or interest groups would sound "fire alarms" triggering greater regulator scrutiny. Neither the percentage of turnout in the presidential election nor the percentage of turnout on a referendum on an environmental trust fund were significant at conventional levels, and both were of an opposite sign than the hypothesis would suggest. The greater the level of political activity, the more likely that a facility would be in violation.

Likewise, the measures of the economic condition of the county of the facility were not related to the facility's probability of being in violation. The greater the unemployment in the area, the less likely it was that the firm would be in violation. The sign is inconsistent with the idea that high levels of unemployment might generate greater leniency from the regulators. The coefficient, however, is smaller than its standard error. The sign on the total manufacturing for the country is consistent with what a marginal benefits story might tell: the larger the number of manufacturing facilities in a county, the more likely a regulator might be to inspect and the less likely the facility would be in violation (though again, it is not significant at conventional levels).

Neither of the two variables that were direct proxies for evasiveness were statistically significant, although they were of a sign consistent with an evasion hypothesis. Firms that reported the number of employees as the minimum of a range were more likely to be in violation, although the magnitude of this coefficient is quite small. Likewise, firms that underwent any form of previous administrative action (and thus displayed a propensity to be a "bad actor") were also more likely to be in violation. The coefficient here is large, but no larger than its standard error.

Our story with respect to the ignorance hypothesis as the cause of facilities' failure to file is better supported by the estimates. We conjectured that larger firms (measured by the log of the sales volume) would be more likely to have a dedicated environmental staff responsible for learning about regulatory requirements. The coefficient on sales volume is statistically significant at $p < .05$, and quite substantial. Facilities in counties where Minnesota regulators had made appearances to publicize pollution prevention were also less likely to fail to file. Thus, as facilities were more likely to possess information about the TRI, the less likely they were to violate its reporting provisions.

Firms that are subsidiaries of other companies were more likely to be able to draw upon the expertise and knowledge of the environmental and legal staff of the company than were firms that stand alone. The parameter estimate is again substantively sizable and statistically significant. The dummy variables denoting whether the facility had some contact with other EPA programs were of mixed signs, and none were significant at conventional levels. Facilities that were listed in the water and Superfund databases were less likely to be in violation, whereas facilities in RCRA and the air database were more likely to be in violation. Firms that were major dischargers of water pollution were much less likely to be in violation than other firms. Again, the more facilities were likely to possess information about TRI, the less they were likely to violate its reporting provisions.

It is possible that the reason our results are stronger with respect to the ignorance hypothesis rather than evasion is related to the relative novelty in 1990 of the TRI program. The program had such a short history of implementation that facilities may not have had much information on which to project expected fines for avoiding compliance with the reporting requirements. Or firms may have been prescient in projecting that likely fines would be extremely low (none of the 142 firms identified in the 1991 survey effort were fined by Minnesota regulators for their failure to report). The general point stands: when one models the propensity of a regulated entity to be in violation or compliance, one must model the probability that the firm is aware of the regulatory program at the outset. The detection phase of the model is consistent with our beliefs about regulator familiarity with facilities. Plants in counties where regulators

Table 3.2. *Total and Average Releases and Transfers for Violators and Filers, Drawn from Toxics Release Inventory for Minnesota, 1990*

	Totals		Means	
Category	Violators	Filers	Violators	Filers
Stack air emissions[**]	1,695,969	41,148,866	11,382	94,378
Fugitive air emissions[*]	1,086,399	7,140,239	7,291	16,377
Total air emissions[**]	2,782,368	48,289,105	18,674	110,755
Water releases[**]	328	797,084	2	1,828
Land releases	150,355	1,435,889	1,009	3,293
Publicly owned treatment works (sewer) transfers[**]	160,496	4,476,721	1,077	10,268
Off-site transfers[**]	642,777	3,768,215	4,314	8,643
Total releases[*]	2,933,051	50,522,074	19,685	115,877
Total transfers[*]	803,273	8,244,936	5,391	18,910
Total releases and transfers[*]	3,736,324	58,767,010	25,076	134,787

Totals in pounds of releases or transfer, for 1990. There were 149 violators and 436 filers for these calculations.

[*]$p < .05$, [**]$p < .10$

had visited facilities to examine pollution prevention opportunities were more likely to be known to state regulators and hence drawn from the Dun and Bradstreet list of facilities to be surveyed about their chemical use. Facilities owned by older companies were also more likely to be detected using the EPA list, and this effect is statistically significant in a one-tailed test at the $p < .10$ level. The goodness of fit for our model by conventional measures is quite acceptable.[30]

Table 3.2 provides additional information about facilities that violated the TRI and the magnitude of nonreporting.[31] After Minnesota engaged in efforts to track down violators, more than one quarter of the facilities eventually reporting for 1990 were facilities that had originally failed to submit TRI forms. Though a large number of facilities were added to the TRI by the Minnesota ERC reporting program, these plants accounted for only a small fraction (6%) of the total releases and transfers in the 1990 Minnesota TRI. Table 3.2 compares the violators caught by Minnesota regulators with the filers in terms of the total amounts and the average amounts of toxic releases and transfers. The most striking feature of the table is that the figures are much lower for violators than for filers in all categories of releases and transfers. The average number of chemicals subject to TRI reporting is also smaller for violators (two per facility) than filers (three). Those facilities that failed to file TRI reports in 1990 but were later caught were on average much smaller polluters than plants already reporting. If one were to compare the TRI submissions of violators caught using the EPA's list of facilities with those of plants detected through other sources, one would not see statistically significant differences between the average pollution levels for any of the releases and transfers.

Though a substantial number of facilities were thus added to the Minnesota TRI through enforcement actions, these facilities turned out to be relatively small polluters. If the results from Minnesota were extrapolated to other states, then finding additional nonreporters might not increase the TRI figures substantially in percentage terms. Note, however, that Minnesota could be an outlier because its mix of industries differs from that in other states and because a higher fraction of facilities may have complied with the law to begin with because of the strong environmental laws in the state.[32] The fraction of nondetected noncompliers detected by Minnesota ERC is not far from the estimated national average, nonetheless. Of the 585 eventual filers of 1990 Minnesota TRI forms, 149 were noncompliers (26%), compared with the estimated national noncompliance rate of 33%.

Overall, our results show the importance of examining the "street level" phase of regulatory politics. Most models of environmental enforcement are derived from economic theories of crime and punishment in which the legal standards are known to all parties. Indeed, most principal agency models of compliance assume that the agent is fully aware of the principal's request. The results of our detection-controlled model indicate that a large fraction of facilities subject to environmental reporting may fail to file toxic reports (though these plants account for only a small percentage of total releases), that ignorance and evasion help explain noncompliance, and that regulators using normal detection means may be biased toward detecting facilities with which they are already familiar. Information asymmetries already play a large role in regulatory models: members of Congress may vote on the details of technical policies with the knowledge that voters remain rationally ignorant of the details, regulators may act on the basis that hidden actions and information allow them some freedom from congressional oversight, and regulated firms make compliance decisions in part based on the likelihood that enforcement agencies will not detect the level of compliance chosen. With the increasing use of programs in which information provision decisions are delegated to the regulated community, the failure of firms to be informed about regulatory requirements should be added to the list of information problems in regulatory politics. Ignorance of the law may be no defense, but it may provide an increasing explanation for noncompliance in an expanding regulatory universe.

Exercising Property Rights to Pollute

Although analyses of the TRI program's early years of operation often focus on companies and plants, the operation of right-to-know provisions may also depend on an additional set of actors – individuals in the communities surrounding facilities. Pollution generates numerous types of expected costs for a firm: expenditures on compliance with regulations, fines for rule violations, liabilities for health and natural resource damages, and compensation to communities surrounding polluting facilities. The incentives for a company to engage in pollution reduction may depend on who bears pollution risks, because imposing costs on a firm will often involve collective action. Firms may face higher expected costs in areas where residents are more likely to exercise their property rights to the environment. Regulatory inspections or county zoning battles over externalities, for example, may be more likely in areas where citizens engage more in collective action. If the private costs of pollution to a firm were linked to social costs through a liability system, then incentives for pollution reduction would also be linked to the size of risks generated by emissions. In a Coasian world, residents could costlessly negotiate with a firm so that it would internalize the damage arising from its pollutants.[33] In a world of incomplete information and imperfect monitoring and enforcement arising from transaction costs, however, there is no guarantee that incentives to reduce pollution will relate to the magnitude of contaminant risks.

This section provides empirical evidence that incentives for firms to reduce toxic emissions do depend both on the magnitude of cancer risks arising from their pollution and who bears these risks. Included in the TRI's yearly information on plant-level emissions of more than 300 chemicals are data on carcinogens released through air emissions. The release of the TRI information changed the benefits and costs of polluting, changes that differed across facilities depending on the nature of the pollution and the surrounding community. I use pollution and community information from 1988, the earliest year of accurate TRI data, to examine here how reductions in pollution releases subsequent to the release of the information differed depending on the dangers generated by the emissions. I combine the TRI data on the air releases of emissions that are carcinogenic with information on local populations to generate estimates of individual and population cancer risks from these contaminants. Controlling for the quantity of air toxics released in 1988, I find that plants whose emissions generated higher numbers of expected cancer cases reduced their emissions more between 1988 and 1991. This indicates that the combination of pollution reduction incentives created by command and control regulation, information provision programs, and liability concerns did lead firms to consider cancer risks as they made emission level choices. The type of residents surrounding a facility also affected decisions about pollution reduction. The higher the voter turnout in the area, a proxy for residents' willingness to engage in collective action, the greater the reductions in a plant's release of air carcinogens. This underscores that the likelihood that property rights are exercised and pollution reduced may depend on underlying variations in the probability communities will engage in collective action. Analyses of environmental regulations that focus on how property rights are defined rather than exercised may miss variations in environmental protection that arise from differences in political activity among the residents surrounding polluting facilities.

Related Research

The chemicals tracked in the Toxics Release Inventory are covered by an array of pollution laws, including hazardous waste, clean air, clean water, and toxic substances legislation. EPA and state regulators use the TRI data to target facilities for compliance inspections, which means that higher emissions may translate into higher expected fines and compliance costs (U.S. EPA 1995). Investors use the data as indicators of a company's future pollution costs. Firms with higher TRI figures experienced negative, statistically significant abnormal stock returns upon the first release of the information in 1989 (Hamilton 1995a), and those with the largest negative returns reduced their subsequent emissions more (Konar and Cohen 1997). Community groups, which have the ability to raise the costs of operating facilities in their neighborhoods through zoning measures or court suits, have used the TRI figures to negotiate "good neighbor" agreements in which facilities establish pollution reduction targets (MacLean and Orum 1992). In a 1993 survey of more than 200 corporate counsels, more than 50% indicated that "pressure from community activists had affected their companies' conduct – sometimes forcing a reduction in pollution" (Lavelle 1993). Between 1989 and 1994, more than 200 reports, primarily by public interest groups, used the TRI data to focus attention on pollution patterns (Orum 1994).

Firms thus face pressure for pollution reduction from numerous sources. Little empirical work exists on how companies react to variations in toxicity and risks across chemicals, although the evidence available indicates that firms do take these factors into account in their production decisions (Ringleb and Wiggins 1990, Ashford et al. 1993). A case study of hazardous waste reduction at Allied Signal, a major chemicals producer, found that the dangers posed by particular chemicals were factored into decisions about where to invest in pollution reduction. According to analysis of how environmental decisions were made in one of the company's facilities in Hopewell, Virginia:

Waste reduction ideas that passed the test of technical feasibility were ranked. Preference went first to projects actually reducing or eliminating hazardous waste, second to those recycling or reusing waste, and last to plans for waste treatment.... Projects eliminating very large amounts of emissions were favored, of course, but many others that promised only small or unknown improvements were also approved. The rationale that Drake [the facility's Superintendent of Environmental Control and Industrial Hygiene] presented to the financial analysts guarding the plant's operating and capital budgets was reduction of toxicity. Many substances on the TRI were far more toxic than ammonium sulfate, for instance, and thereby greater health risks to the populace and the environment. Cutting emission of such substances, even in small increments, reduced Hopewell's liability risks in a disproportionate manner.[34]

A firm's consideration of chemical risks will in part depend on expectations of how regulator behavior varies with risk. The literature on how regulators react to the specific risks associated with different chemicals is also sparse. Cropper et al. (1992) found that the EPA's decision to cancel or permit the continued use of carcinogenic pesticides depended in part on the maximum individual incremental lifetime excess cancer risk from the chemical. Van Houtven and Cropper (1993) found that in setting standards for hazardous air pollutants, the EPA was more likely to choose a regulatory option as the number of annual cancer deaths it reduced grew larger. Regulators thus appear to react both to population risks (i.e., total expected cancer cases) and individual risks (i.e., the maximum level of risk for an exposed individual) in traditional command and control regulation.

Research in environmental regulation and related work in occupational safety and health does offer some predictions on how firms whose emissions data are public may react to scrutiny in economic and political markets. Studies of hazardous waste handling show that polluting firms do consider the potential for political action among residents bearing externalities (Hamilton 1993, 1995b); regulators cleaning up hazardous waste sites also appear to respond to the level of political activity in the surrounding area (Viscusi and Hamilton 1999). A number of studies demonstrate that plants do respond to regulator visits and the prospect of expected inspections by altering their amounts of pollution emissions (Magat and Viscusi 1990) or adjusting their levels of workplace safety (Bartel and Thomas 1985, Viscusi 1986, Scholz and Gray 1990, Gray and Jones 1991).[35] Research on firms' reaction to the TRI data in particular reveals that companies with larger emissions were more likely to join a voluntary pollution reduction program sponsored by the EPA (Arora and Cason 1995). A number of questions about facility-level pollution decisions remain, however. Do plant managers consider the risks to human health from their carcinogenic air emissions in making pollution reduction decisions? Do facility officials care how risks arise, for example, do they focus on expected cancer deaths or are they also influenced by risk equity issues such as the maximum individual risk created by pollutants? What role does politics play in the reduction of emissions at the facility level? Answering these questions is an important part of analyzing the exercise of environmental property rights and the determinants of pollution reduction decisions.

Modeling Pollution Reduction

The release of the TRI data changed firms' incentives to pollute because the information gave regulators, investors, and communities surrounding facilities new information about pollution patterns. Changes in pollution incentives with the release of information differed across facilities depending on factors associated with the benefits and costs of pollution reduction. The analysis here examines how firms responded to the release of TRI data in 1988 by modeling changes in the release of air carcinogens between 1988 and 1991 as a function of pollution and community characteristics that affected the change in firm incentives with the publication of the TRI data. The dependent variable meant to reflect changes in pollution patterns will generally be calculated in terms of changes in pounds of pollutants released. The analysis focuses on pounds of pollutants because the TRI data are reported in pounds, the scrutiny generated by the information release often focuses on pounds of emissions released, and the variable selected directly by a firm making pollution decisions will often be pounds of emissions released.

The relationship between a firm's pollution decision and the community exposed to potential contaminants will depend on whether and how a company is led to consider the costs of its externalities. Consider that the damages arising from a company's pollution will depend on factors such as the toxicity of the chemicals released, the number of residents surrounding a facility and their physical capital exposed to pollution damage, and the levels of contaminants released. Translating health effects and property damages into claims for compensation or pressure for pollution reduction, however, may often require collective action among exposed residents. Knowing the degree that damage arises from a given company's pollution may depend on whether a firm's pollution figures are public information. Upon the release of the TRI information, a firm would engage in more pollution reduction the greater the toxicity of its contaminants, the larger the number of individuals exposed, and the larger the potential for collective action among residents.

If the release of the TRI data focuses attention on the dangers to human health posed by emissions, then TRI release patterns should show evidence that facilities trade off the costs of pollution reduction with the potential benefit to firms of lowering risks to human health. Plants that reported air emissions of carcinogens in the 1988 TRI were chosen for analysis here because commercially available models exist that allow the calculation of expected cancer deaths from these emissions. Although 1987 was the first year of TRI reporting, the 1988 data were chosen as the base year because of questions about the reliability of the first year of reported data. Of the 75 air carcinogens with emissions reported in the 1988 TRI, 16 had sufficient information on the potency of the chemical in inducing cancer and sufficient TRI data so that facility-level risk assessments could be conducted. For the resulting sample of 2,788 facilities with positive 1988 air releases of these 16 carcinogens, the number of expected cancer cases and the maximum individual lifetime cancer risks posed by emissions of each air carcinogen were calculated for a total of 3,504 risk pathways at these plants. This means that if a plant released three different air carcinogens, it could contribute three risk pathways to the analysis. The pollution pathway level analysis focuses on incentives for pollution reduction by examining two questions – did plants whose releases posed greater risks to human health in 1988 have greater reductions in emissions from 1988 to 1991, and did the nature of the communities bearing these risks affect emission reductions?[36]

In the analysis of pollution pathways, three different measures of pollution reduction are used for robustness. The first dependent variable analyzed in the ordinary least squares (OLS) regressions is the 1988 level of the specific air carcinogen minus the 1991 level of the air carcinogen reported by the plant in the TRI. Human health risks were estimated with Riskpro, the risk assessment model described below, for 3,504 releases of air carcinogens at 2,788 facilities in 1988. In the 1991 TRI data, 2,502 of these pollution pathways appear again in the reported figures; 1,191 of the air releases had increased or stayed the same in comparison to 1988, 1,219 had decreased but remained positive, and 92 were reported as decreasing to zero for 1991. The first OLS regressions with the change in air carcinogen releases between 1988 and 1991 as the dependent variable were run for all emission pathways in 1988 that had data for 1991. Facilities that did not report in 1991, which accounted for 1,002 pollution pathways in 1988, could have reduced the manufacture or use of the chemical so that they did not meet reporting thresholds or could have eliminated use of the chemical altogether. A second set of OLS regressions incorporates these pathways by treating the missing data as evidence of reductions. For those 1,002 pathways with 1988 data but no 1991 information, 1991 releases were assumed to be zero. The OLS regressions with the change in emissions between 1988 and 1991 were then run to include these additional pathways as evidence of even more reductions. A third set of OLS regressions uses the percentage change in the emission of the carcinogen between 1988 and 1991 as the dependent variable. This set of regressions also includes a specification that treats missing pathways in 1991 as evidence of the reduction of emissions for the carcinogen to zero.

Because costs of pollution reduction may vary with the amount of emissions, the 1988 level of emissions and its square term are included as independent variables in the equations modeling reductions. If the marginal costs of pollution reduction decline as emissions increase, then one would expect larger reductions between 1988 and 1991 at larger polluters. Because costs of pollution reduction vary with the production process involved, the regressions contain dummy variables to control for which chemicals were released and what industry the facility operated in (i.e., two-digit SIC code dummies were included for industries that accounted for at least 3% of facilities in the sample). Expected costs arising from fines may vary with the intensity of regulatory scrutiny, so dummy variables for EPA regions and a Southern dummy variable were included. State air quality control expenditures per capita for 1988 were also included as a control for the intensity of regulatory requirements and enforcement[37]

The benefits to society of reduced pollution include a reduction in expected cancer cases arising from air emissions at a facility. For each air carcinogen released by a facility in 1988 in the sample, a commercial risk assessment model (Riskpro) was run to estimate the number of additional cancer cases in the area generated by 1988 emission levels of the carcinogen continued over a time period of 70 years. A larger number of expected deaths may generate greater potential liability in court cases, stronger pressure from communities or environmentalists, or more intense scrutiny from regulators. The estimated cancer deaths are thus included to capture the potential incentives for firms to take into account the risks to human health posed by their emissions. Because regulators exhibit preferences over both the level of population risks (i.e., expected deaths) and the levels of individual risks (i.e., what is the risk posed to an individual), the maximum individual lifetime risk to residents near the plant is also included because plants may face more incentives to reduce as individual risk levels increase because of government concerns with risk equity. More attention may be focused on some of the air carcinogens because they are more toxic if inhaled, independent of the number of people exposed to the pollutant. The inhalation slope factor, a measure of toxicity, is included to capture the scrutiny that may vary with the degree of danger associated with a substance.[38]

The expected number of cancer cases arising from a facility's release of an air carcinogen and the maximum individual lifetime risk were calculated by using Riskpro, an environmental modeling system (General Sciences Corporation 1990). For each air carcinogen release, the latitude and longitude of the plant, the identity of the chemical, and the amount of air emissions reported in the TRI for 1988 were entered into the model. A default stack height of 10 m was assumed. This information allows the model to use regional air and wind data to calculate the dispersion of the chemical and the resulting concentration of the chemical in the surrounding area. The area of impact is assumed to be a circle around the facility with radius of 50 km, which is further divided up into 160 blocks for analysis. The latitude and longitude information is combined with 1980 census data by Riskpro to estimate the populations exposed to the plant's releases. Assuming that the 1988 level of emissions is continued over the lifetime (70 years) of plant neighbors, the model calculates the lifetime average daily dose of the chemical inhaled by a resident in each block surrounding the facility. This figure is then multiplied by the slope factor for the chemical, a value derived from a dose–response curve that represents the risk of cancer per unit dose of the chemical. This is a number determined by the EPA that is expressed in units of $(mg/kg/day)^{-1}$. The resulting lifetime excess cancer risk from the air pollutant for each block is multiplied by the resident population for each block to derive the number of cancer cases in the area from the release. The model then computes the total number of expected cancer cases arising from exposure over 70 years to levels of pollution equal to the 1988 cancer air emissions from the plant for residents within 50 km. The maximum individual lifetime risk among the residents in the blocks surrounding the facility is also calculated.[39]

The risk figures derived from this environmental modeling are based on many assumptions. The latitude and longitude data should be viewed as an assumption. Even though they are reported by facilities in their TRI submissions, these figures are often only an approximation.[40] Pollution from point sources (e.g., smokestacks) and nonpoint sources (e.g., leaks) were assumed to be released by a single smokestack 10 m high. Actual concentrations of exposures to residents from leaks could thus be higher than that indicated by assuming a 10-m stack height. Cancer risks were estimated assuming that 1988 emissions would be continued for a "lifetime" of 70 years, though operation at such a steady state would be unlikely. The figures do present a relative measure of the risks posed by air carcinogens, however, so the relative incentives for pollution reduction based on health risks are captured by the expected cancer deaths and maximum individual lifetime cancer risks associated with 1988 levels of air emissions.

The regression models of pollution reduction include expected cancer cases and the maximum individual lifetime risk estimates from Riskpro. Increases in the maximum individual risk (MIR) should increase incentives for pollution reduction, either through an increase in expected deaths or through a separate valuation (as in regulatory matters) of the maximum risk levels experienced by individuals. The regressions, however, analyze the impact of MIR holding expected deaths constant.[41] MIR may increase with expected deaths remaining constant if the number of people affected within the radius decreases. If this were the case, and if the likelihood that firms incorporated human health damages depended on the number of people affected, then the incentives for pollution reduction could be lowered with MIR increasing and expected deaths remaining constant, because this would mean fewer people would be potentially affected by the risk. Fewer people exposed could translate into less community pressure or lower regulatory pressure because fewer constituents were involved. If facilities also incorporated risk equity issues into their damage assessments, because of public pressure or pressure from regulators concerned about MIR, then this could still result in an increasing MIR, leading to increasing incentives for pollution reduction. With the specification that examines the impact of MIR with expected deaths constant, therefore, the expected sign of MIR is indeterminate. Toxicity is included as a separate variable in some specifications to test for whether, controlling for the impacts of exposure at a particular facility, chemicals known to be more dangerous in general are reduced more.

Though emissions from carcinogens result in damages to society, the likelihood that facilities will incorporate these damages into their pollution decisions may depend on the ability of residents affected to engage in collective action. Residents affected by pollution may engage in concerted activity to pressure facilities, contact regulators or legislators about the pollution, or turn out at the polls and cast ballots based in part on their environmental concerns. The percentage of residents 18 and older in the county that turned out to vote in the 1988 presidential election is included in the regressions to proxy for the probability that a community will engage in collective action to pressure polluting facilities (see Hamilton 1993 for evidence that voter turnout in a community helps predict whether commercial hazardous waste capacity will be expanded in a county). The more politically active a community, the more likely firms will be to incorporate the damages from their pollution and hence the larger the reduction in pollution between 1988 and 1991. To distinguish the level of political activity from the level of support for environmental programs, I also include the percentage vote in the county for the Republican candidate in the 1988 presidential election. I also add controls, discussed below, associated with potential difference among residents' valuation of environmental amenities.[42]

Aside from concerns about collective action, facilities have other incentives to consider the type of community that bears risks associated with emissions. Residents with higher incomes or home values may have a higher willingness to pay for the environment or be able to claim more damages to human or physical capital from pollution.[43] The greater the median house value or household income in the zip code area of the facility, the greater the incentives may be for a facility to reduce. The higher the education levels in the community (represented here by the percentage of those adults aged 25 or older in the zip code with associate, bachelor, or graduate/professional degrees), the more likely residents may be informed about risks, which may translate into higher compensation demands or greater likelihood of pressure on a firm to reduce. The percentage of the plant's zip code residents who are black is included in the regression to see if the variations in polluter behavior found in the environmental equity literature on differences in pollution exposure by race are evident in decisions relating to air emissions (see Goldman 1994,

Hamilton 1995b). Total population in the zip code may reflect the number of residents who may pressure regulators or firms to reduce emissions.[44] The percentage of the residents in cities may influence pollution reduction because it may be another measure of property values at risk or a measure of the concentration of residents who may be directly affected by emissions from a facility. Dispersion of population in rural areas could result in less pressure on a facility to reduce if fewer residents were affected by the emissions. Census variables reflecting all these considerations are included as independent variables in the analysis.

The publication of the TRI data has focused public attention on the aggregate number of pounds of many different pollutants released by a facility as a measure of problems associated with a plant's pollution. The OLS regressions of pollution pathway level changes in releases of the air carcinogens between 1988 and 1991 thus treat quantity reductions of many different types of air carcinogens similarly. Firms may face different incentives for pollution reduction, however, for particular air carcinogens. For the ten air carcinogens that had at least 40 observations available, separate regressions were run for each chemical with a pared down specification to determine whether the changes in air emissions of a given chemical from 1988 to 1991 were related to estimated deaths from the carcinogen and the level of political activity among those exposed to carcinogenic risks.

Results

Establishing what the change in release of air carcinogens between 1988 and 1991 would have been in the absence of TRI reporting requirements is difficult, in part because good data do not exist on the release of many of the carcinogens prior to the institution of the TRI. If one looks at the releases of general classes of air pollutants during the 1980s, one generally finds much smaller percentage drops in releases of these air pollutants than for the specific air carcinogens tracked in the TRI. For example, annual percentage growth rates in million metric tons of air pollutants released per year between 1980 and 1990 were −1.9% for particulates, −.7% for sulfur oxides, −1.8% for nitrogen oxides, −1.9% for volatile organic compounds, −3.2% for carbon monoxide, and −9.3% for lead (Hahn 1994). Thus one may conclude that TRI releases of air carcinogens declined at a faster rate between 1988 and 1991 than the rate of decrease in emissions for many classes of air pollutants for the 1980s overall. One cannot easily determine what percentage of the drop in TRI emissions is a result of the distinct impact of information provision. Determining the impact of an information program such as the TRI is difficult because publicly available pollution data for most of the pollutants in the TRI were not available prior to the start of the program. The analysis here does not isolate the independent impact of the TRI on reduction decisions. It rather examines whether firms, given multiple incentives for emission reduction from command and control regulation, information provision, and the liability system, consider the magnitude of risks and the nature of those who bear these risks in their decisions about the reduction of air carcinogens.

Releases and transfers of TRI chemicals overall declined by 31% between 1988 and 1991. Air releases of suspected carcinogens dropped 35% during the same period, from 300,425,000 pounds to 194,983,000 pounds. Tables 3.3 and 3.4 offer evidence that firms did take into account both the threats to human health and the potential for collective action in exposed communities in determining levels of pollution reduction for air carcinogens between 1988 and 1991.[45] The unit of analysis in these tables is the release of a particular air carcinogen at a plant; for a facility with multiple air carcinogens, each carcinogen would contribute a separate observation to the sample. The average release for an air carcinogen reported in the TRI data dropped from 54,400 pounds per release pathway in 1988 to 50,500 in 1991.

Table 3.3 examines the influences on the change in emissions of an air carcinogen between 1988 and 1991, using multiple measures of reductions for robustness. In specifications (1) and (2), the dependent variable is the change in air carcinogen emissions measured in pounds between 1988 and 1991. Specifications (3) and (4) treat pathways that were missing in 1991 as evidence that the emissions for that carcinogen were reduced to zero and include these additional pathways in the analysis. Specifications (5) and (6) focus on the percentage reduction of air carcinogen releases between 1988 and 1991, with specification (6) treating missing 1991 pathways as evidence of reductions to zero.

The results in Table 3.3 provide strong support for the hypothesis that firms take into account the risk of their pollutants in making reduction decisions. Controlling for the level of air pollution emitted in 1988, a facility with a higher expected number of deaths due to release of the carcinogen had greater reductions in emissions between 1988 and 1991. In other words, the most hazardous plants in terms of human carcinogenic health risks reduced their emissions more. For the 3,504 air carcinogen pollution pathways in the sample, the mean number of cancer deaths

Table 3.3. *Determinants in Facility-Level Changes in Air Releases of Carcinogens, 1988 to 1991*

	1988–91, lbs. (1)	1988–91, lbs. (2)	1988–est 91, lbs. (3)	1988–est 91, lbs. (4)	1988–91, % (5)	1988–est 91, % (6)
Facility air release of carcinogen, 1988 (lbs.)	0.44*** (0.08)	0.43*** (0.08)	0.70*** (0.07)	0.69*** (0.07)	0.03** (0.02)	0.02** (0.01)
Facility air release of carcinogen, 1988 (lbs.), squared	0.18e-7 (0.18e-7)	0.19e-7 (0.18e-7)	-0.19e-7 (0.18e-7)	-0.18e-7 (0.18e-7)	-0.55e-8** (0.27e-8)	-0.33e-8*** (0.16e-8)
Estimated cancer cases from air carcinogen	6,982.6** (3,033)	7,123.9** (3,192)	8,266.1*** (2,325)	8,526*** (2,435)	474.07 (766.5)	337.21 (587.7)
Maximum individual risk	-0.46e7 (0.33e7)	-0.42e7 (0.33e7)	-0.11e8*** (0.29e7)	-0.99e7*** (0.3e7)	0.39e6 (0.71e6)	0.5e6 (0.59e6)
Inhalation slope factor $(mg/kg/day)^{-1}$		0.63e7*** (0.25e7)		74.47 (89.22)		
State air control expenditures per capita, 1988 $	2,331.7 (4,306)	3,172 (4,344)	2,161.6 (3,164)	-0.17e-1 (0.78e-1)	3,761* (2,175)	2,362.2 (1,578)
Southern state	45,404 (46,520)	49,040 (47,270)	17,409 (34,060)	16,131*** (5,439)	-35,844 (40,250)	-25,726 (29,300)
% County voter turnout 1988 presidential election	1,155.8* (702.5)	1,203.1* (713)	890.79* (534.8)	0.32e-2 (0.46e-1)	1,114.1* (657.3)	839.13* (498.3)

	(1)	(2)	(3)	(4)	(5)	(6)
% Republican county presidential vote 1988	−309.39	−322.21	−118.36	−0.82	383.44	260.81
	(344.9)	(347.9)	(261.2)	(0.73)	(656.4)	(453.9)
Total persons in zip code, 1990	−0.12	−0.14	−0.12	0.17e9***	0.34*	0.25
	(0.17)	(0.17)	(0.14)	(0.68e3)	(0.2)	(0.15)
Median household income, 1989	−0.02	0.11	0.03	194.68	−0.82	−0.52
	(0.43)	(0.44)	(0.32)	(135.1)	(0.76)	(0.51)
Median house value, 1987	0.79	0.49	−0.02	−0.26e-1	0.11	0.09
	(0.13)	(0.13)	(0.09)	(0.69e-1)	(0.11)	(0.08)
% Population in cities	298.72	296.53	233.48*	0.11e10**	−181.83	−130.08
	(185)	(183.4)	(138.2)	(0.53e9)	(123.3)	(87.55)
% Black population, 1990	115.79	109.97	54.47	−0.59e-5	146.93	122.82
	(133.4)	(135.1)	(108.8)	(0.47e-4)	(117.8)	(94.8)
% College graduates, 1990	−185.01	−242.96	63.99	0.16e-2	383.61	219.04
	(319.5)	(324.2)	(242.9)	(0.74e-1)	(336.8)	(210.5)
Adjusted R^2	.40	.40	.52	.52	.005	.005
Number of facility chemical releases	1,996	1,983	2,784	2,784	1,996	2,784

Note: The dependent variable in the OLS regressions (1)–(4) is (facility 1988 release of a given air carcinogen − facility 1991 release of the air carcinogen), whereas in (5) and (6), the dependent variable is expressed in % terms (e.g., 1988 release−1991 release=1988 release × 100). In specifications (3), (4), and (6), if 1991 air releases were missing, they were assigned to be 0 in the calculations of emission changes. Each specification also generally included an intercept, dummies for EPA regions, and industry controls for SIC codes. Specifications (1), (3), (5), and (6) also included chemical-specific dummies. White standard errors are in parentheses.
*** Significant at the 1% level; ** significant at the 5% level; * significant at the 10% level.

Table 3.4. *Determinants of Facility-Level Changes in Air Releases of Carcinogens, 1988 to 1991, by Chemical*

Chemical	Facility Air Release of Carcinogen, 1988 (lbs.)	Estimated Cancer Cases from Air Carcinogen	% County Voter Turnout 1988 Presidential Election	% Republican County Presidential Vote, 1988	Southern State	Mean Dependent Variable (lbs.)
1,2-Dichloroethane	−0.06	97,126***	70.87	323.87	−25,769	4,184
	(0.13)	(30,160)	(949.8)	(656.5)	(26,320)	
N = 87						
Adj. R^2 = .28						
1,3-Butadiene	0.33*	3,112.9	844.83*	−661.83	13,933	16,939
	(0.20)	(2434)	(496.3)	(492.0)	(28,070)	
N = 138						
Adj. R^2 = .54						
Acrylamide	0.16	595.4***	10.28**	−1.02	−49,305**	−972
	(0.13)	(166.4)	(4.48)	(3.6)	(825.6)	
N = 40						
Adj. R^2 = .99						
Acrylonitrile	0.42***	9,121.8***	331.67	−277.11	35,529**	16,550
	(0.07)	(1,765)	(523.4)	(238.3)	(17,040)	
N = 86						
Adj. R^2 = .78						
Benzene	0.71***	−18,731	487.72	−478.92	−34,424***	16,509
	(0.11)	(21,320)	(407.9)	(388.6)	(10,250)	
N = 368						
Adj. R^2 = .73						

Carbon tetrachloride	0.75***	12,747***	371	104.73	−8,064.5	19,441
	(0.10)	(4,760)	(315.8)	(240.4)	(18,650)	
N = 83						
Adj. R^2 = .94						
Chloroform	0.33**	−7,725	2,169.3*	2,073.3	73,479	11,952
	(0.16)	(18,190)	(1,220)	(1,358)	(64,930)	
N = 154						
Adj. R^2 = .20						
Dichloromethane	0.55***	−688,000	996.7	−1,433.3**	13,457	−2,085
	(0.10)	(664,300)	(1.352)	(694.5)	(21,350)	
N = 1078						
Adj. R^2 = .34						
Epichlorohydrin	−0.77***	1,460,000***	32.63	2.87	2,847.4	718
	(0.26)	(222,600)	(315.3)	(155.7)	(4,336)	
N = 63						
Adj. R^2 = .57						
Propylene oxide	0.91***	−204,000***	13.66	188.73	−832.74	17,485
	(0.05)	(78,880)	(150.3)	(143.4)	(2,663)	
N = 94						
Adj. R^2 = .97						

Note: Each row is an OLS regression with the dependent variable defined as (facility 1988 release of a given air carcinogen − facility 1991 release of the air carcinogen). Each specification generally included an intercept; regional dummies for EPA Regions 4, 5, and 6; and industry controls for SIC Codes 28 and 29. White standard errors in parentheses. *** Significant at the 1% level; ** significant at the 5% level; * significant at the 10% level.

associated with continued air emissions at 1988 levels was .3 deaths (standard deviation 3.1, minimum 0, maximum 149) and the mean maximum individual risk was 3.3e-4 (standard deviation 2.2e-3, minimum 3e-10, maximum 6.9e-2). Specifications (1) through (4) reveal that for each expected additional cancer death, emissions of the air carcinogen between 1988 and 1991 declined by approximately 7,000 to 8,000 pounds. This indicates that as pollution figures became public, facilities did incorporate human health risks into pollution prevention plans (although no claim is made that the facilities made optimal trade-offs of expected damages from air emissions versus the costs of pollution reduction).

The coefficient on maximum individual risk is negative and statistically significant in specifications (3) and (4) of Table 3.3. Although command and control regulators might increase pressures for reduction as the maximum individual risk increased because of equity concerns, this evidence indicates that pressures for pollution reduction may be lower for firms as the MIR increases. This could be because, holding expected deaths constant, as the MIR increases, the number of individuals affected by the pollution may decrease, which would result in fewer individuals to pressure the facility or regulators for reduction. Specification (2) indicates that pressures to reduce pollutants also varied with toxicity. The higher the inhalation slope factor for the air carcinogen, the greater the reduction in emissions between 1988 and 1991.

As voter turnout in the area surrounding a facility increased, emissions declined. This indicates that for a given level of pollution, facilities may be more likely to engage in reductions if they believe that the affected parties are likely to engage in collective action to force firms to internalize the cost of their pollution. Voter turnout is statistically significant in five of the six specifications. The impact of collective action is evident even after one controls for other socioeconomic measures of the communities surrounding facilities, such as median household income, percentage of college graduates, and percentage of votes for the Republican presidential candidate in 1988. For a one percentage point increase in the voter turnout rate in the county surrounding the plant, emissions of the air carcinogen declined by between 900 and 1,200 pounds between 1988 and 1991.

Across all specifications, carcinogens released in higher amounts in 1988 were reduced more between 1988 and 1991. This is consistent with declining marginal costs of pollution reduction for the air carcinogens in the sample. None of the other variables in the table was consistently statistically significant.[46] Community variables such as the median house-hold income or percentage college graduates of the residents in the zip code surrounding the plant had no impact on emissions. The percentage of the population who were black, a variable that often plays a role in environmental equity studies, was not statistically significant in these models of air carcinogen emission reductions. Although plants do take into account the nature of who bears the risks of their contaminants, it is the likelihood that residents will engage in collective action and thereby force plants to incorporate the costs of their pollutants that affects plant decisionmaking.

Because discussions of reductions of TRI chemicals are often framed in terms of pounds of " pollutants" reduced, Table 3.3 analyzes the reductions in quantities of the 16 air carcinogens together in one sample. Table 3.4, however, analyzes the pollution patterns by individual pollutant.[47] For each air carcinogen with sufficient pathways to include in a regression analysis, a separate model was run with the difference between the 1988 level of releases for the carcinogen and the 1991 level of emissions as the dependent variable. The results indicate that the influences of risks and collective action are still evident when pollution reductions are examined on a chemical-by-chemical basis. The coefficient on the estimated number of cancer cases generated by the air carcinogen was statistically significant in six of the models, with five positive coefficients and one negative one. Controlling for the level of a chemical's releases in 1988, reductions were greater where estimated cancer deaths resulting from exposures were higher. Voter turnout was positive and statistically significant in three of the ten equations, which indicates for some chemicals, reductions were greater where collective action was more likely. If the ten chemicals in the table are ranked in terms of their toxicity (as measured by their slope factors), among the top five most toxic chemicals, voter turnout was statistically significant for three of these contaminants. Collective action may play a stronger role for chemicals likely to be toxic enough to attract community or regulator scrutiny. In seven out of the ten equations, the statistically significant positive coefficient on 1988 releases indicates that the reductions in emission levels for the given chemical were larger for plants with larger initial emission levels. This is consistent with declining marginal costs of pollution reduction for these pollutants. For acrylamide and benzene, reductions were lower in plants in Southern states, perhaps reflecting differences in environmental policies or regulator enforcement. Overall, the results in Table 3.4 support the hypotheses that both the magnitude of risks and the political activity of those likely to be exposed influence toxic reduction decisions.

Conclusions

Progress in pollution reduction is often publicly tracked through counts and announcements of "pounds of pollution" released in a given year by a facility or firm. Some analysts worry that a focus on quantities of pollution released obscures the fact that for a given quantity of pollution, the risks arising will differ depending on the toxicity of a chemical, the dispersion of a contaminant based on wind and topography, and the number of people exposed to the pollutant. The analysis here reveals that contrary to these concerns, for the case of air carcinogens, firms do not treat all pounds of emissions equally in their pollution reduction decisions. Controlling for the quantity of pollution released, I find that as pollution data became public, facilities reduced emissions more the greater the human health risks posed by emissions. These results do not indicate that firms trade off the costs of pollution reduction optimally with the benefits of health protection. The results do provide statistical evidence that expected cancers and individual cancer risk levels arising from contaminants influence private pollution reduction decisions.

Facilities face multiple pressures to reduce pollution, from regulators, investors, environmentalists, and local residents. In a world without transaction costs in which companies are liable for contamination, polluters and residents can costlessly negotiate the compensation for damages. In a world in which the property rights to be free of pollution may depend on collective action, however, the exposure of residents to contaminants may depend on their ability to engage in collective action. Political action may thus be necessary to invoke environmental protection laws. This may be true for multiple reasons. Legislators and regulators may be more responsive to their most active constituents. If environmental regulators wait for constituents to "pull a fire alarm" before they inspect facilities or pressure companies for reductions, then areas with more active residents may enjoy higher levels of regulator responsiveness.[48] Zoning battles may also require community organization. Firms may be influenced more by the prospect of a court case brought by organized residents.

If these hypotheses are true, then firms will care about who bears the risks of their pollutants. The results here suggest this is the case, because emissions were reduced more in communities with higher voter turnouts. The degree to which firms may engage in pollution reduction may depend on the likelihood that collective action will lead them to internalize their externalities. Studies of regulation in general and environmental regulation in particular should thus examine not only how rules are defined but also how property rights affecting firm decisions are likely to be invoked and exercised. In the next chapter, I examine a related issue, namely how politics can affect over time the exact definition of what a regulation requires firms to do in reporting their toxic emissions.

FOUR

Politics of Expansion and Contraction

In the textbook story of rulemaking, Congress delegates decisions to an agency explicitly through directions in legislative text and implicitly through omissions of details in the language of a bill. Administrative procedures, the rules that govern rulemaking, affect how an agency will use the notice-and-comment process to resolve questions left open by Congress. When the dust settles, the agency publishes the final rule in the *Federal Register*, and the language devised becomes part of the *Code of Federal Regulations*. The requirements in the *CFR* become the rules of the road for the agency to enforce as law.

The lives of environmental regulators would be much simpler if rulemaking followed the textbook. The real dilemmas involved in agency decisionmaking, however, often lie in the rest of the story. The complexity of a regulator's task starts first with the delegation of decisionmaking from Congress. As political scientist Ken Shepsle has pointed out, Congress is a "they," not an "it."[1] Regulators at EPA in search of direction from "Congress" might get conflicting advice from Democrats and Republicans, from party leaders in the House or Senate, and from members of contending oversight committees. Which "Congress" should the regulators pay heed to, the one that drafted the authorizing legislation or the one that today apportions the agency's budget and holds oversight hearings? Add into this calculation the fact that EPA has multiple principals.[2] The President appoints the head of the agency to carry out administration policy. The courts deliver orders that compel certain policies and inhibit the pursuit of other objectives. The ultimate principals in the chain of government decisionmaking, the voters, may at times put in a direct appearance in the rulemaking process. The logic of collective action correctly predicts that most will not. Yet their surrogates will, whether they are environmentalists representing green consumers or corporate associations protecting revenues or jobs in particular industries. The continual struggles among the groups that influence the EPA can yield continual changes in how a given regulation is defined and enforced.

The evolution of the TRI program shows how regulatory requirements change over time with changes in the ideologies of policymakers. When the President and EPA Administrator were both Republicans from 1989 through 1992, the first expansion of the TRI reporting requirements came about through legislation (the Pollution Prevention Act of 1990) passed by a Democratic House and Senate. Once Democrats gained control of the executive branch with the election of Bill Clinton, the EPA Administrator and Vice President became advocates for expansion of right-to-know provisions. In 1994, the actions initiated by EPA Administrator Carol Browner resulted in the addition of 286 chemicals to TRI reporting. In 1997, the EPA required seven more industries to report their toxic releases and transfers. When Republicans gained control of the House and Senate in 1995, they tried (unsuccessfully) to reduce the scope of TRI reporting through major regulatory reform proposals that were passionately debated but never passed and signed into law. Once Republicans regained control of the presidency in the election of George W. Bush, the EPA began public stakeholder discussions of ways to reduce the reporting burdens associated with the TRI.

Those who lost legislative and formal rulemaking battles had other avenues to pursue to alter the impact of the TRI. Industry groups filed numerous lawsuits claiming that the EPA had erred in expanding the reach of reporting requirements. In most cases, the courts deferred to the agency's discretion and upheld most of the EPA actions that added to company reporting. Overarching restraints on the formation of regulations, such as the Regulatory Flexibility Act (requiring impact analysis on small businesses), the Paperwork Reduction Act, and the approval process of the Office of Management and Budget (OMB), played a part in the development of formal TRI rules.

The EPA also took a number of informal actions that magnified the impact of the TRI. As in many environmental programs, the EPA used guidance documents to spell out the technical details of reporting requirements. In Barrick Goldstrike Mines v. Whitman, 260 F. Supp. 2d 28 (U.S. District 2003), U.S. District Court Judge Thomas Penfield Jackson agreed with the plaintiff that the EPA was using guidance documents in TRI as if they were formal rules, which would allow the agency to expand reporting without going through the notice-and-comment process. In the 33/50 Project, the EPA targeted 17 chemicals and publicly invited companies to pledge significant reductions of these chemicals by 1995. The EPA also undertook demonstration projects with the TRI data and placed the results or methodology on the web. These included combining data on production information and regulatory compliance from nearly 650 plants in five major industries with TRI data in the Sector Facility Indexing Project and developing software to estimate the relative risk from TRI plants in the Risk-Screening Environmental Indicators project. These were all examples of the agency focusing attention on particular chemicals, plants, and areas through activities other than formal rulemaking.

In this chapter, I trace out how the TRI reporting requirements changed over time by examining the fate of right-to-know proposals in the EPA's formal rulemaking process, Congressional activity, presidential politics, court decisions, and informal agency activity. The results show that the amount and detail of TRI reporting expanded markedly after the first public release of the data in 1989.

Change through Rulemaking

Congress delegates decisions to regulatory agencies in part to save time and, occasionally, to shift the blame for controversial policy choices. Legislators also prefer to put off the resolution of disputes because of uncertainty that exists when programs are initially crafted. Even if representatives might want to privilege the interests of environmentalists or industry groups, working out details in legislative text may be hard because of what might change in the future, such as scientific knowledge about the impact of pollution or compliance technology for firms. Interest groups may not know their own preferences over policy when bills are being written, because their ideas about what is desirable in the future depend on actions to be taken later by regulators.

The McNollgast authors show in a series of articles that administrative procedures in rulemaking provide a way for Congress to deal with uncertainty and control later action by regulators.[3] They point out that the Administrative Procedure Act (APA) and subsequent court cases interpreting it create political constraints on regulators. Proposed rules are announced ahead of time in the *Federal Register* so the public can provide comments. Regulators must respond to information provided by commenters when issuing a final rule. If they fail to grapple with substantive objections raised by public commenters, regulators run the risk of seeing their rules overturned by courts as "arbitrary and capricious" exercises of power. A set of executive orders and laws require agencies in rulemakings to conduct regulatory impact analyses for major rules, consider the impact of a proposed action on small business, and take into account the paperwork requirements created by a rule.[4] The OMB tracks the paperwork burden and reviews the analyses supporting a rule. Additionally, legislators can create special requirements within each bill that govern the criteria that regulators use in the rulemaking to implement a program.

When Congress passed EPCRA in 1986, the text contained detailed specifications on which facilities (e.g., plants with ten or more full-time employees in manufacturing industries that produced or used a chemical in amounts above a specific threshold) and what chemicals (e.g., the 300+ chemicals listed in a report by the Senate Committee on the Environment and Public Works) were covered.[5] Legislators also explicitly delegated to the EPA Administrator discretion to expand and contract the scope of TRI reporting. The text of the bill, however, defined the bounds of this delegated authority. The EPA Administrator could add chemicals through rules if the Administrator determined that lab tests or epidemiology studies provided "sufficient evidence" that a chemical caused acute human health effects at the concentrations likely to exist from emissions "beyond facility site boundaries," could be anticipated to cause cancer in humans or generate chronic health effects, or caused "significant adverse effect on the environment" because of the substance's toxicity and persistence or bioaccumulation. Finding any of these effects would allow an Administrator to add a chemical to the TRI list. At the same time, the Administrator could delete a substance if she found that there "was not sufficient evidence to establish any of the criteria" used to add chemicals. The legislation also provided interested parties with an avenue to change reporting by filing a petition with the Administrator, who would have 180 days to initiate a rulemaking to add or delete the chemical or publish an explanation of why the petition was denied.

Some of the restrictions on the Administrator's power clearly aimed to limit future changes in the scope of the TRI. The Administrator can change the frequency of reporting but "may not modify the frequency to be any more often than annually." The number of substances added to the TRI list on the basis of the environmental damage criteria could "constitute in the aggregate no more than 25 percent of the total number of chemicals on the list." The language of the bill indicated that the Administrator "may" add a chemical if one of the enunciated human health or environmental damage criteria were met, but the text did not require this action. Other aspects of TRI rulemaking procedures tipped toward increasing the amount of information provided. Petitions from a governor were treated differently depending on whether the petition was to add or delete a chemical from the reporting list. A governor's petition to remove a substance was treated in the same manner as a request from any other party. If a governor petitioned to add a chemical, however, the substance was automatically added to the list unless the Administrator took action within 180 days to start a rulemaking or to explain why the proposed chemical failed the criteria for adding substances. The Administrator could revise the threshold that triggered reporting, but the legislation limited the likelihood that the Administrator could reduce the scope of reporting by significantly increasing the threshold. The text required that a "revised threshold shall obtain reporting on a substantial majority of total releases of the chemical at all facilities." EPCRA also instructed the Administrator to request within five years a study from the National Academy of Sciences (NAS) on the use of mass balance analysis to monitor the management and release of chemicals.[6] This ensured the provision of a study on a potential and controversial extension of chemical reporting.

The rulemakings that implemented EPCRA from 1987 through 2004 show that broad provisions of the APA did influence the expansion and contraction of the TRI. The final rule notices in the *Federal Register* contain lengthy responses from the EPA to points raised by commenters. Petitions to add and delete chemicals were addressed in the *Federal Register* by the EPA with detailed references to summaries prepared by the agency on the evidence from scientific studies on chemical toxicity and harms. The overarching rulemaking requirements are also evident in the Regulatory Impact Analyses (RIAs) conducted on major TRI rules, the analyses of impacts on small business triggered by the Regulatory Flexibility Act, and the discussion generated by the Paperwork Reduction Act of the time required to fill out the TRI forms. The EPA's implementation of the TRI in rulemakings appears to follow the path laid out by the enacting Congress. A runaway agency might either add many chemicals to the list without regard to chemical toxicity or environmental damage or delete a substantial fraction of the substances in the name of cost reduction for industry. Neither of these extremes took place, as evidenced in part by the absence of frequent, successful court challenges by industry or environmental groups to the rulemaking procedures.

The text of EPCRA reflects a desire to provide communities with information on potentially harmful chemicals while considering the potential costs to industry. The balancing of likely benefits from reported releases with costs of data provision is evident in exemption of facilities with fewer than ten full-time employees and the annual threshold of 25,000 pounds of chemical manufacture or production or 10,000 pounds of chemical use that a plant would have to hit before needing to file a TRI report. The agency's use of discretion in TRI rulemakings follows a similar path of expanding the amount of chemical information provided by the TRI while balancing the likely costs to industry of information collection. When faced in rulemakings with questions about EPCRA's language, the agency often chose interpretations that expanded the reach of the TRI. Though the statute focuses on chemical toxicity, the agency also added chemicals that were not directly toxic but interacted with the environment to create toxic effects. The agency asserted the authority to add these substances based on "indirect toxicity." The EPA added entire categories of chemicals to the TRI at times, asserting that the power to add a chemical also covered the ability to add classes of chemicals. The agency's expansion of reporting to plants beyond the manufacturing SIC codes was made in part on the Administrator's authority to add more SIC codes to the TRI reporting requirements. The EPA's rejection of the notion that the agency needed to use risk assessments or exposure data to prove harms in each chemical listing case allowed the agency to add substances to the TRI list more readily.

The EPA also used discretion to reduce reporting when the gains from information were judged less than substantial. In petitions to add chemicals, the EPA used low production volumes (a standard not mentioned directly in the statute) to conclude that little would be gained by adding a substance to the list. Similarly, the agency developed in 1994 a new reporting threshold that meant that a facility did not have to file a Form R if aggregate releases of the chemical were 500 pounds or less and the plant manufactured or otherwise used the chemical in amounts of less than 1 million pounds per year. This exemption allowed a plant to file a shorter declaration (Form A) that saved industry and the EPA transaction costs. The prime new TRI initiative by the Bush II administration was the start of stakeholder dialogues in 2002 and 2003 on proposals the EPA might pursue to reduce TRI reporting costs, including higher reporting thresholds for small businesses, expanded eligibility for plants to file a Form A, the creation of a new option whereby plants could simply report that there were no significant changes in their TRI data from a base year, or the greater use of range responses as an option on the TRI reporting forms.

Table 4.1 charts the fate of proposals to delete chemicals from the TRI list from 1987 to 2003. In the early years of the program, companies and industry associations offered many petitions to remove chemicals from

Table 4.1. *Proposed Delisting of Chemicals from TRI Reporting List*

Chemical(s)	Petition Proposed by	Date Petitioned/Final	Final Action
Butyl benzyl phthalate	Monsanto Corporation	1-12-87/2-17-95	Delisted
Ortho-phenylphenol	Dow Chemical Company	4-27-87/10-29-87	Denied
Cobalt and compounds; manganese and compounds; and nickel and compounds	Hall Chemical Company	5-28-87/12-3-87	Denied
Titanium dioxide	E. I. du Pont de Nemours and Company; SCM Chemicals, Inc.; Didier Taylor Refractories Corporation; Kemira Oy	8-24-87/2-19-88 and 6-20-88	Delisted
Acid blue 9 (both the diammonium and disodium salts)	Ecological and Toxicological Association of Dyestuffs Manufacturing Industry (ETAD)	10-5-87/10-7-88	Delisted
Melamine	Melamine Chemicals, Inc.	10-7-87/3-29-89	Delisted
Sodium hydroxide (solution)	The Chlorine Institute, Inc.	4-22-88/12-14-89	Delisted
Ethylene and propylene	Chemical Manufacturers Association	7-13-88/1-27-89	Denied
Sodium sulfate (solution)	Hoechst Celanese Corporation	8-9-88/6-20-89	Delisted
Cyclohexane	Chemical Manufacturers Association	9-9-88/3-15-89	Denied
Aluminum oxide (nonfibrous)	Aluminum Association	9-30-88/2-14-90	Delisted
Ammonia, ammonium sulfate (solution), ammonium nitrate (solution), water dissociable ammonium salts	Allied Signal, Inc.	1-23-89/6-30-95	Ammonium sulfate (solution) and ammonium nitrate (solution) delisted, aqueous ammonia limited to 10% and should be reported under the ammonia listing (qualifier to ammonia listing as a separate action at the same time)

Cadmium sulfide and cadmium selenide	SCM Chemicals, Inc.	4-14-89/10-19-89	Denied
Decabromodiphenyl ether	Great Lakes Chemical Corporation	5-15-89/11-3-89	Denied
Chrome antimony titanium buff rutile	Dry Color Manufacturers' Association	6-27-89/1-8-90	Denied
Terephthalic acid	Amoco Corporation	7-27-89/12-10-90	Delisted
Barium sulfate	1) Petroleum Equipment Suppliers Association and 2) Dry Color Manufacturers' Association (DCMA), Chemical Products Corporation	1) 8-7-89 and 2) 9-18-89/5-23-91	Withdrawal of proposed rule
Antimony tris (iso-octyl mercaptoacetate)	Synthetic Products Company	9-5-89/2-13-90	Denied
Zinc borate hydrate	U.S. Borax Research Corporation	9-7-89/3-20-90	Denied
Sulfuric acid	American Cyanamid Company (petition withdrawn 6/4/90) and Ecolab, Inc. (this petition incorporated by EPA into existing petition review process)	12-12-89/6-18-90	Denied
Phosphoric acid	1) Ecolab, then Fertilizer Institute and 2) EPA after U.S. District Court of D.C. reversed EPA denial of petition from The Fertilizer Institute (TFI) to delete	1) 12-14-89 and 2) 11-9-90/ 1) 6-25-90 and 2) 6-27-00	1) Withdrawn and 2) delisted
Zinc sulfide	Andrews & Kurth, on behalf of Ore & Chemical Corporation	1-29-90/8-1-90	Denied

(continued)

Table 4.1 (*continued*)

Chemical(s)	Petition Proposed by	Date Petitioned/Final	Final Action
Sulfuric acid	American Cyanamid Company	12-24-90/6-30-95	Delisted liquid forms
Chromium (III) oxide	California Products Corporation	5-21-91/11-22-92	Denied
Hydrochloric acid	BASF, E. I. du Pont de Nemours, Monsanto Corporation, and Vulcan Materials	9-11-91/ 7-25-96	Modified by deleting nonaerosol forms
Acetone	Eastman Chemical Company and Hoechst Celanese	9-24-91/6-16-95	Delisted
Barium sulfate	1) Chemical Products Corporation (CPC) and 2) Dry Color Manufacturers Association (DCMA)	1) 9-24-91 and 2) 11-6-91/6-28-94	Delisted
1) Chromium; 2) nickel; and 3) copper in stainless steel, brass, and bronze	1) Russell Harring Cutlery; 2) Bath Iron Works Corporation; and 3) Stillwater Fasteners, Inc.	1) 6-12-92; 2) 9-25-92; and 3) 10-1-92/6-29-93	All denied
Di-n-octyl phthalate	Vista Chemical Corporation	1-28-92/10-5-93	Delisted
1) Copper phthalocyanine compounds (substituted with only hydrogen and/or bromine and/or chlorine) and 2) copper phthalocyanine pigments (blue 15, green 7, and green 36)	1) Color Pigments Manufacturers Association (CPMA) and 2) The Dry Color Manufacturers Association (DCMA)	1) 3-5-93 and 2) 6-1-88/ 1) 4-11-95 and 2) 5-23-91	Delisted
Manganese and manganese compounds	American Iron and Steel Institute (AISI)	10-20-93/8-24-95	Denied

	EPA initiated	7-5-94 (final)	Redefined category list
Glycol ethers category (at least surfactant glycol ethers)			
Monosodium methanearsonate and disodium methanearsonate	ISK Biosciences Corporation	10-18-94/4-20-95	Denied
Di-(2-ethylhexyl) adipate (DEHA)	Chemical Manufacturers Association	1-18-95/7-31-96	Delisted
Diethyl phthalate (DEP)	Fragrance Material Association	2-7-95/7-29-96	Delisted
Zinc oxide	American Zinc Association	4-4-95/9-12-95	Denied
Polymeric diphenyl methane diisocyanate (PMDI)	Polyurethane Division of the Society of Plastics Industry (SPI)	8-15-95/3-5-97	Denied
Copper metal	National Electrical Manufacturers Association (NEMA)	8-17-95/10-18-96	Denied
Barium compounds category	Chemical Products Corporation (CPC)	6-28-96/1-3-97	Denied
Methyl isobutyl ketone (MIBK)	Ketones Panel of the Chemical Manufacturers Association (CMA)	4-23-97/2-23-99	Denied
Chlorosilanes, DMP, and bronopol	CMA and several other plaintiffs brought suit about the 286 chemicals added	1-12-98/4-22-98	Delisted
Chromite ore and unreacted ore component of its processing residue from Transvaal region of South Africa	Elementis Chromium LP	1-26-98/5-11-01	Delisted
Acetonitrile	BP Chemicals Inc. and GNI Chemicals Corporation (GNICC)	2-4-98/3-5-99	Denied

reporting requirements. Because the original set of 309 individual chemicals and 20 chemical categories covered by the TRI had been established by Congress, EPA had not had to determine for the purposes of EPCRA whether these substances were toxic or met the criteria that chemicals added to the list would have to meet. Through petitions to delist, companies could force the EPA to examine the scientific evidence on a chemical's harms and provide responses to questions about the interpretation of lab or epidemiology studies. The early years of the program may also have seen relatively more delisting petitions because the administration from 1987 through early 1993 was guided by Republicans, who might be more likely to interpret evidence in a manner similar to industry participants in rulemaking. When the EPA published in 1989 the first TRI report (covering releases in 1987), 1 chemical had already been delisted prior to the 1987 data collection, 3 had been deleted before the 1988 reporting, and 4 were proposed for delisting.[7]

The chemicals subject to delisting petitions were often those that generated large numbers of TRI reports. Of the top 25 chemicals with the largest TRI releases and transfers in 1988, 12 were the subject of petitions to the EPA by firms or associations seeking to get the substances removed from reporting.[8] These chemicals accounted for 53% of the total releases and transfers in 1988. In terms of the top 25 chemicals as measured by the number of TRI forms filed in 1988, 14 of these substances (accounting for 38% of all TRI forms) were subject to delisting petitions. Although some of these petitions were denied, the EPA did choose to act and delist substances on the original congressional list. As of January 1994, the EPA had deleted 12 chemicals and added 16 to the TRI reporting list.[9]

Many of the petitions to delist are filed, unsurprisingly, by firms that manufacture or use the chemicals. In cases in which production may be concentrated in one or a few firms, those companies will be the ones to file the petition to delist. When Monsanto petitioned the EPA to delist butyl benzyl phthalate, it had a clear incentive because its Bridgeport, New Jersey, plant was the sole U.S. producer of the chemical.[10] Although ammonium sulfate was manufactured at an estimated 70 plants owned by 61 different companies, it was Allied Signal that filed the petition to delist ammonium sulfate (solution) from the TRI. The company's Hopewell, Virginia, plant accounted for nearly half of the U.S. total production capacity of the chemical.[11] The actions initiated by a single firm can have a large impact on reporting. In 1989, Hoechst Celanese Corporation successfully petitioned the EPA to delist sodium sulfate solution. The EPA delisted the chemical after finding that the chemical did not "meet the listing criteria related to acute human health effects, chronic health effects, or environmental toxicity."[12] The chemical was on the TRI for only the first year of reporting, 1987, when its 12 billion pounds of releases and transfers accounted for 53% of national TRI totals. The delisting actions of a few firms can also trigger large regulatory battles. When Eastman Chemical Company and Hoechst Celanese petitioned the EPA (successfully) to delete acetone from the TRI, a four-year regulatory battle began that generated 51 comments (with 29 supporting the EPA's proposed rule to delete acetone and 22 objecting).[13]

EPA's response to the petitions to delist depended on the agency's reading of the evidence on toxicity, health effects, and environmental harms. After the Chemical Manufacturers Association petitioned the EPA in 1988 to delete cyclohexane, the agency denied the petition after determining,"By contributing to ozone pollution, cyclohexane meets the criteria of section 313(d)(2) for both acute and chronic health effects, as well as for ecotoxicity effects."[14] When the EPA received three petitions (from DuPont, SCM Chemicals, and Kemira) to delist titanium dioxide, the agency issued a proposed rule to delist the chemical in part because "the weight-of-evidence is not sufficient to support a determination that TiO_2 can reasonably be anticipated to cause cancer in humans ... or can reasonably be anticipated to cause any significant adverse health or environmental effect."[15] During the notice and comment process, the Natural Resources Defense Council (NRDC) opposed the delisting and asserted that the agency had made mistakes in interpretation of cancer bioassay research and human epidemiology studies. The agency responded to the NRDC comments in the final rule and reiterated its assessment that the chemical did not meet the criteria for listing.[16] The agency proved willing to change its decision when presented with new information. The EPA originally in 1991 denied two petitions to delist barium sulfate. Yet when the agency later received petitions from the Chemical Products Corporation and Dry Color Manufacturers' Association that contained additional information on the impact of barium sulfate in the environment, the EPA changed its assessment and delisted the chemical.[17] The agency at times reversed its decisions because of court challenges. In 1998, the EPA deleted several chemicals and categories from the TRI to comply with a court order arising from a suit brought by the Chemical Manufacturers Association.[18]

The most controversial reduction in TRI reporting to date arose from petitions filed by the Small Business Administration (SBA) and the

American Feed Industry Association (AFIA). In 1991, the SBA petitioned the EPA to exempt plants with only small amounts of releases
and transfers from reporting. The AFIA asked that facilities in the feed
industry (SIC 2048) be relieved from reporting because they had very
low releases and transfers. In 1994, the EPA proposed and adopted a
rule in response to these petitions that established an alternate reporting
threshold for TRI reporting for plants with relatively small amounts of
reportable chemicals. Specifically, plants with annual reportable amounts
of a TRI chemical that did not exceed 500 pounds and that manufactured
or used 1 million or fewer pounds of the chemical did not have to file a
Form R. They could simply file a certification form (later called a Form
A) that noted that they qualified for this reporting threshold. In 1994,
the EPA was adding 286 chemicals and categories to the TRI, so the
alternate threshold was a way to offset partially the expanded reporting
demands.[19] The agency finalized the rules adding substances to the TRI
list and reducing the reporting threshold on the same day, November 30,
1994.

The threshold proposal attracted approximately 500 comments, with
400 from firms or industry associations and the rest from "environmental
and labor organizations, public interest groups, state program officials,
and private citizens." Those opposing the threshold noted the potential
loss of information on hazardous chemicals in communities and urged
the EPA to retain the reporting requirements. In its Regulatory Impact
Analysis, the agency estimated that the reduced reporting costs would
save industry a total of $21.5 million per year and save the agency approx-
imately $800,000 in reduced transaction costs. The agency estimated that
4,500 plants would not have to file any Form Rs with the new threshold
and that 7,100 other plants would be able to convert at least one Form
R into a simple certification statement. The agency noted that a total of
23,600 TRI reports could be replaced with the certification, which meant
much lower paperwork for firms. The EPA estimated using 1992 data
that the relaxed reporting would reduce TRI reportable amounts by only
2.5 million pounds, approximately .01% of the national TRI totals for that
year.

Whereas efforts to reduce reporting costs of the TRI originated from
private sector petitions during the Bush I and Clinton administrations,
the second Bush administration made burden reduction their main new
TRI initiative. In October 2002, the EPA issued a notice in the *Federal
Register* inviting people to participate in an online discussion called the

"Stakeholder Dialogue on the Toxics Release Inventory."[20] In November 2003, the agency began phase 2 of the dialogue and said it was "seeking suggestions and ideas on a number of burden reduction options including, but not limited to: establishing higher reporting thresholds for small businesses or for certain classes of facilities or chemicals; modifying the eligibility requirements of the Form A Certification Statement to expand its use; creating a new form allowing facilities meeting certain criteria to certify to no significant change in reporting in the current year as measured against a designated baseline year; and using range codes in . . . Form R."[21]

Framing the discussion of the program as one of burden reduction generated many complaints about the operation of the program. In a dialogue posting, Glen Barrett of the American Petroleum Institute noted:

One of API's member companies has 50 bulk petroleum terminals that filed 498 Form Rs last reporting year, of which 119 were for zero releases. Filing these 119 zero release reports required over 1,000 hours of effort. API requests that EPA determine the number of zero release reports that the agency receives, assess their practical utility, and consider eliminating the need to file them.[22]

Michael P. Walls of the American Chemistry Council noted that in terms of agency guidance on TRI compliance:

EPA must understand . . . that the guidance is frequently as complex as the reporting questions which give rise to them. . . . The single largest problem with respect to guidance . . . is the frequent changes, due to EPA's ongoing or revised interpretations of the regulations, intended and inadvertent changes in the massive collection of questions and answers (Q&A), and the responses of EPA's contractors to inquiries.[23]

Tracy Glaser of the Timken Company focused on the problem that what the TRI terms "releases" may never be released to the environment, noting:

The result of these major overstatements in the amounts of toxics reported as released to the environment is that the public (by assuming that anything reported as a toxics "release" is a toxic they are actually exposed to) has highly inaccurate information regarding the extent of the problem of toxic releases and thus is primed to support more burdensome regulations to address a "problem" that has been artificially inflated by inappropriate and inaccurate EPA data. This inaccurate information is also used to press lawmakers and the EPA itself to adopt more burdensome law and regulation, resulting in public policy targeted at a chimera rather than a reality.[24]

Table 4.2. *Proposed Additions of Chemical Information to TRI Reporting Requirements*

Chemicals/Information	Proposed by	Date Proposed/Final	Final Action
10 Chemicals: 2,3-dichloropropene, dinitrobenzene, p-dinitrobenzene, allyl alcohol, diethylamine, isosafrole, o-dinitrobenzene, creosote, dinitrotoluene, toluenediisocyanate	EPA	4-21-89/12-1-89	9 chemicals added
7 Ozone-depleting chemicals: CFC-11, CFC-12, CFC-14, CFC-15, halon 1211, halon 1301, and halon 2402	Three governors (Kean, Kunin, and Cuomo) and the Natural Resources Defense Council	1-9-90/8-3-90	Added
Ozone-depleting chemicals, hydrochlorofluorocarbons (HCFCs)	Natural Resources Defense Council, Friends of the Earth, Environmental Defense Fund	12-3-91/12-1-93	Added 11 HCFCs separately and not as a category
List of 80 chemicals and 2 chemical categories	Gov. Mario Cuomo and the Natural Resources Defense Council	3-4-92/12-1-93	Partial grant of petition: added 21 chemicals and 2 categories
List of 313 chemicals	EPA	1-12-94/11-30-94	Added 286 chemicals

7 industry groups to list of industry groups subject to reporting requirements under 313: metal mining, coal mining, electric utilities, commercial hazardous waste treatment, chemicals and allied products-wholesale, petroleum bulk stations-wholesale, solvent recovery services	EPA	6-27-96/5-1-97	Added 7 industry groups to the list of industry groups subject to reporting requirements under EPCRA 313
PBTs; dioxin and 27 dioxin-like compounds, and vanadium	EPA (PBTs and vanadium); Communities for a Better Environment (dioxin)	5-7-97/10-29-99	The EPA lowered PBT reporting thresholds, adding a category of dioxin and dioxin-like compounds, adding certain other PBTs, removing fume or dust qualifier from vanadium and, adding vanadium except when contained in an alloy
Lead and lead compounds	EPA	8-3-99/1-17-01	Lowered reporting thresholds for lead and lead compounds
Diisononyl phthalate category	Washington Toxics Coalition (WTC)	2-29-00	No final action

Commenting on the industry complaints in the dialogue about the use of the term *releases* in the TRI, Rich Puchalsky of the Grassroots Connection declared:

Detailed analysis of the fate of each pollutant stream is impossible, which is why TRI reports pounds of chemicals released, not risk numbers. "Linguistic detoxification" – lobbying EPA to change the words it uses to describe pollution – will always be preferred by industry to real pollution prevention, because it's cheaper.[25]

As an additional step to reducing the transaction costs of filing the TRI, the EPA developed the Toxics Release Inventory–Made Easy (TRI-ME) software. This program leads facilities through the reporting form, provides guidance assistance, checks for common mistakes, generates printed forms, and allows plants to send the information to the EPA over the Internet through the Central Data Exchange of the EPA. Nearly 90% of the 84,000 TRI Form Rs containing data for 2002 were generated by facilities that used TRI-ME.[26] In a July 2002 *Federal Register* notice complying with the Paperwork Reduction Act, the EPA estimated that the TRI annually involved 88,117 responses that generated 2,356,900 burden hours at a cost of $101.9 million. The agency indicated it had revised its estimate of the number of hours necessary to complete a Form R from 47.1 hours to 14.5 hours and attributed the decline to computerization at facilities, better guidance, and greater industry familiarity with TRI. The agency noted that TRI-ME software reduced record keeping, form completion, and submission time totals by 25%.[27]

Whereas most of the efforts to scale back the data collected by the TRI came from industry, Table 4.2 shows that the EPA initiated most of the attempts to expand the information provided to the public. The environmental groups and governors who petitioned the EPA did add more chemicals to the list than the number deleted by industry petitions. The largest expansions of the reporting requirements, however, came in three actions generated by the EPA: the proposal to add 313 (later pared down to 286) chemicals to the TRI, the addition of seven new industries to the program, and the lowering of reporting thresholds for persistent bioaccumulative toxic (PBT) chemicals and for lead. In these actions, the agency drew on broad interpretations of the language of EPCRA to justify decisions. The agency frequently quoted legislative history, conference reports, and *Congressional Record* statements to show that the discretion exercised was consistent with "congressional intent."[28] The major expansions of the TRI came during the Clinton administration.

Table 4.3. *2001 TRI Figures, in Pounds*

	Total On-Site Releases	Total Off-Site Releases	Total On- and Off-Site Releases	Total Transfers for Further Waste Management
1988 core chemicals from manufacturing industries	991,176,014	415,971,142	1,407,147,156	2,810,612,740
Chemicals and industries added after 1988	4,571,428,872	136,287,815	4,707,716,687	1,236,173,272
TOTAL	5,562,604,886	552,258,957	6,114,863,843	4,046,786,012
Percentage accounted for by core chemicals	17.8	75.3	23.0	69.4

The willingness of the agency to use discretion to expand the reach of right-to-know provisions reflected both the green ideology of the Administrator and those higher in the administration (including Vice President Gore).

Table 4.3 shows the large impact on the TRI program from the expansions achieved in the notice-and-comment rulemaking process. For reporting year 2001, total on- and off-site releases at TRI facilities totaled 6,114,863,843 pounds.[29] If reporting had been limited only to the core chemicals on the list in 1988 and the plants in the original set of manufacturing SIC codes, then the public would have received data on only 23.0% of the release totals for 2001. Total transfers for further waste management in 2001 totaled 4,046,786,012 pounds. The core 1988 chemicals and original manufacturing industries generated 69.4% of this figure. The addition of new chemicals and industries to the TRI thus accounted for three fourths of the total releases and one third of the total transfers for waste management reported in 2001.

The first expansion of the list of TRI chemicals came from a proposal by the EPA to add ten chemicals based on their carcinogenicity or chronic toxicity. After inviting comments on a proposed rule to add ten substances, the EPA in a final rule published in 1989 added nine of the chemicals to the reporting program. Comments submitted by Hoechst Celanese questioning the study used to establish the toxicity of diethylamine caused the agency to defer action on that substance.[30] As envisioned in the administrative procedures set up through EPCRA, interest groups were able to petition the EPA successfully to add substances. Eleven hydrochlorofluorocarbons (HCFCs) were added in 1993 as the result of a petition from the Natural Resources Defense Council, Friends of the Earth, and the Environmental Defense Fund to add HCFCs. Industry commenters objected to the addition because the chemicals exhibited low or no direct toxicity. The agency's use of discretion to expand the TRI was evident in how the final rule on HCFCs justified the listing on the basis of "indirect toxicity." As the agency explained:

The information on health effects induced by HCFCs has been reviewed by the Agency and generally supports the contention that these chemicals exhibit low or no direct toxicity. The concerns about these chemicals are based on their depleting effect on stratospheric ozone and the resulting increase in penetration of UV-B radiation, causing the adverse environmental and human health effects listed.... EPCRA allows EPA to add a chemical to the section 313 list if the chemical is "known to cause or can reasonably be anticipated to cause" certain adverse human health or environmental effects. EPCRA does not limit EPA to considering only effects caused directly by a toxic chemical. EPA believes that indirect effects can and should be considered in determining whether or not a chemical should be subject to reporting under section 313.[31]

The deckstacking embodied in the different treatment of petitions from governors did come into play in additions made in 1990. On January 9, 1990, the EPA got a petition from three governors (Kean of New Jersey, Cuomo of New York, and Kunin of Vermont) and the NRDC asking for the addition of seven ozone-depleting chemicals. The legislative text of EPCRA specifies that for petitions from a governor to add chemicals, the substances are automatically added to the list unless the agency takes action within 180 days by starting a rulemaking or issuing an explanation of why the substance failed to satisfy the listing criteria. When the agency failed to meet the statutory deadline (July 8, 1990), the substances automatically joined the TRI list. On August 3, 1990, the agency did issue a final rule in which it affirmed that the evidence did indicate the seven chemicals satisfied the listing criteria. In response to an invitation in March 1990 to comment on the governors' petition, the EPA had received 39 comments on the ozone proposal, with 2 supporting the additions and 37 opposed. Industry commenters focused on the lack of evidence of direct toxicity for the chemicals. The agency stated that the ozone-depleting chemicals were indirectly toxic: the chemicals deplete the stratospheric ozone, which increases the penetration of UV-B radiation, which causes adverse human health and environmental effects. Making the case that indirect effects, though not mentioned in the EPCRA text, were a valid listing criteria, the EPA said:

The statute and the legislative history do not specifically preclude the considera-tion of indirect effects in evaluating whether or not a chemical meets the statutory criteria for listing under section 313. In fact, the statute grants the EPA broad dis-cretion in granting or denying petitions to modify the list. EPA believes that indirect effects can and should be considered in determining whether or not a chemical should be subject to reporting under section 313.[32]

The treatment of a second governor's petition shows the ability of environmentalists to use administrative procedures to expand reporting and the agency's use of discretion to balance the benefits of informa-tion provision with the cost of reporting. In March 1992, Governor Mario Cuomo of New York and the NRDC petitioned the EPA to add 80 chemi-cals and two chemical categories, all of which were already on the list of RCRA toxic wastes, to the TRI list. In September 1992, the EPA partially granted the petition by proposing the listing of 68 chemicals and two chemical categories; the agency omitted 12 of the chemicals from the proposed listing because the information available indicated they did not meet the EPCRA toxicity criteria. In the final rule, the EPA ended up adding only 21 chemicals and two chemical categories. For 18 of the chemicals originally listed in the proposed rule, the EPA chose not to put them in the final rule listing because it determined that "no evidence was found that they are manufactured or imported in quantities of at least 10,000 pounds at any one facility." The manu-facturing threshold for listing, which was discussed in the proposed rule, drew fire from environmentalists and public interest groups. Thirty-one commenters urged the EPA to focus only on toxicity in listing and not consider whether a chemical was actually produced or used in sufficient amounts to generate TRI reporting. In response, the agency noted that the language of the bill indicated that a chemical "may be added" if cer-tain criteria were met, implying that the agency did not have to add a chemical, even if the toxicity criteria were satisfied. The agency noted:

...while the statute specifies generally accepted scientific principles, laboratory tests, and other studies as the permissible bases for making a toxicity determi-nation under section 313(d)(2), EPCRA does not preclude the Agency from considering other information, such as production volume, when exercising its discretion when responding to a petition to list or not list a chemical that may meet the toxicity criteria.[33]

Although some commenters challenged the addition of the two chemical categories on the premise that only individual chemicals could be added, the agency responded that "the statutory authority to add 'a chemical' to the list may be reasonably interpreted to include the authority to add groups or categories to the list, particularly in light of the fact that the original list by Congress in section 313(c) of EPCRA included 20 chemical categories.... "

The three largest expansions of EPCRA came from three different types of EPA-initiated action: the adding of chemicals, the coverage of new industries, and the broadening of information provision by lowering the threshold of chemical production or use that triggered facility reporting. In January 1994, the EPA proposed adding 313 chemicals and chemical categories to the EPCRA list. The agency began with a list of chemicals either regulated under a set of U.S. environmental statutes or designated by reports as possible, probable, or known carcinogens. The agency then applied three screens to the chemical set. Did evidence indicate the chemical was toxic? Was the substance produced or used in volumes likely to trigger reporting? Did a hazard evaluation indicate the chemical would meet the statutory criteria spelled out in EPCRA? A technical review summarized the evidence for why each of the 313 chemicals was proposed for listing, a review that included data on "adverse acute and chronic toxicity, carcinogenicity, mutagenicity, developmental and reproductive effects, neurotoxicity, and environmental effects."[34]

The proposed rule elicited 286 comments, from predictable sources: 136 from industry (e.g., firms), 60 from trade associations, 32 from environmental groups, 15 from individual citizens, 3 federal agencies, 7 state agencies, and 13 from public interest groups and other groups.[35] Aside from general feedback on the rule, the EPA got specific technical comments for 110 of the proposed chemicals or categories. Industry commenters argued that the agency should have used more stringent screens in determining substances to list. Eastman Chemical Company argued that even if a chemical met the production volume screen, the EPA should consider not placing a substance on the list if the number of likely Form Rs was small. The EPA responded:

While the Agency has determined to not list chemicals for which no reports would be submitted, EPA believes that it is appropriate to add chemicals to EPCRA section 313 for which even a small number of reports are likely to be submitted nationally. In such cases, the reporting facilities will still provide important information to the surrounding communities.

Industry commenters also urged the agency to conduct exposure assessments and risk assessments to ascertain the likelihood and magnitude of harms arising from a potentially listed chemical. The EPA rejected this interpretation of its duties under EPCRA, noting that the conference report on EPCRA had said:

The Administrator, in determining to list a chemical under any of the above criteria, may, but is not required to conduct new studies or risk assessments or perform site-specific analyses to establish actual ambient concentrations or to document adverse effects at any particular location.[36]

The agency declared that:

This passage indicates Congress did not intend to require EPA to conduct new studies, such as exposure studies, or perform risk assessments, and therefore did not consider these activities to be mandatory components of all section 313 decisions.

The EPA said that the language of EPCRA required exposure to be considered for listing under the acute human health criteria, because the bill says the agency must consider if "a chemical is known to cause or can reasonably be anticipated to cause significant adverse acute human health effects at concentration levels that are reasonably likely to exist beyond facility site boundaries." The other listing criteria (e.g., chronic human health or environmental damage), which did not mention concentration levels and site boundaries, did not require assessment of exposure factors. The agency noted, however, that it was not prohibited from considering exposure in assessing these criteria too. The EPA took the overall position that discretion to consider particular factors such as production volume and exposure did not mean that industry could force the agency to define and use these factors in particular ways in listing decisions.

In the final 1994 rule, the EPA added 286 of the initially proposed 313 chemicals and categories to the EPCRA list. The Regulatory Impact Analysis performed on this final rule indicated that adding the 286 chemicals would for the first year of additional reporting create $99 million in industry costs, which would decline to $49 million in future years once plants had become familiar with what chemicals were covered and had estimated their releases for a year. The additional costs to the EPA of collecting and processing the data on the 286 chemicals was estimated to be $1 million per year.

In June 1996, the EPA proposed adding seven industries to EPCRA reporting: metal mining, coal mining, electric utilities, commercial hazardous waste treatment, chemicals and allied products – wholesale, petroleum bulk stations – wholesale, and solvent recovery services. A large section of the *Federal Register* notice was devoted to the rationale for the agency's authority to add industries to TRI reporting. The EPA noted:

The limited list of chemicals and facilities identified in the original legislation was meant as a starting point, or core program. Congress recognized that the TRI program would need to evolve to meet the needs of a better informed public and to fill information gaps that would become apparent over time. In implementing the expansion of the TRI program, EPA is pursuing the course set by Congress.[37]

The agency quoted from an August 8, 1995, directive from President Clinton that called for a "continuation on an expedited basis of the public notice and comment rulemaking proceedings to consider whether, as appropriate and consistent with section 313(b) of EPCRA, 42 USC 11023(b), to add to the list of Standard Industrial Classification ("SIC") designations of 20 through 39...." The EPA noted that the 1991 GAO report on the TRI, which had been required by EPCRA, criticized the agency for not using its statutory authority to add more types of facilities to the TRI program. The proposed rule notice pointed out that the actual text of EPCRA says:

The Administrator may add or delete Standard Industrial Classification Codes ... but only to the extent necessary to provide that each Standard Industrial Classification Code to which this section applies is relevant to the purposes of this section.

EPA noted that the Conference Report restated this:

[EPA's] authority is limited, however, to adding SIC codes for facilities which, like facilities within the manufacturing sector SIC codes 20 through 39, manufacture, process or use toxic chemicals in a manner such that reporting by these facilities is relevant to the purposes of this section.

The agency turned to the Conference Report again for a description of the purposes of the TRI:

The information collected under this section is intended to inform the general public and the communities surrounding covered facilities about releases of toxic chemicals, to assist in research, to aid in the development of regulations, guidelines, and standards, and for other similar purposes.

Finally, the EPA in the proposed rule quoted a statement from Congressman Edgar, identified as a "principal architect of EPCRA":

... the reporting provisions in this legislation should be construed expansively to require the collection of the most information permitted under the statutory language. Any discretion to limit the amount of information reported should be exercised only for compelling reasons.... For too long, the public has been left in the dark about its exposure to toxic chemicals.

After making the case for its statutory authority, EPA proposed adding seven industries based on its determination that plants were likely to be involved with a TRI chemical; that facilities in the industries were likely to manufacture, process, or otherwise use these chemicals; and that the reporting requirement would generate information.

Though the agency had held extensive outreach before issuing the proposed rule, comments streamed in during the notice-and-comment process. Part of this reflected the increased ease of participation, given that comments now could be emailed (email was first mentioned in a *Federal Register* notice dealing with EPCRA in 1995; the Internet and EPCRA were mentioned in a 1994 notice). The proposed industry rule drew 2,715 comments, which included 470 industry, 86 trade association, 60 environmental group, 1,875 individual citizen, 5 federal agency, 43 state agency, 108 public interest group, 18 labor group, 14 university, and 36 association comments. Industry commenters tried to narrow the set of facilities added. Commenters representing mining firms argued that mining did not meet the EPCRA criteria of "manufacturing" or "processing," so mining should be exempt. In reply, the agency noted:

Had Congress intended to exclude mining activities, EPA believes it reasonable to conclude that Congress would have expressly provided such an exemption. In the absence of such exemptions, EPA believes Congress intended the phrase "manufacturing, process, or otherwise use" of toxic chemicals to encompass a broad scope of activities involving toxic chemicals, the reporting of which would be relevant to the public-information purposes of section 313.[38]

Others urged the EPA to add industries only in cases in which plants were likely to generate significant risks to public health. Again, the EPA rejected this narrowing:

In passing EPCRA, Congress determined that it is for the public to take the information reported on the use and releases and other waste management of toxic chemicals, and to determine whether there is a need for any response given other factors, such as economic and environmental conditions, or particularly vulnerable human or ecological populations. Congress did not intend the federal government to consider these local factors prior to determining whether certain information should be made available to the public, or prior to determining whether an industry group should be added.

The EPA also defended its revised interpretation of *otherwise used*. With the new set of industries being added, EPA revised the definition of *otherwise used* to include "treatment for destruction, disposal, and waste stabilization" when a facility receives chemicals from other facilities for waste management. Overall, the EPA did not change its decisions about which industries to add during the notice-and-comment process. EPA estimated that the new industry provisions would generate 42,500 new TRI reports from 6,300 plants, whereas the revision of *otherwise use* would generate 3,600 reports from 360 manufacturing plants. First-year industry incremental compliance costs were estimated at $226 million, but dropped to $143 million annual costs in later years.

Through a final rule proposed and adopted in 1999, the EPA used its discretion in a different manner to expand TRI reporting. Concerned about the effects of chemicals that persist in the environment and accumulate in organisms (i.e., bioaccumulate), the EPA proposed to lower the reporting thresholds that trigger the filing of TRI reports. Section 313 contained thresholds for the manufacture, production, or use of chemicals and provided that the "Administrator may establish a threshold amount for a toxic chemical different from the amount established" in the bill.[39] Commenters attacked the agency for lowering the threshold on the basis that the legislation did not explicitly say the agency could decrease the threshold. The EPA responded that the general purposes of the TRI would guide its decisions about thresholds, noting:

Because Congress provided no prerequisites to the exercise of EPA's authority to lower the thresholds, and little explicit guidance, EPA looked to the purposes of section 313 to help guide the exercise of its discretion.[40]

After reviewing the scientific studies on persistence and bioaccumulation and responding to criticisms of the proposal, the EPA went ahead and adopted lower reporting thresholds on the manufacture, production, or otherwise use of 18 chemicals on the TRI. These lower thresholds ranged from 100 pounds for chemicals such as aldrin and trifluralin to 10 pounds for mercury and chlordane. The rule also responded to a petition from Communities for a Better Environment by adding dioxin and dioxin-like compounds and establishing a reporting threshold of .1 grams for these substances.[41] The costs associated with the rule were estimated to be substantial. An estimated 11,300 facilities would file nearly 20,000 additional Form Rs because of the lowered thresholds and addition of dioxin. The first year's incremental industry costs were estimated to be $145 million, with later annual industry costs from the rule change dropping to $80 million. EPA's annual additional costs from the rule were estimated at $1.6 million.

In August 1999, the EPA proposed to lower the reporting thresholds for lead and lead compounds because of their persistence in the environment and bioaccumulation. On January 17, 2001, during the last week of the Clinton administration, the EPA issued a final rule that lowered the reporting threshold for lead to 100 pounds. The EPA noted that:

Several commenters allege that under EPA's interpretation of EPCRA section 313(f)(2), Congress did not provide an "intelligible principle" for determining whether or how much to lower a statutory threshold, thereby rendering this provision unconstitutional as an improperly broad delegation of legislative power.[42]

EPA rebutted this critique by showing how the text and legislative history provided implicit guidance for the threshold decision, noting:

... the Agency's choice of revised thresholds was governed, and ultimately constrained, by EPCRA section 313's overriding purpose, which is to provide government agencies, researchers, and local communities, with a comprehensive picture of toxic chemical releases and potential exposures to humans and ecosystems.

Regulatory analysis again indicated this rule would generate substantial costs: 9,800 plants would submit new Form Rs at a first-year cost of $80 million and a subsequent annual cost of $40 million. The analysis conducted under the Regulatory Flexibility Act estimated that nearly 4,100 small businesses would be affected by the lead threshold rule, but that no small business would bear annual costs more than 1% of annual revenues after the first year of the program. In fall 2001, the agency conducted workshops to help companies comply with the new lead rules. The agency also posted a draft guidance document on lead reporting to stimulate public comment on the development of its recommendations on how to comply with the rules.[43]

The agency was required to estimate the likely impact of additional reporting requirements in the rulemaking process as part of the Regulatory Impact Analysis and as part of the process of estimating paperwork burdens for OMB under the Paperwork Reduction Act. In a 2002 notice in the *Federal Register* related to EPA's submission of an information collection request to OMB, the agency noted that it had often overestimated the impact of new TRI reporting requirements. EPA said that:

...the 1997 program change for industry expansion estimated 39,033 responses would be submitted, but only 12,567 responses were actually submitted. Likewise, the 1999 program change for PBT chemical thresholds estimated 19,990 responses would be submitted, but only about 7,000 responses were actually submitted.... The prediction of 9,813 additional reports for lead and lead compounds may prove to be an overestimate, as with EPA predictions for past rules.[44]

Not all of EPA's efforts to expand reporting resulted in regulatory changes. In 1993, the first year of the Clinton administration, the EPA started the TRI- Phase 3 project (with *3* denoting the next step after the 1994 addition of chemicals to the TRI (phase 1) and addition of industries (phase 2)). The agency held public meetings in 1994 and 1995 to focus on the potential for collection of chemical use data. In October 1996, the EPA issued an Advance Notice of Proposed Rulemaking (ANPR) in the *Federal Register* seeking comments on the agency's consideration of collecting more information than currently done under EPCRA or the Pollution Prevention Act (PPA) of 1990. The agency defined chemical use data as "the information most commonly described as materials accounting data: amounts of a toxic chemical coming into a facility, amounts transformed into products and wastes, and the resulting amounts leaving the facility site."[45] EPCRA had required the EPA to request a NAS study on mass balance accounting, the evaluation of chemical throughput at a facility. Although the EPA interpreted the NAS study as inconclusive on the desirability of requiring mass balance reporting, the agency said the study did note that materials accounting (e.g., collecting information on chemical inputs and production process at a facility) might be helpful. In the 1996 notice, the agency asked for comments on potential data elements the EPA might seek on chemical use. From the origin of EPCRA to the present, industry has opposed the collection of detailed chemical use information at the plant level for many reasons, including costs of reporting, confidential business information, and accuracy of the data. Although the EPA did expand the TRI through chemical additions, industry expansion, and the lowering of reporting thresholds, to date, the agency has not translated the query about chemical use data into a proposed rule.

Congressional Action, and Inaction

Congressional action on toxics right-to-know issues did not end with the passage of EPCRA. Once the EPA created the regulations defining the TRI reporting system, Congress members shifted their activities to monitoring implementation. Oversight committees held hearings to critique the EPA's operation of the TRI, budget decisions were made that encouraged the program to expand or contract, and bills were introduced to augment or pare down the information required under TRI. During the Bush I administration, Congress passed the only specific legislation to expand the TRI – the Pollution Prevention Act of 1990. Committee hearings held during the time showcased the frustration of EPCRA's sponsors with the failure of the agency to expand the chemicals or industries covered. Bills were introduced to increase through legislation the scope of the TRI. The Clinton administration EPA took heed of calls to increase toxics reporting and expanded through rulemaking the number of chemicals and industries in the TRI. Once Republicans gained control of the House and Senate in 1995, however, the change in principals resulted in congressional attempts to rein in the TRI. During the summer of 1995, congressional debates over regulatory reform contained many proposals to reduce the reach of the TRI, though these measures ultimately did not make their way into law. With the Bush II administration, Republican congressional leaders did not attempt a direct legislative revision of the TRI. Numerous oversight hearings were held, however, that allowed stakeholders to voice their frustration with TRI initiatives, especially the lowering of the lead reporting threshold in 2001. Although not attracting significant attention or controversy, Congress did constrain the TRI program during the Bush II administration through the power of the purse. The TRI program budget dropped 39% in nominal terms between FY 1997 and FY 2004, with the majority of the decline coming between FY 2001 and FY 2004.

During the Bush I administration, the EPA got the TRI off the ground with the first release of data in 1989. Congress members used hearings on EPCRA as a forum to oversee the agency's implementation and to push for an expansion of reporting. Table 4.4 lists congressional hearings on toxics reporting from 1988 to 2004. In the aptly titled Senate Environment and Public Works subcommittee hearing *Oversight of the Emergency Planning and Community Right to Know Act of 1986* (May 26, 1988), legislators focused on whether EPA had sufficient resources to gather the incoming 1987 data, develop a public report, and ensure compliance with reporting. Testifying at the hearing, Rep. James Florio noted:

I am not convinced that the EPA has set aside the proper resources to enforce this law and ensure compliance. In its fiscal 1989 budget request, EPA said it needs only three fulltime people in Washington office and eight in regional offices to work on enforcement over the next two years. It is inconceivable that 11 people will be able to enforce the law on 30,000 facilities nationwide.[46]

Table 4.4. *Congressional Hearings on Toxics Reporting, 1988 to 2004*

Committee/Subcommittee	Hearing Title	Date
House Public Works and Transportation/Water Resources	Reauthorization of Superfund	March 26–28, May 1, July 24, and 25, 1985
House Energy and Commerce/Health and the Environment	Toxic Releases Control Act of 1985	June 11 and 19, 1985
Senate Small Business	Community Right-to-Know Legislation and Its Regulatory and Paperwork Impact on Small Business	June 18, 1985
House Energy and Commerce/Commerce, Transportation, and Tourism	Superfund: Right-to-Know and Hazardous Wastesite Cleanup	December 20, 1985
Senate Environment and Public Works/ Superfund and Environmental Oversight	Oversight of the Emergency Planning and Community Right-to-Know Act of 1986.	May 26, 1988
House Government Operations/Information, Justice, and Agriculture	Federal Information Dissemination Policies and Practices	April 18 and 23 and July 11, 1989
Senate Environment and Public Works/ Superfund, Ocean, and Water	Oversight of Right-to-Know Pollution Data	May 10, 1989
House Energy and Commerce/Transportation and Hazardous Materials	Hazardous Waste Reduction Act	May 25, 1989
House Energy and Commerce/Transportation and Hazardous Materials	Pollution Prevention and Hazardous Waste Reduction	May 31, 1990
House Government Operations/Government Information, Justice, and Agriculture	Creative Ways of Using and Disseminating Federal Information	February 19 and June 4, 1992
Senate Environment and Public Works/Superfund, Ocean, and Water	Expansion of the Right-to-Know Program	June 27, 1991
House Energy and Commerce/Transportation and Hazardous Materials	Solid Waste Disposal Act Reauthorization	March 10 and 16, 1992
House Commerce/Health and Environment and Oversight and Investigations	Internet Posting of Chemical "Worst Case" Scenarios: A Roadmap for Terrorists	February 10, 1999
House Commerce/Health and Environment	Chemical Safety Information and Site Security Act of 1999	May 19 and 26, 1999
House Small Business/Regulatory Reform and Oversight	EPA Rulemaking: Do Bad Analyses Lead to Irrational Rules?	November 8, 2001
House Small Business/Regulatory Reform and Oversight	The TRI Lead Rule: Costs, Compliance and Science	June 13, 2002
House Resources/Energy and Mineral Resources	Toxic Release Inventory Impact on Federal Minerals and Energy	September 25, 2003

In a Senate subcommittee hearing one year later entitled *Oversight of Right-to-Know Pollution Data* (May 10, 1989), senators pressed EPA officials on implementation issues relating to data accuracy and accessibility and the attempts to catch nonfilers. Commenting on the EPA's lack of budgeted enforcement personnel, Senator Lautenberg declared:

I can tell you, since I was one of the drafters, this is just not enough to convince lots of people that there is a commitment by EPA and by the administration to get this job done, and unless we really get on the ball with tough enforcement, aggressive enforcement, and numbers of enforcement actions, there are going to be lots of people who are going to yawn at this thing and say, What the heck? Our chance of getting caught is fairly slim, and the penalties, if we do get caught, are not very severe.[47]

In a House subcommittee hearing later in May 1989, EPA Administrator Reilly testified that he was "proud of our effort to create the Toxic Release Inventory on the rapid schedule mandated by Congress," though he did estimate that roughly a quarter of covered facilities were not filing reports.[48]

Some of the oversight hearings featured industry participants critical of aspects of the TRI. In a House subcommittee hearing on pollution prevention in May 1990, the executive director of the Environmental Health Coalition in San Diego, Diane Takvorian, noted the need to expand TRI to cover nonmanufacturing facilities and federal facilities. She also submitted a report using TRI data entitled *Communities at Risk: Your Right to Know about Toxics in San Diego*. Bill Anderson, executive vice president of the Industrial Environmental Association in San Diego, testified:

First, to this "Communities at Risk" report, we believe that the unnecessary alarmist nature of the report seeks to maintain a "Chicken Little" atmosphere with the general public. Now, unfortunately, when the sky is not falling, that atmosphere is unfair to the public and to the industrial community. More importantly, it is counterproductive and it has the potential to paralyze progress and to waste an awful lot of time and money in providing solutions to problems that do not exist instead of focusing the effort where it is necessary and where it will do the most good. ... Their report makes no effort to educate the public about the appropriate and responsible use of chemicals. Rather, it leaves the impression that all chemicals are dangerous and should be eliminated.[49]

The first, and to date only, legislative alteration of TRI reporting requirements came through the passage of the budget reconciliation bill in October 1990. Tucked into this budget measure was the Pollution Prevention Act of 1990 (PPA). The act required EPA to develop a strategy to encourage pollution prevention, that is, the elimination of waste before it is produced. The text of the legislation required the EPA to add particular data elements to the TRI information form so that the public could gain information on a facility's efforts to prevent pollution. As the agency described the new data elements in the *Federal Register*:

Facilities must provide information on: the quantity of the chemical (prior to recycling, treatment, or disposal) entering any wastestream or released to the environment; the quantities of the chemical recycled at the facility or elsewhere; the quantities of the chemical treated at the facility or elsewhere; information on source reduction activities and methods used to identify those activities; the quantities of the chemical released in one-time events not associated with production processes; the quantities of the chemical expected to enter any wastestream or be recycled in future years; and a production ratio or activity index for the reported chemicals.[50]

Senators noted during debate that EPA Administrator Reilly, the National Roundtable of State Waste Reduction Programs, the Chemical Manufacturers Association, the National Wildlife Federation, and the National Toxics Campaign Fund had all praised the measure.[51] The act was based on a bill (S. 585) introduced by Sen. Frank Lautenberg, one of the original architects of EPCRA. Whereas the first TRI forms had contained an optional section on waste minimization activities at a plant, the PPA expanded on the type of source reduction activities tracked and made the information collection mandatory. The production index allowed one to estimate how pollution had changed relative to production at a facility over time. Estimates of future activities could help plants form strategies aimed at reducing releases and transfers down the road. Overall, legislators hoped that the expansion of the TRI through the PPA would focus public attention more on pollution prevention.

In June 1991, Sens. Frank Lautenberg and Dave Durenberger held a Senate subcommittee hearing entitled *Expansion of the Right to Know Program* that focused on a legislative draft they were circulating that would expand the number of chemicals, widen the industries required to report, and collect chemical use data from plants. Explaining his frustration, Senator Lautenberg noted:

We knew in 1986 that we could enhance the benefits of Right-to-Know by covering more facilities and more chemicals, and that's why we provided EPA with the power to do so in the 1986 law. We are now in the fifth year of the Right-to-Know program, but EPA has yet to take the steps to require additional types of facilities to report under the law, and it has required emissions data on only an additional 16 chemicals.... Congress provided EPA with initial mandates about types of facilities and specific chemicals but, recognizing that the program would require some start-up time, Congress deferred to EPA to take the next steps. EPA's inaction, coupled with the clear benefits of the Right-to-Know program, convinced us that it is time to expand the law.[52]

Linda Fisher, EPA assistant administrator in the Office of Pesticides and Toxic Substances, defended the operation of the TRI program in the hearing. She noted that:

... we do appreciate the fact that the TRI program needs to be expanded in the coming years. Expansion must be designed, though, with caution and planning. The Right to Know More Act of 1991, your proposal, proposes to expand on all three fronts at once. To extend the list of chemicals reported, to require more facilities to report, and to require new information from the facilities could paralyze our current system.[53]

During the hearing, Deborah Sheiman of the Natural Resources Defense Council noted how NRDC and 15 other public interest and environmental groups had recently released a report called *The Right to Know More* that argued for broad expansion of the TRI. In a submitted statement, the Chemical Manufacturers Association (CMA) voiced opposition to the draft bill. The CMA noted that the bill would add close to 500 chemicals to the TRI. Not surprisingly, the association argued in favor of the (longer) administrative process for any expansion of the TRI. The CMA statement noted:

... EPA already has the statutory authority to add these chemicals. It is a mistake for Congress to randomly almost triple the size of the current list without a scientific evaluation of the chemicals involved. Such an evaluation can best be done in the administrative process. And it must be done in a reasonable, phased process that allows EPA, the States, and the regulated community to adjust to the increased burden over time.[54]

The CMA also opposed the collection of chemical use data at facilities, noting:

How would data on the consumption or use of these chemicals benefit the public?... The only possible answer is that the data would be virtually meaningless and lead to unnecessary worry or fear about the production of useful and beneficial products to a modern high-technology society.[55]

Frustration by the original supporters of EPCRA and others with the pace of TRI expansion translated into the introduction of a number of bills in the early 1990s (see Table 4.5, which lists proposed legislation on toxics reporting from 1988–2004). Rep. Gerry Sikorski (D-Minn.) authored the Community Right-to-Know More Act of 1991, which attracted 160

Table 4.5. *Proposed Legislation on Toxics Reporting, 1988 to 2004*

Bill Number	Bill Title	Sponsor	Date Introduced
H.R. 2800	Waste Reduction Act of 1988	Wolpe (D-Mich.)	June 25, 1987
H.R. 1457	The Waste Reduction Act	Wolpe (D-Mich.)	March 15, 1989
S. 585	Pollution Prevention Act of 1989	Lautenberg (D-N.J.) et al.	March 15, 1989
S. 816	Toxics Release Prevention Act of 1989	Durenberger (R-Minn.)	April 18, 1989
S. 585	Pollution Prevention Act of 1990	Lautenberg (D-N.J.) et al.	October 25, 1990
S. 761	Hazardous Pollution Prevention Planning Act 1991	Lieberman (D-Conn.), Durenberger (R-Minn), and Lautenberg (D-N.J.)	March 21, 1991
H.R. 2880	Community Right-to-Know-More Act of 1991	Sikorski (D-Minn.) et al.	July 11, 1991
S. 2123	Right-to-Know-More Act of 1991	Lautenberg (D-N.J.)	November 27, 1991
S. 2360	Toxics Release and Pollution Prevention Act of 1992	Durenberger (R-Minn.)	March 17, 1992
S. 980	Hazardous Pollution Prevention Planning Act 1993	Lieberman (D-Conn.)	May 18, 1993
S. 343	The Comprehensive Regulatory Reform Act	Dole (R-Kans.) et al.	February 2, 1995
H.R. 4234	Public Right-to-Know and Children's Environmental Health Protection Act	Pallone (D-N.J.)	September 27, 1996
H.R. 1636	Children's Environmental Protection and Right-to-Know Act of 1997	Waxman (D-Calif.)	May 15, 1997
S. 769	Right-to-Know-More and Pollution Prevention Act of 1997	Lautenberg (D-N.J.)	May 20, 1997
S.857	A Bill to Amend the EPCRA of 1986 to Cover Federal Facilities	Coverdell (R-Ga.)	April 22, 1999
H.R. 1657	Children's Environmental Protection and Right-to-Know Act of 1999	Waxman (D-Calif.)	May 3, 1999
S. 1112	Children's Environmental Protection Act	Boxer (D-Calif.)	May 24, 1999
S. 855	Children's Environmental Protection Act (reintroduced)	Boxer (D-Calif.)	May 9, 2001
S. 940	Leave No Child Behind Act of 2001	Dodd (D-Conn.)	May 23, 2001

cosponsors. The party breakdown of the cosponsors, 142 Democrats and 18 Republicans, shows how expansion of reporting was a partisan issue. Sen. Frank Lautenberg introduced the Right to Know More Act of 1991, which attracted four cosponsors. Sen. Dave Durenberger sponsored the Toxics Release and Pollution Prevention Act of 1992. Senator Lieberman (D-Conn.) introduced the Hazardous Pollution Prevention Planning Act of 1993. These bills placed a number of ideas up for debate: expansion of the TRI to cover chemicals found in other environmental statutes; coverage of additional industries outside manufacturing; the need for federal facilities to provide surrounding communities with toxics information; the desirability of having plants provide data on what chemicals they used in the manufacturing process; and the encouragement of the development of pollution prevention plans at facilities. Some of these proposals were later embraced by the EPA once control of the White House shifted from Republicans to Democrats. None of these proposals, however, generated sufficient support to pass on the floor of the House or the Senate.

As Congress members discussed revision of the TRI in the early 1990s, their debates often echoed positions adopted by environmentalists and industry officials. Arguing for more toxics use reporting (TUR), Paul Orum of the Working Group on Community Right to Know declared in 1991:

There is a need to look inside the plant gates.... We shouldn't be waiting to release chemicals over the fence line as pollution before triggering right-to-know reporting. We should also be triggering the right-to-know law in the use of these chemicals during manufacturing.[56]

Manik Roy of the Environmental Defense Fund also argued in 1992 in favor of toxics use reporting, pointing out:

The amount of toxic chemical used is directly related to public health and environmental risk presented by use of the chemical.... If it is important to report the quantities of toxic chemical released to the environment, why is it not also important to report the quantities of toxic chemical transported to and stored at a facility and shipped as product?[57]

The Chemical Manufacturers Association's director of environmental programs, however, criticized such reporting because it would involve "some very sensitive business information" that would allow competitors to divine proprietary information about technology and production processes.[58] Capturing the depth of industry opposition to toxics

use reporting, Margaret Rogers, manager of government relations/
environmental policy at Dow Chemical, asserted in 1992:

We are extremely concerned about the push to focus on toxic chemical use.... We
will mightily resist efforts to make public policy on our reporting of use. We have
drawn a line in the sand on that one.[59]

Part of the legislative action on toxic reporting came in committee votes on other bills. In consideration of the reauthorization of the
Resource Conservation and Recovery Act (RCRA) in spring 1992, the
House Energy and Commerce Committee transportation and hazardous
materials subcommittee rejected an amendment by a 9-to-8 vote that
would have required utilities to file toxic emission reports. The subcommittee on a 13-to-4 vote also killed an amendment that would have
required utilities to file plans for voluntary toxic use reduction.[60] In April
1992, the Senate Environment and Public Works Committee adopted
in a 13-to-4 vote an amendment by Senator Lautenberg to expand the
TRI to cover 250 more chemicals.[61] In May 1992, the Senate Environment Committee approved a RCRA bill text on a 12-to-5 vote that contained provisions expanding the number of TRI chemicals and requiring
toxic use reporting. The bill ultimately failed to pass because multiple parties were critical of its provisions. The chairman of the CMA
declared:

We're disappointed in the bill.... There has been insufficient debate on costs,
environmental benefits, and the rationale for some of the approaches they've
taken.[62]

The legislative director of Clean Water Action also expressed disappoint-
ment with the RCRA bill, noting, "Oil, chemical, paper, and beverage
companies made sure that the bill did nothing to force them to reduce,
reuse, or recycle their wastes."[63]

When President Clinton assumed office in 1993, efforts to expand the
TRI shifted from the legislative arena to EPA rulemaking. The EPA
developed proposed rules to add chemicals and industries to the TRI.
Legislators who favored right-to-know expansion encouraged the administration's efforts. In March 1993, 54 senators wrote to Clinton urging him
to issue an executive order requiring federal facilities to report under the
TRI program.[64] Though right-to-know proponents had been unable to
win passage of legislation on federal facility reporting, senators saw the
support of President Clinton as a way to achieve quickly through executive

order what had been debated for years. Clinton did sign an executive order in August 1993 requiring federal facilities to participate in the TRI reporting program.

In the wake of the 1994 midterm elections, control of the House and Senate committees and subcommittees transferred from the Democrats to the Republicans. The shift in interests of EPA's congressional principals is evident from their League of Conversation Voters (LCV) ratings. Each year, the LCV calculates the percentage of time a legislator votes in favor of the environment on a set of bills the LCV selects. In the Senate, chairmanship of the Environment and Public Works Committee passed from Sen. Max Baucus (1994 LCV score, 92%) to John Chafee (1994 LCV score, 85%). The chairmanship of the subcommittee dealing with Superfund and waste management went from Frank Lautenberg (92%) to Robert Smith (8%). In the House, chairmanship of Natural Resources went from George Miller (92%) to Don Young (0%). In Energy and Commerce, control passed from John Dingell (62%) to Thomas Bliley (0%).[65] The changing of the guard led to a rapid change in the types of questions that legislators were asking about the TRI.

In 1995, numerous bills and amendments were proposed that would have slowed or reversed environmental regulation and/or the expansion of the TRI. Sen. Don Nickles proposed a bill to create a 45-day period after a rule became final during which Congress could veto the measure.[66] A proposed House bill would have installed a seven-month retroactive moratorium on rules, which would have stopped the November 1994 TRI expansion. Press reports indicated the CMA was "quietly" supporting the moratorium proposal.[67] A House appropriations subcommittee voted in July 1995 to cut the EPA budget by one third and included 17 "riders" that constrained the agency's implementation of particular programs, including a provision to limit the gathering of TRI information and to remove the 286 chemicals recently added.[68] When the bill came to the floor, 51 Republicans (many from the Northeast) joined Democrats in voting for an amendment to strike these 17 riders. The amendment passed 212 to 206, which was described in the trade press as "a stinging defeat for the conservative House Republican leadership, which previously had little trouble pushing through legislation restricting the ability of federal agencies to write and implement regulations."[69] The House leadership engineered a second vote, in which the amendment to delete the riders failed on a tie vote of 210 to 210. House and Senate conferees ended up dropping the 17 riders from the final bill, but *Chemical Week* noted that Rep.

Jerry Lewis (R-Calif.) "managed to place a handful of the riders in the report that accompanies the bill, including one that instructs the EPA not to expand the Toxics Release Inventory to include data on chemical use."[70] Although Senator Lautenberg feared the language, which did not have the force of law, might constrain the EPA, Lewis declared he was not sure the move would affect the EPA because, "They have demonstrated a willingness to ignore the Congress in the past."[71] The attempts to constrain the TRI process through the budget process angered Lynn Goldman, assistant administrator of EPA's Office of Prevention, Pesticides, and Toxic Substances (OPPTS), who told a meeting of chemical company representatives in October 1995, "Today we are looking down the barrel of a shotgun that your industry has placed in the hands of the House of Representatives."[72]

In the Senate, efforts to change the TRI came through debate over the Dole-Johnston regulatory reform bill, which would have required cost-benefit and risk assessment analyses for rules imposing more than a $50 million cost on society.[73] The bill also required the EPA to drop the TRI chemicals added in November 1994 unless the agency could establish that the removal "presents a foreseeable significant risk to human health or the environment."[74] When Senator Lautenberg introduced an amendment to strike provisions in the bill, making it harder to list substances on the TRI, the Senate voted 50 to 48 to accept Senator Dole's motion to table (i.e., kill) the Lautenberg proposal.[75] Of the 50 senators who voted to kill the Lautenberg measure, 47 were Republicans and 3 were Southern Democrats (Johnston and Breaux from Louisiana and Heflin from Alabama). Of the 48 no votes, 41 were Democrats and 7 were (moderate) Republicans (Chafee, Cohen, Jeffords, Kassebaum Baker, Lugar, Roth, and Snowe). A Democratic alternative regulatory reform bill was killed on a vote of 52 to 48.[76] Though the Dole-Johnston bill generated contentious debate and considerable media coverage, this regulatory reform proposal did not make its way into law.[77]

The summer 1995 battle to alter the TRI marked a high point of industry attempts to have Congress reverse decisions made by EPA rulemakings. Tracing the source for the TRI provision in the reform bill, the *Wall Street Journal* asserted:

The language [scaling back the Toxics Release Inventory] was crafted by an aide to Sen. Bennett Johnston (D-La.), co-author with Sen. Dole of the latest version of the bill, after Sen. Johnston met with representatives of BASF Corp., a unit of BASF AG, Germany, to discuss the matter. A spokesman for Sen. Johnston denied that the senator inserted the language at BASF's behest.[78]

Evidence that industry helped craft the TRI language in the bill comes from a June 5, 1995, letter from the president of the Louisiana Chemical Association, Dan Borne, to Senator Johnston, in which Borne says:

It is my understanding that you will be meeting with Dr. J. Dieter Stein, Chairman and CEO of BASF Corporation on Tuesday, June 6th. Dr. Stein will probably want to discuss specific language that addresses this problem [EPA's addition of chemicals to TRI]. I have looked at the amendment and believe it addresses our concerns.[79]

In an article laying out the BASF activities entitled "Special Interests, Special Access," the Working Group on Community Right-to-Know pointed out that BASF's plant in Geismar, Louisiana, produced the chemical NMP, which had been added to the list in the November 1994 final rule. BASF and other producers of NMP eventually chose to sue the EPA to delist NMP in October 1995, after attempts to reverse the expansion of the TRI through legislation collapsed.[80] If the provisions in the Dole regulatory reform bill (S. 343) had passed, the Working Group estimated that the list of chemicals covered by the TRI would drop by 90%.

Reactions to the political battles over TRI varied. Explaining why some companies pushed hard for a comprehensive regulatory reform bill featuring cost-benefit and risk assessment requirements, Glenn Ruskin of Ciba noted, "Some people say this may be the only opportunity we get so let's go for it all."[81] Lynn Goldman, EPA assistant administrator in OPPTS, expressed anger with industry attempts to use legislation to reverse EPA's TRI actions. She complained, "When we had a Democrat-controlled Congress and had senators that were planning to expand TRI by writing new statutes, the industry was very supportive of the idea that this should be done administratively and not by Congress."[82] In an interview with *Chemical Week* about the failure of the regulatory reform bill to pass in the Senate, Senator Johnston indicated the measure did not pass because some interests tried for too much in the bill. The interview transcript noted:

What provisions went too far? JOHNSTON: The TRI provision was one of those. While I can understand [industry's concern over the addition of chemicals] and was trying to change that, I think it cost us more that it was worth.

Do you think industry concerns about the addition of chemicals and the possible addition of chemical use reporting to TRI are best addressed legislatively? JOHNSTON: Some of the regulations go too far, but it's probably not worthwhile to attempt to change them legislatively. I don't think it would be successful, and it might highlight the issue.[83]

Johnston was correct that the legislative efforts to roll back TRI had made the issue prominent for environmentalists. Of the fourteen votes on the environment selected by LCV to create its 1995 Senate voting scorecard, one was Lautenberg's amendment to strike the TRI provision from the regulatory reform bill and two related to votes to cut off debate on the full bill. Of twelve House votes used by LCV to create the 1995 House scorecard, two dealt with votes to remove the 17 riders (including the TRI provision) from the EPA appropriations bill.[84]

During the second Clinton term, sharp partisan divisions in Congress made it unlikely for TRI legislation to pass. In 1997, Rep. Henry Waxman introduced the Children's Environmental Protection and Right to Know Act of 1997, which would expand the TRI to include data on chemical use at plants and change reporting thresholds for substances presenting significant risks to children. The bill attracted 147 cosponsors, split between 132 Democrats and 14 Republicans, but did not advance. Senator Lautenberg introduced a similar bill covering toxics use reporting in the Senate in 1997. In 1999, Congressman Waxman again introduced a toxics use bill and Senator Leahy offered a bill to require utilities to report mercury emissions in the TRI. None of these expansion measures came to a vote on the House or Senate floor. Efforts to roll back the TRI through regulatory reform, however, were not repeated either. As *Chemical Week* assessed the political environment in Washington in January 1999:

With Republicans holding only a six-vote majority in the House and a five-vote majority in the Senate, the chemical industry is not anticipating regulatory reform action by Congress this year. Efforts to streamline regulations or overhaul Superfund, for example, require bipartisan support – an increasingly rare commodity following President Clinton's impeachment by the House on a party line vote last month.[85]

Discussions of the advantages and drawbacks of the TRI came up during congressional debate over the posting on the Internet of plant worst-case scenarios for chemical releases that facilities had to file under the Clean Air Act Amendments of 1990. Witnesses at congressional hearings frequently referred to the benefits to the public from the accessibility of the TRI.[86] The title of one of the hearings in 1999, *Internet Posting of Chemical "Worst Case" Scenarios: A Roadmap for Terrorists*, foreshadowed the final vote in Congress to restrict the EPA from posting on the Internet the information on potential hazards from chemical plant disasters. Paul Orum of the Working Group on Community Right-to-Know criticized keeping the information off the Internet, declaring in 2000 that:

Keeping information off the Internet will not protect communities.... This is a know-nothing, do-nothing response to dangerous practices in the chemical industry.[87]

In the post-9/11 consideration of chemical plant safety, legislators did continue to try and maintain the provision of full TRI data to the public. In debate over a bill requiring plants to submit vulnerability assessments and plans for security to the Department of Homeland Security, Sen. Barbara Boxer added an amendment (adopted without objection) that would prohibit publicly available data such as the TRI from being declared classified as part of new legislative action.[88]

During the Bush II administration, the most significant congressional activity on the TRI involved oversight hearings critical of EPA decisions made (primarily) in the Clinton years. The title of the November 2001 House Committee on Small Business Subcommittee on Regulatory Reform and Oversight hearing summarized the tone of congressional questioners: *EPA Rulemaking: Do Bad Analyses Lead to Irrational Rules?* Subcommittee Chairman Mike Pence began the hearings with a primer on how rulemaking procedures are designed to guide agencies:

The polestar of the rulemaking process is that the regulations must be rational. When Congress passed the Administrative Procedure Act in 1946, it believed that the process of notice, comment and agency response to the public comment would be sufficient conditions to insure a rational outcome. After the regulatory onslaught of the 1970s, which saw the creation of the EPA and the enactment of many statutes that EPA implements by rulemaking, Congress and the executive branch determined that further refinements were necessary.... In 1980, Congress enacted the Regulatory Flexibility Act. The Act represents another tool in the decisional calculus designed to develop rational rules. The RFA requires federal agencies to consider whether their proposed or final regulations will have a significant economic impact on a substantial number of small businesses. If the regulations do have a sufficient impact, the agencies are required to consider whether less burdensome alternatives exist that achieve the same objective.[89]

Each of the five witnesses at the hearing focused on failures in the EPA's approach to conducting analyses for rulemakings. Andrew Bopp, executive director of the Society of Glass and Ceramic Decorators, testified about the rule lowering the TRI reporting threshold for lead and lead compounds. He faulted the EPA for failing to consult more closely with his industry before the development of the rule, indicated that the EPA in its assessment of the rule's impact underestimated the number of hours necessary to complete the TRI form, and asserted that the EPA's conclusion that there would be no first-time filers in SIC 32 because of the threshold change was incorrect. Making the case for greater EPA sensitivity to small business reporting concerns, Kopp said:

It is important also to note that none of these small businesses employ environmental compliance staff to handle such complicated burdens.... EPA's estimate of the time necessary to compile and complete the TRI forms of 111 hours per year does not remotely correspond with reality for small glass and ceramic decorators. Remember, this is a rule that is supported by more than 500 pages of instructions and guidance.[90]

Kopp urged the committee to require agencies to meet with small businesses before the development of rules. Randall Lutter of the American Enterprise Institute offered systematic reforms to overcome the problem that EPA program offices supervise the economic analyses of the rules they propose, including the development of a separate office in EPA to conduct regulatory analyses and a requirement that another agency review EPA's economic analyses and risk assessments in the case of significant rules.

In June 2002, the House Subcommittee on Regulatory Reform and Oversight convened again to hold an oversight hearing whose title telegraphed its focus: *The TRI Lead Rule: Costs, Compliance, and Science*. Chairman Pence began with a summary that outlined frustration with the rule that lowered the TRI reporting threshold for lead:

Today, we are not talking about further reductions of children's exposure to lead in paint or other major remaining sources of concern that have been identified. Today, we are talking in this hearing about a paperwork regulation that will at best provide some new information about the uses of lead that present no real risk for human health at a significant cost to small businesses and to the EPA. At worst, one could argue, this rule will provide inaccurate information about lead usage and divert important resources away from more pressing public health and environmental needs.... This is not EPA's finest hour, I would argue, after a great and I think colossal achievement in the reduction of lead exposure to children in this country. It stands in stark contrast to those reductions. This paperwork rule is also estimated to cost businesses between $70 and $100 million in the first year of implementation.[91]

Kim Nelson, assistant administrator for environmental information, explained that in the final lead rule, the agency had presented scientific evidence that lead was both persistent and bioaccumulative. She indicated that the EPA was going to seek a review from the Science Advisory Board on whether lead should be considered highly bioaccumulative, which could result in a further lowering of the reporting threshold from the 100-pound level adopted in the final rule. Noting the short time period that plants had to learn about and file reports under the new threshold rule, she said that the agency would focus on compliance assistance (e.g., getting information out on how to comply) rather than "direct enforcement" actions in the first year of reporting. Dennis McGuirk, president of a trade association for the electronic interconnection industries, offered a critical view of the EPA's lead outreach:

...unfortunately, EPA did not finalize the guidance until January of 2002, after the entire first reporting year had passed. The guidance is long, it is confusing, and often times it is conflicting.[92]

Hugh Morrow, president of the North American office of the International Cadmium Association, detailed concerns about the EPA's application of the PBT criteria to metals. He noted that in July 2000, a letter from members of the House Science Committee declared because of questions about scientific validity, "We strongly encourage EPA as soon as possible to refer for SAB [Science Advisory Board] review the issue of the scientific soundness of applying PBT concepts to metals." In February 2002, the EPA did announce that the agency would try to develop a more comprehensive approach to the assessment of risks from metals. The EPA's Science Advisory Board noted the connection between this review and the TRI, declaring:

Discussions between the agency and external stakeholders, as well as concerns expressed formally as part of the Toxics Release Inventory lead rule making, have demonstrated the need for a more comprehensive cross-agency approach to metals assessments that can be applied to human health and ecological assessments.[93]

Morrow noted the apparent incongruity of the EPA enforcing a rule while searching for more scientific evidence to sustain it. As he put it:

I know they are convening the SAB and that is going to move forward, but at the same time the TRI lead rule is moving forward, and it seems to me that it really should not be in place if its basis is in fact the concept that lead is a PBT.[94]

In September 2003, the House Resources Committee Subcommittee on Energy and Mineral Resources held an oversight hearing entitled *The Toxic Release Inventory and Its Impact on Federal Minerals and Energy*. Industry witnesses again criticized the EPA's TRI reporting requirements governing lead and the mining industry. Fern Adams, representing the association of the electronic interconnection industries, criticized the EPA for not creating during the development of the lead rule a Small Business Advocacy Review Panel as required for rules with significant impact under the Small Business Regulatory Enforcement and Fairness

Act. Adams noted that in the first year (2001) of the new lead thresh-old, 40% of those who were new TRI lead filers reported zero releases and that the median reported lead release was one pound. Represent-ing utility interests, Richard Bye of Texas Genco complained that when companies placed coal combustion by-products into waste management units, the TRI called these "releases." He argued that this gave the pub-lic the false impression that the material was escaping into the environ-ment. Urging a change in how wastes were described, he said, "What the TRI Program sorely needs is a 'Truth in Reporting' standard in which English words are given the meaning used by ordinary citizens in every-day communication."[95] Mining representatives complained that EPA had failed to change TRI reporting requirements in response to two court decisions limiting the scope of mining reporting. Summarizing frustration with the agency, Peter O'Conner of AngloGold North America (a mining firm) said:

... distortion of Congressional intent has occurred because EPA continues to treat naturally-occurring metals and metal compounds in dirt and rock that are moved and deposited at a mine site the same as releases of man-made chemicals from an industrial plant. That approach leads to enormous reported numbers which give the public an inaccurate and misleading picture of chemical releases in their community.[96]

O'Conner noted that treating metals in rock and dirt moved during mining as releases had made mining the industry with the largest releases in 2001 (accounting for 45% of TRI releases). He also noted that the addition of mining had:

... erroneously turned states with any significant mining industry into the nation's so-called "dirtiest" states. Nevada, for example, went from 44th in TRI "releases" in CY 1997 to 1st in CY 1998 and thereafter....[97]

Perhaps because of the lessons learned from 1995, Republicans in Congress did not actively try to reduce the scope of TRI reporting through legislation in 2001 to 2004. In May 2001, Sen. Barbara Boxer intro-duced the Children's Environmental Protection Act, which would have expanded the TRI by requiring reporting on toxics that involved spe-cial risks to children. The law would have required that small releases of lead, mercury, dioxin, cadmium, and chromium be reported and required the EPA to identify other chemicals with special risks to children. The measure did not come up for a vote.

In introducing the Agency Accountability Act of 2001 in May 2001, Sen. Kit Bond singled out the EPA's lead rulemaking for criticism.[98] Bond noted that the EPA estimated in the proposed rule phase that 5,600 small businesses would be affected by the lowered reporting threshold, that first-year compliance cost for a small business would range between $5,200 and $7,500, and that total first-year implementation cost would be $116 million. Using a decision rule based on compliance cost as a percentage of firm revenues, however, the EPA certified that the rule did not have a "significant impact" on small businesses. This in turn meant the EPA did not have to meet additional analytical requirements about the rule's impact on small entities under the Regulatory Flexibility Act. Bond's bill attempted to restrict agency discretion in making the decision about "significant impact." The measure would require an agency to publish its decision to certify that a rule would not have a significant economic impact on small businesses in the *Federal Register*, which would then allow small businesses to offer evidence to the contrary. Describing how the EPA would declare rules did not have a significant impact on small businesses, Bond said:

That is how most of the bad regulations get through. EPA was infamous for doing that and saying it didn't have any impact. The regulation comes down to small business, which says we are getting killed. Then they have to fight the battle. Then they have to go to court and prove that they are impacted and the EPA didn't pay any attention to them.[99]

The bill required an agency to describe the economic analysis behind its certification decision, allowed small entities to go to court for review of the decision, and asked the chief counsel for advocacy of the Small Business Administration to define through a rulemaking what terms (e.g., "significant economic impact" or "substantial number of small entities") agencies would have to use in determining whether small businesses are impacted. Making clear his desire to limit the discretion of agencies to avoid the RFA requirements, Bond noted:

Frankly, if it were clear that agencies were doing what Congress intended for them to do, then this bill would be unnecessary. If they were doing adequate analysis in reaching out to small business now, then this act will have no impact on how they promulgate their regulation. . . . Unfortunately . . . there is overwhelming evidence that agencies are not treating this obligation seriously, and we must tell them in forceful terms that we really meant it when we said 5 years ago [in the Small Business Regulatory Enforcement Fairness Act of 1996]: You have to pay attention to small business. . . . Had EPA done what it should have done in the lead TRI rulemaking, there would not be the litigation we are seeing now, and it would have saved businesses and the Government untold sums of taxpayers' dollars.[100]

Though the bill did not pass, the issue of whether the EPA violated administrative procedures in its development of the lead reporting rule was pursued through a lawsuit (described later in this chapter).

Presidential Action

Part of a president's ability to influence regulatory policy lies in his ability to fill the political appointee positions in federal agencies. Research shows that enforcement and other regulatory decisions can rapidly shift when leadership changes in an agency.[101] A president can also influence environmental policy by altering the actions of government agencies that have environmental effects. Although the TRI reporting program was first implemented during the term of President George H. W. Bush, he did not personally champion the program in speeches or press conferences. In the spring of 1993, expectations by environmentalists were high for action by President Clinton. The U.S. Public Interest Research Group "called on Clinton to fulfill his campaign promise to expand reporting to all toxic chemicals used and produced, and require companies to develop pollution prevention plans."[102] On Earth Day 1993, President Clinton gave a speech announcing the preparation of an executive order that would establish a voluntary goal for federal agencies to reduce their release of toxics by 50% by 1999. In August, Clinton signed Executive Order 12856, which established the toxic reduction goals for federal agencies, required departments to develop pollution prevention strategies, and required federal facilities that manufacture, process, or otherwise use toxic chemicals to report their releases and transfers under EPCRA.[103] Using the executive order mechanism allowed Clinton to increase TRI reporting quickly without seeking legislative change. Federal facility data thus became part of the annual EPCRA information release starting with 1994. For 2000 TRI data, 153 federal facilities (with 83 owned/operated by the Department of Defense, 21 by the Department of Energy, and 17 by the Tennessee Valley Authority) submitted 646 TRI forms, totaling 81.4 million pounds of on- and off-site releases. The public data release for 2000 noted that federal facility on- and off-site releases for chemicals tracked in 1998 and 2000 had actually increased 22.4% during those years.[104] In Executive Order 13148, issued in April 2000, the President established goals for federal agencies to reduce their TRI releases and off-site transfers by 40% by 2006.[105] Although President Clinton was unable to get strong pollution prevention and chemical management legislation passed, he tried through these executive orders to encourage facilities controlled by the government to focus on pollution prevention.

Clinton also used the executive order in symbolic politics as a way to signal to Congress and the public his support for the environment. During the summer of 1995, the Republican-controlled House and Senate debated regulatory reform measures that, among other things, would have reduced the scope of TRI reporting. Clinton signed an executive order on August 8, 1995, that required government contractors to comply with EPCRA reporting requirements, thereby insuring that if Congress later reduced the scope of the TRI, companies doing business with the government would still have to report on a wide array of chemicals. As the president's press secretary, Mike McCurry, explained the battle between Congress and the President:

The President today will act, using his presidential authority, to protect the country, protect the nation's environment at a time when Congress seems determined to eviscerate all those laws on the books that are designed to protect the health and safety of Americans and protect the pristine quality of our environment. He believes he can use his executive power today, acting by executive order, to ensure that those who emit toxic chemicals into communities continue to report and disclose those emissions as they have been required to do since 1986 under passage of the Community Right to Know Act. The President's executive order today will require those who would do business with the federal government to continue to report on over 650 toxic chemicals that are emitted. He will also instruct the Administrator of the Environmental Protection Agency to expedite rulemaking on other areas, including facilities and other chemical use that could broaden the scope of the executive order that he will outline today.[106]

President Clinton announced the signing of the executive order during a speech in Baltimore, during which he outlined the advantages of the EPCRA:

The Community-Right-to-Know Act does not tell companies what they can and can't produce. It doesn't require massive bureaucracy. It doesn't affect every company, just those in certain industries. It's carefully focused on a list of 650 specific dangerous toxins. About 300 of those have been added since this administration came into office, I might add. And over 100 of them are known to cause cancer. This law works, as you have heard.[107]

After Senator Dole led the legislative battles in 1995 to revise the TRI, President Clinton frequently referred to right-to-know as a way to demonstrate that he favored innovative ways to protect the environment.

In the January 1996 state of the union address, President Clinton declared:

To communities we say, we must strengthen community right-to-know laws requiring polluters to disclose their emissions, but you have to use the information to work with business to cut pollution. People do have a right to know that their air and their water are safe.[108]

Campaigning in Kalamazoo, Michigan, in summer 1996, Clinton told the audience:

We're also going to expand our community right-to-know law to make more information, practical information, available to families easier and faster. Right-to-know will protect you here in communities like Kalamazoo because you can find out what's dangerous to your families. Once there is a right-to-know law, companies think twice about what they do. In the decades since we've passed the first one, businesses have reported reducing toxic emission by 43 percent. Right-to-know works. Don't be fooled about it; it makes a big difference.[109]

Clinton also included a reference to toxic information in his acceptance speech at the Democratic National Convention.[110] Assessing why Clinton stressed TRI in his campaign frequently, a reporter for the *Washington Post* concluded in October 1996 that:

For a centrist Democrat like Clinton, the TRI is an almost perfect government program: It is low-cost, it imposes a relatively light burden on the private sector compared with more "command-and-control" environmental laws like the original clean air and water acts, and it achieves significant results without the heavy hand of government intervention. Yet it is no accident that when Clinton talks about community right to know, he often speaks in virtually the same breath of loosening the government's regulatory grip on business – worshiping, like his opponent Dole, at the altar of "common sense" environmentalism that balances real risks against real-world costs. His administration, Clinton said in his Baltimore speech last year, has done "more than anybody in 25 years to try to streamline regulation, reduce the burden of excessive regulation, get rid of dumb rules that don't make sense."[111]

Vice President Al Gore championed the expansion of the TRI during the Clinton years. In a June 1996 press conference when the 1994 TRI figures were released, Gore announced the proposal to increase the number of reporting facilities by 30% by adding seven industries to the reporting requirements.[112] In 1998, he asked the EPA to choose testing procedures that would identify chemicals that posed special risks to children and called on the agency to speed up its assessment of whether persistent bioaccumulative toxics (PBTs) should be covered by TRI reporting.[113] When the 1998 TRI data (the first to contain the seven additional industries) were announced in May 2000, Gore praised the information release, noting:

Putting basic information about toxic releases into the hands of citizens is one of the most powerful tools available for protecting public health and the environment in local communities. This is why this Administration has dramatically expanded the public's access to this vital information. Citizens now have more information than ever at their fingertips to help protect their communities, their health and their children's health.[114]

Ironically, the TRI played a role in the 2000 elections as a source of information for campaign statements and advertisements. Accepting the endorsement of environmentalists in October 1999, Al Gore used rankings from the TRI to note that Texas, home to Governor George W. Bush, was "No. 1 for toxic releases into the air, into the water and into the soil. For the first time ever, Houston, Texas, is taking over the top spot as the city with the worst smog pollution in America."[115] A television ad run by the Sierra Club in New Hampshire during the primary season included text references to the TRI to support the narrator's claims that:

Houston is the city with America's dirtiest air. Texas leads the nation in air and toxic pollution. And in the four years George W. Bush has been governor, the number of smog alert days increased dramatically. The health of more kids has been put at risk. And 11-year-old Billy Tinker's asthma is worse. Call George W. Bush. Tell him it's time to clear the air.[116]

The Republican National Committee ran ads noting that "George Bush is cleaning up Texas," and cited TRI information to back up the claim.[117] The Sierra Club then produced a response ad, which included citations to TRI data released in May 2000 to back up claims made by a narrator that:

Fact is, Texas isn't the nation's leader in reducing toxic pollution . . . 23 states did a better job. Fact is, toxic air and water pollution increased in recent years in Texas. Fact is, Texas leads the nation in toxic pollutants released to the air. Call George Bush at 512-463-2000. Tell him to clean up Texas' air and water.[118]

On the day (January 20) that George W. Bush became President in 2001, his White House chief of staff, Andrew Card, issued a memo halting the publication of news rules in the *Federal Register* so that they could be reviewed by the new administration and delaying for 60 days new rules already announced but not yet in effect. This included the lead TRI reporting threshold rule that had been published on January 17, 2001.[119] The regulatory freeze affected 175 regulations, including 70 that were final but not yet in effect and almost 35 that were termed major rules because of their impact on the economy.[120] In February and March 2001, the Bush administration announced decisions to back out from the Kyoto global warming treaty, reduce the stringency of rules governing mining on federal property, and revise Clinton administration regulations that would reduce the amount of arsenic deemed acceptable in drinking water. This generated much criticism for the President's environmental policies. A Roper poll found the public split on Bush's handling of the environment, with 37% registering approval and 40% disapproval. A survey by CBS News determined that 59% opposed the President's choice "not to reduce carbon dioxide emissions."[121]

When the EPA announced in April 2001 the decision to go ahead with the implementation of the TRI lead reporting rules, many commented that the decision reflected a response to criticisms of the President's environmental policies. As *Los Angeles Times* reporter Elizabeth Shogren put it:

The choreography of the announcement on the lead-reporting regulation appeared to reflect at least some sensitivity to the criticisms. While many similar announcements of this scale have been made through agency press releases, Tuesday's announcement was made personally by EPA Administrator Christie Whitman, standing behind the lectern in the White House briefing room. "What we want to make very clear to the American people is that this administration, this president cares about these issues," she said. "This administration has an extraordinarily good environmental record."[122]

On the day of the announcement, environmentalists still criticized the President's policies. Allen Mattison of the Sierra Club commented, "This is more of a case of Bush deciding he will not stand in the way of a real protection and trying to claim that's environmental leadership."[123] In March, 73 trade associations and groups had argued in a letter to the EPA Administrator that the rules should be withdrawn. Tom Sullivan of the National Federation of Independent Business announced the group would file suit to challenge the lead rule, arguing that "it's going to harm small business."[124]

Whereas the release of the annual TRI figures during the Clinton administration often involved the EPA Administrator or Vice President Gore, the Bush administration downplayed the event. As an article in *Chemical Week* entitled "TRI Publication Method Prompts Environmental Complaints" noted in April 2001:

EPA published the 1999 edition of the toxic release inventory (TRI) on its Web site last week, eschewing the formal press conference common during the Clinton

Administration. The shift prompted charges from right-to-know activists that the Bush Administration is trying to limit public access to TRI.[125]

The absence of references to the TRI by administration officials reflected the fact that expanding the reach of the TRI was not on the agenda. The major new TRI initiative undertaken by the Bush administration in 2003 was the stakeholder dialogue focused on how to decrease the reporting burdens generated on industry by the program.

Courts as a Policy Forum

Parties dissatisfied with the outcomes of rulemakings or other agency actions can seek to reverse EPA decisions through court cases.[126] Interest groups who do not like the substance of an EPA rule cannot challenge the outcome on the basis that they believe the agency made the wrong trade-off between environmental protection and reporting costs. They can, however, reverse a substantive decision made by the agency on the grounds that the EPA did not follow the proper procedure in arriving at its decision. The Administrative Procedure Act, laws such as the Regulatory Flexibility Act, the specific language of EPCRA, and court precedents create the background rules that govern rulemaking. Firms or trade associations unhappy with the outcome of a rule can challenge the EPA in court on many grounds: the EPA did not interpret its statutory authority correctly, failed to respond to comments adequately, did not analyze the proper scientific data accurately, or acted in an arbitrary and capricious manner. A successful challenge may lead the courts to reverse an agency decision directly. Interest groups may also have an incentive to file a court challenge in the hope that by the time a decision is referred back to an agency, control of the executive branch may have shifted to a more sympathetic party. Finally, interest groups may use court challenges as a signal to agencies that they will fight future potential policies. Industry groups in particular may also benefit if meeting the analytical and resources demands involved in court cases forces agencies to limit their new initiatives because of finite staff and monetary resources.

Industry challenged most of the EPA's large-scale expansions of the TRI, though the agency prevailed in most of the major suits. The Chemical Manufacturers Association (CMA) filed a complaint in U.S. District Court in 1995 seeking to stop the listing of more than 150 of the 286 chemicals added to the TRI by the EPA. When the suit was brought, Paul Orum of the Working Group on Right-to-Know observed that, "It's clearly intended to keep EPA busy rather than expanding right-to-know along the lines of President Clinton's recent directive."[127] Lynn Goldman, assistant administrator of the Office of Prevention, Pesticides, and Toxic Substances, complained about the adversarial strategy adopted by the chemical industry in its filing of the court case and support for congressional bills to hobble the TRI, noting, "I've been fair about dealing with industry's petitions to delist chemicals from the TRI, and I've taken a lot of heat for some of my decisions."[128] The CMA and three other parties (National Oilseed Processors Association, Troy Corp., and the NMP Producers Group) argued that the EPA's rulemaking was invalid because the agency did not consider whether chemicals listed because of their long-term effects were likely to be present in sufficient quantities to cause harm. They argued that the agency needed to consider exposure factors, a component of risk assessments, when listing chemicals that caused environmental damage or chronic health effects. The agency responded in part that the statutory language only required exposure considerations for chemicals listed for acute health effects.

In 1996, Judge Gladys Kessler ruled in the EPA's favor in Chemical Manufacturers Association v. Browner et al., 924 F. Supp. 1193 (U.S. Dist. 1996). Summarizing the judge's ruling, the *Toxic Chemicals Litigation Reporter* noted:

Judge Kessler found . . . that the legislative history and statutory language suggests that Congress intended the EPA to consider exposure when listing a chemical known to cause acute health effects, but that it is not required to consider exposure when listing a chemical known to cause chronic health effects or environmental damage. The EPA has consistently applied a policy of considering exposure only for chemicals that exhibit a low or moderately low toxicity, but not for chemicals exhibiting a high or moderately high toxicity and therefore that [sic] its actions were not arbitrary and capricious, she ruled. "The fact that it is EPA's policy to consider exposure on some instances and not in others does not make the policy arbitrary, so long as there is a reasonable rationale for the policy and therefore for the agency's exercise of its discretion," she said.[129]

In the challenges in the individual lawsuits to the listing of specific chemicals, Judge Kessler determined that the agency had considered the weight of evidence in the listings. She noted that, "While some of the explanations of the agency are too sparse for this court's liking, there is no question that the basic steps on the agency's decision-making path can be reasonably discerned."[130] After the decision, one environmentalist declared that, "What the chemical industry hoped to achieve, had they won, was the ability to dispute all the E.P.A.'s listing decisions in the future with endless legal challenges over the levels of risk and exposure."[131] Even after the decision, Jeffrey Van of the CMA insisted, "We believe the agency cut corners and that some of the substances don't belong on the list."[132] Viewing the litigation as part of the long-run strategy of resisting the full expansion of the TRI to cover chemical use (i.e., the TRI phase III proposal, meant to follow the first phase of chemical expansion and second phase of industry expansion), Bayer Corporation's Vice President/Environmental Control Lee Hughes said, "If we don't stand up now, phase III could just roll over us."[133]

In 1997, the U.S. Court of Appeals for the District of Columbia Circuit rejected the CMA's appeal and upheld the adoption of the rule adding 286 chemicals to the TRI. CMA and the other appellants had made at least four objections to the rulemaking: that the EPA used toxicity requirements inconsistent with EPCRA; that the agency did not use its own guidelines in listing chemicals; that the EPA had failed to consider whether human exposure would take place for substances listed based on chronic health effects; and that the EPA had not established what the criteria were for human exposure consideration. The appeals court found "that appellants have established neither unlawfulness, arbitrariness, capriciousness, nor a misrepresentation of EPCRA."[134] In defending the EPA's decision not to use exposure criteria in certain listings, the judges noted:

It is not the case that the congressional language mandating listing of a chemical that is "known to cause or can reasonably be anticipated to cause in humans" the enumerated adverse effects unambiguously incorporates the likelihood of contact between humans and the chemical.[135]

In the case of two chemicals, bronopol and DMP, the appeals court reversed on complaints about the listing and instructed that the decisions on these two chemicals be remanded to the EPA. The appeals court found that for bronopol, the agency's method of differentiating between acute and chronic effects was "at least questionable" and that for DMP, the agency had based the listing on 1960s studies from the Soviet Union that had been assigned low confidence by the Interagency Testing Committee. The appeals court found, "Any one of the flaws indicated in the Soviet studies (by the ITC) would render the study invalid under EPA regulations."[136] Lynn Goldman, EPA assistant administrator, declared overall, "The decision validates that our approach to the statute is reasonable. It's a marvelous precedent for the program."[137] Cynthia Lewis, the lawyer for the NMP producers, complained that the appeals court "treated [this] as a routine case of deferring to an agency's technical judgments" and lamented that, "It will encourage EPA to think they can pursue these expansions without being as careful as we think they should be."[138]

The EPA won another EPCRA victory in 1997 in The Fertilizer Institute v. Browner et al., No. 96-273-JJF (D DE, Aug. 8, 1997), in which Chief U.S. District Judge Joseph J. Farnan, Jr. of the District of Delaware ruled against the trade group's challenge to the listing of nitrate compounds on the TRI. The Fertilizer Institute (TFI) had claimed that the agency failed to provide sufficient rationale for the listing of nitrate compounds and failed to respond to the TFI comments. The judge found that:

...the EPA's proposal was adequate to provide the public and interested parties, particularly sophisticated commenters like TFI who are familiar with nitrate compounds, with sufficient notice that the EPA was proposing to list nitrate compounds because of their chronic effects on an infant's body...and the record provided sufficient notice of the scientific basis of the EPA's decision.[139]

The judge noted that the EPA had responded to comments adequately and that the explanation for the agency's action was "well supported in the four studies that the EPA specifically relies on."[140]

When phase II of the TRI expansion, the addition of industries, landed in the courts, the EPA again prevailed. In Dayton Power & Light Co. v. Browner, 44 F. Supp. 2d 356 (U.S. Dist. 1999), the U.S. Court of Appeals for the District of Columbia in 1999 rejected power company complaints that the EPA administrator erred in adding electric utilities to TRI reporting because they were not "operationally similar" to plants in the manufacturing sector on the TRI. The court held that "toxic chemicals are released into the environment by the production of electricity, and...the public should be informed of these emissions."[141] The court held that including electric power plants "falls squarely within EPA's statutory authority" and noted that EPCRA "expressly authorized the EPA to encompass facilities into the TRI program to the extent necessary to further the purposes of the TRI reporting program."[142]

Industry did prevail in suits that affected the implementation of the TRI. In Steel Company v. Citizens for a Better Environment, 118 S.Ct. 1003 (U.S. S.Ct. 1998), the Supreme Court effectively reduced the incentives for groups to file citizen suits against companies that fail to file TRI reports.[143] In 1995, Citizens for a Better Environment (CBE) sent a notice to Steel Company, correctly noting that the firm had not filed TRI forms as required by EPCRA. Though the firm did file the reports upon receipt of the notice, CBE pressed on with the suit and asked for the right to inspect the plant, for civil penalties to be assessed against Steel Company, and for attorney fees and other costs incurred by the environmental group. The Supreme Court decided for the Steel Company and held that CBE lacked standing to bring the case. The precedent that companies could simply file TRI forms if they got a notice of a citizen suit and thereby prevent a citizen group from recovering fees reduced the incentives for environmental groups to bring these types of EPCRA suits.

In 1999, the U.S. District Court of Appeals ruled in favor of The Fertilizer Institute in a suit against the EPA. In 1990, TFI had petitioned the agency to delist phosphoric acid, arguing that the substance is not toxic. In June 1998, the EPA denied the petition, noting that phosphoric acid can help stimulate the growth of algae in water, which can lead to a drop in oxygen levels and thus harm to fish. Judge Gladys Kessler agreed with the TFI that phosphoric acid was not toxic because it does not directly cause the harm to the fish. Lois Epstein of the Environmental Defense Fund worried that:

The court appears to be saying that if something is transformed in the environment, you cannot hold anyone responsible. ... It's as if the court doesn't understand the importance of the chemical and biological transformation process.[144]

The president of TFI, Gary D. Myers, hailed the decision, noting:

The court has recognized our argument that EPA's use of the term "toxic" is overly broad and ambiguous. This victory represents not only a victory for more rigorous science in the regulatory process, but also removes an administrative burden from our industry.[145]

The Clinton EPA eventually decided not to appeal the court decision. In response to the court decision, the EPA issued a proposed and then final rule delisting phosphoric acid from the TRI.

Challenges to the EPA's ability to use guidance and exercise discretion were upheld in a case brought by Barrick Goldstrike Mines. Metals mining was added to the TRI in the 1997 industry expansion. The EPA historically used a de minimis exception in TRI that meant if a "toxic chemical in a mixture amounts to less than 1 percent, the substance is not counted toward the manufacturing, processing, or 'otherwise used' threshold for releases."[146] In its guidance document for metals mining facilities in January 1999, the EPA noted that substances in waste rock did not qualify for the de minimis exemption because the waste rock was not manufactured, processed, or otherwise used. This meant that Barrick would have to file TRI forms for trace chemicals found in waste rock moved during mining. Barrick sued the EPA, arguing that the revision to the de minimis exception had been made without a rulemaking. The U.S. Court of Appeals accepted in Barrick Goldstrike Mines v. Browner et al., 342 U.S. App. D.C. 45 (U.S. App. 2000), the company's argument that the EPA's guidance document was subject to review as a final agency action. Even though the agency's position had only been stated in a guidance document and letter, the court noted that "the finality of EPA's position is clear enough." The court pointed out, "If Barrick does not conform to EPA's view in fulfilling its reporting obligation it will be subject to an enforcement action and fines."[147] The use of guidance documents to make policy decisions is a topic controversial in EPCRA and other environmental programs, for it allows the agency to avoid the constraints imposed on its decisions by notice-and-comment rulemaking.[148]

After the appeals court remanded the case back to the district court, Judge Thomas Penfield Jackson ruled in 2003 that the court could "find no basis for concluding that Barrick has created and therefore manufactured the impurities contained in the ore."[149] He held that the toxic chemicals in the waste rock should be eligible for the de minimis exemption from TRI reporting if they constituted less than 1% of the rock. Carol Raulston of the National Mining Association praised the decision, noting:

It was not congressional intent for substances that naturally occur ... in the rock in minimal amounts to be part of our TRI reports simply by the mere fact that we move that material. ... We in no way manufacture anything with that rock.[150]

The Bush administration's decision not to appeal the decision meant that the mining industry could reduce their reports of heavy metals released into the environment. Criticizing the agency, Lexi Shultz of the Mineral Policy Center declared:

The decision and the EPA's failure to appeal fly directly in the face of the fundamental principle that the public has a right to know about dangerous toxins that are being put into the environment. ... By not appealing the decision, the agency is allowing the mining industry to wrap the dumping of chemicals, such as hundreds of millions of pounds of arsenic, in a shroud of secrecy.[151]

In 2000, mining had ranked as the largest releasing industry on the TRI list. The Mineral Policy Center estimated that the waste rock exemption created by the court decision could reduce industry reports by nearly half.[152]

The decision to expand TRI information by lowering the reporting threshold for lead, a decision made in a final rule from the Clinton administration and affirmed by the Bush administration, attracted immediate court challenge. In Ad Hoc Metals Coalition v. Whitman, a coalition of industry groups asked in 2001 that the rule be set aside because of the EPA's alleged violation of the Administrative Procedure Act and the Regulatory Flexibility Act. The industry asserted many failures in the EPA's lead rulemaking: EPA used a methodology that was scientifically unjustified to categorize lead and lead compounds as persistent, bioaccumulative, and toxic (PBT); the criteria used by the agency were not appropriate for lead; EPA greatly underestimated the number of small businesses affected by the rule; the agency used inadequate economic analysis in the rulemaking; the EPA made the reporting apply to a period prior to the date the regulation went into effect; and the EPA went beyond its statutory authority in reducing the reporting thresholds.[153]

Informal Agency Activity

In a world where information is abundant and attention scarce, EPA tried to magnify the impact of the TRI data by concentrating public scrutiny on a subset of chemicals, facilities, and risks. The actions the agency took were informal, in the sense that they did not involve the full notice-and-comment rulemaking process and depend on the strict enforcement of regulations. Consistent with the aims of an information provision program, the EPA tried to increase the power of the TRI by generating awareness about a subset of the substances and plants. Three agency actions demonstrate how the EPA tried to shine a spotlight on particular polluters: the 33/50 Program; the Sector Facility Indexing Project; and the Risk-Screening Environmental Indicators project.

The EPA Administrator has so-called soft power to draw people together to focus on particular pollution problems.[154] Part of this arises because the Administrator can use traditional command and control regulatory powers to examine the pollution behavior of companies. Part of this arises because the Administrator can harness media attention through speeches and press conferences. Describing his reaction to the early TRI data, William Reilly, EPA Administrator from 1989 to 1992, said in 1991:

When we saw the toxic release inventory information associated with 40 plants, I invited the CEOs of the companies that owned those plants to EPA and told them, "Look, we don't have the legal authority to take immediate action against your plants. But the risks from these releases are very, very high. What do you propose to do about it?" . . . They brought their releases down 83% in these plants.[155]

In 1991, EPA initiated a voluntary pollution reduction program first termed the Industrial Toxics Project and later called the 33/50 Program. The agency chose a set of 17 chemicals from the TRI and invited companies to commit to reducing releases and transfers of the substances by 33% (relative to a 1988 baseline) by 1992 and 50% by 1995. EPA initially focused on inviting a set of between 500 and 600 large firms in February and March of 1991 to make commitments under the program. When CEOs of major firms sent letters to the EPA Administrator responding with their pledges, they often issued press releases to generate coverage of their environmental programs. The headlines of these press releases from May 1991 read like a roster of major manufacturers: "DuPont Subscribes to EPA Emissions Program"; "Dow Announces Commitment to Exceed EPA Request for Emission Reductions"; "Cyanamid to Reduce Emissions by 50% by 1995"; "Kodak Will Participate in New EPA Initiative to Cut Target Emissions in Half"; "Amoco Joins Voluntary EPA Program to Reduce Toxic Emissions 50% by 1995."[156] On July 19, 1991, EPA Administrator Reilly heralded the first results from the 33/50 Program by announcing that 236 companies had already committed to reductions of more than 200 million pounds of releases.[157] In an interview with the *Greenwire* in June 1991, Reilly noted that the TRI program helped companies make commitments to reduce releases because the information generated press coverage and public scrutiny, informed CEOs of pollution they did not know about, provided data on chemicals that could generate liabilities through Superfund, and spurred some companies to technological innovations. Reilly said the voluntary programs worked in part because of traditional regulation:

In all of the communications, when we talk about voluntary programs, we make very clear that the firm foundation of it all is a very vigorous and continuing enforcement effort. That has been our highest priority. We are very proud that we set records for enforcement in virtually all categories of civil, and criminal enforcement in 1989. We broke records in 1990. I hope we continue to break them.[158]

In assessing the 33/50 Program in a 1999 final report, the EPA noted that from a 1988 baseline of 1.496 billion pounds of releases and transfers for the 17 chemicals, firms had reduced this figure to 672 million in 1995, a reduction of 55.1%.[159] The agency noted that the biggest reductions in 33/50 chemicals came for two ozone-depleting chemicals, carbon tetrachloride and 1,1,1-trichloroethane, that the U.S. had eventually banned production of to comply with the Montreal Protocol. The agency noted that reported source reduction activities (i.e., pollution prevention) were greater for 33/50 chemicals than for other TRI substances and that reductions for 33/50 chemicals occurred at a higher rate than those for other TRI substances in the year after the program stopped. Of the 509 large firms initially invited to participate in March 1991, 64% agreed. The agency eventually invited more than 7,500 companies with plants involved with 33/50 chemicals to participate, and 1,294 made commitments.

Environmentalists were more critical of the 33/50 Program. In a May 1994 report entitled *Pollution Prevention . . . or Public Relations? An Examination of the EPA's 33/50 Program*, the Citizens Fund reported on results from a survey of manufacturing plants in the 33/50 Program. The group found that many of the reductions of releases and transfers from the 1988 baseline stemmed from actions taken before the initiation of the 33/50 Program. The Citizens Fund report noted that reductions came for a variety of reasons, including the ban of ozone-depleting chemicals, public scrutiny generated by the release of the TRI data in its first years of operation, pollution control laws, and plant shutdowns and other production changes. The Citizens Fund faulted the agency for not pursuing a national pollution prevention program more aggressively.

The growth of data accessibility on the Internet led to another TRI initiative, the Sector Facility Indexing Project (SFIP). Under this program, the agency focused attention on approximately 650 plants within five industries: oil products, automobiles, paper, steel, and other metals. In the SFIP database maintained on the EPA website, the agency combined data on plant TRI releases, compliance histories with environmental regulation programs, production capacity figures, and census data on the neighborhood surrounding the plant. The information lowered the costs to answering questions about which plants generated more pollution for a given level of output and what facilities potentially exposed different types of communities to risks. Describing the development of the SFIP in 1997, a front-page *New York Times* article said:

The ambitious project is the latest and in some ways the most innovative step so far in a steady campaign by the Clinton Administration to expand "right to know" initiatives: environmental programs that seek to inhibit pollution not with red tape and fine print, but merely by exposing polluters to possible pressure from a well-informed public. . . . But as far as the affected industries are concerned, it might as well be called the Scarlet Letter Initiative, because they fear that it will unfairly brand some of them as polluters.[160]

Josephine S. Cooper of the American Forest and Paper Association asserted that, "The concern we have is that the data that is in there, if it is not accurate and properly characterized, can mislead and misinform the public."[161] Industry opponents particularly objected to the proposal (not implemented in the SFIP) that the agency would multiply the number of pounds of a chemical release by a toxicity factor to give an indication of the relative harms generated by facilities. The EPA publicly launched a website for the SFIP in May 1998. In a December 1999 evaluation report, the EPA noted that the site had generated more than 4,100 user sessions per month.[162] Environmental groups using the SFIP to generate reports and analyses included the Council on Economic Priorities, Ecology Center of Ann Arbor, Environmental Defense Fund, Environmental Working Group, and Friends of the Earth. EPA offices reported using the data to identify likely TRI nonreporters and to develop enforcement strategies within some of the targeted industries.

The EPA's provision of data on the Internet often provoked criticism from industry. As early as 1997, the EPA Envirofacts database brought together facility level information gathered from multiple agency databases, including the TRI. Mark Greenwood, a former EPA official who went on to be the counsel for the industry-based Coalition for Effective Environmental Information, noted in April 1997:

The information age introduces a new set of policy tools, capable of imposing swift and irretrievable impacts, for which there are no clear ground rules about fair play.... That reputation [of a firm on the Internet] will only be fair if it is based on accurate information, and some of EPA's databases are flawed.[163]

The EPA's chief information officer, however, noted that the only information available from the agency online would be that which the public could already be entitled to through the Freedom of Information Act. He also said a division director within the EPA had to sign off for the inclusion of a data element on the website. The SFIP project demonstrated how potential accessibility could drive improvements in the data too. In August 1997, the EPA gave plants that would be covered in the SFIP information from the environmental records that would be posted online. Nearly two thirds of the profiled plants responded to the EPA's invitation to give comments on the data, and corrections were submitted to be made in the data.[164]

EPA data on the Internet received a powerful transformation when Environmental Defense Fund (EDF) started the Scorecard website (www.scorecard.org) in 1998. The website allowed an individual to analyze TRI releases easily by zip code or facility. The website also posted indicators of the relative harms posed by a facility's releases by expressing the chemical releases in terms of pounds of benzene and toluene releases. Though the EPA was slow to employ a relative hazard measure it had worked on for eight years, Mark Greenwood observed, "I don't think EPA could get a benzene equivalence index like EDF's through its Science Advisory Board, whereas EDF just does it."[165] Assessing the impact of Internet pollution data, *Chemical Week* concluded in October 1998:

With the introduction of the Environmental Defense Scorecard website and risk management plans (RMPs) due in June 1999, companies have been forced to come to terms with a reality about environmental reporting: Information about plant operations is reaching more people than ever before – and it is environmental groups and regulators that are doing the most to spread the word.[166]

Commenting on the EDF impact, Mike Pierle of Solutia noted:

Clearly, the EDF website is going to drive companies to make more data available on the Internet.... If EDF has accomplished anything it's to get companies to think faster about what data are best suited for presentation on the Internet and about alternate formats that may be more meaningful to the stakeholder.[167]

By 2000, the EDF website was providing estimated cancer risks from almost 6,000 plants, based on air releases tracked under the TRI. David Roe of EDF commented that the government ought to give the public such detailed health risk assessments and observed, "Perhaps the fact that Scorecard is now doing it will break the ice."[168]

The EDF website calculation of cancer risks in part relied on another of the EPA's programs to generate scrutiny on TRI facilities, the Risk-Screening Environmental Indicators Project (RSEI).[169] The RSEI model is a software program that allows a user to calculate a risk-related indicator of the dangers arising from TRI releases at a facility. The model incorporates information on the amount of TRI release from a plant, the toxicity of the substance, the likely transport of the chemical in the environment and exposure routes for humans, and the number of individuals likely exposed to the chemical. The EPA to date has made the model available as a software package. Although the agency has so far not been willing to present on the Internet calculated cancer risks likely to arise from individual TRI plants, the RSEI has allowed regulators to examine the relative hazards posed by particular plants and industries to particular communities and regions.[170]

Conclusions

The evolution of the chemicals and industries covered by the TRI follows a path of partisan politics. When Republicans controlled the White House and EPA from 1989 through 1992, environmentalists tried to expand the implementation of EPCRA through added legislation. Once President Clinton came to power, the EPA Administrator expanded the number of chemicals and industries subject to reporting. Industry officials frustrated by the rapid growth in reporting chose other avenues to block the EPA actions, including court cases and protracted congressional battles to restrict the TRI through regulatory reform legislation. Once George W. Bush became President, the terms of debate shifted yet again as the EPA sought input from stakeholders on how to reduce the reporting burden generated by the program.

The evolution of the TRI also shows how politicians affect the level of public debate over public information provision. In an era of expansion of the Toxics Release Inventory, President Clinton, Vice President Gore, and EPA Administrator Carol Browner all praised the perceived effectiveness of the TRI. When Republicans in Congress staged a high-profile battle over regulatory reform in 1995, the adverse public reaction played a role in the eventual defeat of legislative measures that would have limited the impact of the TRI. The administration of George W. Bush did later constrain the implementation of the TRI, but did so through actions less likely (compared to legislative reform) to attract broad public scrutiny, such as gradual budget cuts and reductions in enforcement.

Although the outcomes of elections determined the ultimate directions the TRI program followed, another set of influences also affected the implementation of the program. These influences, common to any environmental regulatory program, follow a partially predictable pattern associated with the birth and growth of a regulation. In the following chapter, I explore the factors – public opinion, media coverage, enforcement actions, and office politics – that influence the thousands of decisions that go into the actual operation of a regulatory program.

FIVE

Life Cycles in the Regulatory Environment

The evolution of the Toxics Release Inventory program reflects the life cycles inherent in many elements of the regulatory environment. A common set of factors influences the course of an environmental regulation: public opinion; media coverage; inspection and enforcement decisions in the field and interpretations rendered by administrative law, state, and federal judges; and office politics (both within the EPA and across other federal agencies). These factors vary predictably across the life of a regulation, as evidenced by the history of the TRI program.

High levels of public concern with toxics fueled the passage of EPCRA. The toxic reporting program set in place by legislation continued even as public attention waned. Media coverage of the TRI program spiked in the popular press in 1995 and 1996, during the legislative battles over the TRI and the presidential election. Releases and TRI policy in subsequent years garnered less media coverage, in part because the novelty of the information provision program had declined and because the Bush II administration did not make TRI a high-profile policy. In the trade press aimed at industry readers and environmentalists, the TRI continually generated coverage because policy continued to change over time. Inspection and enforcement actions in the early years of the program were trumpeted by the EPA, in part as a way to convey reporting requirements to industry. In later years, agency officials focused limited enforcement resources on particular chemicals or industries as a way to improve compliance. Enforcement decisions and rulemaking actions generated disputes, whose resolutions by administrative law judges and by state and federal courts helped refine expectations about reporting requirements. When the Bush II administration came into office and Republicans gained control of both the House and Senate, the budget for the TRI program dropped dramatically. Across administrations, OMB played a more active role at the times when the executive branch focused more on the costs rather than the benefits of environmental regulation. The debates in 2003 and 2004 about information requests made in the TRI reflect the ability of both OMB and small business lobbies to press the case for reduced reporting burdens on industry.

In this chapter, I analyze how each of these four factors that influence the regulatory environment – public opinion, media coverage, enforcement actions and decisions by judges, and office politics – changed over time and influenced the development of the TRI.

Public Opinion

In his classic 1972 article *Up and Down with Ecology – The "Issue Attention Cycle,"* Anthony Downs noted that some issues follow a path of growing and then waning public attention, defined by stages he identified as the pre-problem stage, alarmed discovery and euphoric enthusiasm, realizing the cost of significant progress, gradual decline of intense public interest, and the post-problem stage.[1] He presciently observed:

The greater the apparent threat from visible forms of pollution and the more vividly this can be dramatized, the more public support environmental improvement will receive and the longer it will sustain public interest. Ironically, the cause of ecologists would therefore benefit from an environmental disaster like a "killer smog" that would choke thousands to death in a few days.[2]

Twelve years later, the chemical accident at the Union Carbide plant in Bhopal, India, on the night of December 2 to 3, 1984, left more than 2,000 dead and ignited a debate in the United States over the public's right to know about chemicals at industrial plants. A subsequent chemical leak in August 1985 at the Union Carbide plant in Institute, West Virginia, also generated media coverage.[3] Table 5.1 shows in January 1985, 35% of the respondents in a national poll mentioned the accident in India when asked whether they remembered recent news reports about the chemical industry, whereas 32% said they did not recall any recent stories about chemicals.[4] By 1989, only 6% of respondents mentioned Bhopal (perhaps because of the passage of time), and 50% of respondents indicated they did not recall any particular news reports about chemicals or the chemical industry. In October 1985, as Congress considered right-to-know legislation as part of the Superfund amendment debates, a significant fraction

Table 5.1. *Public Awareness of Chemicals and Right to Know*

Do you happen to remember any particular news reports or stories you've seen or read recently about chemicals or the chemical industry? (If yes, ask: What do you remember them saying?) (1,500 survey participants)

	1985 (Jan.)	1985 (Oct.)	1986 (Oct.)	1989 (Oct.)
Yes, Bhopal, India; Bhopal disaster; 2,000 dead in India	16%	13%	7%	6%
Yes, chemical leak in Bhopal killed thousands, toxic spill in India, thousands died in India because of gas leak	11%			
Yes, Union Carbide disaster/gas leak, caused thousands to die in India	8%			
Yes, hazardous chemical dumps, illegal toxic waste dumps discovered	4%	12%	12%	7%
Yes, Agent Orange, Vietnam herbicide, veterans dying from Agent Orange	4%			
Yes, effects on humans, people living near dumps getting cancer	2%	2%	2%	2%
Yes, transportation problems, train derailment caused chemical spill	2%	3%	2%	1%
Yes, specific chemical dumps: Times Beach, Love Canal	2%			
Yes, other	2%	11%	10%	6%
Yes, don't know (vol.)	1%	1%	1%	1%
No	32%	36%	44%	50%
Not sure	8%	7%	7%	9%

There's been a lot of discussion recently about an issue called toxic "right to know." Simply put, this issue concerns the question of whether companies should be required to disclose to their employees, and to the general public in some cases, the names and the potential hazards of any toxic chemicals and substances used in the workplace or on the job. Have you heard about the issue of toxic right to know? (If yes, ask: How familiar are you with it?) (1,500 survey participants; October 1985)

Yes, very familiar	Yes, somewhat familiar	Yes, not too familiar	Yes, not familiar at all	Yes, don't know	No, never heard	Not sure
5%	23%	19%	11%	3%	33%	3%

of the public reported that they had heard about the issue. Thirty-one percent of respondents said they were very or somewhat familiar with the issue of right to know, whereas 33% said they had never heard of the issue.

The attention to toxic chemicals and toxics policy generated by the Bhopal and Institute accidents is evident in other polling data from 1985. When respondents were asked in January 1985, "How likely to do you think it is that a similar accident (leakage of a toxic substance) could occur from an industrial plant or facility in the United States," 25% said very likely and 43% somewhat likely.[5] A September 1985 Harris survey featured the following question:

Union Carbide, the chemical company that had a plant disaster in (Bhopal) India, where 200,000 people were injured and over 2,000 people were killed, recently had another leak of toxic gas at its plant in Institute, West Virginia. The leak caused 135 injuries. How serious a danger do you feel are these leaks from chemical plants such as these – very serious, somewhat serious, not very serious, or not serious at all?[6]

Seventy-two percent of respondents indicated they viewed it as a very serious danger. In a July 1985 poll, 66% of respondents indicated their opinion was closer to the statement "toxic air emissions are a serious health threat," versus 15% who believed "toxic air emissions are not a serious health threat" and 19% who indicated they did not know. When asked about policy options, 80% of survey respondents in an August 1985 poll said that laws and regulations "to control the dumping and disposal of toxic chemicals" were "not strict enough." A survey sponsored by *Time* in September 1985 asked:

In order to reduce the chances of such an accident (at a chemical plant in which hundreds of people are killed or injured) happening, do you think we should: Prohibit companies from producing certain toxic materials?[7]

Fifty-one percent of respondents indicated they would support such a prohibition, versus 41% who said the policy should not be adopted.

Survey questions specifically about right-to-know policies were very rare after 1985. News media polls focused survey questions on the general category of toxic/hazardous waste and the specific policies linked to cleaning hazardous sites under the Superfund program. A CBS/New York Times poll in September/October 1986, for example, asked, "Regardless of how you usually vote, do you think the Republican party or the Democratic party is better . . . at handling the problem of toxic waste?"[8] Twenty-four percent of respondents during this midterm election period rated the Republicans as better able to handle the problem, versus 33% for the Democrats. An ABC News survey in January 1989 before the inauguration of George H. W. Bush asked, "Thinking now of Bush's first term in office, do you expect the Bush administration to make substantial progress or not in . . . dealing with toxic waste and other environmental problems?"[9] Fifty-seven percent of respondents indicated that they felt that Bush "will make substantial progress" versus 38% who said he "won't make substantial progress."

Table 5.2 shows that public interest groups active on environmental issues were more likely to ask survey questions relating to right to know. The responses could help environmentalists target campaign messages and demonstrate to politicians the potential support associated with environmental positions.[10] In a September 2000 survey commissioned by the League of Conservation Voters, Al Gore earned high ratings for his work on toxic waste.[11] In a March 2000 poll sponsored by Democracy Corps, George W. Bush's record on toxic emissions raised very serious/serious doubts about him for 54% of respondents. At a time (i.e., May 2001) when the Bush II administration was generating significant criticism for its environmental policies, the League of Conservation Voters Education Fund asked respondents directly about their feelings about right-to-know laws and determined that 65% responded positively to the statement that strong right-to-know laws were needed. In March 2002, the LCV Education Fund Environment Survey found that a senator's vote to limit the public's right to know about chemicals was the most frequently chosen reason among a list of reasons to oppose a senator.

The priority of environmental problems on the public agenda changes over time.[12] When asked, "What would you say are the two or three most important issues or problems facing the nation today that you would personally like to see the federal government in Washington do something about?," 11% of respondents mentioned the environment, pollution, or toxic wastes in a July 1990 NBC News/Wall Street Journal poll.[13] This dropped to 3% in a January 1999 survey. When asked whether they "personally worry" about "contamination of soil and water by toxic waste," 69% of respondents indicated they worried a great deal in a May 1989 Gallup poll; this figure dropped to 53% in March 2002.[14] Within the set of environmental problems facing the country, right-to-know laws can be seen as affecting many problems, including air and water pollution, hazardous waste contamination, and toxic chemical exposures. If one focuses narrowly on the survey responses that mention "toxics," polling data indicate that within the overall set of environmental concerns,

Table 5.2. *Survey Questions on Politics and Toxic Waste*

Let me read you a series of statements that could be used to describe George W. Bush. For each statement, please tell me whether this description, if accurate, raises very serious doubts, serious doubts, minor doubts, or no real doubts in your own mind about George W. Bush.... Under Governor Bush, Texas has become the number one state in toxic emissions and cancer risk from pollution, with more than half of the state population living in areas that fail to meet federal ozone standards. Environmental Protection Agency records indicate that industrial emissions increased 10% during Bush's first term as governor, and last year, Houston passed Los Angeles as the smog capital of the United States. Does that raise very serious doubts, serious doubts, minor doubts, or no real doubts in your own mind about George W. Bush? (1,000 survey participants; March 2000)

Very serious doubts	Serious doubts	Minor doubts	No real doubts	Don't know/refused
21%	33%	21%	18%	7%

Let me read you some things that are being said about Al Gore on the environment. For each one, please tell me whether it is a very convincing, fairly convincing, just somewhat convincing, or not at all convincing reason to vote for Al Gore (for President in 2000)... For nearly a quarter-century, Al Gore has led the fight to protect public health from pollution. As a congressman, Gore was one of the first to tackle the issue of toxic waste, helping pass a law to clean up more than 1,000 toxic dump sites that threatened communities across the country. In addition, Gore and the administration launched tough public health standards to protect 140 million people from potentially harmful microbes in drinking water. (1,023 survey participants; September 2000)

Very convincing	Fairly convincing	Just somewhat convincing	Not at all convincing	Not sure/refused
28%	23%	22%	20%	7%

Let me read you some statements that have been made by elected officials, and for each one, I want you to tell me whether you feel positively or negatively about that statement. I want you to use a zero-to-ten scale, with ten meaning you feel extremely positive about the statement, and five meaning it makes no difference to you... The elected official says the public has a right to know what is in their water and air and we need tough laws to ensure that people have this information. Chemicals and toxics are released into the water, air, and ground every day, and too many companies doing the polluting refuse to make public what they are doing. We need strong right-to-know laws to protect the public's health and well-being. (1,000 survey participants; May 2001)

0–2 (Negative)	3–4	5 (Makes no difference to me)	6–7	8–10 (Positive)	Don't know/refused
4%	4%	10%	16%	65%	1%

From the list you just heard (of positives that describe a senator), which stood out as the most convincing reason to oppose this senator? ... Vote to limit public's right to know/keep information from the public/withholding information from the public/did not let people know about chemicals being released into the air and water; putting nuclear waste in one place/nuclear repository in Nevada/shipping radioactive waste across country on trains; exempted corporations from cleaning up toxic sites, polluted areas; took campaign contributions from special interests/bought off; did not make companies clean up messes/pollution; cut funding for EPA (Environmental Protection Agency) inspectors/environmental inspections; voted against tougher laws for the environment. (1,000 survey participants; April 2002)

Vote to limit public's right to know/keep information from the public/withholding information from the public/did not let people know about chemicals being released into the air and water	25%
Putting nuclear waste in one place/nuclear repository in Nevada/shipping radioactive waste across country on trains	13%
Exempted corporations from cleaning up toxic sites, polluted areas	12%
Took campaign contributions from special interests/bought off	9%
Did not make companies clean up messes/pollution	6%
Cut funding for EPA inspectors/environmental inspections	6%
Voted against tougher laws for the environment	3%
Everything/all	5%
Nothing/no reasons/wouldn't support	3%
Other	1%
Not sure/don't know/refused	15%

the attention to toxics has declined over time. When asked, "Now, thinking about the environment, what do you think is the single most important environmental problem facing the country today?," 9% of respondents indicated hazardous/nuclear waste, dumping toxic chemicals, and hazardous chemicals in July 1990.[15] This declined to 5% of respondents in October 1994. When asked, "What's the most important environmental problem facing this country today?" in April 2001, only 2% said hazardous/medical/nuclear/toxic/waste dumping.

Overall, public opinion on toxics right-to-know policies follows Downs's issue attention cycle. The Bhopal disaster in December 1984 focuses media attention on chemical safety and stimulates Congress members to introduce right-to-know legislation. National polls in 1985 reflect high levels of public concern with toxics, at a time when hazardous waste policies are also attracting attention as the Congress attempts to amend Superfund legislation. Congress acts in December 1985 to include the EPCRA provision creating the TRI as an amendment to the broader Superfund bill. In 1986, the final version of the bill passes. In later years, few questions about right to know are included in national surveys, demonstrating in part the likely waning interest in the topic. Yet the regulatory program created by the initial burst of public attention in 1985 continued to generate interest and controversy within the set of interest groups and environmental lobbies active in rulemakings and court cases. The TRI did resurface in public debates at times, often in the context of partisan politics. President Clinton and Vice President Gore highlighted the expansion of the TRI to distinguish their support for the environment from Republicans such as Sen. Robert Dole. George W. Bush's administration let stand the lead reporting threshold rule in 2001 at a time when his environmental policies were under attack. Within the set of environmental problems, however, public attention to toxics and right to know appears to have declined over time from the high levels in the mid-1980s.

Media Coverage

Media coverage of the Toxics Release Inventory program began with a burst of stories when the 1987 data were first released by the EPA on June 19, 1989. The analysis in Chapter 2 shows that for 134 companies whose TRI releases I found covered in newspaper reports in 1989, 40% of those firms were first mentioned in stories about TRI releases on June 19 or 20, 1989. For the set of 450 publicly traded firms whose stock price reactions to the TRI are analyzed in Chapter 2, only 50 generated articles in 1989 in the newspapers tracked in Lexis or in the *Wall Street Journal*. These firms, however, accounted for 71% of the total emissions and transfers generated by the 450 publicly traded companies. Though journalists concentrated on a small subset of firms, their stories covered a large fraction of the potential pollution tracked in the TRI. Chapter 2 also shows whether a company's releases were written about was predictable based on likely reader interests. For a given level of releases and transfers, if emissions were concentrated in a few facilities, the company was more likely to be written about. More Form Rs, denoting more chemicals, translated into a higher probability of coverage. Journalists were also more likely to write about a firm if the fact that it was a polluter might be new information. Controlling for other factors, companies in industries with reputations for high emissions (e.g., chemicals or primary metals) were less likely to generate TRI stories in 1989. The more Superfund sites a company was involved in, an indicator of pollution activity, the less likely a company was to get written about in TRI stories.

In this section, I focus on how media coverage of a regulatory program differs between the popular press and the trade press. To analyze general news coverage, I examine stories in the Lexis Major Papers file, which contains information from 53 major city or national newspapers (32 of which are in the United States). To capture the publications read by those involved in industry and in environmental regulation, I analyze coverage in the Industry News file in the Business News section of Lexis. This file contains articles from specialized trade journals such as *Chemical Week*. I first discuss trends over time, though this analysis comes with a caveat. Lexis files from more recent dates are likely to contain more publications. This means if one sees coverage declining in recent years, one may have more confidence in concluding that stories have decreased, whereas increases over time may in part be a function of expanded Lexis coverage. To control for this problem, I also picked five major newspapers with coverage in Lexis back to 1989 and separately analyzed their coverage of the TRI. The prime focus of analysis, however, will be on the types of stories presented in the general versus business press. To conduct this, I developed a list of likely words journalists might use in framing TRI stories and counted the number of TRI stories that used different types of words.

Another work by Anthony Downs, his book entitled *An Economic Theory of Democracy*, offers insight into why coverage of a regulatory program should differ across the general versus trade press.[16] Downs identifies four different information demands that people express. Producers want information for business decisions, consumers seek data about purchase decisions, viewers and readers desire some stories for entertainment and diversion, and voters need details that help them choose politicians and policies. Markets for the first three types of information may work relatively well, because if individuals do not seek out the information, they may not get the desired benefits of better informed decisions.[17] The market for public affairs information, however, may suffer because individuals may not demand voter information. The probability that their vote will matter is so low that individuals do not invest in gathering information to make political choices. Their choice to remain rationally ignorant makes sense at the individual level – why invest in learning about global warming if your vote or protest will not directly affect the decisions about this policy? There will be some market for political coverage: some people feel a duty to be informed; others believe the details of politics are intrinsically interesting; and horse-race coverage, scandal stories, and human interest angles can also attract readers and viewers. However, the implications of rational ignorance may mean that journalists, constrained by market demand, will not offer detailed analyses of policy issues.

Coverage of the TRI should vary across publications depending on the types of information demands the outlets are aimed at satisfying. Trade press publications will be read by those with a demand for details that will help them make producer decisions. The list of those with a need to know about changes in TRI regulations is long and includes environmental compliance managers in manufacturing, general business managers in industries such as chemical production, environmental lawyers, public interest group regulatory affairs specialists, and government officials (e.g., congressional and agency staff). General newspapers serve a broader audience who may have all four information demands related to the TRI. Business pages may cover TRI program changes, green consumers and investors may seek out information on company pollution records, readers may find stories about toxics intrinsically interesting, and voters may learn about candidate stands on the environment through stories about right-to-know legislation. Major newspapers overall may be more likely to stress the entertaining aspects of the TRI, such as stories that focus on disaster, risk, corporate misdeeds, or political conflict. The pressure to entertain will be greater on journalists targeting the general reader. Reporters writing for trade outlets can afford to offer more details on the TRI precisely because their readers may use those details in making decisions about environmental compliance or policy.

Table 5.3 reports the number of articles with the words *Toxics Release Inventory* in the text by year in the Major Papers and Industry News files. Coverage in the general newspapers peaked in 1995 and 1996, during the time that Congress debated changes to the program and President Clinton and Vice President Gore championed the program in election-year speeches. Trade press articles mentioning the TRI peaked in 1999 and 2000, when disputes arose over the implementation of the expansion of TRI reporting. In both types of media outlets, coverage of the TRI declined with the start of the Bush II administration. This reflects the fact that the EPA and Bush II administration did not choose to emphasize the right-to-know program and that other events, such as the war on terrorism and invasion of Iraq, crowded out environmental stories.[18] Analysis of the smaller set of newspapers with full coverage in Lexis from 1989 to 2003 also indicates that the Bush II years had fewer TRI stories than the mid-1990s had.[19] For *USA Today*, coverage of the TRI peaked in the first year of operation. For 1989, there are seven *USA Today* articles in Lexis, with headlines such as "The Chemicals Next Door," "Toxic Disaster Is Possible; Lax Rules Drawing Attention," "Talking about Toxic Waste Is Chic," and "Where You Can Get Data."[20] From 1997 through 2003 there were a total of seven TRI articles in *USA Today*, evincing the declining prominence of the program in general newspapers.

Table 5.3 also shows the frequency of TRI articles that contain words associated with different ways to view the program. In both the general and trade press, a higher percentage of articles contain the word *risk* than use the word *cost*. This may reflect the fact that the potential for negative health outcomes is more interesting than stories about regulatory cost. Articles containing the word *industry* are much more likely in both venues than those with the word *environmentalist*. Though activists tried hard to place environmental justice (e.g., the distribution of pollution across demographic and social groups) on the EPA's agenda, only 2% of the newspaper and 1% of the trade press articles referred to the topic. Although the few TRI environmental justice articles there were in the major newspapers declined to zero in 2001 to 2003, the regulatory actions of the mid-1990s (e.g., the signing of an executive order on environmental justice by President Clinton) stimulated activities that were still covered in the business press in the Bush II administration.

Compared with coverage in the trade press, TRI articles in major newspapers were much more likely to mention two words – *environmentalist*

Table 5.3. *Media Coverage of the Toxics Release Inventory, 1988 to 2003*

General News – Major Papers Lexis File

Search Terms		Article Counts															
	1989	1990	1991	1992	1993	1994	1995	1996	1997	1998	1999	2000	2001	2002	2003	Total	%TRI
Toxics Release Inventory	16	8	27	25	41	46	64	74	58	42	37	32	21	30	26	547	
& Risk	3	1	6	3	10	10	23	17	15	17	19	13	6	10	4	157	28.7
& Community	8	3	17	13	15	13	30	33	17	17	17	11	8	9	13	224	40.9
& EPA	14	7	23	18	31	33	45	55	39	33	29	31	17	25	24	424	77.5
& Cost	2	0	3	4	11	11	20	20	7	12	8	2	4	2	5	111	20.3
& Industry	11	8	21	19	38	39	56	64	56	36	34	26	16	26	20	470	85.9
& Environmentalist	2	0	10	1	11	5	15	23	13	8	8	11	3	9	10	129	23.6
& Prevention	1	0	3	5	10	9	10	10	4	10	4	0	1	1	2	70	12.8
& Environmental justice	0	0	0	0	0	0	2	2	2	1	0	2	0	0	0	9	1.6
& Cancer	5	2	6	6	8	13	11	9	9	15	8	7	3	7	4	113	20.6
& Rule	1	0	7	3	3	7	19	15	9	3	7	1	8	6	7	96	17.5

Business News – Industry News Lexis File

Search Terms			Article Counts															
	1988	1989	1990	1991	1992	1993	1994	1995	1996	1997	1998	1999	2000	2001	2002	2003	Total	%TRI
Toxics Release Inventory	1	19	36	94	102	95	132	133	170	174	154	176	214	139	101	103	1843	
& Risk	0	1	4	16	16	17	30	49	40	38	51	66	72	41	37	25	503	27.3
& Community	1	12	22	47	51	30	63	45	63	65	57	81	69	54	37	44	741	40.2
& EPA	1	18	35	82	77	69	98	104	142	132	120	158	195	126	89	96	1542	83.6
& Cost	0	2	3	14	29	21	33	48	54	55	34	48	34	27	24	15	441	23.9
& Industry	1	13	20	73	88	70	106	110	125	137	131	53	73	110	78	89	1277	69.3
& Environmentalist	0	1	3	14	15	10	14	11	16	23	12	28	38	16	18	30	249	13.5
& Prevention	0	8	4	30	36	43	40	35	33	28	27	20	21	10	11	9	355	19.2
& Environmental justice	0	0	0	0	0	2	5	0	0	2	2	1	2	5	3	2	24	1.3
& Cancer	0	3	2	9	4	4	4	15	9	8	23	31	29	20	18	14	193	10.5
& Rule	0	2	2	13	17	5	26	41	53	54	19	61	26	47	15	28	409	22.2

and *cancer.* Whereas 24% of the general newspaper articles contained the word *environmentalist,* only 14% of the business news outlets did. This may be in part because reporters for major papers were more likely to write stories about conflict, in which industry and environmentalists are both mentioned as part of a policy battle. Journalists writing TRI articles for a general audience were much more likely to mention cancer, which factored into 21% of the major paper articles and 10% of the trade press. If journalists in major papers need to frame their reports in more interesting ways to attract a general reader, a greater focus on *cancer* may generate reader attention.[21] General news stories mentioning the TRI were as likely to mention cancer (21%) as cost (20%).

Business news articles are more likely to use words associated with the details of policy, factors that might bore a general reader but help an environmental compliance manager, regulatory affairs specialist, or lawyer. Trade press articles were more likely to feature mentions of the EPA. The TRI articles in the business press were slightly more likely to refer to prevention, as in pollution prevention programs, and slightly more likely to refer to cost. Trade press notices about the TRI were more likely to refer to a rule, which is consistent with the type of coverage that chronicled the passage of a regulation through the rulemaking process and into the implementation phase. The articles in the industry press were twice as likely to refer to costs (mentioned in 24% of articles) than to cancer (10%).

The creation of the TRI database dramatically lowered the cost to reporters of writing stories about toxic pollution. Prior to EPCRA, manufacturing firms often did not track their toxic releases and transfers or have an incentive to provide these data to the public if they did. The change in property rights to information brought about by the TRI forced industry to create and share data on toxics with the government, which in turn provided the information to the public and reporters. One of the earliest newspaper articles to use the TRI data appeared in the Louisville *Courier-Journal* on November 27, 1988. The reporter, Scott Thurm, examined the paper TRI forms filed with the state of Kentucky on 1987 releases. Describing how he put the story about TRI releases in Kentucky together, Thurm related:

When I asked state officials to see the reports, they were being stored, largely unread, in cardboard boxes on the floor of an office in Frankfort.... To make sense of the reports, we chose to transfer selected information from the written copies to a computer form we developed. Our form included the name and county of the facility, how much of the chemical was released to various media, how company officials had arrived at these figures, whether the waste streams had been treated before they were released, and whether the company had taken steps to minimize waste of that chemical.... All of the information was typed into an IBM-compatible portable personal computer that I carried each day to the State Department of Environmental Protection. I chose to input all of the data myself, which took about six days, spread over about three weeks.[22]

By summer 1989, the EPA's TRI data were available on computer tapes. In its July 31, 1989, article "The Chemicals Next Door," *USA Today* labeled its examination of the TRI as an "exclusive report" and trumpeted its "three-month investigation" and the "USA TODAY computer analysis of recently released 1987 Environmental Protection Agency records."[23] The spread of the personal computer and growth of the Internet dropped the cost of accessing the TRI dramatically. By 2002, for example, the *Buffalo News* could carry a piece entitled "The Internet Helps Us Keep an Eye on the Industries Next Door," in which a local doctor could describe how to use the EPA's TRI Explorer website to search for chemical data on local plants such as the Huntley plant, Bethlehem Steel, and Chemical Distributors.[24]

Media scrutiny of company releases is one of the primary ways that the TRI can create incentives for firms to reduce pollution, a topic explored more in depth in the next chapter. Summarizing in 1992 the press coverage of the TRI in the early years of the program, MacLean and Orum determined:

Most stories fall into one of two categories: in-depth analyses of specific places or companies, or yearly overviews of TRI data. Many articles adhere to a common format, presenting the three "sides": environmentalists, regulators and industry. As with most news stories, reporters prefer to illustrate the release data with political controversy or human drama. TRI challenges many reporters to use new data management tools. A preliminary review of 100 stories, all from large urban dailies, found that less than 20 percent of the reporters accessed the TRI database themselves. Often, however, citizen organizations serve as an important link to the public by interpreting the data in advocacy reports that are covered in the press.[25]

Overviews of the influence of the TRI often refer to the role that the media play in reporting on particular firms, publicizing the findings of advocacy group reports, and covering the political battles relating to the program.[26] As a public policy program, the TRI faces the same set of problems associated with coverage of many regulatory policies: the lack of expressed demand for policy-relevant information by voters (i.e., rational ignorance) and the effect this has on the number of stories written; the tendency to emphasize danger (i.e., risk, cancer) and drama (i.e., political battles) to produce entertaining stories about policy; the lack of training for journalists to get the skills necessary to cover the beat; and the variation in the costs of writing about a policy area depending on the willingness of government officials to provide information on a particular area.[27]

Enforcement Policy

Concern over whether firms would file TRI reporting forms is evident in the wording of the legislation creating the program. The text of EPCRA provides a civil penalty of up to $25,000 for each violation by a firm of the 313 reporting requirements. The law also allows citizen suits to be filed against facility owners or operators who fail to submit a 313 reporting form to the EPA. As Chapter 2 related, congressional supporters of the TRI pressed the EPA in oversight hearing discussions in 1988 on whether the agency had adequate resources to find noncompliers.[28] In the June 1991 GAO report on TRI implementation, the GAO estimated that 36% of plants that should have filed TRI forms for the 1988 reporting year did not; pointed to problems with EPA enforcement, such as inefficient targeting for inspections and slow resolution of cases; and noted that the EPA acknowledged at least 10,000 facilities were not complying with the law. The GAO investigators said, "Some EPA and state officials told us that, despite their efforts to publicize the inventory program, many small to medium-sized facilities remain unaware that it exists or are uncertain whether their manufacturing activities or the chemicals they use obligate them to report."[29] The analysis in Chapter 3 confirms that for many noncompliers, ignorance of the law rather than evasion may explain the failure to file the proper TRI form.

One way to spread the word about compliance with a new regulatory program is through publicity. A week after the first TRI data were released, the EPA announced on June 26, 1989, that 42 companies were being fined a total of $1.65 million for failing to report under TRI. The story landed in the A section of the *Washington Post*, in an article that explained that the EPA had levied nearly $4 million in total fines relating to failure to file TRI reports. EPA Administrator William K. Reilly stressed the importance of compliance, noting:

These companies have a legal responsibility to provide the data.... We will not allow non-reporting companies to thwart the right of citizens to find out which toxic chemicals are being released into their communities.[30]

Throughout the early 1990s, the EPA sought to publicize its EPCRA enforcement actions. Regional EPA offices would often put out press releases aimed at local and environmental editors about the actions. For example, in October 1990, *PR Newswire* carried a press release datelined San Francisco from the EPA Region 9 office entitled "EPA Proposes $566,000 in Fines under Right-to-Know Law." Announcing civil complaints and assessed penalties against eight plants for failing to file in 1987 and 1988, the director of the air and toxics division of the EPA western office warned:

Companies that violate the law will be severely penalized and must suffer the financial consequences. The proposed penalties have been assessed against these eight facilities because they failed to estimate and report releases of toxics to the air, land, and water.[31]

The press releases often grouped the cases by state to provide an angle for local newspapers. On January 24, 1991, for example, *PR Newswire* carried EPA press releases entitled "Four New Jersey Firms Agree to Improve Facility Operations to Benefit Environment; EPA Collects $45,000 for Right-to-Know Violations" and "Six New York Firms Agree to Improve Facility Operations to Benefit the Environment; EPA Also Collects $34,275 in Penalties."[32] Trade press outlets were more likely than general newspapers to carry news about TRI enforcement in the later years of the program, in part because their readers would have an incentive to keep current on environmental compliance issues. A brief June 1993 *Chemical Week* article, entitled "EPA Seeks $2.8 Million in TRI Violations," noted the number of civil penalties and total fines announced by the EPA for reporting infractions.[33] *Rubber and Plastics News* carried in June 2000 an article entitled "EPA Fines Kirkhill for Skipping Report," which noted that the EPA had fined the company $35,700 for skipping a year of reporting.[34]

Table 5.4 shows that the EPA did ratchet up quickly the number of inspections conducted to see if facilities were complying with the reporting requirements of EPCRA Section 313. The first TRI reports (cataloguing 1987 data) were due on July 1, 1988. The number of EPA inspections jumped from 153 in 1988 to 768 in 1989. The inspection totals stayed relatively high throughout the Bush I administration. EPCRA 313 inspections peaked in fiscal year 1993 at 836. As the program matured, inspections went down in the mid-1990s, during a time when agency TRI resources were focused on the rulemakings expanding the inventory. Inspections dropped to their lowest level, 321, in the first year of the Bush II administration.[35] In terms of EPCRA 313 case settlements and

Table 5.4. *EPCRA Enforcement over Time*

A. EPCRA Section 313 Inspections

Year	# Inspections	Year	# Inspections	Year	# Inspections
1988	153	1993	836	1998	584
1989	768	1994	548	1999	513
1990	701	1995	612	2000	472
1991	666	1996	571	2001	321
1992	774	1997	473		

B. Dollar Values of Enforcement Actions, EPCRA Statute Based

Year	Criminal Penalties Assessed	Civil Judicial Penalties Assessed	Administrative Penalties Assessed	Dollar Value of Injunctive Relief	Dollar Value of SEPs
1995	0	39,977	4,084,188	141,437	8,707,770
1996	0	1,373,700	4,090,324	698,560	5,133,681
1997	0	0	5,183,747	2,435,393	7,646,285
1998	0	524,084	4,640,551	4,822,104	26,262,598
1999	0	0	3,802,384	528,264	4,151,296
2001	15,000	12,957	3,515,780	334,689	3,711,428
2002	0	225,000	3,100,756	582,589	1,223,257

C. Dollar Values of Enforcement Actions, EPA Totals

Year	Criminal Penalties Assessed	Civil Judicial Penalties Assessed	Administrative Penalties Assessed	Dollar Value of Injunctive Relief	Dollar Value of SEPs
1995	23,221,100	34,925,472	36,054,174	906,637,052	103,840,773
1996	76,660,900	66,254,451	29,996,478	1,429,849,730	65,810,214
1997	169,282,896	45,966,607	49,178,494	1,895,323,837	85,442,922
1998	92,797,711	63,531,731	28,263,762	1,976,759,053	107,853,506
1999	61,552,874	141,211,699	25,509,879	3,424,223,733	236,798,552
2001	94,726,283	101,683,157	23,782,264	4,396,018,367	89,134,956
2002	62,252,318	63,816,074	25,859,501	3,936,692,345	57,906,341

Note: All years refer to fiscal years. Dollar values are in nominal terms. SEPs, Supplemental Environmental Projects.

total final administrative fines assessed, 1990 marked the high point over the period FY 1989 to 1995. In FY 1990, the EPA settled 193 enforcement cases for a total of $4,186,428 in final assessed administrative penalties.

Table 5.4 also records other enforcement activities under EPCRA for FY 1995 to 2002, though these dollar totals refer to actions taken under all sections of EPCRA (not simply the reporting requirements in Section 313). Starting in FY 1995, the EPA's annual enforcement report carried a table on the dollar value of enforcement actions by statute. The figures demonstrate first that criminal penalties are rarely involved in EPCRA cases. EPCRA cases will at times involve the agreement by companies to devote a given amount of money to a "supplemental environmental project" (SEP), which may involve pollution reduction or prevention. Table 5.4 shows that the dollar value of SEPs undertaken as part of EPCRA cases peaked in FY 1998 at $26,262,598 and reached a low point in FY 2002.[36] Assessed administrative penalties peaked at $5,183,747 in FY 1997 and hit a low point in FY 2002 of $3,100,756. These low measures of EPA enforcement activity in FY 2002 in EPCRA are also reflected in lower levels of total EPA enforcement activities during FY 2002. All dollar values in this table are presented in nominal terms. If they were converted into constant dollars, the declines would be more pronounced.

In his review of the literature on environmental enforcement, Mark Cohen (1999) notes that although inspection probabilities and fines are relatively low, most analysts believe that compliance rates with many aspects of environmental regulation are relatively high in the United States.[37] He points out that many factors may influence environmental compliance decisions: gains from noncompliance; belief by company officials that compliance is the right thing to do (i.e., social norms); community pressure; fear of damage to company brand name from noncompliance; overestimation of likely inspection probabilities; deterrence value of criminal sanctions; and regulator strategies that may condition future inspections and treatment based on current behavior. Helland (1998) does find some evidence that compliance today with environmental regulation does make future inspections at a plant less likely.

The TRI fits this general description of compliance with environmental regulation. In the early years of the program, at least two thirds to three fourths of facilities were estimated to comply with the TRI reporting requirements. Inspection probabilities were relatively low. Consider the year that inspections peaked, FY 1993. With 836 inspections, a plant might consider the probability of being inspected at between .036

(836 inspections/23,000 TRI filers) or .027 (836 inspections/[23,000 TRI filers and 7,600 nonfilers]).[38] The average final administrative fine levied in a TRI settlement case was $24,180 (i.e., $2,852,935/118 cases) in FY 1993. The expected value of fines for noncompliance would be $725 (i.e., .03 inspection probability × $24,180 fine) for a plant. If one takes the EPA's 1992 estimate (provided to the OMB under the Paperwork Reduction Act) of four forms per facility and nearly 53 hours per form, the expected number of hours required simply to fill out the TRI forms would be 211 hours.[39] If the plant paid an average wage of $20 per hour to those assembling the TRI data and filling out the forms, then the costs of TRI paperwork alone would be $4,220.[40] If the firm does not file and is caught, it will have to pay a fine and file the paperwork. A firm considering expected costs of $725 in fines and $127 in paperwork (.03 × $4,220) with noncompliance versus $4,220 with compliance might be better off not filing simply to save on the paperwork costs. Noncompliance also brought other benefits to a firm, such as avoiding public scrutiny and the pressure to reduce emissions. Yet if a firm were caught, costs might also be greater if there were firm reputation damage.[41]

The EPA penalty policy for violating the Section 313 reporting requirements attempts to match agency response with gravity of harm and create incentives for firms to comply with the information provision requirements. Simple revisions to the Form R reports already filed that occur when a facility gains new information and revises an estimate would not usually trigger EPA action. The EPA might issue a notice of noncompliance to a plant if the reports were incorrectly assembled or invalid data were submitted. Civil administrative fines would be triggered by actions (in descending order of severity) such as failure to file a TRI form, data quality errors, or failure to maintain adequate records relating to TRI at a facility. The EPA factors in the extent of the harm created by these levels of action. The extent relates to the amount of TRI chemical manufactured, processed, or otherwise used at the facility, the number of employees at the plant, and the gross sales of the parent company. The larger the chemical amount, plant size, or parent company, the more likely the violation will trigger a higher penalty. These gravity-based factors are combined to yield an estimated penalty, which can then be adjusted up or down based on factors such as whether the facility volunteered the violation, the plant or parent company had a previous history of EPCRA violations, the facility is cooperative during the enforcement process, the company will undertake a "Supplemental Environmental Project" (SEP), and the violator can afford to pay the fine. Although the 2001 penalty policy indicates that the most serious violations could merit a fine of $27,500 per day, the fines assessed indicate that the EPA's adjustments render fines lower than this hypothetical maximum.[42]

To see the challenges for the EPA in enforcing the 313 reporting requirements, consider the resources available to the agency. In 2004, there was generally one person in each of EPA's ten regions with responsibility to work on the paperwork associated with TRI inspections. Within each region, there were one to two people assigned to conduct the inspections, who were often individuals who had retired with significant experience in environmental policy and had come back to work for the EPA as inspectors.[43] In the early days of the TRI program, environmental groups such as the Atlantic States Legal Foundation used the citizen suit provision of EPCRA to bring cases against companies that failed to file TRI forms.[44] These suits generated agreements that brought additional TRI reports, publicity about the reporting requirements, and legal fees for the public interest groups. In Steel Company v. Citizens for a Better Environment, 118 S.Ct. 1003 (S.Ct. 1998), however, the Supreme Court ruled in 1998 that once a company contacted by an environmental group had filed its delinquent TRI forms, a group did not have standing to sue and could therefore not get its legal fees paid.[45] This meant environmental groups would in essence have to fund their own citizen suit investigations without the prospect of reimbursement, which effectively led to the demise of EPCRA citizen suits.

Concentrating enforcement actions on particular chemicals or industries is one way the EPCRA enforcement officials have tried to maximize the impact of their scarce resources. In 2000, the EPA launched the National Nitrate Compliance Initiative. The agency had discovered in 1999 that many facilities that filed reports for nitric acid did not file reports for nitrate compounds, which the agency believed would be coincidentally manufactured when nitric acid was neutralized. The EPA chose to focus on nitrates in part because the chemical can cause serious human health risks and damage to lakes and streams. The agency first mailed an "Enforcement Alert" newsletter to facilities, reminding them of the need to report nitrates that were coincidentally manufactured and encouraging them to self-disclose their violations. Though some facilities did come forward and file TRI forms for nitrates, many of those suspected of violations did not. The agency eventually sent likely violators a "Show Cause Letter" that gave a plant the choice to demonstrate they were not in violation or accept a settlement agreement that involved a $5,000 fine per company (or $1,000 per firm for those with fewer than 100 employees) and a promise to conduct an EPCRA compliance audit that would stress reporting of coincidental production of chemicals. The EPA's final report on the initiative catalogued the results:

... nearly 600 companies agreed to audit more than 1,000 facilities for EPCRA Section 313 regulatory obligations and to pay administrative penalties totaling more than $1.4 million. As a result, EPA, the public, and our state partners received more than 7,000 revised or original TRI reporting forms that documented the release, transfer, and other waste management of 420 million pounds of nitrates that previously had been unreported.... As a result of the initiative, 508 facilities submitted 5,794 reporting forms for chemicals other than nitrates.[46]

The agency also noted that the initiative had identified this large number of noncompliers without a large number of (costly) on-site inspections.

Although the nitrate initiative generated many TRI reports, it also sparked severe criticism from industry, especially among small businesses that had neglected to file. In May 2000, Sen. Christopher Bond sent a letter endorsed by 15 trade associations (including the Chemical Manufacturers Association) to EPA Administrator Carol Browner. Signaling that there might be repercussions from the EPCRA enforcement initiative, Bond (who chaired the Senate Appropriations subcommittee dealing with the EPA budget) noted in his letter:

Such generous use of enforcement resources on a data quality concern with no direct impact to actual environmental conditions faced by communities suggests a surplus of enforcement resources.... That the agency has such an abundance of enforcement resources that it can devote enforcement attention of this magnitude to reporting data quality issues is an important fact to know as we continue through the agency's appropriation season.... Facilities were trying to do the right thing by reporting to the TRI and would have done the right thing if they had known and understood their obligations.... EPA efforts to inform the regulated community of this obscure requirement clearly failed in this case.[47]

The next major EPCRA enforcement initiative focused on an issue, the late filing of TRI reports, that did not disproportionately affect small businesses.

Table 5.4 shows that EPCRA inspections reached their lowest level (since 1988) in 2001, with 321 inspections. Analyses of environmental enforcement across programs in the Bush II administration found a decline from enforcement levels of the 1990s. In a December 2003 article entitled "Fewer Polluters Punished under Bush Administration, Records Show," Seth Borenstein of Knight Ridder reported:

Knight Ridder examined EPA data in 17 categories and subcategories of civil enforcement since January 1989 and compared the records of the past three administrations. In 13 of those 17 categories, the Bush [II] administration had lower average numbers than the Clinton administration. And in 11 of those categories, the 2003 average was lower than the 2001 average, showing the trend increasing over time. "It tells you somebody's not minding the enforcement store," said Sylvia Lowrance, a 24-year EPA veteran who was the agency's acting enforcement chief under Bush from January 2001 to July 2002.[48]

Many factors can slow the pace of environmental enforcement. One agency official referred to "invisible brakes" that were placed on active enforcement in the Bush II administration. The absence of a person to fill the slot for assistant administrator for enforcement and compliance assurance during parts of the administration slowed work. Career officials did not receive direct orders to stop enforcement. However, they determined that it was easier to slow the progress of cases rather than to push for active efforts at a time when the President was not actively pushing a strong environmental agenda. Another factor reducing enforcement was resources. In an August 2002 report triggered by a query from a Democratic representative (James Oberstar), the GAO found that the EPA had 1,559.7 FTE (full-time equivalent) enforcement positions in FY 2001 and was projecting a drop to 1,350.3 under the President's proposed budget for FY 2003. Describing how anticipations of budget cuts had affected hiring, the GAO noted that Office of Environmental Compliance and Assurance officials said "managers were probably inclined not to fill all vacancies, anticipating that FTE positions would soon need to be reduced under the fiscal year 2002 budget."[49]

The judgment calls of EPCRA enforcement officials in the field are not necessarily the final word on a case. Companies can appeal decisions to administrative law judges in the EPA. From 1989 to 2003 there were 48 cases dealing with EPCRA Section 313 decided by administrative law judges. Years with the most cases came as the agency was implementing the interpretations of expanded EPA reporting (e.g., 1995 saw eight cases and 1998 had ten cases).[50] Issues dealt with in these cases included how fines were calculated, what constitutes a release, whether chemicals were used/processed above threshold levels, how facility size is determined, and the application of the EPCRA penalty policy. Most of these cases ended with the decision of the administrative law judge. There were 32 federal court cases dealing with EPCRA Section 313 between 1991 and 2003, but most of these dealt with challenges to rulemaking (as described in Chapter 4) rather than challenges to the enforcement policy.[51]

Office Politics

Bureaucratic politics influence the operation of the TRI in at least three ways: intra-agency interactions among different program offices in the EPA; interagency struggles between the EPA and other executive branch offices and agencies such as the Office of Management and Budget (OMB); and the battles for resources within the agency and within congressional committees, which result in the budget figure that each year defines the TRI program's resources.[52] The overall EPA office containing the TRI program has changed over time, starting with the Office of Pesticides and Toxic Substances (1989–1991), Office of Pollution Prevention and Toxics (1992–1999), and Office of Environmental Information (2000–current). The Toxics Release Inventory Program Division within the Office of Environmental Information currently leads the effort to assemble the TRI data, advance TRI policies, and aid firms with compliance. Responsibility for enforcement rests with agency officials in the Office of Enforcement and Compliance Assistance.

Intra-agency interests come into play in the TRI in the development of rules. During the Bush I administration, all regulations went through a development process that included the circulation of a proposed rule to all offices before being delivered to the EPA Administrator's office for review and signature. As Donald Elliott, EPA general counsel from 1989 to 1991, described the process:

This system provided one final opportunity for members of the Agency other than those that had originally drafted the rule to review and question it. It was rare that one of the media program offices would question a rule drafted by another of the media offices, but it did occasionally occur. More frequently, however, the economists at what was then the Office of Policy Planning and Evaluation, or the lawyers at the Office of General Counsel or Enforcement, or sometimes even the scientists at ORD [Office of Research and Development] would question the basis for a rule or other action that one of the program offices was proposing during this internal review.[53]

This broad internal review at the senior official level was eliminated in the Clinton administration. The staff from different EPA offices, however, continued to be involved in the development of proposed TRI rules. In the development of a proposed regulation, TRI program officials would lead a working group that would draw upon staff from multiple offices and disciplines to help develop a rule. In the rule finalized in 1994 that added 286 chemicals to the EPCRA reporting requirements, for example, agency toxicologists provided analysis of the scientific evidence of possible harms associated with the chemicals and economic analysts contributed assessments of the impact of the additional reporting requirements. This internal review process helped TRI officials draft regulations in a way that might anticipate some of the criticisms likely to be offered by those outside the agency once a rule was proposed.

The drafting of TRI regulations also generated interagency conflicts. The Department of Energy, for example, asserted that it already tracked information on utility emissions when the agency was expanding the TRI to cover utilities. The Small Business Administration continually urged the agency to consider the reporting costs imposed on small businesses. The agency outside the EPA with the greatest impact on TRI regulations, however, is the Office of Management and Budget (OMB). OMB has at least three tools to influence the course of a regulatory program, and all three have been applied in the case of the TRI. Under Executive Order 12866, OMB must review proposed and final rules to determine in part if the analysis laying out the benefits and costs of the rule have been conducted correctly and if lower cost regulatory alternatives have been adequately considered. The executive order gives the OMB Office of Information and Regulatory Affairs (OIRA) 90 days to review a regulation, though this can be extended.[54] OIRA can return a rule to an agency for further work if it believes the rule and supporting analysis are not consistent with EO 12866. A second tool used by OMB is the prompt letter from OIRA, which can identify areas an agency should consider working on in terms of the development, implementation, or modification of a rule. A third power wielded by OMB comes from the 1980 Paperwork Reduction Act, which requires OMB to review and approve/disapprove an agency's request to collect information. If OIRA does not approve a form's use, then the agency may not collect the data and individuals cannot be penalized for failing to provide the information.

OMB typically carries more influence in Republican administrations, a trend evident in the influence of OMB on TRI regulations. In March 1992, OMB rejected, using its Paperwork Reduction Act power, the Form R proposed by EPA that would have collected the new information required under the Pollution Prevention Act of 1990 (PPA). According to an analysis offered in *Chemical Week*:

OMB says the EPA package defines "waste stream" too broadly; ceases to consider energy recovery as recycling; seeks more source reduction data than the law requires; and requires reporting all TRI chemicals "affected" by source reduction.[55]

The impasse between the EPA and OMB created a quandary for facilities facing a July 1, 1992, deadline to report on their pollution reduction activities. In May, the Chemical Manufacturers Association sent out its own form to members to use for reporting PPA data, whereas environmentalists and public interest groups worked on their own version of the form.[56] At the end of May 1992, OMB and EPA agreed to a single-page addition to Form R to cover the pollution prevention information, a page that required the provision of 47 data elements. Assessing the resolution, an industry trade journal noted:

In resolving the dispute, the agencies skirted a major obstacle by omitting an official definition of wastes. Industry had objected that EPA's proposed definition was "unclear," notes Sharon Eisel, an environmental issue manager at Dow Chemical USA. In avoiding the issue the EPA is, in effect, allowing industry to determine what should be considered a waste – at least for the time being. That should simplify the reporting task to some extent.[57]

Although the agency could not extend the reporting deadline beyond July 1, the EPA indicated it would not start enforcement actions against firms if they filed their TRI forms by September 1.[58]

During the Clinton administration, OMB review influenced the formulation of TRI regulations at a minimum through anticipation. EPA officials working on TRI regulations would conduct the regulatory analyses of the impact of rules with an eye toward review by OMB. Often in proposed rules, the agency would invite comments on two or three alternative approaches, in part because OMB often favored the inclusion of multiple options at the draft stage. Coverage of OMB in the press in 1997 shows that the agency continued to assert its review power. As *Chemical Week* reported in March 1997:

The White House Office of Management & Budget (OMB) is delaying an EPA rule that adds seven nonmanufacturing industries, including chemical wholesalers and distributors, to the Toxics Release Inventory.... OMB is sympathetic to arguments by the National Association of Chemical Distributors (NACD...) that EPA has overstated releases of TRI chemicals by its members because of a faulty report by one distributor in Massachusetts. The Small Business Administration supports NACD and says the industry should be excluded given the high cost of reporting. Environmental groups are pressuring EPA to hold steady.[59]

The dispute spilled over into congressional hearings, with the president of the NACD testifying in an April 1997 subcommittee hearing of the House Committee on Small Business about how "the Agency's apparent failure to perform sound cost-benefit analysis allowed it to prepare a rule that is not cost-justified with respect to distributors."[60] President Clinton resolved the dispute by announcing on Earth Day (April 22, 1997) that chemical wholesalers and distributors would be included in the seven industries required to report to the TRI under a new rule (which EPA Administrator Browner signed later that day). Assessing the politics, *Chemical Week* noted:

Clinton's move broke a deadlock between EPA, the Small Business Administration, and the White House Office of Management and Budget (OMB) that has held up issuance of the final rule since February.... OMB blocked the rule partly because the National Association of Chemical Distributors (NACD) argued that TRI reporting costs would equal the net income of some small members. Susan Hazen, EPA director/environmental assistance, maintains the rule will not have a "significant impact on a substantial number of small businesses."[61]

OMB played an even more active role in trying to influence the TRI program in the Bush II administration. In March 2002, the administrator of OIRA, John Graham, sent Kim Nelson, the EPA assistant administrator for environmental information, a prompt letter encouraging the EPA to take several actions to improve the use of EPA's environmental data.[62] He encouraged the EPA to speed up efforts to establish a single facility identification number that a plant could use in all its EPA reports, which the agency had been working on since at least 1995. He also asked the EPA to make the TRI data more readily available to the public, noting that 2000 TRI data would not reach the public until spring 2002. Graham indicated that the agency should stress that respondents were responsible for making sure the data were quality controlled, which would cut down on the checking the EPA performed on the information. The letter highlighted the regulatory actions that OMB wanted EPA to expedite. In a response letter, Nelson noted that the EPA was working on projects in all the areas identified by OIRA and said that the combination of the TRI-ME software (which had technical assistance built in to reduce errors) and the Central Data Exchange would increase the speed with which the EPA received and released the TRI data.[63]

OMB provided another outlet for industry groups to register their complaints about the TRI. The agency accepts comments on regulations and meets with groups interested in proposed and final rules. When OMB asked in May 2001 for suggestions on regulatory changes that would increase net benefits from regulation, the Mercatus Center proposed that the agency review the TRI PBT rule.[64] The center criticized the EPA for expanding the TRI without duly considering the utility of the information provided or the size of the risks involved in the releases and transfers. The 2001 TRI lead reporting rules, which generated congressional hearings and a lawsuit, also prompted industry to contact OMB. The National Federation of Independent Business included the TRI lead reporting regulations as one of its top priorities for regulatory reform in a list of proposals given to OMB.[65]

The Bush II OMB also used its powers under the Paperwork Reduction Act to gain leverage on the operation of the EPA's TRI program. Under the PRA, OMB usually approves information collection requests for a period of two to three years. In 2002, OMB only approved the EPA's Form R for a period of eight months. This forced the agency to come back again to gain approval of the TRI form and allowed OMB to stress the need it perceived for EPA to reduce the reporting burden in TRI. The agency initiated several electronic stakeholder dialogues about ways to improve the TRI, with the phase II dialogue in 2003 to 2004 explicitly focused on "Burden Reduction Options." In an agency discussion paper posted to stimulate comment, the EPA outlined numerous ways that reporting costs could be reduced: higher reporting thresholds for small businesses, which would reduce the likelihood they would need to file; expanded use of the Form A option; and creation of a "no significant change" statement that would allow a firm to certify that its TRI releases and transfers had not significantly changed from the previous year.[66] *Chemical Week* directly linked the EPA focus on burden reduction with OMB, reporting in October 2003:

EPA says it is working on changes to the Toxics Release Inventory (TRI) that would reduce the burden on industry – a mandate from the White House Office of Management and Budget (OMB), which says EPA has not come up with an adequate way to lessen the workload associated with TRI. The proposed changes will be made public following OMB's review, industry officials say. EPA is required to send its proposed TRI information request form to the OMB every three years for approval.[67]

When the OMB provided the EPA in January 2004 with a two-year approval for its information collection request to use the Form R in the TRI program, the OMB terms-of-clearance letter specifically linked future reviews of the TRI form with EPA efforts at burden reduction:

This ICR is approved for two years. OMB understands that EPA is exploring options for reducing the burden of this collection while still maintaining the practical utility of the data, and is currently accepting public comments on a discussion draft of various burden reduction options. OMB supports this effort and looks forward to an update on progress in this area when it reviews the next ICR submission.[68]

The *Federal Register* notices by the EPA of its submission to OMB for approval of the Form R data collections provide over time a picture of how estimated TRI reporting burdens changed. The September 1990 notice estimated that completing a Form R would take 29 hours and that the estimated annual reporting burden was 3,672,500 hours.[69] After the pollution prevention data were added to the form, in September 1992, the EPA estimated 53 hours to complete a Form R and an annual reporting burden of 6,470,000 hours. In December 1999, the EPA estimated that Section 313 reporting generated 27,235 respondents, the average response entailed 52 hours to complete, and total burden hours were 7,321,441 hours. In December 2002, the agency estimated that Form A, used for certifying that a facility's chemical release and production mean that it does not have to file a Form R, would involve each year 5,451 respondents and generate 172,313 burden hours (for a cost of $7.57 million). In October 2003, the EPA estimated that Section 313 reporting would generate 84,000 responses, involving 2,432,898 reporting burden hours and a total of $111.3 million in labor costs. The agency noted that it had adjusted the estimate of time to complete a Form R from 47.1 hours to 14.5 hours. Industry officials, however, contended that the reporting burden was much higher. Michael Walls, senior counsel for the American Chemistry Council, said in November 2003:

The Toxics Release Inventory comes at significant cost and burden. We estimate the TRI costs the U.S. $600 million a year.... The burden is in collecting the data – monitoring it, checking it, and all that. You don't just scratch down a few numbers and send them to the EPA.[70]

Whereas expansion of the TRI was a hallmark of the Clinton administration, the policy options nominated for discussion by the EPA in the stakeholder dialogue revealed the focus of the Bush II EPA on scaling back the TRI. OMB, SBA, congressional Republicans, and industry associations all offered advice on how to reduce reporting burdens. Glen Barrett of the American Petroleum Institute voiced support for a switch to biennial reporting that "would cut the burden in half."[71] Rep. Jim Gibbons (R-Nev.) argued for a reduction in reporting coverage, noting that in terms of the reporting requirements for mining, "I'm questioning whether the EPA really believes that the simple moving around of dirt is a proper thing to include in the Toxics Release Inventory."[72] After testifying about TRI and mining reporting at a House hearing in 2003, EPA

Assistant Administrator Kim Nelson admitted, "It's a struggle to find the fine line between reducing the burden and providing information."[73] Examining the potential battle over the TRI policy options the EPA was proposing for discussion in fall 2003, Paul Orum of the Working Group on Community Right-to-Know commented:

This is EPA proposing an industry wish list of options to change the nation's preeminent right-to-know law.... Depending on what goes forward, this could be a significant weakening of the program.[74]

A major battle that the TRI program lost over time involved its budget.[75] Funding for the TRI program is close to a rounding error in the EPA's budget. In FY 2004, the EPA's total budget was $8.37 billion; the TRI program division's share of that was $6,653,000.[76] The proportion of the EPA paperwork burden generated by the TRI is also relatively small. In FY 2003, the OMB estimated that the EPA's paperwork requirements for business and government officials generated 147.24 million hours in time spent filling out and filing paperwork.[77] In its October 2003 application to the OMB for continued approval to use the Form R to collect TRI information, the agency estimated annual hours spent filling out these forms to be 2,432,898.[78] This reporting burden generated annual estimated labor costs, however, of $111.3 million. In addition, firms faced expenses from the TRI associated with the costs of public and regulator scrutiny and changes in operations that might arise from that scrutiny.

Over time, those frustrated with the reporting burdens generated by the TRI found a way to change the program other than through direct legislative alterations to the regulations. From FY 1997 to FY 2004, the budget for the TRI program dropped 39% in nominal terms. Table 5.5 shows that reporting center operations, the part of the program that receives and processes the data, took up the majority of the TRI funds each year. Funding for each of the parts of the TRI declined between FY 1997 and FY 2004. Petitions and rules had the largest percentage drop, which is not surprising given the shift in the Bush II administration away from any ideas about expanding the TRI. The sharpest drops in total TRI funding occurred during the Bush II years, a time when the agency also started a dialogue focused on reducing the reporting burden (and perhaps scope) of the TRI data. A new budget category added, the TRI-ME section, marked the agency's investment in software that facilitated industry's electronic filing of TRI forms.

The significant drop in the TRI budget has focused the TRI program division on maintaining the provision of public information with fewer

Regulation through Revelation

Table 5.5. *TRI Program Division Budget ($M)*

Budget Category	FY97	FY98	FY99	FY00	FY01	FY02	FY03	FY04
Reporting center operations	7,477	7,214	7,046	6,260	6,011	4,958	4,743	4,643
Compliance assistance	950	1,113	1,075	508	983	866	541	443
Data analysis & outreach	1,311	956	695	520	438	408	482	482
Petitions & rules	385	297	275	25	2	30	28	28
Data quality	450	320	355	40	100	110	108	108
Regional senior environmental employees	300	300	300	405	250	300	250	250
TRI-ME			79	1,692	1,275	878	1,011	700
TOTAL	10,873	10,200	9,825	9,450	9,059	7,550	7,163	6,653

Note: Dollar values are in nominal terms. Data provided by U.S. EPA Office of Environmental Information in response to a Freedom of Information Act request.

resources. One way that costs have been reduced, for industry and the EPA, is through electronic delivery of information. The EPA's Toxics Release Inventory Made Easy (TRI-ME) software was tested in reporting of 2000 data and distributed with the paper TRI forms starting with the 2001 data. The software leads a facility operator through a set of questions that helps with filling out the TRI form and provides easy access to guidance information. The agency estimated in 2003 that 90% of TRI reports will be filed using TRI-ME and that the software will reduce the costs of filling out and submitting the forms by 15%.[79] The software is also designed to reduce reporting errors. The EPA's Central Data Exchange allows a facility to submit the data over the Internet. This process has reduced transaction costs significantly. A TRI form submitted through the CDX takes the agency 4 minutes to process, versus 45 minutes for information submitted on hard copy. The TRI-ME software builds in data checks so that the EPA does not have to devote as many resources to checking the data filed.

The rapid availability of the industry reports has also allowed the agency to speed up release of the data. For example, the statutory deadline for firms to provide the EPA with 2003 information is July 1, 2004. By November 2004, the agency plans to have the 2003 data filed electronically with the EPA available for search on the EPA Envirofacts database. Agency resources are also being conserved through the abandonment of the publishing of a large national overview report each year. Starting with the 2002 data, released in June 2004, the EPA will provide a short ten-page summary reporting national trends in TRI data. Analysts will be pointed to the TRI Explorer dataset to conduct their own inquiries with the newly released TRI information. The late reporting enforcement initiative complements these advances, because making sure that firms report by the July 1 deadline assumes a greater importance when the industry data are being provided to the public more quickly by the EPA.

Conclusions

The implementation of the TRI program shows how aspects of the regulatory environment change over time in predictable ways. The high level of public interest that generates a piece of legislation such as EPCRA may dissipate over time, even as the regulatory program it creates lives on. Media coverage in the general press often focuses on political battles, such as 1995 attempts to pass regulatory reform legislation and the 1996 election year focus on TRI in speeches by President Clinton. The trade press continued to cover the TRI when it fell out of public view, in part because the implementation of the expanded reporting requirements continued to generate disputes within the regulatory community. The direction of TRI policy changed with the election of George W. Bush and the Republican control of Congress. Budgets shrank, inspections dropped, and the focus of agency policy debates became how to reduce the reporting burden. Throughout the debate over the expansion and contraction of the TRI, environmentalists and industry officials offered their opinions on the program's impact. In the next chapter, I analyze the research by academics on the impacts of the TRI.

SIX

The Impact(s) of the TRI

The TRI data have generated growing activity in at least one sector of the economy – academia. Scholars use the information to examine how information provision may affect polluter behavior. Through statistical studies, they explore how investors, residents, reporters, and regulators may learn from toxics information. Researchers have drawn on the TRI to analyze questions such as why companies engage in voluntary pollution reduction and why firms may fail to report their emissions or provide accurate estimates. Nonprofits, particularly environmental groups, have catalogued in case studies the many ways that lower information costs translate into increased attention to toxic releases and transfers. The detailed plant-level data in the TRI, coupled with the mapping technology of GIS software, have added increasing information to debates over environmental equity. The example of the TRI has also led to the spread of information provision programs in countries outside the United States. In this chapter, I analyze the evidence to date on what the TRI shows about the impact of information as a regulatory tool.[1]

Changes in Decisionmaking

Statistical tests of the impact of the TRI often use differences across states to investigate how information provision may affect polluter behavior. The studies that use the state as the unit of observation allow researchers to examine how differences in state laws and public pressure may affect toxic releases and transfers.[2] Grant (1997) examines TRI emissions by state from 1989 to 1991 and concludes that "states that have right-to-sue laws or that provide substantial funding for right-to-know programs have significantly lower rates of toxic emissions over time."[3] Yu et al. (1998) note that states varied widely in policies they adopted relating to information provision and toxics. They construct an index of state information activity based on a survey of state toxic offices done by the National Conference of State Legislatures and note that:

> More information, more informational outlets, more easily available information, and information more integrated with other data (such as geographic or income information) can be expected to inform a larger portion of the public and in more depth regarding toxic threats or problems in their area.... Whether the pressure is actually exerted or is merely rendered more feasible by accessible information, company behavior can be expected to be influenced.[4]

They include in their analysis a control variable for the 17 states that had adopted specific provisions to enforce EPCRA (whose text requires companies to report to EPA and the state a plant is located in). They also measure the degree to which a state required companies to engage in pollution prevention activity. Examining changes in total TRI releases in a state between 1992 and 1993, they find all three of these state policy variables affect reported changes in releases. States with efforts to spread toxics information, enforce EPCRA, or encourage pollution prevention had greater reductions in state-level TRI totals.

Maxwell, Lyon, and Hackett (2000) view some firm voluntary actions to reduce emissions as strategic efforts to preempt more costly regulation. They analyze changes in a measure of TRI releases between 1988 and 1992 at the state level and conclude:

> ... that states with higher initial levels of toxic emissions and larger environmental group membership reduced toxic emissions more rapidly. In this situation, firms have relatively low marginal abatement costs, consumers value abatement highly, and consumer organizing costs are low. Since the threat of mandatory regulation is high while the marginal cost of self-regulation is relatively low, it makes good sense for firms to engage in voluntary emissions reductions.[5]

Kraft, Abel, and Stephan (2004) study a set of TRI facilities (N = 11,353) reporting in both 1991 and 1997 and partition these based on changes in their total TRI releases and in their production-related waste (with PRW defined as "the sum of all toxic wastes generated across a firm's production processes that a facility reports as recycled, recovered for energy, treated on and off-site, or released on and off-site").[6] They find that 16.7% of the plants had decreased releases but increased PRW between 1991 and 1997, 41.0% decreased both releases and PRW, 34.4% reported higher releases and PRW, and 7.8% increased releases but decreased PRW. For each state, they calculate the ratio of the number of facilities expanding releases to the number reducing releases and compute the same ratio using PRW figures. They find that states with higher conservation group membership per 1,000 residents and states with less ideologically polarized politics had higher ratios of plants reducing toxic releases. This would be consistent with plants in these states facing (or anticipating) more pressure from environmentalists to reduce their TRI releases. Overall they conclude from regression analyses focusing on explaining differences in state patterns of TRI reductions that:

... the lack of significant results across most of our independent variables, is itself telling. Arguably, our broad argument about the influence of information disclosure programs remains viable: decision-making is most critically influenced closer to the source – either through interactions with the community or within facilities (and companies) themselves. State differences can mediate some of what happens at the local level, but only partially.[7]

Many of the statistical studies of the TRI that take the firm as the unit of analysis focus on two questions – How have investors reacted to release of the TRI? and What factors motivate firms to undertake voluntary pollution reduction activities such as participating in EPA's 33/50 Program? The literatures on both topics attempt to isolate the impact of information provision from other influences on firms, and both are explored in more detail below. The existence of the TRI data has also allowed analysts to explore how concerns about liability affect corporate decisionmaking. Grant and Jones (2003) point out that firms may attempt to shield themselves from liability for environmental harms by having their subsidiaries engage in more pollution-intensive production. If something goes wrong at a plant owned by a subsidiary, the parent company may be less likely to be held liable than if it had owned and controlled the facility directly. Examining 1990 TRI data for more than 2,000 plants in the chemical industry, they find that facilities that were listed as subsidiaries did have higher TRI emission rates.[8] They note, "This is consistent with the argument that because parent firms are no longer liable for the environmental damage caused by their subsidiaries, the latter are under less pressure to manage effectively their toxic chemicals."[9] Khanna, Kumar, and Anton (2002) use the TRI data to study the environmental performance of a sample of S&P 500 companies. They find:

... firms with poorer environmental performance, i.e., having a high level of toxic emissions per unit sales in the past and being currently listed as PRPs for a larger number of Superfund sites were more environmentally efficient. This suggests that the threat of liabilities, adverse public reactions to high on-site toxic release intensity and a greater potential for reducing end-of-pipe disposal for firms with high off-site transfers per unit sales did motivate firms to change their production processes to make them more efficient and less wasteful.... [10]

Much of the TRI research still in progress uses facility-level TRI information and detailed economic census data on plant production activity to examine the distinct impact of information provision on plant behavior.[11] Facility-level TRI data can also, however, be used to answer other questions. Chapter 3 uses plant compliance data from 1990 EPCRA reporting in Minnesota to show that ignorance of the law rather than evasion probably explains why facilities failed to file TRI reports. The analysis also shows that plants that did not initially report in the early years of the program were small polluters; the eventual addition of their reports did not substantially increase the Minnesota TRI figures. Chapter 3 also uses facility level TRI data to show that decisions about reductions in toxic emissions depend on the magnitude of danger arising from the pollution and who bears pollutant risks. Controlling for the quantity of air toxics released in 1988, I found that plants whose emissions generated higher numbers of expected cancer cases did reduce their emissions more between 1988 and 1991. The nature of the community bearing the pollution risk also affected plant activities. The higher the voter turnout in the area, a proxy for residents' likelihood of collective action, the greater the reductions in a plant's release of air carcinogens. The results in Chapter 3 do not establish the independent effect of the TRI. They rather show that given the multiple influences of regulation, information provision, and liability concerns, plants do take into account the size of risks and the nature of who bears the risks in making decisions about the release of air carcinogens.

Helland and Whitford (2003) use TRI data from 1987 to 1996 to examine the incentives that regulators have to treat facilities differently depending on their location. They note that pollution from plants in counties that border other states may be less likely to concern regulators if the effects of the pollution spill over to residents from other states (who are not their constituents). They find that:

... facilities' emissions into the air and water are systematically higher in counties that border other states. These results are consistent with the hypotheses that jurisdictional considerations are an important determinant of pollution incidence.[12]

They point out that higher emissions in border counties might arise if state regulators were less intensive in their enforcement of regulations or less likely to write stringent pollution permits for plants whose negative effects spill over into other jurisdictions.

Santos, Covello, and McCallum (1996) explored the impact of the TRI through a survey (N = 229 respondents) of plants in the pulp and paper, chemical, and refinery and petroleum industries. The questionnaires provided interesting baseline information about these TRI facilities: 63% were within 500 feet of homes, businesses, or recreation areas; 61% indicated they displayed visible aspects of production (e.g., smoke plumes); and 42% indicated they had experienced high-profile environmental problems with media attention. Most plants surveyed indicated changing their actions because of the TRI. As the authors report:

Most facilities (84%) reported that their facilities pay more attention to hazardous and toxic substances as a result of SARA Title III.... Two-thirds (65%) said Title III was effective, including 17% who said it was very effective. The vast majority of facilities (91%) indicated that SARA Title III had increased production costs.[13]

The plants did not report extensive public requests for TRI information. According to the questionnaire results:

Less than 10% of the facilities said that the public had requested information on emergency response plans or on SARA Title III releases. Only 17% of those surveyed say the number of requests from the public has increased over the past 5 years.[14]

Eighty-one percent of the facilities said that the Superfund Amendments and Reauthorization Act (SARA) Title III caused "needless public concern." Consistent with the idea that the TRI generates scrutiny, nearly half the plants reported that they had increased efforts to communicate with the community as a result of SARA Title III.

The EPA's Risk-Screening Environmental Indicators (RSEI) model offers analysts another way to examine the impact of the TRI. The model estimates a "surrogate dose for each square kilometer of the U.S. weighted by the relevant toxicity for the chemical and the population" and produces a risk score for each of these geographic units. Shapiro (2003) uses TRI air emissions from 1988 and 1996 to calculate what factors influenced changes in risk scores in square kilometer cells surrounding TRI plants in areas of industrial production. Focusing on changes in risk scores, he finds that "better-educated neighborhoods seem to have been better able than lesser-educated regions to overcome the obstacles to finding and utilizing the TRI data in its initial years to encourage greater emission reductions in their neighborhoods."[15] He finds that in general, "those with higher incomes are better able to elicit changes in manufacturing facility behavior to improve neighborhood air." Shapiro notes that areas in states with more stringent traditional environmental policies and more spending on air quality and air emission programs experienced increased reductions in air toxics, consistent with information provision and traditional regulation working as complements. State programs to disseminate pollution information also increased TRI emission reductions. Overall, these results show the impact of bottom-up (e.g., neighborhood) and top-down (e.g., state policy) factors on changes in the generation of TRI releases.

Assessments of the EPA's 33/50 Program demonstrate the difficulties of isolating the precise impact of information provision on company actions. The section on informal agency action in Chapter 4 describes the basic details of the program. In 1991, the EPA targeted 17 TRI chemicals for reduction, announced a goal of reducing releases and transfers of these chemicals of 33% by 1992 and 50% by 1995 from a baseline of 1988 TRI data, and invited companies to gain recognition by submitting commitments to the agency to reduce these chemicals. TRI data for 1995 show that overall releases and transfers of the 17 chemicals dropped by 55.1%, from 1.496 billion pounds in 1988 to 672 million pounds in 1995.[16] Many theories were offered for why firms might commit to reduce pollution voluntarily: the desire to curry favor with regulators, who can engage in enforcement actions under other environmental programs; an ability to gain credit for reductions already made (i.e., the 1988 baseline meant actions in 1989 and 1990 would already allow firms to claim progress in 1991 toward the goals); an attempt to please green consumers; and the need to reduce emissions of some chemicals because of command and control regulatory actions (i.e., the United States had banned production of carbon tetrachloride and TCA by January 1, 1996, to comply with the Montreal Protocols). Eventually, almost 1,300 companies made commitments to the 33/50 Program. These firms accounted for 13% of all the eligible companies but accounted for greater than 60% of releases and transfers of the targeted chemicals in the base year of 1988. Among the group of between 500 and 600 large firms included in the first round of invitations in 1991, 64% accepted the participation invitation and made commitments.

Arora and Cason (1995) study the decision about whether to participate in the 33/50 Program for 302 firms in the seven manufacturing industries with the largest releases and transfers of the 17 targeted chemicals. As of February 1992, 93 had elected to participate and 209 had not joined. They find that, controlling for other factors, a firm was more likely to join the larger the company (measured by employment), the greater the aggregate TRI releases, and the lower the concentration of sales in the industry. In a broader study of decisions among more than 6,000 companies about whether to participate in 33/50, Arora and Cason (1996) again find that larger firms and those with higher TRI releases were more likely to join. Firms with more contact with consumers, defined as those with higher normalized advertising expenditures, were also more likely to join, suggesting that reputations with consumers were influential. The degree that firms had already reduced these chemicals between 1988 and 1990 did not, surprisingly, influence whether they made commitments in 1991 (despite the fact that they could have claimed credit for these earlier reductions). Poor records of compliance with command and control regulations also did not predict who would join. Videras and Alberini (2000), however, find that within a set of 218 manufacturing firms on the S&P 500 those identified as potentially responsible parties at more Superfund sites or involved in corrective actions (e.g., cleanups) under RCRA were more likely to join. They also find that companies seeking publicity through publishing their own environmental reports were also more likely to join 33/50.[17]

If "good" firms join voluntary programs like 33/50 to gain credit for efforts they would already be likely to undertake, then the programs might have little ultimate impact on the release of toxic chemicals. Research on the exact impacts of the 33/50 Program on releases and transfers is mixed.[18] Khanna and Damon (1999) study the impact of the 33/50 Program on firms in the chemical industry. They focus on 123 firms in the chemical industry, of which 75 joined and 48 did not participate. The Chemical Manufacturers Association (now called the American Chemistry Council) had already adopted a voluntary program called Responsible Care in 1988, under which CMA member firms agreed to responsible management of chemicals and agreed to pursue pollution prevention strategies (measured in part by levels of TRI releases reported each year). This meant that CMA member firms might be more likely to already be engaged in practices that would make 33/50 participation less costly. Studying the decision by chemical firms to join the program, Khanna and Damon conclude:

... firms that participate are those that expect larger benefits or have relatively lower costs of participation. This included firms that stand to benefit from increased consumer goodwill, from reducing potential liabilities by changing their current pattern of pollution generation, and from lower costs of abatement in the future under the proposed MACT regulations. Firms that had initiated efforts to control toxic pollution because of encouragement by the CMA, had assets closer to retirement, and could substitute other chemicals for 33/50 chemicals more easily had lower costs of participation and were more likely to participate.[19]

For the firms in the chemical industry, they model the many company-specific factors that influence the amount of releases and transfers of 33/50 chemicals. They then include a variable that reflects the predicted probability a company will join 33/50. They estimate that "a 10% increase in the probability of participation of a firm reduces its 33/50 releases by 5.1%."[20] Aggregating the expected reductions that they estimate are due solely to participation in 33/50, they find for their sample of chemical industry firms, the existence of the 33/50 Program meant that total expected releases and transfers were reduced in 1991 to 1993 by 28% relative to 1990 levels.

Gamper-Rabindran (2004) draws less sanguine conclusions based on analysis of plant-level data for TRI facilities in manufacturing SIC codes. She models both the decision to join the 33/50 Program (finding that plants owned by publicly traded companies were more likely to join) and the impact of program participation on reported releases. Gamper-Rabindran notes that the mandatory phase-out of 2 of the 17 TRI chemicals accounted for a significant fraction of the reported reductions in the 33/50 Program. She also takes public health factors into account by indexing the TRI figures by EPA's chemical toxicity weights. She finds that:

... controlling for participants' self-selection into the program, relative to non-participants, participants do not reduce their health-indexed emissions of target chemicals in several key industries. Where reductions are detected in selected industries, participants' increased off-site transfers to recyclers give reasons to question whether this program truly reduced emissions. Moreover, the program did not reduce emissions in less politically active communities.[21]

Vidovic and Khanna (2003a) also raise questions about the ultimate impact of the 33/50 Program in their study of participation at the firm level for a sample of 264 companies. They conclude that "the decline in emissions observed by the EPA is more likely to be the continuation of an earlier trend, rather than result of the 33/50 Program."[22]

The reactions of stock prices to release of the TRI data and the subsequent reaction of firms to these price changes provide clear evidence that information provision can cause changes in polluter behavior. The initial release of the TRI did provide investors with new information about toxic emissions. For the 1987 TRI data, nearly three quarters of total releases and transfers reported by firms came from publicly traded companies.

The results in Chapter 2 show on the first day the TRI data were released by the EPA to the public (June 19, 1989), the average abnormal return in the stock market for companies with TRI reports was negative and statistically significant. Companies listed in the TRI lost on average $4.1 million in stock value on the first day the data were released. The larger the number of chemical forms filed, the greater the drop in stock market value for a company. These impacts were lessened for companies that investors already knew had significant environmental liabilities, such as firms with exposure at Superfund sites or companies in the primary metals industry.

Konar and Cohen (1997) point out that stock prices may drop upon the release of TRI data if relatively high emissions per dollar of firm revenue signal inefficient production, attract the attention of community activists, drive away green consumers, or generate scrutiny (and potential fines) from regulators. They identify the 40 firms with the largest negative abnormal stock market returns on June 19, 1989, and analyze how these companies reacted to their penalty in the market. These companies were among the worst at controlling their toxic emissions, ranking in the top one third in terms of emissions per dollar of company revenue in their industries. Yet these firms with the most negative stock market reactions were not the largest TRI releasers in terms of total pounds of emissions. This is predictable, because companies with well-established track records for pollution (perhaps because of their size or business line) might not generate surprises for investors if they report high TRI figures. Konar and Cohen establish that those top 40 firms with the largest negative abnormal returns did go on to change their actions. Comparing TRI data for 1989 versus 1992, they find that the top 40 companies reduced their TRI emissions per dollar of revenue more than other firms in their industries. They also found that the top 40 companies made "other significant attempts at improving their environmental performance by reducing the number and severity of oil and chemical spills ... and ... [had] a lower chance of receiving higher fines from the government in subsequent years."[23] They conclude, "New information concerning a firm's toxic emissions that has a significant effect on market valuation is likely to induce that firm to significantly reduce subsequent emissions and to otherwise improve its environmental performance."[24]

Khanna, Quimio, and Bojilova (1998) show that repeated provision of the TRI can provide new information to investors each year, because comparisons across years allow investors to see how firms change over time and relative to each other. They examine a subset of 91 firms in the chemical industry and find that for the day after the release of the TRI data in June 1989, abnormal returns were not statistically significant, consistent with prior knowledge by investors that chemical firms were heavy polluters. In each of the years 1990 to 1994, however, they find that "repeated provision of the TRI information causes these negative returns to be statistically significant in the years 1990–1994, particularly for firms whose environmental performance worsened over time and relative to other firms."[25] They also find evidence that firms with greater declines in market value went on to reduce their on-site TRI releases and increase their transfer of waste off-site. Though some analysts refer to this shifting as a "toxic shell game," these authors point out, "Since a very large part of the off-site transfers by the chemical industry, over the period studied, were for recycling and energy recovery..., the substitution of abatement for on-site discharges by these firms could reduce the net risks associated with toxic waste generation and lead to positive net benefits for society."[26] They find that the overall effect of market losses on later firm aggregate TRI figures (e.g., on-site releases and off-site transfers) is not statistically significant.

The TRI data also allow one to trace out the relationship between firm financial performance and environmental performance. Konar and Cohen (2001) use data on the market value of S&P 500 firms in 1989 to estimate a company's intangible asset value, which will arise from factors such as brand name and goodwill. They show that a bad environmental record translates into a lower intangible asset value for a company. They estimate that, on average, the firms in their sample had a reduction of $380 million in market value because of poor environmental performance, measured by TRI emissions per revenue dollar in 1988 and number of pending environmental lawsuits in 1989. They calculate that "a 10% reduction in emissions in toxic chemicals results in a $34 million increase in market value" for firms in their sample.[27] Patten (2002) shows that one avenue that investors can use to learn about environmental performance is firm 10Ks, the financial reports that publicly traded firms must file each year with the Securities and Exchange Commission. For 122 of the 500 firms reporting the largest TRI figures in 1988, Patten examines environmental disclosure in 1985 versus 1990 10K reports. He finds that after the creation of the TRI (i.e., 1990), firms were more likely to engage in environmental disclosure in their financial reports and that the disclosure provided was more extensive as measured by a content analysis.

The logic of collective action predicts that most people most of the time will remain rationally ignorant about the TRI and will not seek out the data. The 1991 GAO study of the TRI's initial implementation confirmed this. In a 1990 survey of reporting facilities, the GAO found that 77% said they had not received any direct inquiries from the public for information about toxic releases. In a survey of residents in three counties commissioned by the GAO, researchers found that less than 20% of residents definitely knew that toxic emission reports were available from the government. Bearing out the logic of collective action that interest does not equate with action, the GAO survey "disclosed that most people in these counties – 69 to 75% – would be interested in learning about toxic chemical releases from the government."[28] Atlas, Vasu, and Dimock (2001) surveyed residents in two counties in 2001 and found that 10.9% of respondents said they had heard of the Toxics Release Inventory. When asked if they were familiar with a fictitious source of environmental information, the Chemical Compliance System, 16.3% of respondents said they had heard of this (nonexistent) data source. Pointing out that 46.8% of those who said they were aware of the TRI also indicated awareness of the made-up database, the authors conclude that the set of people actually aware of the TRI is probably lower than the 10.9% figure.

A subset of the public has an added incentive to care about release of the TRI data, the homeowners surrounding TRI facilities. Residents can recognize polluting facilities through many means: visible emissions; noise and odors generated by production; and conduits for waste release and transfer, such as smokestacks, storage lagoons, and trucks rumbling out of facilities. Several researchers have investigated whether the information provided under EPCRA generated *new* information to residents and home buyers, who may already be familiar with some of the drawbacks of nearby manufacturing plants. Bui and Mayer (2003) analyze repeat sale housing price indices and total TRI emissions at the zip code level for Massachusetts. Using the zip code data, they conclude that "the introduction of TRI reporting had virtually no effect on housing prices, and – even more surprisingly – ... subsequent reductions in aggregate reported emissions between 1987 and 1990 have no significant effect on house prices, either in the aggregate or when disaggregated into the most hazardous types of chemicals or the most noxious air emissions."[29]

Oberholzer-Gee and Mitsunari (2003) use data on individual home sale prices from June 1988 to June 1990 in five counties in the Philadelphia area and match the homes to the number of TRI facilities and level of emissions in the surrounding quarter-mile rings. They conclude that the TRI did change risk perceptions, noting (p. 20):

The predicted effect of pollution on home values in the Philadelphia area did change after the release of the TRI data, a finding that is consistent with changes in underlying risk perceptions. On average, the predicted prices declined indicating that home buyers revised risk perceptions upward. These learning effects are fairly local. Our evidence indicates that risk perceptions remained the same for sources that are very close by, and pollution does not appear to impact property values if the sources are at a distance of more than a mile. The latter finding is consistent with Bui and Mayer who investigate average effects for larger geographic areas (2000).

They find that the impact on housing prices of pollution depends on distance from the TRI plant. Their estimates imply (p. 21), "For sources within a distance of one-quarter mile, a one-standard deviation increase in toxic emissions typically leads to a decline in prices of about 1%." Overall, their study suggests that residents had underestimated the extent of nearby pollution, that the release of the TRI data caused risk perceptions to rise, and that these learning effects pertain to the residents relatively close (e.g., within a mile) to plants.

Despite the logic of collective action, some individuals do participate in environmental politics. Their actions, such as making contributions, writing letters, and volunteering, make the work of citizen groups possible. Lynn and Kartez (1994) conducted a survey of active TRI users that included 67 responses from public interest groups (e.g., citizen or environmental organizations). Among the citizen groups, 85% reported using the data to exert public pressure on facilities, 79% to educate affected residents, and 75% to lobby for legislative or regulatory changes. Low reported uses included preparation for court litigation (15%) or emergency planning (13%). When asked if "your organization's efforts to provide information about the TRI in written reports, phone, mail, and personal contacts, or any other means" had to their knowledge resulted in a specific type of action, 87% of the citizen group respondents said their efforts had generated media coverage.[30] Fifty-eight percent of the citizen groups indicated that "source reduction efforts were effected at plants" because of their work, and 51% reported that their activities had prompted industry-citizen meetings. Though the number of individuals knowing and acting on the data are low, these results indicate that those environmentalists who used the data did take action to generate scrutiny on facilities and try to change plant pollution decisions. Companies factoring in the risk of public or regulator backlash from TRI-reported emissions would thus need to estimate the likelihood (which could be greater for larger firms or companies with very high releases) they would be targeted by environmentalists.

The analyses in Chapters 2 and 5 indicate that the TRI did provide information to another group, reporters. Chapter 2 showed that in the initial year the TRI data were released, 1989, most publicly traded companies with TRI releases that I examined did not garner media coverage tracked in Lexis or the *Wall Street Journal*. Those that did get covered, however, accounted for 71% of total releases and transfers in the sample analyzed. Journalists were more likely to write about a firm the higher the number of Form Rs filed and less likely if evidence already existed that the firms were polluters. Thus firms in the chemical industry and those listed as potentially liable at a higher number of Superfund sites were less likely to be written about. Chapter 5 shows that what journalists chose to cover about the TRI depended on their market niche. Reporters for general newspapers were more likely to focus on potential risk (e.g., more likely to use the word *cancer* in TRI articles) and on the debate between industry and environmentalist perspectives. Trade press journalists were more likely to focus on the details of policy that might interest industry readers concerned about environmental regulation and compliance. These journalists were more likely to refer to the EPA, write about rules, discuss pollution prevention, and focus on costs more than cancer.

The counts of chemical quantities in the TRI also provide researchers with data that enable them to study the impact of other policy instruments. Sigman (1996a) uses TRI data on chlorinated solvent wastes from 1987 to 1990 to analyze the impact of state taxes on the generation or management of hazardous wastes. She estimates that without these state taxes that wastes generated would be 5% to 12% greater and that the taxes encouraged plants to use treatment rather than land disposal for waste management (a desirable result because chlorinated solvent wastes are frequently found migrating off-site via groundwater at Superfund sites). She also finds (1996b) that for chlorinated solvent wastes, greater hazardous waste management costs lead firms to increase their air emissions of the chemical, demonstrating that when companies face constraints in one media of pollution, they can substitute into releases via another media. Snyder (2003) uses the TRI to study how company decisions changed when 14 states adopted management-based regulations in the 1990s, which required firms to have review and planning processes relating to waste and to develop strategies related to pollution prevention. She finds using a panel dataset of more than 31,000 manufacturing facilities that those plants subject to management-based regulations had greater decreases in TRI releases and a higher likelihood of source reduction efforts.[31] Khanna and Anton (2002) analyze the adoption of comprehensive environmental management programs by firms and find that companies with higher on-site and off-site TRI releases per unit of sales were much more likely to engage in these management programs. They point out that high releases can attract both regulator attention and public scrutiny, which can create incentives to reduce costs by setting up more internal environmental management practices.

How accurate are the TRI data? Research shows that this depends on what data elements in the TRI are involved, the degree of precision expected in reporting, and whether one defines accuracy in part by the conclusions about likely chemical risks the public might make based on the data. The EPA generated a series of annual data quality reports in which investigators visited sites to survey how well the TRI forms were completed. Site visitors would walk through plant calculations and decisions to assess whether they agreed with choices made in filling out the forms. For the data quality report for 1994 and 1995, 101 plants were surveyed. The EPA concluded that at these sites:

Facilities generally determine thresholds correctly over 90 percent of the time. Errors are generally evenly split between failing to report chemicals that exceed thresholds, and reporting those that do not.... Most facilities in all industry sectors (greater than 80%) used an appropriate methodology to most accurately estimate releases.... Facility and site surveyor release estimates were in good agreement, calculated to be within +/−3% for most SIC codes.[32]

The EPA data quality report for 1996 found that many reporting errors derived from mistakes that could be remedied by providing facilities with more information and guidance. The report identified errors such as overlooked container residue, failure to identify the type of facility that receives a transfer, incorrect assessments over whether a chemical is being recycled or reused, and incorrect use of source reduction definitions.[33] Analyzing the EPA's data studies, Susan Dudley of the Mercatus Center noted they suggest that, "while in the aggregate, the TRI reflects the number of pounds of listed chemicals released, releases reported on a facility basis may contain such large errors that make them unreliable for site-specific analysis."[34]

Other researchers have used surveys and interviews to investigate how reported changes in TRI data should be interpreted. The title of the 1990 report by Poje and Horowitz, *Phantom Reductions: Tracking Toxic Trends*, highlights their conclusion about reported reductions early in the TRI program. They contacted officials at 29 plants that generated nearly a quarter of the 1987 TRI toxic emissions and asked about the reported 39% reduction in releases and transfers these facilities indicated in their 1988 TRI figures. Poje and Horowitz note, "On the basis of extensive interviews with plant officials, we conclude that most of the largest decreases in toxic emissions resulted from changes in reporting requirements, analytical methods, and production volume, and not from source reduction, recycling, or pollution abatement."[35] Natan and Miller (1998) conducted a phone survey of the 80 plants that had for at least one chemical reported very large reductions in TRI figures between 1991 and 1994. In examining the TRI waste management figures about how waste is handled in the production process, they "found that just one type of paper change, redefining on-site recycling activities as in-process recovery, which does not have to be reported, accounted for more than half of these facilities' 1991–1994 reported reductions in the amounts of TRI chemicals they generated in waste."[36] In terms of the TRI figures on amounts of chemicals more likely to reach the environment, they concluded:

Reductions specifically in the release and disposal category, however, were much more likely to be real. Changes in plant operations and production levels accounted for 92% of the facilities' reductions in release or disposal.[37]

Comparisons across years and plants provide another way to assess the accuracy of the data. When the EPA changed reporting guidelines on transfers for off-site recycling for the 1988 TRI reports so that firms were less likely to report these transfers, environmentalists used the earlier information from 1987 data to conclude, "Under EPA regulatory policy, companies are shipping roughly 200 million pounds of toxic chemicals to 'recycling' facilities without having to report these transfers under the toxics-release inventory."[38] In analyzing TRI data in late 1999, the EPA noted that some plants reporting treatment of nitric acid also reported the coincidental manufacture of nitrate compounds arising from this treatment. Other facilities reporting nitric acid treatment, however, did not file reports on nitrate compounds. The suspicion that 600 facilities might be failing to file TRI forms about this coincidental manufacturing led the EPA to launch the National Nitrate Compliance Initiative in 2000, which (as described in Chapter 5) ultimately made the TRI data more accurate by adding more reporters.[39] In conducting a review of the transfer of firm pollutants to wastewater treatment facilities (called "publicly owned treatment works" or POTWs in the TRI program), the EPA's Office of Inspector General found that industrial users had overstated transfers to POTWs by a total of 1,163,258 pounds because they were incorrectly listing chemicals sent to commercial recovery or recycling units as sent to POTWs. The Office of Inspector General issued a report calling for improved TRI reporting and concluded, "While the number of errors noted was small, they made a significant impact on determining trends in transfers to POTWs."[40]

For 12 of the TRI chemicals, the EPA also collects chemical concentration levels from a system of air pollution monitors across the country. Comparing the data from monitors with the self-reported changes in TRI figures, de Marchi and Hamilton (2004) find that the large drops in air emissions reported by firms in the TRI between 1988 and 2000 are not always matched by similar reductions in average measured chemical concentrations from air pollution monitors.[41] They also use a concept called Benford's Law, a property of some collections of numbers in which the first digit is most likely to be a 1, and then a 2, and then a 3, so that the overall probability of a number starting with the digit D is given by log $(1 + 1/D)$. Analysis of the chemical concentration data from the monitors indicates that these pollution data generally follow Benford's Law. The emission data can be easily transformed into concentration data through a dispersion model, so the Benford pattern should also appear in the TRI data. De Marchi and Hamilton find, however, that the self-reported data in the TRI do not always follow Benford's Law for such heavily scrutinized chemicals as lead and nitric acid. This suggests that plants may not be accurately estimating their air releases for some TRI chemicals.[42]

Snyder (2004) focuses on a potential bias in TRI release figures that arises because a facility is only required to file TRI reports if its manufacture or use of a chemical exceeds a particular threshold. A facility reporting TRI releases in one year might not file a report in the following year if its chemical use was below the reporting threshold. Analysts focused on aggregate TRI figures might interpret the drop in reported emissions as evidence of environmental progress, although the actual emissions of TRI chemicals from the nonreporting facility could actually be the same as in the previous year (or higher/lower). Snyder combines information from the TRI with data on chemical use and reasons for nonreporting generated by the Massachusetts Toxics Use Reduction Act (TURA). Examining the impact of threshold reporting triggers on TRI data in Massachusetts, she concludes:

First, a potentially significant share of the decrease in observed releases may be due to facilities no longer being legally obligated to report releases because their use of the chemical is below the reporting threshold. Second, the reporting thresholds may also skew the cross-sectional rankings of facilities. In particular, facilities that appear to be lower releasers or good environmental performers based on TRI releases may actually not be better than other facilities with higher releases. . . . The rankings are considerably less wrong about identifying the worst facilities.[43]

Whereas academics use statistical tests to trace the effects of the TRI, nonprofits and government agencies often point to case studies as evidence of the impact of the TRI. Stories about emission reductions at a particular plant may not prove causation, because multiple factors (including information and scrutiny generated by the TRI) may lead a given facility manager to reduce releases. The collections of case studies about the TRI, however, are helpful in proving that the data are used by specific groups involved in environmental policy and in describing the many channels through which TRI information flow in the private and public sectors.

Ten case studies collected by the Working Group on Community Right-to-Know in 1991 show that community groups used the TRI to learn about the variety and magnitude of chemical releases at local facilities, to pressure companies for reductions, and to measure the progress of firms who made commitments to reduce. Ranking first on some measure of pollution often generated activism and publicity. Four of the ten case studies involved areas, facilities, or firms ranked first in some dimension of the TRI: Calhoun County, Texas (home to facilities of Alcoa, Union Carbide, BP Chemicals, and DuPont) ranked first in the United States in 1989 TRI land disposal figures; Syntex Chemicals Corporation was the top source of TRI air emissions in Boulder, Colorado; the Ulano Corporation plant generated the most TRI air releases in New York City in 1988, accounting for 17% of the city's TRI releases; and the TRI data identified Raytheon Company as the top emitter of "ozone destroying" chemicals in Massachusetts.[44] In these cases, activists used TRI data to generate media attention, protests, public hearings, government scrutiny, and company responses. In Calhoun County, actions by environmentalists pushed the EPA to require an environmental impact statement from a company (Formosa Plastics Corporation) seeking to increase its permitted emissions by 3,000 tons. After negative media coverage and a public meeting with local citizens, Syntex "signed a good neighbor pledge to cut its 1989 reported toxic air emissions 50% by 1994." On the same day that a report on Ulano pollution was released by the Consumer Policy Institute, the New York State Department of Environmental Conservation announced "that Ulano must begin using a new incinerator to reduce emissions . . . or face stiff fines." After a MassPIRG report using TRI data focused media attention on Raytheon, the company pledged to switch away from ozone depleting chemicals by 1992.

The most frequently cited case of the TRI changing a company's behavior is the reduction of toxic air emissions by Monsanto. On the day before the first Form Rs listing 1987 TRI were due at the EPA, Monsanto Chairman and CEO Richard Mahoney on June 30, 1988, said in a release:

We are announcing today our target: By the end of 1992, we intend to reduce air emissions of hazardous chemicals, worldwide, by 90 percent from those being reported tomorrow. When we reach that target, we will then continue to work towards the ultimate goal of zero emissions. The baseline in the U.S. for this will be the 1987 Title III emissions report. The list of chemicals in that report have been selected as priorities by the federal government, and that is where we will begin.[45]

Monsanto correctly anticipated that the release of the TRI information would focus attention on the magnitude of its releases and transfers. A 1991 article that appeared upon the release of the 1989 TRI data noted:

An environmental advocacy group has ranked Monsanto Co. of St. Louis second in the nation in total volume of toxic pollution from its plants.... A Monsanto plant in Alvin, Texas, ranked No. 1 on the list of individual polluters.... Monsanto's plants around the country combined to release 293.8 million pounds of toxic materials in 1989, second only to Du Pont's 343.6 million pounds, the group said.[46]

The vice president of the environmental group (Citizen Action) that produced the report was quoted in the article as saying, "We can't afford not to reduce and remove these poisons from our environment." He went on to acknowledge, however, that Monsanto was one of the companies already trying hard to reduce TRI emissions. The preemptive measures taken by Monsanto allowed a company spokesperson to comment in the article that, "We became one of the first chemical companies to voluntarily and publicly commit to stringent waste reduction goals on a corporate-wide basis."

Monsanto updated the press on company progress toward the goal. In July 1991, the firm announced it had cut TRI air emissions from its U.S. facilities by 58% from the 1987 baseline. The EPA's assistant administrator for air and radiation praised this effort, saying, "This reflects the most progressive leadership in this area."[47] In July 1993, the firm declared it had met its goal of air toxics reduction by cutting emissions 92% worldwide.[48] The firm estimated that the reductions involved 250 projects and cost $120 million. Plant closings and abandonment of production for some chemicals generated 55% of the cuts. Adding new pollution control equipment contributed 31%, recycling and reuse produced 10%, and 4% arose from new technology and processes. Chairman Mahoney declared, "While there is still much to do, these results indicate we are well on our way to achieving the superior environmental performance to which we aspire."[49] Though some environmentalists worried that parts of the reductions were phantom reductions (i.e., were paper reductions involving reestimation of releases), a researcher for U.S. Public Interest Research Group said, "They have done some truly good things."[50]

Many large companies followed Monsanto's lead. By 1992, the companies that had announced stated reduction goals for particular types of TRI releases (e.g., air or all media; all TRI chemicals or TRI carcinogens) included AT&T, Dow Chemical, DuPont, GE Plastics, Merck, 3M, Occidental Chemical, and Upjohn.[51]

Although the efforts of individual companies show how the TRI moved actors in the private sector, environmentalists also point to instances in which TRI data helped generate changes in legislation and the implementation of regulations. They credit TRI information with helping spur the passage of pollution prevention laws in Massachusetts and Oregon and adoption of air toxics legislation in Louisiana and North Carolina.[52] The information also changed the enforcement of existing laws. For example, a report by Pennsylvania Public Interest Research Group identified AK Steel Corporation as discharging 32 million pounds of nitrates into the Connoquenessing Creek in Butler County, Pennsylvania; at the time, the county was advising that pregnant women and infants not drink water from the creek because of elevated nitrate levels.[53] The report prompted media coverage and government action. The state started to develop a permit to reduce allowable nitrate releases, EPA issued an emergency order to require AK Steel to lower significantly its discharges into the creek, and the company had to provide alternative water sources when the local water plant could not meet the federal standards on nitrate levels.

Others use the TRI data to keep score on how companies are dealing with pollution. The Investor Responsibility Research Center (IRRC) created an Emissions Efficiency Index that uses TRI data as one input. The index is designed to give investors an indicator of which firms may have poor environmental practices, which could translate into liability, costs, and notoriety down the road.[54] Some companies, such as Boeing and Monsanto, post their TRI data on their websites to demonstrate progress they have made in reducing releases. As of July 1994, almost 200 reports had been released (primarily by public interest groups) that used the TRI data to focus on local, regional, and national patterns of releases and transfers.[55] The TRI database has also allowed local activists to analyze how the operation of a facility might impact environmental justice outcomes in their communities.[56]

As its title suggests, the EPA's 2003 study *How Are the Toxics Release Inventory Data Used? Government, Business, Academic, and Citizen Uses* offers the most diverse list to date of TRI case studies. Examining the many different ways the data are used in environmental decisionmaking, the report provides examples of use by a large number of organizations. The catalogue of TRI use is lengthy and varied:

Communities use TRI data to begin dialogues with local facilities and to encourage them to reduce their emissions, develop pollution prevention (P2) plans, and improve safety measures. Public interest groups, government, academicians, and others use TRI data to educate the public about toxic chemical emissions and potential risk. Industry uses TRI data to identify P2 opportunities, set goals for toxic chemical release reduction, and demonstrate its commitment to and progress in reducing emissions. Federal, state, and local governments use TRI data to set priorities and allocate environmental protection resources to the most pressing problems. Regulators use TRI data to set permit limits, measure compliance with those limits, and target facilities for enforcement activities. Public interest groups use TRI data to demonstrate the need for new environmental regulations or improved implementation and enforcement of existing regulations. Investment analysts use TRI data to provide recommendations to clients seeking to make environmentally sound investments. Insurance companies use TRI data as one indication of potential environmental liabilities. Governments use TRI data to assess or modify taxes and fees based on toxic emissions or overall environmental performance. Consultants and others use TRI data to identify business opportunities, such as marketing P2 and control technologies to TRI reporting facilities.[57]

Overviews of the TRI

Overall qualitative assessments of the TRI fall into three categories: analyses that focus on how the provision of information in the TRI may work, political economy examinations that describe the dynamics of the origin and implementation of the program, and policy analyses that end with recommendations for change in the TRI. Stephan (2002) offers five hypotheses about how the TRI could alter market and nonmarket decisionmaking: the TRI may lower information costs and thereby raise the probability that firms face pressure about their pollution patterns; the data in the TRI can stimulate shock if reported levels are higher than anticipated; companies may reduce emissions if they fear negative attention or face the shame (and damage to brand) associated with bad environmental outcomes; the TRI may focus the most attention on the worst polluters; and the information may influence further agenda-setting in politics by changing legislation or the implementation of regulation.[58]

Roe (2000) focuses on the debates about the relative desirability of the form information may take: raw data that can be transformed by end users, or processed data more readily understood by citizens; simple forms such as pounds of pollutants or rankings of pounds or more complex forms such as descriptions of the multiple ways a chemical may enter the environment; single interpretations of a facility's emissions or multiple interpretations; use of a single indicator (pounds) or multiple indicators (e.g., pounds, risk-weighted pounds, risks to human health, possible environmental damages); analyses that stress positive messages (progress) or negative information (failure to reduce); assessments conveyed in absolute terms or relative measures (e.g., total pounds released versus percentage of local air pollution accounted for by a plant); or presentation of new facts (which may shock) versus familiar data through trend analysis. He notes how the form of information presentation favored will depend on the goal of disclosure. Analysts might favor different types of information provision depending on whether the goal is progress toward efficient pollution management, stimulation of citizen action and democratic debate, or creation of effective benchmarks for company performance.

Pedersen (2001) asserts that the TRI should be viewed in terms of "social cost disclosure."[59] He argues that if one identifies changing the social costs imposed by pollution as a primary goal of the TRI, this highlights the inadequacies of the TRI: failure to cover a large set of chemicals under the EPCRA reporting requirements; lack of explicit distinction among the different TRI chemicals in terms of human health risks; and insufficient attention to the likely differences in the dangers posed by medium of release. Criticizing the focus of the TRI on large industrial sources, he notes, "Since a molecule of benzene, or any other chemical, has the same impact whatever the size of the emitting source, most of the points of distinction between large and small sources ... do not apply in the TRI context."[60] He also points out that listings of pounds by medium of release may mislead, because:

A discharge directly into the air or water is far riskier, other things being equal, than a shipment to a landfill for disposal.... Landfill disposal is riskier than legitimate recycling into a new and benign product. A release of pollutants in an area that exceeds air or water quality standards will often be riskier than a release in an area that does not since the environment and human body are often able to tolerate small amounts of pollutants without detectable harm.[61]

As environmental economists, Tietenberg and Wheeler (1998) also use the concept of social costs to analyze information provision about pollution. They start with the framework developed by Coase in his 1960 article "The Problem of Social Cost." Coase pointed out that in the absence of transaction costs, polluters and neighbors will bargain over emission levels until the marginal social benefits of pollution abatement equals the marginal social costs. Information provision can help residents around a plant learn about one input into the environmental damage function, the amount of emissions at a nearby facility. Tietenberg and Wheeler point out, however, that data in environmental information provision programs such as the TRI may be flawed. They note:

Information has both a quantity and quality dimension. Effective risk communication requires that the requisite information be reliable, as well as available. Inaccurate or partial information can be worse than no information at all, if it promotes either a false sense of security or unjustified fears. And firms have incentives to mislead the public, either by overstating their environmental accomplishments or by selective omission (noting the positive outcomes and ignoring or burying the negative ones).[62]

Reviewing the empirical evidence on the TRI and other programs, they conclude that the "current level of evidence provides no guidance on whether disclosure strategies are producing efficient outcomes or not." Among the open research questions they identify are what the rates of return are for investments in information provision, the form that the information should take, and whether the impacts of the programs decrease over time.

Karkkainen (2001) points out that a primary advantage of the TRI data is that they provide a standard measurement (pounds of releases and transfers) to use to monitor firm performance. The existence of a quantifiable indicator allows firms to set goals, provides analysts with a way to chart progress at a facility over time and identify "leaders and laggards" within an industry, and generates pressure for "continuous improvement." To the extent that the TRI data are narrow, incomplete, and unreliable, however, these flaws can be magnified through the focus on the information. Karkkainen points out that if "you manage what you measure," company officials at TRI facilities will have an additional yardstick to monitor performance because of the requirement to create and file the data. He points out that large emissions may especially attract attention in smaller areas, noting that:

Dow Chemical CEO Frank Popoff... contends that his firm is unusually sensitive to environmental concerns because most of its facilities are located in small towns, where "usually we are the biggest game in the local community, and we live under our stacks."[63]

Analyses of the political economy of the TRI offer another way to examine the program. Three authors – Fung, Graham, and Weil – have individually and collectively generated works that offer a general theory of the origin and implementation of information programs and a specific focus on the TRI. Fung, Graham, and Weil (2002, 2003) emphasize that the start of an information provision program may be path dependent. A surprise event such as the Bhopal tragedy may trigger attention to a problem, which may then lead political entrepreneurs to get a policy passed that has concentrated costs and widely dispersed benefits.[64] They point out that information provision programs, also referred to as transparency policies, may need to evolve over time to create a sustained impact. Defining the factors that go into potential success, they note:

A transparency policy shows sustained development when (i) the number of information users grows, (ii) the scope of information reported expands to require more data from more actors, and (iii) the quality of information released as a result of the regulation improves in its accuracy, pertinence, or accessibility.[65]

In later work, they develop what they term the "transparency action cycle." The cycle, which traces out how information can affect outcomes, has six stages: transparency policy, new information, user's perception and calculation, user's action, discloser's perception/calculation, and discloser's response.[66] They point out that information provision programs can succeed if the data end up being routinely incorporated into management routines and decisionmaking processes. They refer to the data that end up being absorbed into the decisionmaking processes because it is relevant and accessible as "embedded information."[67]

Fung and O'Rourke (2000) point out that the public scrutiny generated by the release of the TRI often focuses on the plants and facilities that rank high on some dimension of releases and transfers. They refer to this "environmental blacklisting" as populist maxi-min regulation. As they explain:

"Maxi-min" means that people spend maximum energy targeting the minimum, or worst, environmental performers. Focusing regulatory effort on the worst offenders makes sense from both moral and environmental perspectives. The worst polluters do the most damage to human health and environment and so deserve greatest public pressure and scrutiny.[68]

Mary Graham (2002) stresses that the impact of the TRI in part arose because managers had not previously collected the information required in the reports. She notes that when Richard J. Mahoney, the chairman and

CEO of Monsanto, learned in 1988 that the company's first TRI figures would reach 374 million pounds, he said:

I was astounded by the magnitude of the numbers... I called in Hal Corbet, our vice president for environment, and told him that when I released the numbers I was going to announce that toxic emissions would be reduced 90 percent by 1992. He said we didn't have a clue about how to do that and suggested 50 percent. I said no, the number has got to have a nine in front of it.[69]

Explaining the push to reduce TRI toxics at Monsanto, Mahoney said, "I wanted to get off the list."[70] While facilities were responding to public scrutiny of their releases, Graham also describes how industry officials successfully limited some proposed disclosures about plants. Though the EPA proposed in 1997 to develop a hazard ranking for facilities, industry representatives criticized the methodology, enlisted Senate Majority Leader Trent Lott and others to contact the agency about the proposal, and ultimately dissuaded the EPA from releasing a hazard ranking of facilities.[71] Lobbying by industry, congressional action, and agency concerns about terrorism kept the EPA from posting on the Internet the worst-case scenarios and facility risk management plans firms had to create under the Clean Air Act Amendments of 1990. Graham describes the political compromises built into the design and operation of the TRI and other information disclosure programs. Assessing their overall operation, she reaches a mixed conclusion:

Disclosure systems have been systematically oversold. A disconnect has developed between broad claims by politicians that such systems reduce risks, promote informed choice, and further public participation in government and specific requirements that are limited in design, flawed in execution, and uncertain in effect.[72]

Graham and Miller (2001) show that the simplest version of the TRI story – that public scrutiny led to a 46% reduction in total TRI releases between 1988 and 1999 – should come with many disclaimers: patterns of reduction vary widely across industries, media, and states; progress on some dimensions has slowed from the pace of the early years of the TRI; and regulation, legislation, and market forces may explain some of the pollution reductions attributed to disclosure. They note that TRI releases decreased 37% between 1988 and 1993 and only 10% between 1993 and 1998 (with an additional 4% drop between 1998 and 1999). The slowdown in reductions could come from increasing marginal costs of pollution reduction (e.g., early gains came from cheapest solutions) or increased manufacturing during the economic growth of the 1990s. Graham and

Miller point out that only 23% of manufacturing facilities in the 1999 TRI data indicated they had reduced waste through source reduction. Although air releases of core TRI chemicals had dropped 61%, the Clean Air Act of 1990 encouraged reduction of some of these emissions and the phase-out of some ozone-depleting chemicals under the Montreal Protocol led to other drops in emissions (particularly in 1991–1994).[73] On-site land disposal reported in the TRI actually increased 24% between 1993 and 1998. After many TRI facilities reported increasing the amounts of metals sent to landfills, EPA officials determined by contacting the plants that the shift came about because the increased prices charged by a major metals recycler had led plants to shift their waste to landfills. Overall, the analysis by Graham and Miller shows the importance of looking beyond national aggregates and the need to examine trends at the industry, state, medium, chemical, and facility level to gain an understanding of what forces influence patterns of TRI releases and transfers.

Policy briefs and analysis generated during debates over changes to the TRI also contain assessments of the data. In testimony about the TRI lead rule before a House subcommittee in 2002, Susan Dudley of the Mercatus Center noted the lack of hazard and exposure information in the TRI:

How does information on the pounds of certain chemicals emitted from certain facilities, even if it were perfectly accurate, advance an individual's knowledge of the potential risks he faces living near those facilities? Consider the alarm that might be engendered by the revelation that a plant near one's home emitted quantities of the following toxic, and potentially carcinogenic, chemicals: acetaldehyde, benzaldehyde, caffeic acid, d-limonene, estragole, and quercetin gylcosides. Informed citizens might demand that the facility minimize or prevent the use and release of these chemicals. In fact, these chemicals occur naturally and are likely to be found on a fresh fruit platter of apples, pears, grapes, and mangos.[74]

In comments on the lead reporting rule, Dudley (1999a) urged the EPA to assess the value of the information tracked in the TRI because, "It may find that less data, targeted at higher risk chemicals and facilities, would provide more useful information than more data on more chemicals."[75] She also recommended that the EPA consider reducing the frequency of TRI reporting, explore the accuracy of reported data more in depth, and consider "targeting TRI reporting requirements at sources that comprise the majority of releases" so that other facilities could avoid the reporting burden.[76]

A 2001 report by OMB Watch also provides a critical assessment of the EPA's information provision programs, but the objections voiced generally center on the need to increase and expand data gathered from facilities. The recommendations assembled by this public interest group start with the premise that right to know should be viewed as a right. The report suggests:

EPA should articulate core principles that establish a clear commitment to right-to-know, such as: In our democracy, all members of the public have an enforceable right to anonymous, timely, and unfiltered access to government information at low or no cost. Government has a duty to identify and collect data and information to protect and benefit the public, spur efficiency, ensure accountability, and strengthen democratic processes.[77]

OMB Watch argued for the EPA to improve programs such as TRI by limiting confidential business information claims, auditing the data provided by industry, requiring firms to provide information to the EPA in electronic form, and making environmental data available to the public more quickly. To better involve the public, OMB Watch recommended that the agency create a Public Access Advisory Council and that EPA encourage public participation by supporting greater use of citizen enforcement suits and by funding citizen groups to serve as monitors to check the accuracy of data provided by industry.[78]

TRI and Environmental Equity

Debates about what demographic groups are exposed to relatively high pollution levels and environmental risks predate the first release of the TRI data. Activists and researchers concerned about the distributional impacts of pollution began in the 1980s to use a new term to describe the links between environmental outcomes and race: *environmental racism*. The term first gained prominence with the release of a 1987 report by the Commission for Racial Justice that found "race has been a factor in the location of commercial hazardous waste facilities."[79] The commission's executive director, Benjamin Chavis, concluded that patterns of exposure of minorities to uncontrolled waste sites and commercial hazardous waste facilities were strong evidence of "environmental racism." In 1991, the association between race and pollution became the focus of the first National People of Color Leadership Summit on the Environment. Grass-roots organizers and other environmentalists at the conference announced goals such as a congressional ban on toxic dumping in Indian reservations or other minority communities, the hiring of more minorities by established environmental groups, and a compensation program for victims of environmental damage.

The question of whether pollution levels in minority communities stem from discrimination attracted increasing judicial, executive, and legislative attention. In 1991, at least two suits were filed by neighborhood environmental groups that challenged the siting of waste facilities in minority communities on the basis of civil rights laws.[80] The U.S. Environmental Protection Agency (EPA) established an Environmental Equity Task Force in 1990 to study in part whether minorities experience differences in exposure to waste, incidence of disease associated with pollution, protection from regulatory standards aimed at a "representative" consumer or worker, and levels of regulatory enforcement that may vary by neighborhood. The task force concluded that minority communities do experience "greater than average" exposure to many pollutants, including toxic waste, air pollutants, and lead; that there are few data that link differences in minority mortality rates to most environmental causes; and that the EPA did not then give adequate attention to issues of environmental equity.[81] The chair of the task force rejected the idea that "systematic racism" accounted for disparities in exposure, however, linking these patterns rather to economic factors.[82] In response to the increasing attention to the distributional impact of pollution, the EPA also created an Office of Environmental Equity. In 1992, Rep. John Lewis introduced the Environmental Justice Act (H.R. 5326), a bill designed "to establish a program to assure nondiscriminatory compliance with all environmental, health, and safety laws and to assure equal protection of public health." The measure directed the EPA to study the areas where people faced the highest risk of toxic pollution and ensure that polluting facilities in areas with high toxic pollution were inspected frequently. In February 1994, President Clinton issued an executive order requiring each federal agency to develop an environmental justice strategy.

The increasing availability and accessibility of the TRI data in the 1990s facilitated the debate over equity and pollution risk, an issue that came to be known by the term *environmental justice*. Early research on demography and pollution often proxied exposure to risk by the presence of a hazardous waste TSDF (i.e., treatment, storage, or disposal facility) in an area or the location of a hazardous waste site that qualified for inclusion in the Superfund program's National Priorities List (NPL).[83] The TRI made available for the first time detailed plant-level information on the releases and transfers of toxics from (over time) more than 20,000 facilities. The declining cost of computer power and spread of geographic information systems (GIS) technology meant that the unit of observation in environmental justice studies went from relatively large units (e.g., state, county, zip code) to smaller units (e.g., census tract, census block group, one-mile ring analysis around a plant). The quantities in the TRI data allowed analysts to calculate risks arising from facilities, such as the estimations in Chapter 3 of excess cancers likely to arise from exposure to air emissions of carcinogens tracked in the TRI. The academic literature on environmental justice that draws on the TRI has focused primarily on two questions: what groups live around TRI facilities, and how do the characteristics of community residents affect plant decisions? The policy responses of the EPA to debates about equity and risk also reflect the impact of the TRI, because agency guidance documents now encourage the use of TRI information to study the incidence of pollution.

Economic theories offer many explanations for why exposure to environmental risks from TRI facilities may vary by race: pure discrimination by polluters or politicians in siting decisions; differences in willingness to pay for environmental amenities linked to income or education levels; and variations in the propensity of communities to engage in collective action to oppose the location of potential polluters.[84] A snapshot in time that reports the nature of the neighborhoods surrounding TRI plants cannot provide a causation story for why there is a particular relationship between community demographics and facility location. This in part is because with a single data point, one cannot determine which came first, the people or the pollution.[85] If polluting facilities locate and then degrade the environment, this may shift housing prices and attract low-income residents. Alternatively, firms may choose to locate in low-income areas because expected compensation demands or damages are lower. A snapshot detailing the incidence of pollution today does not provide evidence on the nature of communities when firms were making their location decisions. Studies using current TRI data can, however, answer a different question – which groups bear the risks of living near TRI facilities?

One advantage of using a relatively large geographic unit of analysis is that it allows researchers to focus on national patterns. Millimet and Slottje (1999) develop environmental Gini coefficients to measure inequality across U.S. states in per capita measures of the different types of releases tracked by the TRI (i.e., stack air, fugitive air, water, land, underground injections). They find that states with relatively high proportions of women, minorities, and children are "over-represented in the upper tail of the per capita pollution distribution" and point out that environmental policies that do not take this into account may end up increasing measures of environmental inequity.[86] Daniels and Friedman (1999) analyze 1990 TRI air emissions at the county level and find in regression analysis a "positive relationship between proportion Black and toxic releases to air."[87] They also find evidence of "lower- and higher-income counties experiencing lower levels of toxic releases than middle-income counties."

There are approximately 3,100 counties in the United States, whereas there are about 36,000 residential zip codes. Researchers have used census data at the zip code level to refine the analysis of what groups are more likely to be exposed to TRI releases. Brooks and Sethi (1997) construct an air pollution index at the zip code level that takes into account TRI emissions in and around the zip code and the toxicity of chemicals released. Using 1990 census data for U.S. zip codes, Brooks and Sethi find that minorities, renters, individuals with fewer years of schooling, and people with incomes below the poverty line are more highly exposed to toxic air emissions from TRI facilities. Ringquist (1997) also looks at a national analysis of zip code census data and TRI facility locations and determines:

Even when controlling for background factors, TRI facilities and pollutants are concentrated in residential ZIP codes with large minority populations. Moreover, while other background characteristics provide the most powerful explanations for the distribution and density of TRI facilities, the racial attributes of neighborhoods – more than their class attributes – best account for the remaining patterns in the distribution of environmental risk.[88]

Arora and Cason (1998, 1999) tell a causation story by using census data from 1990 at the zip code level and other information to explain levels of TRI releases in 1993. They conclude, "Releases in non-urban areas of the southeastern US exhibit a pattern suggesting that race might be an important determinant of release patterns."[89] In addition, they find, "Economic characteristics of neighborhoods (such as income levels and unemployment) also affect releases."

Researchers using smaller units, such as census tracts or block groups, often study the distribution of pollution within a smaller area, such as a city or region of a state.[90] Sadd, Pastor, Boer, and Snyder (1999) use GIS technology to study TRI air releases in southern California. They find that census tracts in the metropolitan Los Angeles area that contain a facility releasing air emissions tracked in the TRI had many statistically significant differences from other Los Angeles census tracts. The TRI tracts had higher minority percentages, higher percentages of Latino residents, lower per capita incomes, lower household incomes, a higher percentage of industrial land, a higher percentage of the population employed in manufacturing, and lower housing values. Other researchers have used TRI information and census data to explore potential exposures to pollution risks by examining census block groups and one-mile rings around facilities in Allegheny County, Pennsylvania (Glickman 1994); census tracts in Cuyahoga County, Ohio (Bowen, Salling, Haynes, and Cyran 1995); census block groups in Georgia and Ohio (Kriesel, Centner, and Keeler 1996); census tracts and block groups in South Carolina (Cutter, Holm, and Clark 1996); census tracts or the census blocks within a 1.6-km radius of TRI facilities in metropolitan Phoenix (Bolin et al. 2000); census tracts in the New York City metropolitan area (Fricker and Hengartner 2001); and block groups and other scales of analysis in south-eastern Pennsylvania (Mennis 2002). These studies show that conclusions about how exposure to the risks of TRI facilities varies by race and income depend in part on the geographic unit chosen for analysis and the way that exposure is measured (e.g., presence of a facility, pounds of air emissions released).[91]

The EPA's Risk-Screening Environmental Indicators (RSEI) model combines information on TRI air emissions, chemical toxicity, exposure (i.e., dose), and magnitude of the exposed population to yield a risk-based indicator calculated for square-kilometer cells in the United States. Bouwes, Hassur, and Shapiro (2001) use the RSEI to analyze the distribution of risks from TRI air emissions. They find that of the approximately 10 million square-kilometer cells in the United States and territories, about 773,000 cells were classified as being "impacted by on-site TRI air releases; that is, these cells had both an estimated dose and people living within the cell."[92] Based on their analysis at the cell level, they conclude:

Overall, the RSEI risk-related scores reveal patterns of inequity of concern to environmental justice advocates – higher risk for Blacks and Asians relative to Whites, and in densely populated areas, for Hispanics relative to non-Hispanics. They also reveal that higher unemployment is associated with higher risk.[93]

Matching census demographics of a neighborhood with facility information at the time particular plant decisions are made has allowed researchers to explore the impacts of community characteristics. The analysis in Chapter 3 shows that controlling for the quantity of air toxics released in 1988, plants whose TRI emissions generated higher numbers of expected cancer cases reduced their releases more between 1988 and 1991. The nature of the community bearing the risk also affected firm decisions. The higher the voter turnout in the county surrounding a plant, a proxy for residents' likelihood of collective action, the greater the reductions in a plant's release of air carcinogens. In terms of zip code demographics, variables such as median household income, percentage college graduates, median house value, or percentage black population were not statistically significant in explaining changes in emissions. Wolverton (2002) matches a set of 354 TRI plants in Texas located after 1975 with demographic data at the census tract level from the era when the plants were sited. She finds:

> When the locations of TRI plants for Texas are matched only to current socioeconomic characteristics results are broadly consistent with those of many previous studies and with what the environmental justice literature predicts. . . . When plant location is matched to socioeconomic characteristics at the time of siting, empirical results suggest that, contrary to results cited in the environmental justice literature, race is not significantly related to plant location. Income remains significant and negatively related to plant location. Poverty rates, another variable of concern in the environmental justice literature, remain significant but continue to act as a deterrent to plant location.[94]

The EPA now draws on TRI information in its efforts to implement Executive Order 12898, "Federal Actions to Address Environmental Justice in Minority Populations and Low-Income Populations," which President Clinton signed in 1994. For example, EPA's *Final Guidance for Incorporating Environmental Justice Concerns in EPA's NEPA Compliance Analyses* released in April 1998 refers repeatedly to use of TRI information. Under the National Environmental Policy Act (NEPA), EPA must prepare environmental impact statements (EISs) and environmental assessments (EAs) when the agency undertakes actions that may significantly impact the environment. In analyzing the existing sources of pollution in a community with a proposed project, the guidance indicates, "By consulting maps or photographs that depict the locations of minority or low-income communities, as well as maps of the same geographical area that depict the locations of hazardous waste facilities, Superfund sites, Toxics Release Inventory facility sites, and/or wastewater discharges, analysts and EPA decision makers can gain a general understanding of the spatial relationships between the proposed project and the surrounding communities."[95] The guidance also encourages the use of GIS software to analyze census data and notes that the EPA has made TRI data (e.g., facility location) available "in digitized files for use in GIS applications."

Despite the agency activity relating to environmental justice, a March 2004 report from the EPA's Office of Inspector General found:

EPA has not fully implemented Executive Order 12898 nor consistently integrated environmental justice into its day-to-day operations. EPA has not identified minority and low-income populations addressed in the Executive Order, and has neither defined nor developed criteria for determining disproportionately impacted.[96]

International Information Provision

An unanticipated and growing impact of the U.S. TRI is the adoption of pollution disclosure programs by other countries. After the initial years of the TRI demonstrated how emissions inventories and public data provision could work, in 1992 the United Nations Conference on Environment and Development (UNCED) developed an action plan that encouraged countries to create emissions inventories and to allow the public access to the data.[97] The Organization for Economic Co-operation and Development (OECD) started in 1993 to encourage the 30 industrialized member countries to develop Pollutant Release and Transfer Registers (PRTRs). As the operator of the longest-running and most comprehensive PRTR, the U.S. EPA has often played a role in discussing with representatives of other countries how to establish and operate pollutant disclosure systems.[98] Countries with versions of a PRTR include Australia, Canada, Japan, Mexico, Norway, the United Kingdom, and the United States. Data across countries are at times combined, as in the Commission for Environmental Cooperation of North America's report *Taking Stock 2000: North American Pollutant Releases and Transfers*.[99] The report shows that for the 2000 reporting year, the PRTRs in North America varied in the number of chemicals covered (648 in the United States, 267 in Canada, 104 in Mexico), whether facility reporting was mandatory (yes in the United States and Canada, no in Mexico), and in public access to the data United States and Canada made a facility-level database accessible to the public, whereas Mexico provided the public with annual summary reports that lacked facility-level data and did not make the database publicly available).[100]

Canada's National Pollutant Release Inventory (NPRI) contains self-reported plant-level information on releases and transfers starting in 1993. Researchers have used these data to explore questions of environmental equity (Jerrett, Eyles, Cole, and Reader 1997), the relative toxicity rankings of Canadian industries (Olewiler and Dawson 1998), and the impact of green consumerism on pollution abatement (Antweiler and

Harrison 2003).[101] Harrison and Antweiler (2003) demonstrate the importance of looking at individual facility data in determining what leads companies to alter their emissions. Examining 1993 to 1999 data from the NPRI for nearly 2,500 facilities, they note that on-site releases declined over time by 27%. Looking more closely at the data, they find:

> Just 10 facilities account for 73 percent of the reduction in on-site releases by continuous reporters. Indeed, a single Quebec facility, Kronos Canada, which produces paint pigments, accounts for about half the total reductions. Those dramatic reductions were the result of regulatory enforcement actions by both the federal and provincial governments in the early 1990s. Besides Kronos, many of the facilities that contributed the greatest reductions were pulp and paper mills (Canadian SIC 27). The pulp and paper industry is the only industry that faced new discharge regulations at the national level during this period, and it was also subject to extensive regulatory reform at the provincial level in the early 1990s.... [102]

Their work shows the need to examine pollution trends at the facility, industry, and chemical level to understand why emission patterns may change over time. They also stress how enforcement of traditional pollution regulations can result in emission changes that may later get attributed to the influence of public disclosure.

Afsah, Blackman, and Ratunanda (2000) describe how Indonesia's Program for Pollution Control, Evaluation, and Rating (PROPER) information disclosure system operates. For a set of several hundred facilities generating large amounts of water pollution, the Indonesia Environmental Impact and Management Agency (BAPEDAL) rated each facility starting in 1995 on a five-color scale based on:

> ... plant-level data from pre-existing voluntary pollution control programs, self-reported survey data, and inspection data. Subsequently, ratings have been based on monthly emission reports filed by participating plants. Emissions reports are checked against past reports and against the current reports of similar plants. When discrepancies arise, BAPEDAL conducts inspections to resolve them.[103]

The authors find that between 1995 and 1997, the color rating improved for more than a third of the plants in their sample, with the percentage of plants improving being higher among those facilities initially rated in the two lowest performing categories. When Afsah, Blackman, and Ratunanda surveyed facilities and asked, "How do PROPER ratings create incentives for your firm to improve its environmental performance?," the majority indicated that it was by providing data to plant managers and owners about emissions and reduction opportunities. Respondents also listed external scrutiny as creating incentives, with some facilities ranking pressure from those living around a plant, news media coverage, and the ability of ratings to help in securing ISO 14001 certification as important incentives too.

Conclusions

The TRI data come at a cost and with a price. Estimating, assembling, and submitting the release and transfer data cost facilities personnel time. If the information triggers changes in chemical use or manufacture, there may be additional private costs in terms of source reduction or pollution control. Government resources go into making the data available to the public each year. The price of accessing the TRI data has rapidly declined over time. Interested parties once had to buy magnetic tape copies or pay online use fees to access TOXNET, later could simply purchase a TRI CD, and now can simply use TRI Explorer or Envirofacts to search the TRI data on the EPA's website. Even when the information is freely available on the Internet, it still comes with a price – the time it takes for a person to search the database and interpret the results. The question that the architects of EPCRA faced in passing the right-to-know legislation that created the database was simple – if you build it, will they come?

The research summarized in this chapter shows that the answer is yes for some groups of people. Investors learned about pollution patterns from the initial release of TRI data in June 1989, which caused some firm stock prices to drop. Companies with the largest negative stock price reactions went on to reduce their TRI figures more. In later years, the release of TRI data still moved stock prices, as investors learned about the relative performance of companies in handling TRI releases and transfers. Reporters also took up the data, using it in stories that focused on local firms, national overviews on the trends in emissions, and detailed articles in trade journals about the regulation of toxics. Residents close to plants learned from the release of data, with a drop in housing prices within a one-mile ring of plants showing how the information may have caused residents to adjust their assessments of facility risks upward. Managers inside companies learned about the existence of and magnitude of TRI chemical releases, many of which firms did not track prior to EPCRA because they lacked an incentive to monitor their emissions. Regulators used the data to target enforcement actions and further debates about environmental equity. The vast majority of citizens remained rationally ignorant about the existence and operation of the TRI. For environmentalists, however, the TRI data became a source for national and local reports, for data used in legislative lobbying and political campaigns, and for information used to pressure firms to reduce their TRI emissions.

The separate and exact impacts that the provision of information has on toxic emissions are, to date, unknown. Research on changes in TRI emissions over time suggests, however, that the influence of information provision varies systematically. The impact of the TRI on decisions made at a facility may vary depending on the nature of the surrounding neighborhood, the characteristics of the parent company, the environmental laws in the state, and the enforcement of traditional command and control regulations. TRI emissions were more likely to drop in states with more stringent toxic laws, in states with more active environmentalists, and at plants more likely to face collective action (such as those surrounded by better-educated residents or those with higher voting rates). Companies were more likely to join voluntary pollution reduction efforts such as the 33/50 Program if they had more contact with consumers or were larger firms (and hence had more reputation at risk). Drops in TRI air releases were often encouraged by traditional regulatory instruments, such as the mandatory phase-out of several ozone-depleting chemicals or the attention focused on some toxics by the Clean Air Act Amendments of 1990. Media, environmental group, and public scrutiny often focused on the plants and firms that ranked near the top of some measure of TRI releases. Case studies show how the TRI sparked companies such as Monsanto to pledge reductions in toxics, gave environmental groups such as the Natural Resources Defense Council and the Working Group on Community Right-to-Know the data to highlight poor company performance and poor regulatory decisions, and helped communities identify the source of potential health problems (such as the release of nitrates by AK Steel Corporation into a Butler County, Pennsylvania, creek or the toxic air emissions of the Ulano Corporation plant in New York City).

The operation of the TRI has generated learning and innovation in environmental policy. Debates about air toxics, environmental equity, and source reduction routinely rely now on the detailed data made available in the TRI. The use of information provision as a regulatory tool has gained momentum in other countries, with the spread of Pollutant Release and Transfer Registers (PRTRs) furthered in part by information and advice offered by the U.S. EPA. The popularity of the TRI with environmentalists, the appeal of a policy instrument that offers more flexibility than traditional command and control regulation, and the spread of information provision into other policy areas often lead policymakers to act as if research has clearly established the relative benefits and costs of the program. Yet much still remains to be learned about the TRI, including basic questions such as how accurate the data are and the ways that lower information costs lead to changes in firm behavior. In the following chapter, I explore the lessons that emerge to date from how the TRI has operated and influenced environmental outcomes.

SEVEN

Lessons from and for Regulatory Implementation

Amassing information about information provision is like analyzing analysis. In both cases, gaps in the first stage get magnified in the second stage. Assessing the operation of the Toxics Release Inventory is difficult in part because of its originality and effectiveness. Prior to the passage of EPCRA, firms did not track many of the releases and transfers they would later have to report after this community right-to-know law passed. The toxics data companies did possess prior to 1987 did not often end up in the public domain, in part because it could invite scrutiny, liability, and regulators' attention. Charting the nationwide levels of TRI releases and transfers before the companies had to collect the data is thus infeasible. This rules out measuring the exact impact of information on toxic emissions by looking at trends pre- and post-EPCRA. Yet there are many other ways to investigate the operation and impact of the TRI. In this chapter, I first take a snapshot from the EPA's most recent release of TRI data. I next consider what lessons can be learned from the operation of the TRI as an information provision program. The chapter concludes with an assessment of general lessons for regulatory implementation.

The TRI as a Snapshot

The EPA's June 2004 publication *2002 Toxics Release Inventory (TRI) Public Data Release Report* offers a snapshot of toxics in the U.S.[1] For TRI reporting year 2002, 24,379 facilities filed 93,380 TRI forms. Total on-site disposal and other releases were 4.28 billion pounds for the nearly 650 chemicals tracked under EPCRA. Off-site disposal and other releases totaled 514 million pounds. Because of the information required under the Pollution Prevention Act of 1990, the TRI data contained information on 26.2 billion pounds of production-related waste that was managed by the reporting facilities in 2002. The TRI also contained information on past, current, and future estimated quantities of production-related waste management, data required in part to chart progress over time toward pollution prevention.[2] Individuals in search of detailed plant-level data could go to databases such as Envirofacts and TRI Explorer on the EPA's website.

The EPA's analysis of the 2002 data also examined the reported changes over time in TRI figures. The agency found steep declines in releases between 1988 and 2002: 71.4% in total air emissions, 61.7% in surface water discharges, 33.6% in underground injection, 35.2% in surface impoundments, and 57.4% in total on-site disposal or other releases.[3] Total off-site disposal and other releases (e.g., transfers off-site for disposal) actually grew 6.2%. Overall on-site and off-site disposal and other releases dropped 49.5% from 3.15 billion to 1.59 billion pounds between 1988 and 2002.

The agency tempers this record of progress by noting that reductions can come from "real changes" (e.g., source reduction, pollution control equipment, and changes in production levels) and "paper changes" (e.g., changes in estimation techniques, interpretations of guidance, or reporting definitions).[4] The EPA also ended the overview of 2001 TRI figures with a warning about the limitations of the TRI data: not all toxic chemicals or industries are covered; firms may vary in the estimation techniques used to arrive at the numbers; and releases and transfers do not equate with human exposure. The report noted:

TRI data, in conjunction with other information, can be used as a starting point in evaluating exposures that may result from releases and other waste management activities of toxic chemicals. The determination of potential risks depends upon many factors, including the toxicity of the chemical, the fate of the chemical after it is released, the locality of the release, and the populations that are exposed to the chemical after its release.[5]

The drop in reported TRI figures is a starting point for examining how the program has operated. Divining the impact of the program involves answering a series of questions. What are the goals of the TRI? What is known and unknown about the effects of this information provision on toxic releases and transfers? What indicators would you use to evaluate the impact of information? How would you value changes in public and private sector decisions that arise from the TRI? Putting the answers to these questions together yields a set of lessons from the TRI about regulatory implementation.

Lessons from Regulatory Implementation

The provision of information about toxics can serve intrinsic goals and instrumental goals. The debate in Congress over EPCRA often stressed information provision as a good in and of itself. Legislators in favor of the creation of a community right-to-know law emphasized that citizens had a right to know about potential hazards arising from facilities that manufactured or used toxic chemicals. Congress members stated that people should be able to know about risks from pollution. EPCRA shifted the property rights to pollution from private information held by a firm (if it collected the data at all) to public information assembled and distributed by the government. The language used to describe right-to-know legislation emphasized that knowledge is a good and that government should help inform people about environmental risks.

The data provided in the TRI also have an instrumental value, derived from how the information changes decisions about the environment. Data from the TRI are a means to an end, with the value of this information depending on the degree that it changes perceptions and choices. The harms generated by pollution often do not enter into firm decisions, one reason that these harms are called "externalities" by economists.[6] Markets often underprovide information, because returns to investing in information are low if facts freely circulate once established. Information about harms may be extremely hard to generate if companies have a right to protect information about their production processes from the public. In one sense, the TRI helps address at least two market failures (i.e., too much pollution, too little information) by providing the public with data about potential pollution. People in turn can draw on this information in their role as home buyers, investors, neighbors, readers, and voters.

Congressional debates over EPCRA did not proceed in the language of economics and did not emphasize the exact routes information would take to affect the production of toxic releases and transfers. In rulemakings on EPCRA, the term *externality* was not even used in the EPA's economic analyses of TRI proposals until the November 1994 final rule that added

286 chemicals to the reporting list.[7] In the rule proposed in June 1996 to add seven industry groups to TRI reporting, the agency's economic analysis outlined the market failure rationale for the TRI:

Federal Regulations are used to correct significant market failures. Markets will fail to achieve socially efficient outcomes when differences exist between market values and social values. Two of the causes of market failure are externalities and information asymmetries. In the case of negative externalities, the actions of one economic entity impose costs on parties that are "external" to the market transaction. For example, entities may release toxic chemicals without accounting for the consequences to other parties, such as the surrounding community. The market may also fail to efficiently allocate resources in cases where consumers lack information. Where information is insufficient regarding toxic releases, individuals' choices regarding where to live and work may not be the same as if they had more complete information. Since firms ordinarily have a disincentive to provide complete information on their releases of toxic chemicals, the market fails to allocate society's resources in the most efficient manner. This proposed rule is intended to correct the market failure created by the lack of information available to the public about the releases and transfers of toxic chemicals in their communities, and to help address the externality created when choices regarding toxic chemical releases and transfers have not fully considered external effects.[8]

The economic analysis in the 1996 proposed rule also described how TRI data could remedy market failures:

Through requiring the provision of data on toxic chemical releases and waste management practices, TRI overcomes firms' disincentive to provide information on their toxic chemical releases. TRI serves to inform the public of the toxic chemical releases in their communities. Individuals can then make choices that better optimize their well-being. Some choices made by a more informed public, including consumers, corporate lenders, and communities, may effectively lead firms to internalize into their business decisions at least some of the costs to society of their releases. In addition, by identifying hot spots, setting priorities and monitoring trends, TRI data can also be used to make more informed decisions regarding the design of more efficient regulations and voluntary programs, which moves society towards an optimal allocation of resources.[9]

Although the theory of externalities is well established, the agency declared that estimating the actual benefits derived from the TRI is too difficult to attempt. At the end of the economic analysis of the proposed rule to add the seven industries to EPCRA reporting, the agency noted:

Because the current state of knowledge about the economics of information is not highly developed, EPA has not attempted to monetize the pure information benefits of adding new industry groups to the list of industries required to report to TRI. Furthermore, because of inherent uncertainty in the chain of events, EPA has also not attempted to predict the changes in behavior that result from the information, or the resultant net benefits (i.e., the difference between benefits and costs). EPA does not believe that there are adequate methodologies to make reasonable monetary estimates of either type of benefits.[10]

What do we now know about the impact of the TRI?[11] The research summarized in Chapter 6 shows that the TRI did generate new information about toxics for many groups. Statistical studies show that the TRI provided new information to investors, homebuyers, and reporters. Case studies demonstrate that the managers at many companies learned for the first time the extent of plant-level releases and transfers because of the data generated by TRI reporting. Environmentalists and local community activists used the information to pressure firms to reduce their emissions. Regulators used the data to target enforcement and focus attention on particular sets of industries, chemicals, and plants. The impacts of information provision were not uniform. How facilities responded to the TRI appears to relate in part to the nature of the community surrounding a plant, the type of parent company (e.g., large sales? heavy advertising connection with consumers?), and the underlying command-and-control regulations that may vary by state and by chemical. The existence of the TRI also facilitated many debates, in legislatures about toxic air laws, in communities about the extent of environmental justice, and in academia about the effects of environmental policy that can be measured by TRI figures.

The list of what we do not know about the impact of the TRI is equally long. How accurate are the estimates reported by facilities? Do plants lower their TRI figures by switching to chemicals not tracked on the list, and what impact on risks might this have?[12] What are the exact mechanisms of information transmission in firms and communities that lead to changes in decisionmaking? What percentage of reductions in reported TRI emissions is the result of information provision alone, and what percentages are the result of factors such as the impact of traditional command-and-control regulations or changes in firms' output levels? What factors are most important in amplifying or diminishing the influence of the TRI on facility-level decisions? Many of these questions are the topic of current research, as scholars seek to match TRI data with monitoring concentration reports, census information on plant-level pollution abatement expenditures and production activity, GIS analyses of neighborhood characteristics, state-level variations in environmental policy, and case studies/surveys of plant managers and community activists.[13]

Future research will thus provide more information on what goes on within firms and communities to generate the effects of the TRI.

Assume that we knew the changes in TRI emissions that arose from the impact of information provision. Debate would still exist over what indicators to use to evaluate the program. Those who stressed the intrinsic value of information would look to whether people used the data and whether the information transformed policy debates. Those who focused on the instrumental value of information would look to see what decisions changed because of the TRI. Reductions in the number of pounds of TRI releases and transfers could be one way to measure progress. Toxicity-weighted pounds could be another. Toxics released per unit of industrial production would capture the intensity of pollution and account for shifts in economic activity. Because human health and environmental preservation are the ultimate goals for many TRI proponents, risk assessments could be done that translated TRI air emissions of carcinogens into expected numbers of cancer cases. This would involve assumptions about pollutant dispersion, chemical toxicity, and populations exposed. Similar human health risk assessments could be conducted for each medium of release or transfer, though the number of assumptions required to arrive at an estimate might greatly expand for some media (e.g., assumptions to be made about the likelihood that transport off-site to a RCRA hazardous waste management facility will result in a transport accident or that the facility will eventually leak and generate human exposures). Through this mechanism of risk assessment, changes in expected cancer cases could be estimated from changes in TRI releases and transfers. The costs of the reductions in emissions – in terms of alterations in production technology or expenditures for pollution control – would need to be estimated. The difficulty of amassing these indicators is evident, because costs tend to remain private information with facilities and the benefits of pollution reduction lie in things that do not happen (e.g., cancers that do not appear, environmental damage that does not arise, Bhopal-style accidents that do not happen).

If analysts agreed on the indicators to use, there would still remain the question of what values to employ and what decision rule to adopt in judging the outcomes arising from the TRI. Some environmentalists would focus primarily on the benefits arising from information provision – knowledge, discussion, reduction in emissions, and changed decisions in the private and public sectors. Economists might favor a benefit-cost approach.[14] The net benefits from the TRI would be calculated by placing dollar values on cancers avoided and habitats preserved, eliciting willingness to pay figures to value the intrinsic good associated with consuming information, and surveying firms on the costs of creating TRI information and the costs of changing their production and pollution activities because of the resultant scrutiny. Judgments about the TRI would then turn on estimates of the net benefits generated by the program. The many assumptions and uncertainties involved in benefit-cost analysis have also generated alternative decision frameworks. Legal scholar Daniel Farber recommends an approach he terms *eco-pragmatism*, which he summarizes by the principle, "To the extent feasible without incurring costs grossly disproportionate to any benefit, the government should eliminate significant environmental risks."[15] Frank Ackerman and Lisa Heinzerling reject reliance on benefit-cost analysis and instead offer four principles to guide decisionmaking about environmental (and health) protection:

Use holistic, rather than atomistic, methods of evaluating benefits and costs. Learn from the military: moral imperatives are more powerful than cost comparisons. Adopt a precautionary approach to uncertain, potentially dangerous risks. Promote fairness – toward the poor and powerless today, and toward future generations.[16]

By most readings of the evidence and evaluation frameworks, the TRI program has worked well. The EPA did manage to develop a reporting program and electronic database accessible to the public in the short period of time allotted by EPCRA. The data have generated debates, knowledge, and new ways of looking at the world – the prime components people may have in mind when they say that information is a good in and of itself. The TRI has also had many instrumental uses. Investors, residents, reporters, regulators, and environmentalists all learned new things about toxic releases and transfers from the data. Case studies demonstrate that some companies changed their actions specifically because of the threat of public scrutiny or the contacts from concerned citizens. From these perspectives – did the database work?, did people learn?, did actions change? – the TRI is a success. Given the state of current research on the impact of the TRI, one cannot say what fraction of reported reductions in TRI arose from the provision of information rather than from other factors, such as command-and-control regulation or market-related fluctuations in production. One cannot say if corporate responses to the TRI have been optimal, because detailed data are lacking on the costs of information gathering at the facility level or the costs of pollution prevention measures undertaken. The return to information investment, defined in part by the public health gains from reduced TRI emissions, have not been calculated to date. The evolution of the program, however, has been toward more efficient operation and dissemination. The lower costs of information processing, the greater accessibility of the data on the Internet, and the reductions in transaction costs at the plant level through the TRI-ME software and Internet filing have helped reduce the costs to assembling the data and made it more likely that the data will be used by the public.

Though the exact magnitudes of the TRI's impacts remain to be defined, the analyses in this book do stress a common theme – the impact of information provision about pollution quantities depends strongly on the distribution of other types of information. The initial legislative votes to set up the TRI were influenced by the lack of information voters have about technical amendment votes in Congress. Firm compliance with the TRI in the early years of the program turned on another type of information, the knowledge that the program even existed and imposed reporting requirements. Company incentives to reduce pollutants depended on the degree that environmental information circulated to investors, who in turn bought/sold company shares depending on the release of TRI information. Attempts to reduce the impact of the program were unsuccessful when Republicans led a high-profile fight in Congress to reform risk regulation. But later attempts to scale back the program's reach were successful because they involved less-visible regulatory actions. Finally, concerns about the use of information by terrorists caused the government to reduce the availability of non-TRI chemical release data (such as the scenarios detailing potential chemical hazards at plants that firms had to file under the Clean Air Act Amendments of 1990). Overall, the evolution of the TRI shows how the presence or absence of information aside from the TRI figures affected the impact of the TRI data.

Lessons Learned for Regulatory Implementation

The operation of a single environmental program does not define the success or failure of environmental policy or suggest trends in environmental regulation. The story of the TRI can, however, offer lessons to consider in the operation of other environmental programs. These lessons are crafted as statements, but they could be rephrased as hypotheses to be tested across the application of the broad set of environmental policy tools – command-and-control regulation, information provision, permit trading, or environmental taxes.

Perceived flaws in regulation emerge more from politics than from lack of foresight. The TRI imposes costs that are concentrated on reporting facilities and creates benefits dispersed across the general public. The passage of the bill depended in part on the efforts of political entrepreneurs such as Lautenberg and Stafford in the Senate and Edgar in the House, who championed the right-to-know provisions despite opposition from industries likely to bear reporting costs. The amendment adding the TRI to the Superfund reform bill in 1985 survived by a vote of 212 to 211 in the House, with legislators in districts with more TRI releases and transfers eventually reported under the program more likely to vote against its creation. The design of the TRI thus emerged as compromise forged during political battles. In the 1990s, environmentalists voiced many concerns about the TRI, raising questions about the accuracy of the data, the set of chemicals covered, and the number of industries reporting. Each of these design factors, however, arose from conscious choices made when the legislative text was crafted. In terms of data accuracy, EPCRA Section 313 specifically states, "Nothing in this section requires the monitoring or measurement of the quantities, concentration, or frequency of any toxic chemical released into the environment beyond that monitoring and measurement required under other provisions of law or regulation."[17] The text also defined which industries were covered (i.e., manufacturing industries in SIC codes 20–39) and what chemicals were covered (i.e., those on a list from a report by the Senate Committee on Environment and Public Works). Industry officials later complained about the transaction costs imposed on small businesses by the TRI, yet the text of the legislation in part takes this into account by restricting reporting to facilities with ten or more employees. Criticisms voiced during the operation of the TRI often did not raise new issues about the program. They simply repeated points that were anticipated during the debate over EPCRA, with environmentalists and industry officials criticizing structures they were not able to influence to their liking at the start of the program.

The impact of regulations on the ground varies with changes in who occupies the White House and Congress. Though the Bush I administration worked ably to establish the TRI, the only major expansion of the program during that time period came from the passage of the Pollution Prevention Act of 1990 by a Democratic-controlled House and Senate. Under President Clinton, the EPA broadened the information provided by the EPA through rulemakings that added 286 chemicals and seven industries to TRI reporting requirements. Under the Bush II administration, the agency began a stakeholder dialogue that focused on reducing the reporting burdens created by the TRI. The agency turned its attention on how to maintain reporting with lower transaction costs, through the creation of the TRI-ME software and Internet reporting. The reduction in the TRI program's budget by 39% between FY 1997 and FY 2004 effectively prevented regulators from pursuing new avenues and focused program efforts on maintaining the operation of the TRI with reduced resources. This evolution of the TRI shows how the course of a regulatory program can change depending on which party controls Congress or who occupies the White House.

Administrative procedures, and judicial review, do allow interest groups another shot at influencing the course of regulatory policy. The language of EPCRA built in administrative procedures that allowed petitions to add and delete chemicals from the TRI, and rulemakings resulted in both types of actions taking place. The early years of the program, that is, 1987 to 1989, saw successful petitions to strike chemicals from the TRI list filed by Monsanto, DuPont, the Chlorine Institute, Hoechst Celanese Corporation, the Aluminum Association, Allied Signal, Amoco, and others. Successful petitions in the 1990s to add substances to the TRI included the addition of seven ozone-depleting chemicals sought by three governors and the Natural Resources Defense Council; the coverage of 11 hydrochlorofluorocarbons (HCFCs) based on a petition from the NRDC, Friends of the Earth, and Environmental Defense Fund; and the eventual addition of 21 chemicals and two chemical categories, resulting from a petition from Gov. Mario Cuomo and the NRDC. Though industry court suits challenging EPA's TRI rulemakings were often unsuccessful, some changes in the program did result from court actions (such as the delisting of phosphoric acid as a result of a court case brought by The Fertilizer Institute).

Ideas spread. Ideas are public goods, that is, one person's consumption does not prevent another's consumption, and one can consume an idea without paying for its generation. Once the operation of the TRI in the United States demonstrated how information provision about toxics could work, the idea of Pollutant Release and Transfer Registers (PRTRs) spread rapidly to other countries. The influence of the TRI figures spilled over into many environmental debates. Legislative debate about EPCRA centered on how communities would use TRI figures to learn about local plant risks. Yet the existence of the TRI data sparked many other debates, including state and federal legislative debates about air toxics legislation, environmental equity debates about the distribution of pollution across different demographic groups, and corporate social responsibility debates about the degree that companies should consider their impacts on the environment. The model of information provision provided by the TRI even served as the basis for the creation by the Federal Communications Commission of an Internet-accessible database to track television station offerings of children's educational programming.[18]

Information provision can work. Prior to the creation of the TRI, firms did not often track their toxic releases and transfers and those that did possess some information did not place it in the public domain. The TRI changed the property rights to information about toxics, forced firms to estimate toxics figures, and combined the resulting information into a database made increasingly easy for the public to use. The provision of the TRI data clearly changed behavior. Case studies abound about managers who learned about pollution figures for the first time, communities that placed pressures on facilities for reductions, and regulators that used the data to focus on particular chemicals or facilities. The data helped change discussions about air toxics legislation and environmental equity. Overall, the TRI data became a standard by which actors in the private and public sectors measured companies' environmental performance.

Intermediaries lower the costs to the public of public information. Most people remain rationally ignorant about the existence of the TRI and the data it offers. Though the EPA's TRI Explorer database or the Environmental Defense's Scorecard website are only a click away on the Internet, most people will refrain from searching out the information on toxics in their areas. There do exist intermediaries, however, who lower the costs to the public of understanding the TRI and using the data created under EPCRA. Reporters for general interest newspapers and specialized trade publications use the TRI data to write stories about local polluters, national emission trends, and the evolution of the EPA's information provision programs. Though the majority of companies releasing TRI information in 1989 were not written about in major papers, the majority of emissions and transfers generated by these firms were covered in the articles that did mention TRI company releases and transfers. Environmentalists used the data to develop reports and lists that often focused attention on firms or plants that ranked the highest on some aspect of the TRI data. The actions of a small number of environmentalists can generate scrutiny that benefits a larger number of unorganized but affected residents and workers at TRI facilities.

The impact of information is not uniform. Enforcement of traditional command-and-control regulations often proceeds either on the police patrol model (e.g., regulators walk a beat and examine a sample of plants) or the fire alarm model (e.g., regulators wait for constituents to complain about a plant before inspecting it).[19] Regulation by fire alarm means that the enforcement of rules will vary depending on the nature of the surrounding community. The impact of information provision on a plant's emissions may also vary widely. Facilities in less politically active communities may face less pressure to reduce emissions. Plants associated with larger companies may face more scrutiny. The impact of information may also depend on factors such as state laws that govern toxics and federal legislation that focuses on air emissions of particular chemicals. The influence of the TRI may also vary across time. In some sense, the data have value in part because of what future regulators and residents may wish to know. As evidence on human health impacts increases and data processing becomes cheaper, TRI data can form the inputs into future studies about the effects of toxic exposures.

Regulators learn over time. EPA officials in the TRI program altered their implementation of the regulation in response to changes in technology, input from industry and environmentalists, and signals from Congress and the President. The EPA reduced reporting burdens through the creation of the Form A (which certified that the facility did not use or produce enough toxics to justify a longer Form R) and the development of the TRI-ME reporting software. Information submitted in the rulemaking process helped the EPA to determine which chemicals to add and which to delete when companies, interest groups, and governors filed petitions. The focus on better indicators of facility performance led the EPA to offer the TRI data combined with census data, enforcement data, and production capacity information for the industries covered in the Sector Facility Indexing Project. The EPA's Risk-Screening Environmental Indicators project offers the public the ability to compare relative measures of risks across TRI facilities. The pace and focus of the TRI program has shifted over time depending on political signals too. Regulators pushed to expand TRI coverage when President Clinton and Vice President Gore placed a high priority on right to know. In the Bush II administration, officials in the TRI program shifted gears and focused more attention on how to reduce the costs created by reporting requirements.

Conclusions

The story of the TRI is like a play within a play. The evolution of this information provision program itself is influenced by the structure of information available in politics. The initial votes in Congress to set up the TRI were influenced by the lower likelihood of constituent monitoring of technical amendment votes versus the greater attention devoted to the vote on final passage of the Superfund reform proposal. The administrative procedures established in EPCRA and the APA led the EPA to add and subtract chemicals from TRI reporting based in part on data submitted in interest group petitions. Battles to restrict the scope of the TRI often took place as conflicts over information processing, as OMB questioned the reporting burden estimates offered by the EPA or the Small Business Administration criticized the agency's analysis of regulatory impacts on small firms. When the EPA's political principals heavily favored environmental protection, the agency expanded the information flowing from the TRI. When the emphasis in Congress and the White House shifted toward reducing the costs of regulation, the agency developed ways to reduce the costs of TRI reporting and filing.

Like the plant officials filling out the TRI forms and the environmentalists set to read them, the EPA officials who established the TRI were working with imperfect information. They could not tell how widely the information would be used. Yet the first 15 years of public data releases (1989–2004) show that the TRI did bring new information to the public, did generate learning in many quarters, did change behavior in the private and public sectors, and did alter many policy debates. Research to date has demonstrated the benefits of the TRI, though whether net benefits are positive remains a question open to further study. Trends in the implementation of the program, however, are clearly favorable. Software and hardware advances have dropped the costs of reporting and filing dramatically. The growth of the Internet, progress in GIS technology, and improvements in information processing have all increased the potential benefits of the TRI by broadening public access and deepening the insights made possible by the data. If risk assessment, cost data, and exposure modeling evolve to the point that the net benefits of TRI can be estimated, that will (ironically) be one of the many questions whose answers were made possible by the leap of faith in information provision made by architects of EPCRA and the TRI.

Notes

Introduction

1. U.S. EPA 1989, p. 92.
2. Facility-level data from TRI are available from the EPA at www.epa.gov/triexplorer/ or the Environmental Defense Scorecard website at www.scorecard.org.
3. Descriptions of TRI facilities in Baton Rouge come from observations I made during a visit to the city on March 18–20, 2004.
4. My research assistant, Kim Krzywy, used the public and technical contact names in the TRI Explorer data to phone or email plant representatives to ask them a set of questions about their creation of the TRI data and their overall experience with the program.
5. Email communication from Wilma Subra on March 15, 2004. For an analysis of the roles that citizen groups and experts play in environmental disputes in Louisiana, see Allen 2003.
6. Email communication from Delecia Lafrance on April 13, 2004. When asked about flaws in how the TRI data were created or used, she responded:

   ...limited accuracy, dynamic database (since values can be revised). Taken alone, release values can easily be misinterpreted because small releases are not always equal to low health risks. One must also consider exposure time, chemical toxicity/concentration, media, and type of release.

7. Email communication from Paul Templet on March 10, 2004. For an analysis of the relationship between jobs and the environment, see Templet 1995.
8. Wold 2003.
9. Email communication from Mark Schleifstein on April 6, 2004. In describing his use of the TRI data, he noted:

   In 1989, we took one of the first TRI data lists and put together a zip code map of the New Orleans metro area, listing the top five releases in each zip, their potential health problems, and the companies that released them, etc. We also used the information on a statewide basis to explain which chemicals/materials were being released at the highest

257

levels, etc. This was part of a series looking at the state's chemical industry and what they were doing to reduce emissions. Since then, we've run at least an annual TRI story, sometimes focusing on a particular chemical plant, and more often just giving a rundown on recent actions by the industry. I also use TRI data in reporting on a specific industry, or in focusing on a specific problem. Sometimes, it proves helpful in identifying what chemicals a particular plant is using/producing when reporting on some other issue.

10. The 1987 TRI total of 22.5 billion pounds of releases and transfers includes sodium sulfate. If this chemical, which was later delisted, is dropped from the figures, the national total for 1987 was 10.4 billion pounds. See U.S. EPA 1989, p. 1.
11. The analysis in Chapter 3 does not isolate the distinct impact of information provision. Rather, the tests explore whether firms, given multiple incentives for emission reduction from command and control regulation, information provision, and the liability system, consider the magnitude of risks and the nature of those who bear these risks in their decisions about reduction of air carcinogens.

One. Legislating an Incomplete Contract

1. See Davis and Green 1984 and Davis 1985. The pattern of references to Bhopal shows how attention wanes over time. Searching the *Congressional Record* in Lexis for references to Bhopal yields 83 references in the 99th Congress, 28 in the 100th, 38 in the 101st, 9 in the 102nd, and values declining to 3 references in the 107th Congress.
2. See Dewees 1983, Becker 1983, Campos 1989, Hahn 1987, 1990, and Keohane, Revesz, and Stavins 1998. The analysis in this chapter of voting on the TRI is based on Hamilton 1997.
3. For a discussion of theories (including those of Coase and Pigou) of how to control pollution, see Baumol and Oates 1988.
4. The final bill provided $8.5 billion for waste cleanups, derived its funding from taxes on petroleum and chemical feedstocks as well as a broad tax and general revenues, and contained provisions that established the Toxics Release Inventory, the EPA database containing firms' reports of their toxic emissions.
5. Previous models of congressional voting on the environment presented in Kalt and Zupan 1984, 1990; Durden, Shogren, and Silberman 1991; and Fort et al. 1993 have emphasized multiple influences on the voting decisions of legislators: the district-level incidence of benefits and costs for a representative's geographic constituents; constituent ideology; the representatives' own preferences for policy; and the particular interests of a representative's electoral constituency, both in district (e.g., voters and contributors) and outside the district (e.g., contributors). As Goff and Grier (1993) and Krehbiel (1993) stress, current controversies in this literature include the degree that district-level constituent characteristics averages reflect the "preferences" of a legislator's constituents given the Arrow problem and the fact that representatives may have a distinct electoral constituency. Grier (1993) questions the interpretation of ideology ratings and the degree that previous researchers

have been able to isolate slack in the principal-agent relationship, whereas Stratmann (1991) and Coates (1996) focus on the impact of interest group influence as measured by PAC contributions. Most relevant to this chapter is Hird's study (1993) of House and Senate voting on Superfund reauthorization. In analyzing votes on the level of funding during the Superfund debate, Hird finds that the number of Superfund sites in a state (but not the number in the district), the amount of hazardous waste generated in the state, and a legislator's economic and environmental ideologies (as distinct from those of the member's constituents) influenced voting on the size of the Superfund program. For a discussion of the origins (in the period 1969–1973) of modern environmental laws, see Schroeder 1998.

6. Nelson and Silberberg (1987) examine a similar phenomenon in voting on defense bills, in which congressional voting patterns vary with the degree of anticipated scrutiny. They find evidence consistent with legislators being more likely to vote their personal ideologies on general defense bills than on narrowly focused bills dealing with particular weapons because in the latter case, there are identifiable beneficiaries who will monitor a Senator's votes.

7. For general interest coverage, the Lexis file ARCNWS was searched for articles about Superfund authorization. Specialized coverage was captured through a search of the BNAENV file, which tracks articles from *Environment Reporter, Chemical Regulation Reporter,* and *International Environment Reporter.* The full bill was voted on in the House on December 10, 1985 (the vote modeled in Table 1.1) and again (after the conference committee) on October 8, 1986. The examination of voting on the full bill in Table 1.1 uses the vote on December 10, 1985.

8. Arnold predicts that Congress members will also take into account general constituent interests in voting on technical amendments because these amendments may someday become general election issues. A story from October 1986 about the North Carolina Senate campaign of Rep. James Broyhill indicates how voting on amendments and final passage may be covered in an election. The article quotes a Sierra Club lobbyist as saying that Broyhill "was a leader in opposing aggressive pollution control. He vigorously fought against Superfund in 1984 and 1985." The article then notes that "Broyhill, sensing the high political appeal of Superfund programs, voted for the measure that passed the Senate last week. Ironically, the $9 billion, five-year measure imposes new corporate taxes and a tax on crude oil, provisions that historically run against Broyhill's grain." See Moriarty 1986.

9. Public scrutiny of the pollution figures reported in the TRI has generated adverse publicity for companies and has led many firms to reduce their reported emissions of TRI chemicals. Hamilton (1995a) demonstrates that on the first day the data were released, firms reporting TRI data to the EPA experienced negative abnormal returns on the New York and American stock exchanges as investors gained information about the extent of their pollution control costs and liabilities. This information provision program has led firms to undertake significant pollution reduction programs. The U.S. EPA (1993a) estimated that between 1988 and 1991, total reported TRI toxic releases and transfers dropped by one third. For evidence on compliance with TRI reporting requirements, see Brehm and Hamilton 1996.

10. The EPA refers to the individuals, companies, small businesses, nonprofit organizations (e.g., universities), and government entities notified that they may be liable for cleanup costs at a Superfund site as "potentially responsible parties" (PRPs).

11. A large number of researchers have found that PAC contributions often flow to confirmed supporters rather than marginal legislators. See, for example, Hall and Wayman 1990. One explanation of this pattern from Denzau and Munger (1986) may be that PACs can buy services in the legislative process more cheaply from legislators favorably disposed toward them, perhaps because a legislator's district interests are similar to those of the PAC. Bronars and Lott (1997) present evidence consistent with the view that contributions are made to support politicians with sympathetic interests rather than to buy legislative support. Stratmann (1991, 1992) points out that a PAC may try to influence the election of friends or sway the position of marginal legislators. Stratmann (1991, 1992) and Coates (1996) both estimate simultaneous models of contributions and votes that allow one to test for which strategy a group of PACs may be pursuing and allow one to make claims about the impact of contributions on votes. Under the election-of-friends strategy, there should be a positive relationship between PAC contributions and general support for an industry's position. Stratmann's model indicates that under a vote-buying strategy, contributions should rise with constituency support for an industry, be highest for legislators representing the median constituency interest on an issue, and then decline for legislators representing districts with more voters sympathetic to an industry. This chapter's analysis includes a squared term for PAC contributions, which may capture part of the declining contribution pattern expected under the vote-buying hypothesis. Coates includes a squared term to reflect diminishing marginal productivity of contributions.

12. These patterns should hold whether PACs are trying to reelect friends or sway votes of particular legislators. If PACS were supporting sympathetic legislators who represent their industries' interests, the votes on technical amendments and the ability to exercise influence in committee could be two ways to determine which interests were important for PACs to support. If PACs were trying to buy votes or influence, again technical amendments and committee behavior would be two areas they might try to influence with contributions. Grier and Munger (1991) focus on the importance of committee power to interest groups. For additional analysis of corporate PAC incentives, see Grier, Munger, and Roberts 1994; Romer and Snyder 1994; and Hardin 1998.

13. See Stratmann 1992 and Irwin and Kroszner 1996.

14. See Vandoren 1990.

15. See Table A1.1 for descriptive statistics for these variables.

16. Because 1987 was the first year for reporting TRI data, the pollution figures from this year are thought to be marred by reporting flaws. 1987 data are used because they are from the closest year to the votes and because they are meant to represent the relative magnitude (rather than absolute levels) of toxic pollutants across districts. In the matching of facilities or PRPs to

congressional districts via zip codes, those plants or PRPs in zip codes that were shared across congressional districts were assigned to totals for both districts.

17. The number of PRPs per congressional district is positively correlated (.20, $p = .0001$) with the number of NPL sites per district and positively correlated (.11, $p = .05$) with the percentage of NPL sites in the district with cleanup costs greater than $20 million. Districts with more PRPs may have greater risks from hazardous waste because the PRPs may continue to generate negative externalities in their operation. Total expected liabilities under Superfund in a district may increase with the number of PRPs both because each additional PRP may mean more costs will be borne by entities in the district and because the nature of the sites in the districts with more PRPs means sites in the district will be more expensive.

18. Toxics Release Inventory data are from the U.S. EPA. A list of potentially responsible parties at Superfund sites was obtained from the EPA through the Freedom of Information Act. Superfund site information came from the EPA's CERCLIS database public extract. Environmental group data came from Hall and Kerr 1991. Reagan voting data came from the *Almanac of American Politics* (Barone and Ujifusa, 1987).

19. See Kalt and Zupan 1984, 1990; Richardson and Munger 1990; Hird 1993; and Grier 1993.

20. PAC classifications came from computer data provided to the author by the Center for Responsive Politics, Washington D.C. The 11 companies estimated to pay 70% of the Superfund feedstock tax were Atlantic Richfield, Dow Chemical, Du Pont, Exxon, Mobil, Phillips Petroleum, Shell Oil, Standard Oil of Indiana, Texaco, Union Carbide, and Unocal.

21. NPL sites are assumed to be associated with more support for pollution control, whereas non-NPL sites are associated with less support. This may be because residents around NPL sites are made more attentive to the program, whereas residents around non-NPL sites may not be as sensitized to site risks or the Superfund program. I interpret the significance of the non-NPL sites on the final vote as relating to the interests of voters associated with polluting industries (the source of many non-NPL sites).

22. Note that the squared contribution term is statistically significant on only one of the three amendment votes in Table 1.1 and is not statistically significant in any of the votes in Tables 1.2 and 1.3. This is more consistent with the theory that PACs give to sympathetic legislators.

23. It may be the actual listing of a site on the NPL and subsequent community experience with the remediation process that generate interest in the program. Representatives with more non-NPL sites were actually less likely to vote yes on the reauthorization, suggesting that representatives side with polluter interests or the interests of employees of polluters when residents have not been made attentive through the NPL process.

24. Whether a Congress member was an incumbent in 1984 is also included as a control, because first-term representatives may receive more from these industry PACs if the companies believe their races will be more contested and thus the contributions more appreciated. Media coverage indicates that

chemical industry PACs do take into account (in addition to issue positions) whether a candidate has a "genuine need for campaign money" and a "good chance of winning." See Chemical Week 1984.

25. The pioneering works treating administrative procedures as instruments of political control and legislation as incomplete contracts are McNollgast 1987, 1989, 1994, and 1995. See also Kiewiet and McCubbins 1991, Hamilton and Schroeder 1994, and Epstein and O'Halloran 1999a,b.

26. See Montgomery 1986 and Hadden 1989 for analysis of the evolution of right-to-know provisions. Legislators during the congressional debate over facility reporting often referred to state emission reporting requirements in New Jersey and Maryland as evidence that plants could generate and report pollution information. In addition to studying the TRI, Hadden also describes in detail the emergency planning and notification parts of EPCRA, Sections 311 and 312. In this book, I focus on Section 313 of the bill, which deals with the reporting requirements that gave rise to the TRI.

27. In Superfund hearings (U.S. House 1985a, p. 1582), a representative of the Chemical Manufacturers Association urged:

> National requirements for the disclosure of chemical hazard information should be established throughout the country. This can be done only at the federal level. States should be precluded from imposing their own separate requirements dealing with the communication of chemical hazard information.... If federal disclosure requirements were not given preemptive effect, a vast number of firms would have to prepare differing disclosure documents – possibly responding to conflicting state and local requirements – for use at facilities in different states.

The legislative director of Citizen Action in contrast argued (p. 1636):

> Any federal right-to-know standard must be seen as a floor, not a ceiling. State and local right-to-know laws have been drafted to take into account regional concerns and circumstances and should not be preempted by a federal statute.

28. When an early draft of the Superfund legislation contained a provision that allowed the national right-to-know requirements to override stricter state laws, Ohio Public Interest Campaign successfully lobbied Rep. Dennis Eckart (D-Ohio), a leader on Superfund reform, to support dropping the override. The AFL-CIO also opposed the national override, which was eventually dropped as the House Energy and Commerce Committee considered the legislation. See Brownstein 1985. Rep. Gerry Sikorski (D-Minn.) noted that at least 48 groups had recorded support for the proposal that chronic health hazards be included in the TRI chemicals, groups that included the AFL-CIO, American Lung Association, League of Women Voters, and League of Conservation Voters. Sikorski (U.S. Senate 1990c, p. 4346) noted that opposition to proposals such as community right-to-know legislation had generated a litany of possible objections:

> We are told at different times that a proposal will cause horrendous, incredibly negative consequences, burden small businesses, destroy family farming, cause horrendous paperwork, flat feet, falling arches and hair, and the heartbreak of psoriasis. These horribles are marched in front of us in a manner that would make John Phillip Sousa proud of the parade.

29. In a letter inserted into the *Congressional Record*, EPA Administrator Lee Thomas opposed the Edgar amendment and noted (131 *Congressional Record* 11459):

   > By expanding the coverage of this section to include literally thousands of chemicals, the amendment renders unworkable the entire provision relating to "Extremely Toxic Substances."... The problems inherent in managing data on thousands of chemical substances would be compounded by the number of facilities submitting those data.... The Edgar Amendment would require literally millions of facilities across the country to compile and submit emissions information to local authorities.

   Testifying about right-to-know proposals before the Senate Committee on Small Business (1985, p. 38), an EPA official urged legislators to limit the scope of reporting because:

   > ...we must focus on chemical risks that are of principal concern. The public is not well served, in my opinion, by being overwhelmed with extraneous information. This diverts their attention from the most serious hazards. It is essential to provide a focused chemical list to communities from which they may determine how best to address the potential for serious accident.

   For EPA additional testimony on RTK proposals, see U.S. House 1985b. Rosegrant (1992) further describes support and opposition for EPCRA and provides an excellent history of the early implementation of the TRI.

30. Rosegrant (1992) credits Ronald Outen, Senate Environment and Public Works Committee staff member, with coming up with the idea of a national chemical database of routine chemical releases that would be accessible electronically to the public. Describing the idea of electronic public access, Outen said (p. 3), "I put in the telecommunications part figuring maybe I could trade it for something later.... In point of fact, no one ever challenged it. No one ever understood it. No one ever asked the philosophical question of what the impact would be." He envisioned facility neighbors using the information to track toxic emissions and to press companies to reduce pollution.

31. For the full text of the legislation, see U.S. Senate 1990a. All quotations from the final bill come from this source. U.S. Senate 1990b details Senate debates over the legislation, 1990c records House debates, and 1990d provides the conference committee report.

32. In Superfund hearings in 1985 (U.S. House 1985a), the legislative director of Citizen Action had testified in favor of a combination of specificity and delegation in designing the implementation of RTK legislation. She (p. 1640) noted:

   > We believe that specified lists of substances should be referenced in any federal right-to-know law and that those lists should be as inclusive as possible in order to ensure that any hazardous substances posing potential health and environmental threats are covered. We also believe that a mechanism should be established so that federal agencies, state and local officials, and citizens can petition to have additional substances added to those lists whenever information becomes available that new health threats are posed. And, unlike the case in the OSHA standard, we do not feel that the companies

themselves should be allowed to judge whether hazards exist but that the determination should be made by a government agency after a review of available health and safety information.

This is a clear example of an interest group representative having preferences over administrative procedures because of the impact these procedures ultimately may have on policy outcomes.

33. For discussions of how information provision can work as a policy tool, see Magat and Viscusi 1992, Gormley and Weimer 1999, and Stiglitz 2000. For theoretical discussions of how the TRI program in particular may affect decisionmaking, see Fiorino 1995, Roe 2000, Stephan 2002, Graham 2002, Rothenberg 2002, and Fung, Graham, and Weil 2003. In a House right-to-know hearing in December 1985 (U.S. House, 1985c, p. 12), a Minnesota state representative offered four potential uses for the TRI data: community emergency planning; firefighting; personal choice (i.e., "A person ought to have the right to intelligent, educated personal choice about the relative degree of risk he or she finds personally acceptable"); and epidemiological studies linking disease to environmental risk factors.

34. Harris (1996) and Knight (1999) focus on barriers to environmental audits, whereas Lewis (2000) discusses the role of trade secret protections in right-to-know legislation. For a debate over whether regulations can improve environmental outcomes and benefit firms, see Porter and van der Linde 1995; Palmer, Oates, and Portney 1995; and Ambec and Barla 2001.

35. See *Federal Register*, February 16, 1988, p. 4521.

36. See Olson 1971 for a discussion of the logic of collective action.

37. Hamilton (2004) analyzes in more detail the economic market for public affairs information.

38. For a discussion of how the nature of political competition varies with the dispersion of policy costs and benefits, see the Lowi-Wilson matrix of political competition developed in Baron 2000. Legislators talked frequently during the Superfund reauthorization debate of the wide public support for dealing with hazardous waste issues. As Sen. Lautenberg (D-N.J.) noted (U.S. Senate 1990d, p. 5193) during debate in 1986:

A recent national poll by NBC and the Wall Street Journal indicated that 67 percent of the American people view cleaning up toxic wastes as more important than tax reform. Another poll by CBS and the New York Times indicated that 67 percent of the American people agreed that requirements for cleaning up toxic wastes cannot be too stringent, regardless of the costs. That is quite a mandate for a strong, well-funded Superfund Program.

39. Buckley (1986) describes dissatisfaction voiced by environmentalists and some members of Congress with the slow pace of Superfund implementation in President Reagan's first term.

Two. Defining Terms

1. For a review and test of positive political theories of rulemaking, see Hamilton and Schroeder 1994.

2. Wood and Waterman (1994) explore EPA decisionmaking during the Reagan administration. Posner (2001) examines the political economy of cost-benefit analysis during this time period.
3. See *Federal Register* June 4, 1987, 52 FR 21152. This is the source of all quotations from the description of the proposed rule.
4. See *Federal Register* February 16, 1988, 53 FR 4500, the source of all quotations relating to the final rulemaking.
5. The estimated cost to a facility of getting its latitude and longitude from the U.S. Geological Survey was $22.50. See Hadden 1989, p. 159.
6. U.S. Senate 1990a, p. 132.
7. See Rosegrant 1992, p. 7. This section draws frequently on this source, which is an excellent case study of the early implementation of the TRI.
8. Rosegrant 1992, p. 9.
9. MacKerron and Rich 1987.
10. MacKerron and Rich 1987.
11. U.S. House 1989a, p. 45.
12. U.S. House 1989b, p. 75.
13. Rosegrant 1992, p. 11.
14. U.S. EPA 1989, p. 2.
15. U.S. EPA 1989, p. 31.
16. Jehl 1989, p. 1–3.
17. Lancaster 1989, p. A6.
18. U.S. Senate 1988, p. 19.
19. U.S. Senate 1988, p. 61.
20. U.S. House 1989a, p. 47. The figure of 39 enforcement cases for failure to submit TRI forms comes from U.S. Senate 1989, p. 31.
21. MacKerron and Rich 1988a, p. 22.
22. Lancaster 1989.
23. U.S. Senate 1989, p. 8.
24. MacKerron and Rich 1988a.
25. U.S. Senate 1989, p. 25.
26. Rosegrant 1992, p. 12.
27. Rosegrant 1992, p. 12.
28. Melamed 1988.
29. MacKerron and Rich 1988b, p. 40.
30. McCurdy 1987, p. 3.
31. Rotman 1989, p. 8.
32. MacKerron and Rich 1988b, p. 40.
33. Crow 1988, p. 21.
34. Rosegrant 1992, p. 7. The EPA's Office of Toxic Substances had responsibility for the creation and operation of the TRI program.
35. U.S. Senate 1989, p. 16.
36. Rosegrant 1992, p. 12.
37. Natural Resources Defense Council 1989, p. 1.
38. Koman 1989, p. 5A.
39. Bertelson 1989, p. 8D.
40. Rotman 1989.

41. See Koman 1989, p. 5A.
42. Tyson and Morris 1989, p. 1A.
43. Tyson and Morris 1989, p. 1A.
44. Tyson and Morris 1989, p. 1A.
45. This section is based on Hamilton 1995a. For other articles that use event studies to examine the impact of new information on environmental and corporate outcomes, see Muoghalu, Robinson, and Glascock 1990; Jones, Jones, and Phillips-Patrick 1994; Laplante and Lanoie 1994; and Konar and Cohen 1997.
46. See U.S. EPA 1989.
47. See Natural Resources Defense Council 1989.
48. Some companies reportedly chose to submit high estimates of their 1987 emissions so that they could report lower estimates of their emissions in future years and thereby appear to be engaged in pollution reduction efforts. For a description of TRI data problems see Sheiman 1991.
49. The directories included Corporate Technology Information Services 1991 and Dun and Bradstreet 1991a,b.
50. The total number of publicly held and privately held facilities reported in Table 2.1 (12,700) is much lower than the total of 19,278 reported in EPA data because my facility count is based on the number of different identification numbers associated with the facilities submitting TRI forms. If the Dun and Bradstreet facility ID number is missing from a facility's report on a chemical's emissions, the data are still included in the pollution subtotals and submission numbers associated with the company that owns the facility. The first missing facility ID is counted as a facility for the firm, but after that, additional missing facility IDs are not counted as additional plants for the firm. Hence data on number of facilities associated with firms will underestimate the number of plants owned by a particular company. This, however, does not affect the total pollution figures associated with the company.
51. Note that the differences between the abnormal returns for firms with and without media coverage are not statistically significant for the windows in Table 2.4. The differences between the abnormal returns for firms with and without Superfund sites are not statistically significant, except in the case of the 0–5 window. For that window, the firms with Superfund sites experienced less negative abnormal returns than those without sites, consistent with the hypothesis that investors already had some information about the pollution patterns of PRPs at Superfund sites.
52. If a firm's TRI data revealed that its pollution releases were lower (in absolute terms or relative to other firms) than previously thought, the publication of the TRI data could have generated positive abnormal returns on day 0 as investors revised their estimates of pollution liabilities downward. The negative, statistically significant abnormal returns on day 0 indicate that on average, the release of the TRI information caused investors to increase the estimated pollution costs associated with these firms.
53. Information on number of shares outstanding came from Standard and Poor's 1989.

54. EPA studies (e.g., U.S. EPA 1993a) of the TRI data now take the 1988 data as the base year for comparisons because of problems with the estimates presented for the first year of the program (1987).

55. It was possible for some firms to receive media coverage on the day that the detailed TRI data were first made public by the EPA because some journalists were given advance notice of the data's release by the agency. Fourteen firms in the regression sample were mentioned in articles on June 19, 1989, about the TRI and hence have a day 0 media coverage dummy equal to one in Table 2.5. Because media coverage over the entire year for these firms is modeled in Table 2.3, the question arises whether the media dummy variable here should be treated as endogenous. I estimated an equation for the probability a firm received coverage on June 19, 1989, using a logit specification and then substituted this probability into the model examining the dollar value of abnormal returns. Using a Hausman test to compare this specification with that using a dummy variable for media coverage, I cannot reject the hypothesis that the media coverage variable for day 0 should be treated as exogenous.

Three. Spreading the Word, in the Public and Private Sectors

1. See U.S. EPA 1990, p. 1. Note that the 1987 TRI releases and transfers total originally was 22.5 billion pounds. Once the agency subtracted the amounts for six chemicals that were delisted from the TRI (three of which were among the top 25 TRI chemicals in 1987) and made revisions based on additional facility reports, the 1987 total for the chemicals remaining on the list dropped to 7 billion pounds. This is the figure used to compare with the reported data for 1988. See U.S. EPA 1990, p. 24.

2. U.S. EPA 1991, p. 2.

3. U.S. EPA 1994, p. 195.

4. Citizens Fund 1991, p. 6.

5. Citizens Fund 1992, p. 2.

6. Citizens Fund 1992, p. 14. The report found that more than 70% of the company executives lived in zip code areas with zero TRI releases.

7. The study was written by Deborah Sheiman of the Natural Resources Defense Council. For a study that focused attention on TRI plants releasing ozone-depleting chemicals, see Sheiman, Doniger, and Dator 1990.

8. Lynn and Kartez 1994, p. 514.

9. Lynn and Kartez 1994, p. 515.

10. For a description of state toxic use reduction laws, see Ryan and Schrader 1991. For an assessment of state actions related to EPCRA, see Becker, Fetter, and Solyst 1989.

11. Becker, Fetter, and Solyst 1989, p. VII.

12. Becker, Fetter, and Solyst 1989, p. 20.

13. For a review of economic models of environmental compliance, see Russell, Harrington, and Vaughan (1986). The literature on compliance strategies with regulation is extensive (see Bardach and Kagan 1982; Braithwaite 1985; Shover, Clelland, and Lynxwiler 1986; Sigler and Murphy 1988; and Scholz

and Gray 1990, which discusses the implications of behavioral theories of the firm for compliance). Implementation of environmental right-to-know laws is discussed in Hadden (1989).

14. Although an explicit calculus of consent explains some of the variation in compliance decisions in many regulatory contexts, research by Scholz and Pinney (1995) identifies an important alternative. In their analysis of tax-payer compliance, they find that for many taxpayers, calculus of the costs and consequences of tax evasion interacts with their sense of citizen duty. Taxpayers with an elevated sense of citizen duty are more likely to overestimate the risks of an audit and the expected penalties for noncompliance. This presupposes that the regulated party is aware of a responsibility to comply, an assumption that applies well to taxpayers.

15. The results in this section are derived from Brehm and Hamilton 1996. To denote the joint work, the pronoun *we* is used throughout the discussion of results from the detection-controlled estimation model.

16. This estimate was derived from a confidential telephone survey of more than 3,000 manufacturing facilities that had not filed a Form R for 1987. Respondents at the facilities were asked questions about chemical use and familiarity with the TRI reporting requirements. The study estimated that for the 147,790 manufacturing plants with 10 or more employees in 1987 in the United States that comprised the set of plants potentially covered by the TRI, more than 19,000 submitted TRI forms whereas approximately 10,000 failed to submit such forms, even though they met the TRI criteria. The largest number of nonrespondents were estimated to be in the Standard Industrial Classification Codes (SIC) 20 (food processing), 34 (fabricated metals), and 32 (stone, clay, and glass). Compliance rates were lower for facilities in a medium-size category (20–49 employees) than for small (10–19) or large (50+) plants, because these plants may be large enough to use chemicals past the threshold level but too small to have an environmental compliance staff. Awareness of the TRI program did increase with plant size, rising from 28% of the small facilities to 54% of the large facilities. Compliance rates also varied by region of the country, from a low of 56% in region 9 (California, Arizona, Nevada, Hawaii) to a high of 75% in region 7 (Iowa, Kansas, Missouri, Nebraska).

17. From October 1988 through May 1993, the EPA's regional offices conducted 3,263 EPCRA inspections and issued 683 civil complaints at these facilities, nearly all of which were for nonreporting TRI data.

18. In addition to the Dun and Bradstreet list from the NEISC, the ERC officials also used the Minnesota Directory of Manufacturers to identify firms that had not submitted TRI forms but were in industries likely to use chemicals covered by the TRI. Other sources of firms to include in the regulators' survey were Section 312 reports filed with the state and local fire departments in which plants file forms about chemical storage, the Minnesota Pollution Control Agency's inventory of hazardous waste generators, a database of all point air source polluters exceeding a threshold of 25 tons of volatile organic compound emissions, and miscellaneous tips to the ERC.

19. Our data on 1990 TRI releases and transfers reported in Minnesota come from the database maintained by the state's Emergency Response

Commission. Although the EPA's national TRI database contains all the information entered by facilities on the Form R reports filed under the TRI program, we chose to use the state ERC data because they were more likely to contain data revisions and data reported late (a prerequisite for catching nonreporters who filed their TRI reports late). There was a total of 585 facilities that reported TRI data to the ERC for 1990. The Minnesota ERC also provided us with a list of facilities that were surveyed but were found not to be subject to TRI reporting and a list of plants inspected for TRI violations.

20. Through the Dun and Bradstreet numbers associated with facilities, we were also able to link up the full sample of Minnesota manufacturing facilities with EPA information on whether the facilities were covered under other regulatory programs. Variables were created to indicate the degree of coverage by federal programs dealing with many different pollution pathways: whether the facility possessed a permit under any of four separate federal air pollution programs; whether the facility possessed a handler identification number under the Resource Conservation and Recovery Act (RCRA), which generally indicates that the facility was a generator, treater, storer, transporter, or disposer of hazardous waste; whether the facility possessed a permit under the Clean Water Act's National Pollutant Discharge Elimination System; and whether the facility was listed as a potential site for hazardous waste cleanup in the Comprehensive Environmental Response, Compensation, and Liability Information System (CERCLIS), which tracks sites investigated for possible inclusion in the Superfund program. These variables are helpful in part because the production processes and chemical uses that give rise to the pollution regulated by these programs may also involve the manufacture or use of the set of chemicals requiring TRI reporting.

21. We need to highlight an important distinction. In addition to the facilities that Minnesota regulators detected using EPA's list, there are more than 80 additional facilities that they were able to detect with alternative methods. In our analysis, these additional cases are classified as nonfilers, not as detected noncompliers. We treat these as undetected noncompliers, because our purpose here is to evaluate the typical effect of state regulators using the EPA's normal inspection list, not the special effect of the additional efforts by Minnesota. The true nonfilers are the facilities that fall outside of the reporting requirements. Undetected noncompliers are the facilities that are covered by the TRI requirements, did not file a report, and were not detected by the EPA's usual method. We take advantage of additional information gathered by the Minnesota ERC, which identified some facilities that should have filed among the nonfilers. We use the Minnesota ERC data on the facilities they detected as noncompliers from data sources outside the standard EPA facility list as a check on the predictive accuracy of our model. We treat the additional facilities detected in violation by the Minnesota ERC as undetected noncompliers. For a technical description of our model, see Brehm and Hamilton 1996.

22. Our information on Minnesota TRI filings came from data supplied by the state Emergency Response Commission. Other facility-level data on

coverage in other federal environmental programs are available from the National Technical Information Service or through the Freedom of Information Act from the EPA.

23. Of the 4,087 plants in the sample, 1,523 were generators, 76 were transporters, and 13 handled disposal, storage, or treatment. Eighty-five sites were investigated and found not to be subject or had missing data on whether they were subject to RCRA.

24. RCRA covers substances found to be corrosive, ignitable, reactive, or toxic.

25. The EPA's regulatory impact analyses of the TRI estimated that the cost of completing the TRI forms would be approximately $13,000 to $15,000 per facility for the first year of the program and $8,000 to $9,000 per facility in subsequent years (U.S. EPA 1988).

26. Compliance with TRI may also lead a firm to realize economic benefits, as the compilation of pollution information for the program may lead managers to discover pollution reduction opportunities. The social benefits from reduced pollution, e.g., reduced health effects and increased environmental amenities, might not enter a firm's calculus without public or regulator pressure, but savings on waste disposal or other fees avoided with pollution reduction would affect its pollution decisions.

27. Note that if plants were engaged in calculated evasion of reporting in 1991 their 1990 releases of TRI chemicals, the ability of managers to estimate expected fines would be hampered by the fact that the program had only been collecting pollution data for a few years and hence experience with nonreporting fines could be limited. Ex post, the Minnesota regulators chose not to fine any of 142 facilities they discovered in 1991 that had failed to file TRI forms.

28. We also included a dummy variable for whether the facility was in the stone, clay, or glass industry (SIC 32), because previous research (Abt Associates 1990) indicated that facilities in this industry were more likely to fail to file TRI reports.

29. Variables relating to the ignorance hypotheses also may have interpretations under the evasion model. Coverage under different regulatory programs, such as air, water, hazardous waste, and Superfund programs, may indicate that compliance costs will be higher and hence violation more likely. In part because RCRA requirements may overlap more with the TRI than that of other programs, we have chosen to interpret regulatory contact under programs other than RCRA as relating to information about the TRI and coverage under RCRA as relating to expected compliance costs. Major dischargers under air and water programs could be interpreted as more likely to receive inspections for TRI compliance and hence less likely to violate based on evasion. Because inspections were not generally coordinated across programs and because few inspections were likely, we interpret the size of the polluter under air and water as a measure of regulator contact that makes ignorance of the reporting requirements less likely. Although we interpret facilities associated with larger companies and subsidiaries as more likely to be aware of the program, they also might be less likely to violate based on concerns about greater reputation effects (i.e., the damage to a firm's reputation due to

failure to observe the law may lead to greater lost revenues for larger firms) if they were discovered in violation.

30. We are able to get convergence of our model over the 4,087 observations in 59 iterations. The gradients for all parameters at the last iteration are all less than 10^{-4} in absolute value. The likelihood ratio test (twice the difference between the log-likelihood for our model and the log-likelihood of the model with just the constant terms) is 732, significant at $p < .01$ for the number of parameters in our model. With Minnesota's supplementary survey of facilities failing to file, we have an additional way to measure goodness of fit. Under a grant from the U.S. EPA, Minnesota surveyed more than 1,300 facilities that did not file TRI forms. Their sample was not taken strictly at random, but excluded industrial classifications and firms that the Minnesota ERC decided had a low probability of being in violation. How well did our model discriminate between the true violators (nonfilers who were detected by Minnesota in their survey) and the true nonfilers (nonfilers who Minnesota declared to be legitimate nonfilers on the basis of their survey)? On this score, we do reasonably well. Of the 113 true violators that we have complete information for, our model predicts that 59% of them are in violation. The success of our fit is entirely consistent with reports from Feinstein (1989, 1990) of the success of detection-controlled methods in general, as well as with our own simulations. We should reemphasize that the DCE technology assumes that there are no false positives, or firms that are labeled as violators who are in fact not in violation. False positives are real and important phenomena, illustrated by the administrative and court cases in which firms contest findings of violation. The DCE methodology cannot address this problem.

31. As this chapter notes, environmentalists criticized the early operation of the program as underreporting the release of toxics for many reasons, including the failure of the TRI to require the reporting of many hazardous chemicals regulated under other federal programs, the exclusion at that time of facilities in nonmanufacturing industries (such as electric power plants) from information disclosure, and the large fraction of manufacturing plants that should have filed reports but did not.

32. The small fraction of additional pollution discovered also does not imply that the environmental impacts of the resources expended to discover these plants were inconsequential. From the perspective of social cost-benefit analysis, one would have to calculate and monetize a number of variables to judge the impact of allocating additional effort to unmasking TRI noncompliers: regulators' enforcement expenditures; the costs imposed on private firms to calculate TRI emissions and subsequent pollution reduction expenditures; the impact on firms' emissions, both for new reporters discovered through enforcement actions and for firms influenced by higher probabilities of discovery; the possible reduction in human health risks and other environmental disamenities from emission cutbacks; and the monetized value that one places on the environment benefits from pollution reduction. An additional question one may ask is if further discovery of TRI emissions may be more easily accomplished by searching for nonreporters or by investigating the data quality of current reporters (Minnesota ERC 1992, Radian 1991).

33. See Coase (1960, 1988) for discussions of the influence of transaction costs on the degree that firms will internalize their externalities. Williamson (1979) examines how transaction costs in general affect the design and operation of property rights. Lewis (1996) analyzes how the distribution of information about pollution affects the implementation of possible environmental policies and how the distribution of political power may affect the feasibility of moving toward market-based policies. This section draws on Hamilton 1999.

34. Prewitt and Vietor, 1992, pp. 14–15.

35. Helland (1998) studies the incentives that regulators have in targeting facilities for pollution inspections. For an analysis of agency enforcement strategies in another area of safety regulation, see Olson (1996). Spence (1997) offers a critique of the positive theories of political control that form the basis of many analyses of regulator behavior.

36. If a facility reported a lower level of TRI air emissions for a carcinogen in 1991 than in 1988, this will be referred to as evidence of pollution reduction here because the lower reported level of releases could have come from activities that resulted in lower levels of pollution. Note, however, that reported TRI release figures could be lower because product production dropped, different methodologies for estimation were used, or a plant switched to use of a chemical not tracked by the TRI (Poje and Horowitz 1990). Starting with 1991 data, the TRI contained more detailed information on pollution prevention, so one could analyze the hierarchy of pollution prevention options followed by a plant (e.g., did the facility engage in source reduction, recycling, energy recovery, treatment, or disposal of a given substance?) (U.S. EPA 1994). Here 1988 was chosen as the base year because reporting for the first TRI year (1987) entailed problems as firms became accustomed to the reporting requirements. Some firms were also said to report strategically high emissions in 1987 so that they could report reductions in pollution levels in later years. Because TRI data are self-reported and rarely verified by EPA inspections, firms may be strategic in their responses. In terms of the decision of whether to report TRI emissions, however, nonreporting appears to be a function more of ignorance about the law rather than evasion (Brehm and Hamilton 1996).

37. State air quality control expenditures per capita are treated as exogenous here, although the argument can be made that these expenditures are a reaction in part to levels of air pollutants released in a state. Census variables for the area around a plant are also treated as exogenous, even though a plant's pollution may lower the level of housing prices in an area and thus influence which demographic groups may settle in the neighborhood. Because neighborhood characteristics are proxied for with information at the zip code level, however, this may not be a severe problem because housing price effects from a facility may not strongly influence zip code median values.

38. The chemical dummy variables are dropped from specifications that contain the inhalation slope factor.

39. The Riskpro model calculates cancer risks using assumptions similar to those adopted by the EPA in its evaluation of cancer risks at Superfund sites, such as the general use of a linear low-dose risk equation. For more details on the Riskpro model, see General Sciences Corporation 1990.

40. One study of TRI coordinates in New York determined that 24% of plants submitted correct coordinates, 41% were within 1 mile, 12% were within 1–5 miles, 12% were more than 5 miles off, 7% had no data, and 4% transposed coordinates (U.S. EPA 1993b). Transposed coordinates were corrected before the Riskpro analysis was performed here.

41. Note that expected deaths and maximum individual risks are highly correlated (.84 for the 2,502 pathways with data for 1988 and 1991), which may generate problems of multicollinearity.

42. See Kahn and Matsusaka (1997) for a discussion of what factors influence the demand for environmental goods and the degree that the environment is a normal good. Note that a firm will care about the pollution costs it is forced to internalize through the operation of economic and political markets. Pollution damages will vary among residents because of differences in the value they place on the environment or differences in their human and physical capital exposed to pollution. The voter turnout variable is meant to capture the likelihood that, for a given level of environmental damage, a community will engage in collective action that increases costs for firms. Why communities may vary in this propensity is treated as exogenous here. Possible hypotheses include differences in transaction costs to political activity or the existence of information asymmetries that affect political action. See Hamilton (1993) for a discussion of the use of voter turnout as a proxy for the likelihood of collective action.

43. Portney (1981) presents evidence on the impact of air pollution on housing prices and derives an estimate of a statistical value of life based on housing price hedonics.

44. Note that more residents in an area may mean more constituents to pressure a regulator for reductions. Greater numbers may make collective action less likely, however, so that the net pressure on regulators would be reduced as population size grows. Because I control for collective action probabilities through the voter turnout variable, I believe that the impact of a larger population should be to increase incentives to reduce emissions.

45. Because tests indicated the presence of heteroskedasticity, White standard errors were calculated and reported for the OLS regressions.

46. Some of the variables not reported in the tables were statistically significant. Pollution reduction did vary by industry, with emissions being reduced more for plants in the paper industries. Chemical dummies were statistically significant, with most chemicals being reduced more readily than dichloromethane.

47. From the perspective of residents surrounding a facility, the costs of pollution exposure will vary by chemical because these carcinogens differ in toxicity. From a firm's perspective, the benefits of pollution will vary by chemical because it may be more costly to change the production process to reduce certain carcinogenic emissions.

48. McCubbins and Schwartz (1984) introduce the notion that congressional oversight may involve "police patrols" (e.g., direct examination of a sample of activities delegated to agencies) and "fire alarms" (e.g., establishment of procedures that allow citizens and interest groups to alert Congress and the courts to agency policies they disagree with). Regulators face a similar choice in monitoring firm compliance with pollution laws. Agencies can sample a set of facilities and inspect them for violations, or they can wait for constituents to alert them of potential polluter violations. The ability of residents to engage in collective action becomes particularly important if environmental regulators adopt a "fire alarm" approach.

Four. Politics of Expansion and Contraction

1. See Shepsle 1992.
2. In the principal-agent model, a principal delegates decisionmaking authority to an agent. Although this division of labor allows specialization and frees up the principal, the agent may take actions a principal may not like because of the agent's advantages of hidden action and hidden information. Kiewiet and McCubbins (1991, p. 27) point out that in political principal-agent relationships, four mechanisms are used by principals to control the actions of agents: contract design, screening and monitoring procedures, monitoring and reporting systems, and institutional checks.
3. See McNollgast 1987, 1989, 1994, and 1995. For additional analyses of agency discretion and congressional influence on rulemaking, see Weingast and Moran 1983; McCubbins 1985; Moe 1985, 1987; Calvert, McCubbins, and Weingast 1989; Hill and Brazier 1991; Farber 1992; Bawn 1995, 1997; Spiller 1996; Furlong 1997; Epstein and O'Halloran 1999a,b; Spence and Cross 2000; and Spence 2002.
4. Kerwin (2003) describes the rulemaking process in depth. Gormley and Balla (2004) discuss rulemaking as part of their analysis of theories of bureaucratic accountability and performance. Constraints on agency rulemaking include the Paperwork Reduction Act requirement to estimate the paperwork burden generated by a rule and obtain White House approval for the collection of new information, the Regulatory Flexibility Act requirement for analysis of the impact of a rule on small businesses, and the requirements under Executive Orders 12291 (Reagan) and 12866 (Clinton) that an agency conduct a regulatory impact analysis of the costs and benefits of a major rule. Mendeloff (1988) examines in depth the political process surrounding toxics rulemaking at another agency, the Occupational Health and Safety Administration.
5. For the full text of EPCRA, see U.S. Senate 1990a. All quotations from the bill come from this source.
6. For the study that resulted, see National Academy of Sciences 1990.
7. U.S. EPA 1989, p. 54.
8. See U.S. EPA 1990, pp. 78–79, for listing of the top 25 chemicals for reporting year 1988 in terms of total releases and transfers and forms. Although 1987

was the first year of reported data, 1988 is more often chosen as the base year for analysis because of initial problems with data estimation and collection in the program's first year of operation.

9. *Federal Register* January 12, 1994, 59 FR 1788.
10. *Federal Register* July 20, 1987, 52 FR 27226. The EPA granted the petition to delist in a final rule published in 1995; see *Federal Register* February 17, 1995, 60 FR 9299.
11. *Federal Register* March 30, 1990, 55 FR 12144. The EPA granted the petition to delist ammonium sulfate and made decisions about other listings relating to ammonia in 1995; see *Federal Register* June 30, 1995, 60 FR 34172.
12. *Federal Register* June 20, 1989, 54 FR 25850. For discussion of sodium sulfate in the first TRI report, see U.S. EPA 1989, p. 3. In anticipation of the delisting of sodium sulfate, the EPA presented the 1987 TRI data totals with and without sodium sulfate figures.
13. *Federal Register* June 16, 1995, 60 FR 31643.
14. *Federal Register* March 15, 1989, 54 FR 10668.
15. *Federal Register* February 19, 1988, 53 FR 5004.
16. *Federal Register* June 20, 1988, 53 FR 23108. For statistical analyses of the impact of comments during the rulemaking process, see Magat, Krupnick, and Harrington 1986 and Balla 1998.
17. *Federal Register* June 28, 1994, 59 FR 33205.
18. The EPA removed chlorosilanes, DMP, and bronopol from the TRI list. See *Federal Register* April 22, 1998, 63 FR 19838.
19. For the proposed rule, see *Federal Register* July 28, 1994, 59 FR 38524. Data from the final rule come from *Federal Register* November 30, 1994, 59 FR 61488.
20. *Federal Register* October 15, 2002, 67 FR 63656.
21. *Federal Register* November 5, 2003, 68 FR 62579.
22. See comments at www.epa.gov/tri/programs/stakeholders/comments/dr/DR0055.htm.
23. See www.epa.gov/tri/programs/stakeholders/comments/dr/DR0050.htm.
24. See www.epa.gov/tri/programs/stakeholders/comments/dr/DR0012.htm. There were also complaints made about the accuracy of the information. Joseph Scott of Harvard Custom Manufacturing used the following example:

> How much olive residue remains on a martini glass after consumption of the martini? Nobody really knows unless the glass is subjected to chemical analysis, but anyone could provide a "best estimate" and the results would vary greatly. By the same token, how much lead is in the residues trapped inside the vent pipe for our wave solder machine, on the fan blades, and in the corners of the blower unit? My "best guess" might be 10 mg, while someone else's might be 500 mg. Both would be considered by the TRI as "accurate" while neither might be true.

See www.epa.gov/tri/programs/stakeholders/comments/ca/CA0005.htm.
25. See www.epa.gov/tri/programs/stakeholders/comments/dr/DR0071.htm.
26. See U.S. EPA 2003, p. 4.
27. *Federal Register* July 1, 2002, 67 FR 44213.

28. Public choice analysts stress that because one cannot treat a group as if it were an individual with preferences, the notion that Congress can be treated as a rational person with a measurable intent is problematic, though judges may make this assumption for the purposes of statutory interpretation. There are many problems with reasoning from statements in the *Congressional Record* and vote outcomes to divine "congressional intent," including the use of procedural motions to limit the consideration of alternatives, strategic voting by Congress members (e.g., a vote trade whereby Congress members vote against their preferred outcome to achieve a desired result on another bill), and the question of "who" is "Congress" (e.g., bill sponsors? staff that author conference reports?). For an excellent description of difficulties in using the idea of "congressional intent," see Eskridge 1988. Lupia and McCubbins (2004, p. 25) note, however, "Social choice theory does not prove that legislative intent is meaningless. Instead, it shows that analysts should be cautious when attempting to draw a meaning from a collective choice."

29. Data on TRI figures by chemical groupings and industries are available from www.epa.gov/triexplorer.

30. *Federal Register* December 1, 1989, 54 FR 49948.

31. *Federal Register* December 1, 1989, 54 FR 49948.

32. *Federal Register* August 3, 1990, 55 FR 31594.

33. *Federal Register* December 1, 1993, 58 FR 63500.

34. *Federal Register* January 12, 1994, 59 FR 1788.

35. See *Federal Register* November 30, 1994, 59 FR 61432, the source of all quotations in this paragraph. Note that if all quotations in a paragraph come from a single source, only the first will be footnoted.

36. House Report 99-962, 99th Congress, Second Session, p. 295, as cited in *Federal Register* November 30, 1994, 59 FR 61432.

37. *Federal Register* June 27, 1996, 61 FR 33588.

38. *Federal Register* May 1, 1997, 62 FR 23834.

39. U.S. Senate 1990a.

40. *Federal Register* January 5, 1999, 64 FR 688.

41. For the proposed rule to add dioxin, see *Federal Register* May 7, 1997, 62 FR 24887.

42. *Federal Register* January 17, 2001, 66 FR 4500.

43. *Federal Register* August 21, 2001, 66 FR 43865 discusses the guidance document; *Federal Register* October 29, 2001, 66 FR 54522 announces the lead workshops.

44. *Federal Register* July 1, 2002, 67 FR 44213. Note that government analysts may have an incentive to overestimate costs in RIAs since underestimated cost figures might be more likely to be challenged by industry in court.

45. *Federal Register* October 1, 1996, 61 FR 51322.

46. U.S. Senate 1988, p. 19.

47. U.S. Senate 1989, p. 37.

48. U.S. House 1989a, p. 39.

49. U.S. House 1990, p. 70. For an examination of the role of experts and hearing testimony in the policy process, see Esterling 2004.

50. *Federal Register* September 25, 1991, 56 FR 48474.

51. *Congressional Record* October 27, 1990, 136 CR S 17512.
52. U.S. Senate 1991, p. 2.
53. U.S. Senate 1991, p. 24.
54. U.S. Senate 1991, p. 38.
55. U.S. Senate 1991, p. 39.
56. Schneider 1991, p. A32.
57. Roy 1992, p. 6.
58. Rotman and Begley 1991.
59. Heller 1992, p. 52.
60. *Utility Environment Report* April 3, 1992, p. 1.
61. Davis 1992.
62. Begley 1992a, p. 9.
63. Begley 1992a, p. 9.
64. *Congressional Record* March 23, 1993, 139 CR S 3411.
65. League of Conservation Voters 1994.
66. Begley 1995a, p. 13.
67. Begley 1995b, p. 10.
68. Begley 1995c, p. 15 and Skrzycki 1995, p. B1.
69. Karey 1995, p. 1.
70. Fairley 1995, p. 17.
71. Fairley 1995, p. 17.
72. Stringer 1995, p. 14. In June 1996, The House Committee on Appropriations voted to cut $1.5 million from the EPA budget to stop spending on agency activities related to potential expansion of the TRI to cover chemical use. Rep. Dick Durbin successfully offered an amendment on the House floor to restore the funds. See Orum 1996.
73. This threshold was later raised to $100 million by an amendment vote; see Begley 1995e, p. 16.
74. Cushman 1995, p. 16.
75. Benenson 1995.
76. Begley 1995d, p. 9. For an analysis of the difficulties associated with regulatory reform and Superfund, see Nakamura and Church 2003.
77. In November 1995, President Clinton vetoed a debt-extension bill to which Republicans had attached their regulatory reform proposals (including requirements for agencies to conduct more benefit-cost analyses and risk assessments when considering new rules). See Kenworthy and Lee 1995.
78. See Working Group on Community Right-to-Know 1995, p. 1., which provides information on the Johnston legislative action on TRI.
79. Working Group on Community Right-to-Know 1995, p. 1.
80. Working Group on Community Right-to-Know 1995, p. 1.
81. Begley 1995f, p. 40.
82. Fairley 1996, p. 18.
83. *Chemical Week* July 31, 1996, p. 52.
84. League of Conservation Voters 1996.
85. *Chemical Week* January 6, 1999, p. 23.
86. See U.S. House 1999a and 1999b.

87. Vise 2000, p. A25. For other discussions of attempts to limit public access to chemical plant risk information, see Hulse 2001, Mary Graham 2002, and Clymer 2003.
88. Samuelsohn 2003.
89. U.S. House 2001, p. 3.
90. U.S. House 2001, p. 9.
91. U.S. House 2002, p. 2.
92. U.S. House 2002, p. 15.
93. U.S. House 2002, p. 22.
94. U.S. House 2002, p. 24.
95. U.S. House 2003, p. 6. Bye noted that in July 2003, EPA had moved to change the TRI form to distinguish between "contained disposal" and "uncontained disposal," but argued that the definitions were still faulty because the EPA said waste placed in surface impoundments and some other land disposal units would be classified as uncontained disposal.
96. U.S. House 2003, p. 16.
97. U.S. House 2003, p. 18. Rep. Tom Udall (D-N.M.), however, pointed out that mines did generate contamination, noting that 87 Superfund sites were former mines. See Coyne 2003.
98. As Chairman of the Senate Committee on Small Business, Senator Bond had asked GAO to review the EPA's OPPTS's implementation of the Regulatory Flexibility Act in the lead rulemaking. This resulted in a September 2000 GAO report on the EPA's economic analysis of the impact on small businesses of the proposal to lower the reporting threshold for lead.
99. *Congressional Record* May 9, 2001, 147 CR S 4597.
100. *Congressional Record* May 9, 2001, 147 CR S 4597.
101. See Wood and Waterman 1994.
102. Beamish 1993.
103. *Federal Register* August 6, 1993, 58 FR 41981. Kagan (2001) discusses in detail how President Clinton exerted influence over regulatory decisions through many avenues, including the use of executive orders.
104. U.S. EPA 2002a, pp. 6–1 and 6–9.
105. *Federal Register* April 26, 2000, 65 FR 24595.
106. See the text of the press briefing at www.ibiblio.org/pub/archives/whitehouse-papers/1995/Aug/1995-08-08-EPA-Administrator-Browner-Briefing-on-Executive-Order.
107. See the text of the speech at Clinton 1995 (vol. 2), p. 1215. Clinton also added an anecdote (p. 1216) to his discussion of right-to-know:

    This is an issue that's very personal with me. I've dealt with the whole issue of right-to-know around chemicals for nearly 20 years now, since I was a young attorney general and a train loaded with chemicals in car after car blew up in a small southern town in the southern part of my State where a relative of mine was the sheriff. And it was just a God's miracle that we didn't have hundreds and hundreds of people killed in this little town. And the first thing that occurred to everybody is: Who knew what about what was on the train?

108. Clinton 1996 (vol. 1), p. 84.

109. Clinton 1996 (vol. 2), p. 1403.
110. Clinton 1996 (vol. 2), p. 1415.
111. Kenworthy 1996, p. A1. For an assessment of the role of efficiency and cost-effectiveness as criteria used in environmental regulation in the 1990s, see Hahn, Olmstead, and Stavins 2003.
112. *PR Newswire* June 26, 1996.
113. Foster 1998, p. 33.
114. *PR Newswire* May 11, 2000a.
115. Harpaz 1999.
116. Marks 1999, p. A20.
117. Lester 2000.
118. *PR Newswire* August 11, 2000b.
119. See Pianin 2001, p. A18. For the notice delaying the effective date of the lead rules 60 days (from February 16, 2001, to April 17, 2001), see *Federal Register* February 16, 2001, 66 FR 10585.
120. Weisman and Hall 2001, p. A8.
121. Shogren 2001, p. A1.
122. Shogren 2001, p. A1.
123. Heilprin 2001.
124. Heilprin 2001.
125. *Chemical Week* April 18, 2001, p. 9.
126. For analysis of court challenges to EPA rules in the 1990s, see Schroeder and Glicksman 2001. Garvie and Lipman (2000) study how the prospect of court challenges affects agency decisions in rulemakings.
127. *Chemical Week* August 30, 1995, p. 5.
128. Stringer 1995, p. 14.
129. *Toxic Chemicals Litigation Reporter* June 4, 1996, p. 23212.
130. *Toxic Chemicals Litigation Reporter* June 4, 1996, p. 23212.
131. Cushman 1996, p. 20.
132. Hebert 1996.
133. Fairley 1996, p. 18.
134. *Toxics Chemicals Litigation Reporter* August 11, 1997, p. 25304.
135. *Toxics Chemicals Litigation Reporter* August 11, 1997, p. 25304.
136. *Hazardous Waste Litigation Reporter* August 18, 1997a, p. 32650.
137. Fairley 1997b, p. 13.
138. Fairley 1997b, p. 13.
139. *Hazardous Waste Litigation Reporter* September 15, 1997b, p. 32688. The ruling was later upheld in the U.S. Court of Appeals for the Third Circuit in 1998.
140. *Hazardous Waste Litigation Reporter* September 15, 1997b, p. 32688.
141. *Toxic Chemicals Litigation Reporter* May 3, 1999, p. 6.
142. *Toxic Chemicals Litigation Reporter* May 3, 1999, p. 6.
143. Hecker 1998.
144. Sissell 1999, p. 16.
145. *PR Newswire* April 20, 1999.
146. *Real Estate/Environmental Liability News* August 4, 2000.
147. *Real Estate/Environmental Liability News* August 4, 2000.

148. For a statistical analysis of the agency's use of "informal rules" such as guidance documents and policy memos in hazardous waste regulation, see Hamilton and Schroeder 1994 and Hamilton 1996a. See Stoll 2001 for a discussion of guidance and due process standards.
149. Villamana 2003.
150. Villamana 2003.
151. *Environmental Laboratory Washington Report* June 20, 2003.
152. *Environmental Laboratory Washington Report* June 20, 2003. In the 2001 district court decision in National Mining Association v. U.S. Environmental Protection Agency (Civil No. 97-N-2665; D. Colo.), the judge upheld the EPA's authority to extend section 313 of EPCRA to cover mining operations.
153. U.S. EPA, Toxics Release Inventory Program Division, 2004a.
154. See Nye 2004 (p. x) for a description of soft power as "the ability to get what you want through attraction rather than coercion or payments."
155. *USA Today* April 3, 1991, p. A13.
156. See *PR Newswire* May 1, 1991c,d and May 10, 1991e; and *Business Wire* May 2, 1991a and May 14, 1991b.
157. *PR Newswire* July 19, 1991f.
158. *Greenwire* June 18, 1991.
159. U.S. EPA 1999a. The 17 targeted chemicals were benzene, carbon tetrachloride, chloroform, dichloromethane, methyl ethyl ketone, methyl isobutyl ketone, tetrachloroethylene, toluene, 1,1,1-trichloroethane, trichloroethylene, xylenes, cadmium and cadmium compounds, chromium and chromium compounds, cyanide compounds, lead and lead compounds, mercury and mercury compounds, and nickel and nickel compounds. U.S. EPA 1999a (p. 5) notes that there were 10,167 firms with plants that had 33/50 chemicals.
160. Cushman 1997, p. A1.
161. Cushman 1997, p. A1.
162. U.S. EPA 1999b.
163. Fairley 1997a, p. 43.
164. U.S. EPA 1999b.
165. Fairley, Mullin, and Foster 1998, p. 24.
166. Sissell 1998, p. 51.
167. Sissell 1998, p. 51.
168. *Environmental Laboratory Washington Report* February 17, 2000.
169. *Environmental Laboratory Washington Report* February 17, 2000.
170. For a description of the RSEI model, see www.epa.gov/opptintr/rsie/faqs.html. The agency submitted the original RSEI model for public comments in 1992. The model went before the EPA's Science Advisory Board three times during its development, including an overall methodology review in 1997.

Five. Life Cycles in the Regulatory Environment

1. See Downs 1972. See also Peters and Hogwood 1985 and Henry and Gordon 2001.
2. Downs 1972, p. 46.

3. For media coverage of the Institute accident, see Diamond 1985 and Noble 1986.

4. Unless otherwise indicated, all polling data in this section come from national surveys conducted by various polling organizations that are archived in the Lexis Public Opinion Online file, which contains information from the Roper Center at the University of Connecticut. I will identify the surveys with their Public Opinion Online accession numbers. Surveys cited in Table 5.1 are from surveys #3316544, #314920, #313049, #302584, and #314953.

5. Surveys mentioned in this paragraph are Public Opinion Online #316553, #61884, #318691, #240677, and #137563.

6. Public Opinion Online #61884.

7. Public Opinion Online #137563.

8. Public Opinion Online #18847.

9. Public Opinion Online #2540.

10. Arnold (1990) points out that Congress members care about the potential preferences their constituents may hold on election day. Polling by interest groups on issues before the prime election season can be used to demonstrate to Congress members how constituents might react if a particular issue were highlighted and can give interest groups insight into what political dimensions (e.g., perceptions) to emphasize. For a discussion of the manipulation of political dimensions, see Riker 1986.

11. Surveys in Table 5.2 come from Public Opinion Online #386430, #355905, #385932, and #402980.

12. The priority for political action that individuals place on issues can be a function of the real-world incidence of problems, media coverage, and the emphasis that leaders and interest groups place on a topic. See Iyengar and Kinder 1987, Baumgartner and Jones 1993, and McCombs, Shaw, and Weaver 1997.

13. Public Opinion Online #87222 for July 1990 data, #321223 for January 1999.

14. Public Opinion Online #26290 for May 1989, #400365 for March 2002.

15. Public Opinion Online #299924 July 1990, #289085 October 1994, and #390989 April 2001.

16. See Downs 1957.

17. See Hamilton 2004.

18. For a related discussion of the impact of war and the economy on attention to the environment, see Harden 2004.

19. The five newspapers were *Boston Globe, Christian Science Monitor, New York Times, St. Petersburg Times,* and *USA Today.* The number of total articles across these five outlets mentioning the TRI per year were eight in 1989, two in 1990, 13 in 1991, eight in 1992, two in 1993, four in 1994, 11 in 1995, seven in 1996, two in 1997, seven in 1998, eight in 1999, four in 2000, one in 2001, three in 2002, and three in 2003. For 1989, *USA Today* had seven of the eight articles.

20. See Flavin 1989, Kalette 1989, Tyson and Morris 1989, and *USA Today* 1989.

21. For a discussion of the way media outlets frame stories, see Entman 1993 and 2004.

22. See Environmental Health Center 1989, p. 6. This is a guidebook released in 1989 to help journalists use the TRI in stories.
23. Tyson and Morris 1989, p. A1.
24. Merrill 2002, p. H1.
25. MacLean and Orum 1992, p. 8.
26. For overviews of how TRI data are used, see Working Group on Community Right-to-Know 1994, MacLean 1995, Patten 2002, and EPA 2003b.
27. The low demand for public affairs information may translate into reduced incentives for reporters to acquire training to cover technical subjects involving regulation. See Hamilton 1991. For a description of the particular challenges faced by environmental reporters, see Friedman, Dunwoody, and Rogers 1999 and Nieman Foundation 2002.
28. For example, see the statements by Rep. James Florio at U.S. Senate 1988, p. 19 and Sen. Frank Lautenberg at U.S. Senate 1988, p. 61.
29. U.S. GAO 1991, p. 49.
30. Lancaster 1989, p. A6.
31. *PR Newswire* October 22, 1990.
32. *PR Newswire* 1991a,b. For an analysis of how the press in general cover EPA regulatory actions, see Coglianese and Howard 1998.
33. *Chemical Week* June 16, 1993.
34. See Rasinski 2000.
35. For the years FY 1989–1995, civil complaints issued under 313 peaked in FY 1993. The figures for civil complaints issued under 313 were 124 in 1989, 206 in 1990, 179 in 1991, 134 in 1992, 219 in 1993, 178 in 1994, and 139 in 1995. In terms of settled EPCRA 313 cases and total final administrative penalties assessed, the figures were 1989, 121 ($2,450,561); 1990, 193 ($4,186,428); 1991, 160 ($3,038,135); 1992, 129 ($2,608,651); 1993, 118 ($2,852,935); 1994, 121 ($3,017,279); and 1995, 69 ($1,032,304). See U.S. EPA 1996, p. A-33. Inspection totals for 313 in later years come from the EPA annual *Enforcement and Compliance Assurance Accomplishments Report*. See, for example, U.S. EPA 2000a.
36. For dollar value of enforcement actions, see the yearly editions of the EPA *Enforcement and Compliance Assurance Accomplishments Report*. Note that a report for FY 2000 is not available.
37. Magat and Viscusi (1990) estimate an average compliance rate of 75% in the early 1980s in the paper and pulp industry. For analyses of firm and agency incentives in environmental regulation compliance and enforcement, see Deily and Gray 1991, Spence 2001, Winter and May 2001, Firestone 2002, and Stafford 2002, 2003. Naysnerski and Tietenberg (1992) examine the role of private enforcement in environmental law.
38. The expected probability of inspection would be even lower if the facility believed the EPA was considering an even larger pool of plants as potential nonfilers (and hence possible targets for inspection).
39. For the EPA estimates of the paperwork burden, see *Federal Register* September 10, 1992, 57 FR 41496.
40. Data in U.S. Census 1995 indicate that entry-level positions for chemical engineers with a bachelor's degree paid close to $20 per hour (i.e., $40,000

median salary per year) in 1993. The EPA's 2003 estimate of labor costs in its Paperwork Reduction Act submission to OMB implies a wage rate of $46/hour for those involved in filling out Form Rs. See *Federal Register* October 31, 2003, 68 FR 62069.

41. In its penalty policy statement involving other sections of EPCRA (i.e., sections 304, 311, and 312), the EPA estimates the gains from not filing as avoiding the costs of filling out the forms and uses wage rates of $100/hour for legal work, $37.72/hour for manager time, $27.90/hour for technical analysis, and $16.69/hour for clerical work. See U.S. EPA 1999c.

42. See U.S. EPA 2001.

43. Many of the details about current EPCRA enforcement policies presented here come from a personal interview with Thomas Marvin, EPA Headquarters, Washington, D.C., April 23, 2004.

44. See Smith 1993 for a legal analysis of an early EPCRA citizen suit brought by Atlantic States Legal Foundation.

45. See Green 1999.

46. See U.S. EPA 2002b, p. 1, and p. 9 (Appendix 1).

47. Hess 2000.

48. Borenstein 2003.

49. See U.S. GAO 2002. The counts of FTE positions refer to those involved in civil enforcement, compliance monitoring, and incentive programs (non-Superfund).

50. Counts of federal administrative law judge decisions dealing with EPCRA 313 by year are one, 1989; three, 1991; one, 1992; two, 1994; eight, 1995; two, 1996; five, 1997; ten, 1998; five, 1999; six, 2000; two, 2001; two, 2002; and one, 2003. See the Lexis Federal Environmental Agency Decisions file. Parties may appeal an administrative law judge decision to the EPA's Environmental Appeals Board (EAB). If private parties disagree with the EAB decision, they may take the case to the federal courts.

51. A search of state environmental agency decision files in Lexis yielded 16 cases dealing with EPCRA reporting. A similar search of state environmental law cases yielded 10 EPCRA cases.

52. For details on the intra- and interagency interactions involving the TRI, I draw on personal interviews conducted in Washington, D.C., on April 22–23, 2004, with EPA officials Maria Doa, John Dombrowski, Thomas Marvin, Cody Rice, and Sam Sasnett.

53. See Elliott 2003, p. 56. The review process is also described in Elliott 1994. Ferejohn (1987) and McGarity (1991) explore how the internal structure of agency decisionmaking affects rulemakings.

54. The mean review time in 2001 for the 700 regulations examined by OMB was 58 days. See OMB 2002.

55. Begley 1992b, p. 12.

56. Begley 1992c.

57. Sheridan 1992, p. 69.

58. Sheridan 1992.

59. Fairley 1997c, p. 38.

60. Robins 1997.

61. Fairley 1997d, p. 17.
62. See John Graham 2002.
63. Nelson 2002.
64. OMB 2001. In 2001, OMB also issued guidelines on the quality of data released by agencies, which were revised in 2002. Many environmentalists saw the attempt to place stricter requirements for quality control and to increase public comment on an agency's release of data as a way to raise the costs to the government of providing information. The report, titled "Poisonous Procedural 'Reform': In Defense of Environmental Right to Know," by Echeverria and Kaplan (2002) conveys how some viewed the OMB's efforts to change the way agencies treat the release of reported data.
65. Franz 2002.
66. See U.S. EPA 2003a. For an announcement of the phase II dialogue, see *Federal Register* November 5, 2003, 68 FR 62579. Though it was termed a dialogue, the TRI program officials did not engage in a back-and-forth exchange with commenters during the posting of suggestions and comments from the public. Agency officials feared that responses might be used as guidance and be the subject of future litigation about interpretation of rules.
67. *Chemical Week* 2003, p. 33.
68. OMB 2004.
69. For a description of TRI reporting burden estimates, see *Federal Register* September 26, 1990, 55 FR 39321; September 10, 1992, 57 41496; December 28, 1999, 64 FR 72657; December 4, 2002, 67 FR 72166; and October 31, 2003, 68 FR 62069.
70. Skrzycki 2003, p. E1. For analyses of the accuracy of estimates of regulatory compliance costs, see Hodges 1997; Harrington, Morgenstern, and Nelson 1999; and Hahn and Litan 2002a,b.
71. Skrzycki 2003, p. E1.
72. Heilprin 2003.
73. Heilprin 2003.
74. Skrzycki 2003, P. E1.
75. Carpenter (1996) explores how budget decisions can influence agency actions by signaling the interests of Congress members and the President. Wood (1988) and Wood and Waterman (1991) examine how EPA enforcement dropped in response to budget cuts in the Reagan administration. Brown (1994) offers a formal model of how which party controls the White House affects environmental policy.
76. See Samuelsohn 2004 for a discussion of the EPA's FY 2004 and FY 2005 budgets.
77. Coyne 2004.
78. *Federal Register* October 31, 2003, 68 FR 62069.
79. *Federal Register* October 31, 2003, 68 FR 62069.

Six. The Impact(s) of the TRI

1. For analyses of the advantages and disadvantages of using information provision as a policy tool, see Ashford and Caldart 1985; Beales, Craswell,

and Salop 1981; Sarokin and Schulkin 1991; Barsa 1997; Kleindorfer and Orts 1998; Tietenberg 1998, 1999; Livernois and McKenna 1999; Pfaff and Sanchirico 1999; Sunstein 1999; Bhojraj, Blacconiere, and D'Souza 2000; Gormley 2000; Schroeder 2000; Case 2001; Cohen 2001; Dranove, Kessler, McClellan, and Satterthwaite 2002; Weiss 2002; and Jin and Leslie 2003. Related work on the economics of information includes Milgrom and Roberts 1986, Farrell 1987, and Stiglitz 2000.

2. TRI studies generally treat the existence of state laws as exogenous and interpret the coefficient on a particular law variable in a regression as measuring the impact of the existence of that legislation. If states that pass toxics laws differ in systematic ways from other states and these differences are not well modeled in the analyses, then interpreting the law coefficients as representing only the influence of the policy may be more problematic. For an analysis that uses TRI data to construct independent variables that help explain which states are more likely to have laws that reward firms for voluntarily reporting and correcting environmental violations, see Videras 2003.

3. Grant 1997, p. 859. In cross-sectional analysis of 1991 TRI releases by state, Grant and Downey (1995) find that releases are lower in states with special state right-to-know programs. They report (p. 345), based on data published in 1991, that "20 states have gone beyond the federal requirements of Title III to establish a special program that actively disseminates information on the polluting activities of local manufacturers." In cross-sectional analysis using 1992 TRI data, Terry and Yandle (1997) conclude (p. 438), "The estimates support the notion that highly educated individuals assign a value to lower emissions levels and take action to bring about reductions. Higher population density appears to reduce the cost of responding to TRI; it is associated with lower per capita TRI STACK air emissions." For research on the role of states in federal environmental regulation, see Sigman 2003.

4. Yu et al. 1998, p. 577.

5. Maxwell, Lyon, and Hackett 2000, p. 587. They focus on changes between 1988 and 1992 in the toxicity-weighted pounds of 17 TRI chemicals per $1,000 of shipments (deflated) from seven manufacturing industries in a state.

6. Kraft, Abel, and Stephan 2004, p. 8. They focus their analysis on the 1991 core chemicals to facilitate comparisons across years. In later work, they plan to expand their statistical analysis and incorporate additional evidence from surveys and case studies they will conduct.

7. Kraft, Abel, and Stephan 2004, p. 13.

8. Grant and Jones (2003, p. 168) explain that "our dependent variable, emission rate, is operationalized as the ratio of annual pounds of chemicals released onsite (weighted by their toxicity) to the annual pounds of chemicals stored and used onsite (also weighted by their toxicity)."

9. Grant and Jones 2003, p. 172.

10. Khanna, Kumar, and Anton 2002, p. 22.

11. Author communications with researchers such as Shanti Gamper-Rabindran and Lori Bennear. Combining 1987 TRI information with Census Bureau information on plant-level economic activity at more than 2,100 facilities in the chemical industry, Streitwieser (1994) found (p. 3) that "intra-industry

variation in toxic waste releases is frequently greater than inter-industry variation" and that "certain firms are consistently better... at minimizing toxic releases, either through managerial ability or other unmeasured effects." As outlined in Kraft, Abel, and Stephan (2004), researchers also plan to survey firm decisionmakers, regulators, and environmentalists in selected communities to analyze the mechanisms by which the TRI affects corporate environmental decisions.

12. Helland and Whitford 2003, p. 403.
13. Santos, Covello, and McCallum 1996, p. 60.
14. Santos, Covello, and McCallum 1996, p. 62. Plant community information programs varied by facility size. Fifty-nine percent of plants with 200 or more employees reported having such communication programs, versus less than 20% of plants with fewer than 50 workers.
15. Shapiro 2003, p. 27.
16. U.S. EPA 1999a. Coglianese (undated) notes that the EPA originally called the program the Industrial Toxics Project but changed the name to 33/50 Program after industry objected to the original title.
17. For overviews of firm incentives to join voluntary pollution reduction programs (including 33/50), see Lyon and Maxwell (1999) and Khanna (2001). O'Toole et al. (1997) examine variations across states in 33/50 participation.
18. There is a large literature on why firms join voluntary pollution reduction programs sponsored by government, industry trade associations (e.g., the Responsible Care Program of the Chemical Manufacturers Association), or a third party (e.g., the ISO 14001 environmental standards established by the International Organization for Standardization) and what the impacts of these programs may be. Researchers have also explored why firms may choose voluntarily to adopt environmental management systems. For theoretical models and empirical assessments of these questions, see Arora and Gangopadhyay 1995; Harford 1997; Segerson and Miceli 1998; Wu and Babcock 1999; Case 2000; Alberini and Segerson 2002; Anton, Deltas, and Khanna 2002; and Potoski and Prakash (forthcoming). A series of assessments focus on the Responsible Care Program: U.S. PIRG 1998, King and Lenox 2000; Lenox and Nash 2001, and King and Lenox 2002. Coglianese and Lazer (2003) explore what they term "management-based regulation," in which the government requires firms to undertake a planning process, which may in turn affect decisions because of the information and ideas developed internally through this process. They point to the Massachusetts Toxic Use Reduction Act (TURA) as an example, noting (p. 700), "TURA requires firms that use large quantities of toxic chemicals to analyze the use and flow of chemicals throughout the facilities, develop plans to reduce toxics use, and submit planning reports to state environmental agencies...." Assessing the implementation of TURA, Coglianese and Nash (2004, p. 160) conclude that even though "TURA has had a more limited impact than widely assumed and one that appears unsustainable over the long term, it is nevertheless possible that management-based regulation may still be a more effective strategy in addressing problems that require constant vigilance, such as the prevention of chemical accidents or the management of leaks and spills."

19. Khanna and Damon 1999, p. 16. They point out that the 17 33/50 chemicals were included in the 189 toxics covered by the 1990 Clean Air Act Amendments, which meant they were headed for regulation under Maximum Available Control Technology (MACT) standards by 2000. Khanna and Damon (p. 6) point out that because of this future regulation, firms might seek advantages through earlier reductions and that the flexibility involved in voluntary reductions might help "lower their future costs of compliance with NESHAP" (the National Emission Standards for Hazardous Air Pollutants).
20. Khanna and Damon 1999, p. 19.
21. Gamper-Rabindran 2004, p. 2.
22. Vidovic and Khanna 2003a, p. 3. Vidovic and Khanna (2003b) find using plant level data that the characteristics of the surrounding community generally did influence a facility's decision of whether to join the 33/50 Program. In particular, the higher the median household income in the zip code of the plant's location, the more likely the facility is to participate in 33/50.
23. Konar and Cohen 1997, p. 123.
24. Konar and Cohen 1997, p. 123.
25. Khanna, Quimio, and Bojilova 1998, p. 245.
26. Khanna, Quimio, and Bojilova 1998, p. 245.
27. Konar and Cohen 2001, p. 281. For another analysis using TRI data to explore the relationship between environmental and financial performance, see Cohen, Fenn, and Konar 1997.
28. U.S. GAO 1991, p. 34.
29. See Bui and Mayer 2003, p. 695. Hedonic housing price studies at Superfund sites demonstrate that homeowners do react to the provision of risk information (e.g., the site remedial investigation (RI) report, which contains risk data). Gayer, Hamilton, and Viscusi (2000, 2002) find that residents around Superfund sites are willing to pay a premium to avoid the cancer risks associated with the sites and that housing prices increase after the release of the RI, suggesting that the information lowers the perceived levels of risk. Newspaper publicity about the local sites increased housing prices, suggesting that residents perceived the news as good.
30. Lynn and Kartez 1994, p. 517.
31. Coglianese and Lazer (2003) describe in depth the operation of management-based regulation.
32. U.S. EPA 1998a, p. iv.
33. U.S. EPA 1998b, p. x.
34. Dudley 1999b, p. 7. Dudley also notes (p. 6), "Almost 3 percent of TRI latitudes and longitudes place the facilities in the wrong county, and 0.75% of the facilities are reported to be in the wrong state."
35. Poje and Horowitz 1990, p. 1.
36. Natan and Miller 1998, p. 368.
37. Natan and Miller 1998, p. 368.
38. Working Group on Community Right-to-Know 1991, p. i. Later changes to the Form R made in response to the Pollution Prevention Act of 1990 added more data to the TRI about source reduction and off-site recycling.

39. U.S. EPA 2002b.
40. U.S. EPA 2004c, p. 4.
41. They compare the percentage change in average reported TRI air releases for each of the 12 chemicals with the percentage change in the average concentration of the chemical for monitors surrounding TRI facilities. There may be many reasons why reported TRI releases have dropped for some chemicals more than average measured concentrations. Firms could be strategically overestimating their reductions. However, it may also be the case that monitors are not placed near TRI plants, so there need not be an expected correspondence between emissions and concentrations. Large changes in average TRI emissions could be based on a relatively small number of plants, or sources other than TRI plants could be driving the average concentrations. De Marchi and Hamilton are currently using GIS analysis to link up TRI plants with the monitors that are nearby in order to examine in more detail how reported changes match monitored values at the facility level.

    A report assessing the accuracy of TRI data by the Environmental Integrity Project and the Galveston-Houston Association for Smog Prevention (2004) concluded, "The official TRI... tells only part of the story because it dramatically underestimates the amount of toxic pollution from the petrochemical industry. The Texas Commission on Environmental Quality (TCEQ) has conducted studies which demonstrate the extent to which emissions of toxic chemicals from petrochemical facilities in Texas are underreported. This report applies the TCEQ's findings nationwide and reveals that emissions of toxic chemicals, including known carcinogens such as benzene and butadiene, are four to five times higher than is reflected in the TRI."

42. Accurate data can be obtained about emissions, though this entails a price. Henriquez (2004) points out the role that information technology plays in the EPA's SO_2 emissions trading program. Every emissions unit participating in the program has to have a Continuous Emissions Monitoring System (CEMS) that allows the tracking and reporting of emissions. Henriquez notes (p. 11):

    This technology has provided credibility and facilitated the emergence of a relatively efficient market for SO_2 allowances, despite the expense of deploying the monitoring system – an average annual cost of about $124,000 per unit (including operating and capital costs). Capital and operating costs of CEMS amounted to 7% of total observed compliance costs in 1995. The estimated total additional cost is not insignificant – $48 million to $54 million – but the payoff is high-quality data and documentation of early environmental benefits from emissions reductions.

43. Snyder 2004, p. 75.
44. Case study information in this paragraph comes from Settina and Orum 1991.
45. *PR Newswire* 1988.
46. Lambrecht 1991, p. B1.
47. Steyer 1991, p. B1. This article also noted that Monsanto produced "96 of some 320 chemicals on the EPA list."
48. Kirschner 1993, p. 7.
49. *Greenwire* 1993.

50. Kirschner 1993, p. 7.
51. MacLean and Orum 1992, p. 15.
52. MacLean and Orum 1992, p. 22.
53. U.S. EPA 2003b, p. 7.
54. U.S. EPA 2003b, p. 15.
55. Working Group on Community Right-to-Know 1994.
56. See MacLean 1995 for a description of the use of the Right-to-Know Computer Network (RTK NET) by environmental activists interested in TRI data.
57. U.S. EPA 2003b, p. 1.
58. Stephan (2002) offers an excellent overview too of the empirical evidence on how and why the TRI may work. For discussions of the particular challenges posed by regulating (or calculating) risks from toxics, see Applegate 1992; Macauley, Bowes, and Palmer 1992; VanDoren 1999; Roe 2002; and Farber 2003.
59. Pedersen (2001) in part offers an environmental law critique of the TRI. For other environmental law descriptions of the TRI and information provision, see Wolf 1996, Reitze and Schell 1999, and Durham-Hammer 2004. Jobe (1999) tells the story of the TRI through the lens of electronic database evolution. For a broader analysis of how electronic information provision may affect rulemaking and regulatory policy, see Coglianese 2004. Beierle 1998, 2000 and Beierle and Cahill 2000 explore how public participation works in environmental policymaking.
60. Pedersen 2001, p. 168. Note that the transaction costs of generating the TRI data may vary by facility size.
61. Pedersen 2001, p. 170.
62. Tietenberg and Wheeler 1998, p. 9.
63. Karkkainen 2001, p. 339.
64. Fung, Graham, and Weil (2003, p. 23) emphasize the role played by Sens. Robert Stafford (R-Vt.), Frank Lautenberg (D-N.J.), and Lloyd Bentsen (D-Tex.) in getting the TRI passed in the Senate. Mary Graham (2002, p. 29) relates in detail how environmentalists played a role in interesting Senate staffers in information provision. Prior to Bhopal, a team of analysts at the environmental research organization Inform had been trying to study chemical use at a set of plants. David Sarokin, director of the effort, said, "It became an impossible exercise to put the whole picture together.... Each federal program had a different way of classifying materials and of collecting information from facilities.... Companies generally knew as little about their waste streams as the regulators did. They were providing data that were required by law and weren't generating any information beyond that. Their people simply were not trained to pay attention to waste." After Bhopal, Senate Committee on Environment and Public Works staff member Richard Outen asked Sarokin and Warren Muir to outline for committee staff the case for a standardized reporting system for toxics. In Outen's assessment, "That was a critical meeting.... After that, it was a matter of dragging the proposal through the legislative maze." According to Sarokin, "Once Bhopal got the attention of Congress, the Superfund reauthorization was a train that

was moving and we were able [to] jump on it with this right-to-know car."
These quotations come from Mary Graham 2002 (pp. 29–31), which offers an
extensive analysis of the origins and evolution of the TRI. For an overview
of the use of information in risk regulation, see Graham 2001.

65. Fung, Graham, and Weil (2002, p. 13). They also define (pp. 128–129) four
characteristics of information provided in successful disclosure programs:
metrics that are accepted and well understood, simple formats, data that
"users or intermediaries can be able to rationally react to," and data that can
be compared easily across different sources (e.g., plants).

66. The descriptions of these stages are taken verbatim from Figure 1 on p. 11 of
Fung, Graham, Weil, and Fagotto 2004.

67. Fung, Graham, Weil, and Fagotto 2004, p. 7.

68. Fung and O'Rourke 2000, p. 120. Scorse (2004) uses the addition of new
reporting industries to the TRI in 1998, which affected the relative pollution
rankings of facilities already reporting in the TRI, to explore if relative pollution rankings affect facility behavior. He finds (p. 1) "firms do respond to
pollution rankings and that the magnitude is significant. Facilities in industries originally covered by the TRI reduced their emissions by as much as
hundreds of millions of pounds less than they would have had they not experienced improvements in their rankings brought about by the introduction
of the new highly polluting industries."

69. Mary Graham 2002, p. 22.

70. Mary Graham 2002, p. 23.

71. Mary Graham 2002, p. 58. The Environmental Defense website www.
scorecard.org, developed by Bill Pease at a start-up cost of $1.5 million,
took the TRI data and reinterpreted it in ways that went beyond the EPA's
presentation of the data. Scorecard eventually provided an option to rank
facilities by the cancer risks created by their air emissions.

72. Mary Graham 2002, p. 157.

73. See Mary Graham 2002, Chapter 2 and Graham and Miller 2001 for detailed
discussions of the patterns evident in the TRI data when one goes beyond
analysis of national totals.

74. Dudley 2002, p. 5.

75. Dudley 1999a, p. 11. Assessing in 1997 the EPA's proposed phase III expansion of the TRI to include materials accounting information that would allow
individuals to track chemical use at a facility, Clay (1997) concluded that the
collection of the data could impinge on intellectual property rights, that the
EPA might lack statutory authority to collect the data, and that the information might only be of limited use to citizens. For a discussion of the benefits
of requiring data on the production and use of chemicals at TRI facilities,
see Sheiman 1991. Schierow (1997) outlines both the advantages and disadvantages associated with TRI expansion. Volokh, Green, and Scarlett (1998)
focus on the problems with the design of the TRI.

76. Dudley 1999a, p. 12.

77. OMB Watch 2001, p. 7.

78. OMB Watch 2001, p. 30. As the report explained citizen monitoring, "EPA
could draw from the many community groups that are monitoring water

quality according to EPA guidelines from Louisiana to Alaska. Under this model, strengthened citizen monitors would have authority to recommend that EPA levy fines for significant errors.... EPA could also require submitters to pay for independent audits of their data submissions in order to ensure accuracy and completeness."

79. Commission for Racial Justice 1987, p. xv.
80. Cole 1992.
81. U.S. EPA 1992a,b.
82. Weisskopf 1992.
83. For a review of the early environmental equity literature and examples of analyses that use the expansion decisions of hazardous waste processing facilities, see Hamilton 1993 and 1995b. Hamilton 2005 reviews evidence on environmental equity and the operation of hazardous waste facilities in OECD countries. OECD 2004 analyzes evidence on environmental equity gathered from many different countries and discusses how to incorporate environmental equity into public policies. U.S. EPA 2004f examines international experiences with an array of environmental policies, including information provision programs.
84. For a test of these theories in the context of hazardous waste, see Hamilton 1995b. Hamilton and Viscusi (1999) explore different measures of environmental equity at Superfund sites.
85. For analyses of the role of market dynamics in the relationship between demographics and pollution, see Been 1993, 1994 and Been and Gupta 1997. Banzhaf and Walsh (2004) examine evidence on how communities change over time in response to the actions of TRI facilities and conclude (p. 5), "We find clear evidence of migration correlated with TRI facility emissions and their arrival or exit from a 'community.' Futhermore, we find significant evidence that TRI facilities cause the composition of a community to become less white over time."
86. Millimet and Slottje 1999, p. 25.
87. Daniels and Friedman 1999, p. 244. For other research using TRI figures at the county level, see Cutter and Solecki 1996 (which focuses on toxic air releases in the southeastern U.S.) and Thomas, Kodamanchaly, and Harveson 1998 (which examines the relationships among cancer rates, demographics, and toxic releases in Texas).
88. Ringquist 1997, p. 811.
89. Arora and Cason 1998, p. 413.
90. Iceland and Steinmetz (2003) investigate the differences in analyzing housing patterns at the census tract versus block group level and note (p. 2), "Block groups are clusters of census blocks created by the Census Bureau as a geographic level between blocks and census tracts to permit the release of tabulated data that cannot be presented at the block level for confidentiality purposes. Block groups generally contain between 600 and 3,000 people and never cross the boundaries of states or counties; census tracts consist of one or more block groups. Census tracts, which typically have between 1,500 and 8,000 people, with an average size of about 4,000 people, are defined with local input, are intended to represent neighborhoods (they are designed to be

relatively homogeneous with respect to population characteristics, economic statues, and living conditions)."

91. Zimmerman (1994) describes measurement problems that arise in defining race and ethnicity in environmental equity studies. Bowen (2002) offers a critical review of the environmental justice literature.

92. Bouwes, Hassur, and Shapiro 2001, p. 8. Cutter, Scott, and Hill (2002) use six different measures of toxicity to examine the relative risks of TRI facilities in South Carolina. Graham et al. (1999) use plant-level risk information (i.e., maximum individual cancer risk figures calculated for a set of coke ovens in 1984) and TRI data to study the relative risks of coke plants and oil refineries. They conclude (p. 171), "Rank ordering of facilities by race, poverty, and pollution produces limited (although not consistent) evidence that the more risky facilities tend to be operating in communities with above-median proportions of nonwhite residents (near coke plants) and Hispanic residents (near oil refineries)."

93. Bouwes, Hassur, and Shapiro 2001, p. 18.

94. Wolverton 2002, p. 7. Szasz and Meuser (2000) examine census data from 1960 to 1990 and 1989 TRI data in Santa Clara County, California, in exploring measurements of environmental equity in that area. Hockman and Morris (1998, p. 157) use TRI information as one environmental indicator in a "five year perspective of toxicity, race, and poverty in Michigan, 1990–1995." Gray and Shadbegian (2002) do not employ TRI data but do examine a related question, how regulator activity varies with the nature of the community surrounding a facility. Examining inspections and enforcement actions at approximately 300 pulp and paper mills from 1985 to 1997 they determine:

> The results suggest substantial differences in the weights assigned to different types of people: the benefits received by out-of-state people seem to count only half as much as benefits received in-state, although their weight increases if the bordering state's Congressional delegation is strongly pro-environment.... One set of results was consistently contrary to expectations: plants with more nonwhites nearby emit less pollution.

95. U.S. EPA 1998c, section 5.1.

96. U.S. EPA 2004e, p. i. For a discussion of environmental justice issues in EPA permitting, see U.S. EPA 2000b. Bullard (1990) helped spark debate about environmental equity; see also Bullard 1993. For other analyses relating to environmental justice, see Centner, Kriesel, and Keeler 1996; Foreman 1998; O'Leary et al. 1999; Lazarus 2000/2001; and Tietenberg 2002.

97. For a description of Pollutant Release and Transfer Registers (PRTRs) across the world, see www.epa.gov/tri/programs/prtrs.htm. For an analysis across many countries of voluntary approaches in environmental policymaking, see OECD 2003. Sand (2004) examines the worldwide growth of environmental information disclosure programs. Wiener (1999) explores how the selection of environmental policy instruments works in a global context.

98. See U.S. EPA 2004d.

99. See Commission for Environmental Cooperation of North America 2003. For a proposal to require firms based in the United States or traded on U.S. stock exchanges to disclose detailed information (e.g., data about environmental, labor, and human rights practices) on their operations abroad, see International Right to Know Campaign 2003.
100. Commission for Environmental Cooperation of North America 2003, p. 7.
101. For an analysis of the determinants of environmental disclosure among Canadian firms from 1986 to 1993, see Cormier and Magnan 1999. For analyses using factory pollution information and air pollution data from England and Wales to examine environmental justice issues, see Friends of the Earth 1999, 2001 and McLeod et al. 2000.
102. Harrison and Antweiler 2003, p. 371.
103. Afsah, Blackman, and Ratunanda 2000, p. 8. For an analysis of informal pollution regulation in Indonesia, see Pargal and Wheeler 1996.

Seven. Lessons from and for Regulatory Implementation

1. See U.S. EPA 2004g, the source for many of the TRI figures in this section, and EPA analysis of the 2002 data posted at www.epa.gov/tri/. The scaleback in TRI program resources is reflected in part in the contrast between the 2002 public data report, which totaled eight pages and directed interested parties to online analyses and databases for more information, and the 2001 public data report (U.S. EPA 2003c), which contained more than 350 pages of tables and analysis.
2. According to data in U.S. EPA 2003c, 20.3% of the TRI facilities that filed Form Rs in 2001 indicated they had engaged in source reduction activities. The 2001 public data report aggregated the TRI information by state, industry, chemical, and medium of release. A separate publication (U.S. EPA 2003d) analyzed the data in detail by state and offered lists of the top ten facilities in each state by on-site releases, on-site and off-site releases, and production-related waste management. EPA websites with TRI data include Envirofacts (www.epa.gov/enviro/) and TRI Explorer (www.epa.gov/triexplorer/). For public interest group websites that offer TRI information, see the Environmental Defense's Scorecard (www.scorecard.org) and OMB Watch's RTK Net (www.rtknet.org).
3. The EPA TRI website (www.epa.gov/tri/tridata/tri02/press/sum8802ad1.pdf) notes that the comparisons between 1988 and 2002 data do "not include delisted chemicals, chemicals added in 1990, 1994, and 1995, aluminum oxide, ammonia, hydrochloric acid, PBT chemicals, sulfuric acid, vanadium and vanadium compounds."
4. See U.S. EPA 2003c, pp. 1–20. The report notes (pp. 1–20), "Source reduction is defined in the Pollution Prevention Act of 1990 as any practice that: reduces the amount of any hazardous substance, pollutant, or contaminant entering any wastestream or otherwise released into the environment (including fugitive emissions); and reduces the hazards to public health and the environment associated with the release of such substances, pollutants, and contaminants. Source reduction practices can include modifications in

equipment, process, procedure, or technology, reformulation or redesign of products, substitution of raw materials, and improvements in maintenance and inventory controls."

5. U.S. EPA 2003c, p. ES-26.
6. Baumol and Oates (1988, p. 17) define an externality by two conditions:

> Condition 1. An externality is present whenever some individual's (say A's) utility or production relationships include real (that is, nonmonetary) variables, whose values are chosen by others (persons, corporations, governments) without particular attention to the effects on A's welfare....

> Condition 2. The decision maker, whose activity affects others' utility levels or enters their production functions, does not receive (pay) in compensation for this activity an amount equal in value to the resulting benefits (or costs) to others.

7. See *Federal Register* November 30, 1994, 59 FR 61432. The agency declared in the Regulatory Assessment Requirements section, "The market failure that this rule is intended to correct is the externality created by the lack of information available to citizens about the releases and transfers of toxic chemicals in their communities."
8. See *Federal Register* June 27, 1996, 61 FR 33588.
9. *Federal Register* June 27, 1996, 61 FR 33588. The economic analysis in the proposed rule went on to note:

> If EPA were to take no action, i.e., not add industries to TRI, the market failure (and the associated social costs) resulting from the lack of information on releases and waste management practices would continue. EPA believes that adding the proposed industry groups to the EPCRA section 313 list of facilities will improve the scope of multi-media data on releases and transfers of toxic chemicals. This, in turn, will provide information to communities, empower communities to play a meaningful role in environmental decision-making, improve the quality of environmental decision-making by government officials, and provide useful information to facilities themselves.

10. See *Federal Register* June 27, 1996, 61 FR 33588. The EPA's economic analysis acknowledges that the TRI information generates both intrinsic and instrumental value. The agency asserts:

> There are two types of benefits associated with TRI reporting – direct and follow-on. The first type of benefit is direct, the pure value of information on releases, transfers and other waste management practices. It is expected that this rulemaking will generate benefits by providing the public with access to information that otherwise would not be available to them. The direct benefits of the rule by itself include improvements in access, understanding, awareness and decision-making related to the provision and distribution of information.

> The second types of benefit derive from changes in behavior that result from the information reported to TRI. The changes in behavior, including reductions in the releases and changes in the waste management practices for toxic chemicals, yield health and environmental benefits. These changes in behavior come at some cost to industry, and the net benefits of the follow-on activities are the difference between the benefits of decreased chemical releases and transfers and the costs of the actions needed to achieve the decrease. These follow-on activities, however, are not required by the rule.

11. Esty (2004) provides an excellent overview of the current and future role of information in environmental policy. He traces out how information emerges (or fails to emerge) in particular market and political settings, notes the circumstances under which better data can improve environmental decision-making, and predicts that continued changes in technology will allow information to play an even more prominent role in environmental protection. Coglianese (2004) explores how changes in information technology may in particular affect the rulemaking process.

12. For a discussion of the risk versus risk trade-offs that are often involved in environmental policy, see Graham and Wiener 1995.

13. Personal communications with scholars such as Lori Bennear, Scott de Marchi, Shanti Gamper-Rabindran, and Mark Stephan.

14. See Arrow et al. 1996. For discussions of the issues involved in benefit-cost analysis, see Stavins 2000, Sunstein 2000, Frank and Sunstein 2001, Posner 2001, Hahn and Sunstein 2002, Lowenstein and Revesz 2004, and Sunstein 2004. On issues related to risk regulation, see Sunstein 2003 and Coglianese and Marchant 2004. Bennear and Coglianese (2004) stress the need for more evaluations of how environmental policies have actually worked, noting (p. 2), "Relatively little analysis takes place after decisions have been made and implemented, which is when program evaluation occurs. Yet anyone who takes analysis and deliberation seriously before decisions are made should also take seriously the need for research after decisions are made." For empirical evidence on how violation of environmental policies may affect firm incentives, see the stock market analyses of Karpoff, Lott, and Wehrly (2004), who conclude (p. 2) "that legal penalties, not reputational penalties, are the primary deterrents to environmental violations."

15. Farber (1999, p. 201) summarizes the guidelines that arise from eco-pragmitism as:

   When a reasonably ascertainable risk reaches a significant level, take all feasible steps to abate it except when costs would clearly overwhelm any potential benefits. Meanwhile, take prudent precautions against uncharted, but potentially serious, risks.
   Take a long-range view. Use low discount rates, maintain the responsibility of the current generation to ensure a liveable future, and treat the preservation of nature as an opportunity for long-term social saving.
   Keep in mind the uncertainty surrounding many environmental problems. Adopt coping strategies such as burden-shifting rules, postponement of irreversible decisions, and (when appropriate because of new information) deregulation.
   Overall, keep a sense of balance, while maintaining a firm commitment to environmentalism. Don't put economists in charge of the regulatory process, but take their views seriously as a reality check on overzealous regulation.

16. See Ackerman and Heinzerling 2004, p. 210. For related arguments about risk assessment, benefit-cost analysis, and toxics policy, see Heinzerling 1998, 2002; Heinzerling and Hoffman 2001; and Ackerman and Heinzerling 2002.

17. U.S. Senate 1990a, p. 132. Rothenberg (2002) emphasizes how politics shapes the form of many environmental policies, noting (p. 19):

   The capacity of the United States to produce environmental policy has risen dramatically, but it has been heavily influenced by the fragmented nature of the American political system, as epitomized both by separation of powers and federalism. Given the fragmentation built into the political system, environmental policy often has a disjointed if durable appearance.

List and Sturm (2004) also present evidence on how electoral incentives affect environmental policy.

18. In the mid-1990s, television stations were required to maintain public inspection files that in part listed the children's educational programs they aired to comply with the Children's Televison Act of 1990. I found (see Hamilton 1996b) that the local Fox affiliate in the Raleigh-Durham, North Carolina, market was claiming that episodes of *Geraldo* and *Beverly Hills 90210* were children's educational programming. I filed a comment in August 1995 with the FCC that suggested that the agency create an Internet-accessible database of station claims about educational programming for children, and based my argument in part on the example of information provision in the TRI program. I argued that the database would lower the costs to parents of finding educational programming and lower the costs to monitoring station performance. The idea of using information provision about station behavior was eventually incorporated into the FCC's 1996 final rule on children's educational programming (see *Federal Register* August 27, 1996, 61 FR 43981). The database listing information about children's educational programming offered by stations can be accessed at http://gullfoss2.fcc.gov/prod/kidvid/prod/kv_info.htm.

19. See McCubbins and Schwartz 1984.

Bibliography

Abt Associates. 1990. *Analysis of non-respondents to Section 313 of the Emergency Planning and Community Right-to-Know Act*. Cambridge, Mass.: Abt Associates.

Ackerman, Bruce A., and W. Hassler. 1981. *Clean air, dirty coal*. New Haven: Yale University Press.

Ackerman, Frank, and Lisa Heinzerling. 2002. Pricing the priceless: Cost-benefit analysis of environmental protection. *University of Pennsylvania Law Review* 150: 1553.

————. 2004. *Priceless: On knowing the price of everything and the value of nothing*. New York: The New Press.

Afsah, Shakeb, Allen Blackman, and Damayanti Ratunanda. 2000. *How do public disclosure pollution control programs work? Evidence from Indonesia*. Discussion Paper 00–44, Resources for the Future, Washington, D.C.

Alberini, Anna, and Kathleen Segerson. 2002. Assessing voluntary programs to improve environmental quality. *Environmental and Resource Economics* 22: 157–84.

Allen, Barbara L. 2003. *Uneasy alchemy: Citizens and experts in Louisiana's chemical corridor disputes*. Cambridge, Mass.: MIT Press.

Ambec, Stephan, and Philippe Barla. 2001. *A theoretical foundation of the Porter Hypothesis*. Working Paper, CSEF, Dipartimento di Scienze Economiche, Universita di Salerno, Italy.

Anton, Wilma Rose Q., George Deltas, and Madhu Khanna. 2002. *Incentives for environmental self-regulation and implications for environmental performance*. Working paper, Department of Agricultural and Consumer Economics, University of Illinois, Urbana-Champaign.

Antweiler, Werner, and Kathryn Harrison. 2003. Toxic release inventories and green consumerism: Empirical evidence from Canada. *Canadian Journal of Economics* 36 (2): 495–520.

Applegate, John S. 1992. Worst things first: Risk, information, and regulatory structure in toxic substances control. *Yale Journal on Regulation* 9 (2): 277–353.

Arnold, R. Douglas. 1990. *The logic of congressional action*. New Haven: Yale University Press.

Arora, Seema, and Timothy N. Cason. 1995. An experiment in voluntary environmental regulation: Participation in EPA's 33/50 program. *Journal of Environmental Economics and Management* 28 (3): 271–86.

———. 1996. Why do firms volunteer to exceed environmental regulations? Understanding participation in EPA's 33/50 Program. *Land Economics* 72 (4): 413–32.

———. 1998. Do community characteristics influence environmental outcomes?: Evidence from the Toxics Release Inventory. *Journal of Applied Economics* I (2): 413–53.

———. 1999. Do community characteristics influence environmental outcomes?: Evidence from the Toxics Release Inventory. *Southern Economic Journal* 65 (4): 691–704.

Arora, Seema, and Shubhashis Gangopadhyay. 1995. Toward a theoretical model of voluntary overcompliance. *Journal of Economic Behavior and Organization* 28: 289–309.

Arrow, Kenneth J., Maureen L. Cropper, George C. Eads, Robert W. Hahn, Lester B. Lave, Roger G. Noll, Paul R. Portney, Milton Russell, Richard Schmalensee, V. Kerry Smith, and Robert N. Stavins. 1996. Is there a role for benefit-cost analysis in environmental, health, and safety regulation? *Science* 272: 221–2.

Ashford, Nicholas A., and Charles C. Caldart. 1985. The "right to know": Toxics information transfer in the workplace. *Annual Review of Public Health* 6: 383–401.

Ashford, Nicholas A., James Victor Gobbell, Judith Lachman, Mary Mathiesen, Ann Minzner, and Robert Stone. 1993. *The encouragement of technological change for preventing chemical accidents: Moving firms from secondary prevention and mitigation to primary prevention*. Cambridge, Mass.: Center for Technology, Policy, and Industrial Development, MIT.

Atlas, Mark, Michael Vasu, and Michael Dimock. 2001. *TRI to communicate: An empirical evaluation of the dissemination and impact of Toxics Release Inventory data*. Prepared for the Association for Public Policy Analysis and Management Conference, November 1–3, Washington, D.C.

Balla, Steven J. 1998. Administrative procedures and political control of the bureaucracy. *American Political Science Review* 92 (3): 663–73.

Banzhaf, H. Spencer, and Randall P. Walsh. 2004. *Testing for environmental gentrification: Migratory responses to changes in environmental quality*. Prepared for 2004 AERE Workshop, Estes Park, Colorado.

Bardach, Eugene, and Robert A. Kagan. 1982. *Going by the book*. Philadelphia: Temple University Press.

Baron, David P. 2000. *Business and its environment*. 3d ed. Upper Saddle River, N.J.: Prentice Hall.

Barone, Michael, and Grant Ujifusa. 1987. *Almanac of American politics, 1988*. Washington, D.C.: National Journal.

Barsa, Michael. 1997. California's Proposition 65 and the limits of information economics. *Stanford Law Review* 49: 1223–47.

Bartel, Ann P., and Lacy Glenn Thomas. 1985. Direct and indirect effects of regulations: A new look at OSHA's impact. *Journal of Law and Economics* 28: 1–26.

Baumgartner, Frank R., and Bryan D. Jones. 1993. *Agendas and instability in American politics*. Chicago: University of Chicago Press.

Baumol, William J., and Wallace E. Oates. 1988. *The theory of environmental policy*. 2d ed. New York: Cambridge University Press.

Bawn, Kathleen. 1995. Political control versus expertise: Congressional choices about administrative procedures. *American Political Science Review* 89 (1): 62–73.

———. 1997. Choosing strategies to control the bureaucracy: Statutory constraints, oversight, and the committee system. *Journal of Law, Economics, and Organization* 13 (1): 101–26.

Beales, Howard, Richard Craswell, and Steven C. Salop. 1981. The efficient regulation of consumer information. *Journal of Law and Economics* 24 (December): 491–544.

Beamish, Rita. 1993. *EPA says 37.8 billion pounds of chemical wastes generated in 1991*. Associated Press, 26 May.

Becker, Gary. 1983. A theory of competition among pressure groups for political influence. *Quarterly Journal of Economics* 98 (3): 371–400.

Becker, Victoria, Mary Fetter, and James Solyst. 1989. *Emergency Planning and Community Right-to-Know Act: A status of state actions – 1989*. Washington, D.C.: Natural Resources Policy Studies Unit, Center for Policy Research, National Governors' Association.

Been, Vicki. 1993. What's fairness got to do with it? Environmental justice and the siting of locally undesirable land uses. *Cornell Law Review* 78 (September): 1001–85.

———. 1994. Locally undesirable land uses in minority neighborhoods: Disproportionate siting or market dynamics? *Yale Law Journal* 103 (April): 1383–422.

Been, Vicki, and Francis Gupta. 1997. Coming to the nuisance or going to the barrios? A longitudinal analysis of environmental justice claims. *Ecology Law Quarterly* 24: 1–56.

Begley, Ronald. 1992a. Contentious RCRA bill goes to Senate, includes expanded TRI requirements. *Chemical Week*, 27 May, 9.

———. 1992b. Delays put firms in deadline crunch. *Chemical Week*, 8 April, 12.

———. 1992c. PPA forms tied up in red tape. *Chemical Week*, 20 May, 13.

———. 1995a. Deregulatory action picks up speed. *Chemical Week*, 1 February, 13.

———. 1995b. Regulation reform slows down. *Chemical Week*, 29 March, 10.

———. 1995c. EPA attacked on budget front. *Chemical Week*, 19 July, 15.

———. 1995d. Frustrations mount in effort to scale back regulations. *Chemical Week*, 26 July, 9.

———. 1995e. Senate bill weakened on the floor. *Chemical Week*, 19 July, 16.

———. 1995f. Advocacy conflict with deregulatory Congress; Diverse voices challenge lobbying. *Chemical Week*, 5 July, 40.

Beierle, Thomas C. 1998. *Public participation in environmental decisions: An evaluation framework using social goals*. Discussion Paper 99-06, Resources for the Future, Washington, D.C.

————. 2000. *The quality of stakeholder-based decisions: Lessons from the case study record*. Discussion Paper 00-56, Resources for the Future, Washington, D.C.

Beierle, Thomas C., and Sarah Cahill. 2000. *Electronic democracy and environmental governance: A survey of the states*. Discussion Paper 00-42, Resources for the Future, Washington, D.C.

Benenson, Bob. 1995. Regulations: Senators roll back restriction proposed by regulatory overhaul. *CQ Weekly*, 22 July.

Bennear, Lori Snyder, and Cary Coglianese. 2004. *Evaluating environmental policies*. Faculty Research Working Paper Series, John F. Kennedy School of Government, Harvard University.

Bertelson, Christine. 1989. Computer to spew toxic waste data. *St. Louis Post-Dispatch*, 9 July.

Bhojraj, Sanjeev, Walter G. Blacconiere, and Julia D'Souza. 2000. *Voluntary disclosure in a multi-audience setting: An empirical investigation*. Working paper, Johnson Graduate School of Management, Cornell University.

Bolin, Bob, Eric Matranga, Edward J. Hackett, Edward K. Sadalla, K. David Pijawka, Debbie Brewer, and Diane Sicotte. 2000. Environmental equity in a sunbelt city: The spatial distribution of toxic hazards in Phoenix, Arizona. *Global Environmental Change Part B: Environmental Hazards* 2 (1): 11–24.

Borenstein, Seth. 2003. Pollution enforcement off under Bush, files show. *Pittsburgh Post-Gazette*, 9 December, A-19.

Bouwes, Nicolaas, Steven M. Hassur, and Mark D. Shapiro. 2001. *Empowerment through risk-related information: EPA's risk screening environmental indicators project*. Working Papers Series, no. 18, Political Economy Research Institute, University of Massachusetts.

Bowen, William. 2002. An analytical review of environmental justice research: What do we really know? *Environmental Management* 29 (1): 3–15.

Bowen, William M., Mark J. Salling, Kingsley E. Haynes, and Ellen J. Cyran. 1995. Toward environmental justice: Spatial equity in Ohio and Cleveland. *Annals of the Association of American Geographers* 85 (4): 641–63.

Braithwaite, John. 1985. *To punish or persuade: Enforcement of coal mine safety*. Albany, N.Y.: State University of New York Press.

Brehm, John, and James T. Hamilton. 1996. Noncompliance in environmental reporting: Are violators ignorant, or evasive, of the law? *American Journal of Political Science* 40 (2): 444–77.

Bronars, Stephen G., and John R. Lott Jr. 1997. Do campaign donations alter how a politician votes? Or, do donors support candidates who value the same things that they do? *Journal of Law and Economics* 40 (2): 317–50.

Brooks, Nancy, and Rajiv Sethi. 1997. The distribution of pollution: Community characteristics and exposure to air toxics. *Journal of Environmental Economics and Management* 32: 233–50.

Brown, Courtney. 1994. Politics and the environment: Nonlinear instabilities dominate. *American Political Science Review* 88 (2): 292–303.

Brownstein, Ronald. 1985. Trench warfare. *National Journal* 17 (37): 2047–53.

Buchanan, James, and Gordon Tullock. 1975. Polluters' profits and political responses: Direct controls versus taxes. *American Economic Review* 65 (1): 139–47.

Buckley, James R. 1986. The political economy of Superfund implementation. *Southern California Law Review* 59: 875–909.

Bui, Linda T. M., and Christopher J. Mayer. 2003. Regulation and capitalization of environmental amenities: Evidence from the Toxic Release Inventory in Massachusetts. *Review of Economics and Statistics* 85 (3): 693–708.

Bullard, Robert D. 1990. *Dumping in Dixie: Race, class, and environmental quality.* Boulder, Colo.: Westview Press.

———, ed. 1993. *Confronting environmental racism: Voices from the grassroots.* Boston: South End Press.

Bureau of National Affairs. 1993a. States call for EPA action against companies that fail to report TRI data. *Environmental Reporter*, 19 March, 23: 3015.

———. 1993b. EPA seeks out almost $2.8 million in penalties for chemical release reporting violations. *Environmental Reporter*, 4 June, 17: 542.

Business Wire. 1991a. Cyanamid to reduce emissions 50% by 1995. *Business Wire*, 2 May.

———. 1991b. Amoco joins voluntary EPA program to reduce toxic emissions 50 percent by 1995. *Business Wire*, 14 May.

Calvert, Randall L., Mathew D. McCubbins, and Barry R. Weingast. 1989. A theory of political control and agency discretion. *American Journal of Political Science* 33 (3): 588–611.

Campos, Jose Edgardo L. 1989. Legislative institutions, lobbying, and the endogenous choice of regulatory instruments: A political economy approach to instrument choice. *Journal of Law, Economics, and Organization* 5 (2): 333–53.

Carpenter, Daniel P. 1996. Adaptive signal processing, hierarchy, and budgetary control in federal regulation. *American Political Science Review* 90 (2): 283–302.

Case, David W. 2000. Legal considerations in voluntary corporate environmental reporting. *Environmental Law Reporter* 30: 10375.

———. 2001. The law and economics of environmental information as regulation. *Environmental Law Reporter News and Analysis* 31: 10773.

Centner, Terence J., Warren Kriesel, and Andrew G. Keeler. 1996. Environmental justice and toxic releases: Establishing evidence of discriminatory effect based on race and not income. *Wisconsin Environmental Law Journal* 3: 119–58.

Chemical Week. 1984. Chemical PACs pick their candidates. *Chemical Week*, 30 August, 5.

———. 1993. EPA seeks $2.8 million in TRI violations. *Chemical Week*, 16 June, 65.

———. 1995. CMA files suit against TRI additions. *Chemical Week*, 30 August, 5.

———. 1996. Parting advice: Stay off the radar screen. *Chemical Week*, 31 July, 52.

———. 1999. Washington: Partisan rift thwarts action. *Chemical Week*, 6 January, 23.

———. 2001. TRI publication method prompts environmental complaints. *Chemical Week*, 18 April, 9.

————. 2003. EPA submits plan for easier TRI reporting. *Chemical Week*, 15 October, 33.

Citizens Fund. 1990. *Poisons in our neighborhoods: Toxic pollution in the United States*. Washington, D.C.: Citizens Fund, June.

————. 1991. *Manufacturing pollution: A survey of the nation's toxic polluters*. Washington, D.C.: Citizens Fund, July.

————. 1992. *Manufacturing pollution*. Washington, D.C.: Citizens Fund, August.

————. 1994. *Pollution prevention... or public relations? An examination of EPA's 33/50 program*. Washington, D.C.: Citizens Fund, May.

Clay, Barbara Ann. 1997. The EPA's proposed Phase-III Expansion of the Toxic Release Inventory (TRI) reporting requirements: Everything and the kitchen sink. *Pace Environmental Law Review* 15: 293.

Clinton, William J. 1995. Remarks on environmental protection in Baltimore, Maryland, August 8, 1995. *Public Papers of the Presidents: William J. Clinton*, vol. 2, pp. 1215–18.

————. 1996. *Public Papers of the Presidents: William J. Clinton*, vol. 1 & 2.

Clymer, Adam. 2003. Government openness at issue as Bush holds on to records. *New York Times*, 3 January, A1.

Coase, Ronald. 1960. The problem of social cost. *Journal of Law and Economics* 3 (October): 1–44.

————. 1988. *The firm, the market, and the law*. Chicago: University of Chicago Press.

Coates, Dennis. 1996. Jobs versus wilderness areas: The role of campaign contributions. In *The political economy of environmental protection: Analysis and evidence*, edited by Roger D. Congleton. Ann Arbor, Mich.: University of Michigan Press.

Coglianese, Cary. 2004. *E-rulemaking: Information technology and regulatory policy*. Center for Business and Government, John F. Kennedy School of Government, Harvard University.

————. Undated. *EPA's 33/50 Program: Innovation and impact in toxic emissions reduction*. Preliminary draft, John F. Kennedy School of Government, Harvard University.

Coglianese, Cary, and Margaret Howard. 1998. Getting the message out: Regulatory policy and the press. *Harvard International Journal of Press/Politics* 3 (3): 39–55.

Coglianese, Cary, and David Lazer. 2003. Management-based regulation: Prescribing private management to achieve public goals. *Law and Society Review* 37 (4): 691–730.

Coglianese, Cary, and Gary E. Marchant. 2004. Shifting sands: The limits of science in setting risk standards. *University of Pennsylvania Law Review* 152: 1255.

Coglianese, Cary, and Jennifer Nash. 2004. *The Massachusetts Toxics Use Reduction Act: Design and implementation of a management-based environmental regulation*. Regulatory Policy Program, Center for Business and Government, John F. Kennedy School of Government, Harvard University.

Coglianese, Cary, Richard Zeckhauser, and Edward Parson. 2004. *Seeking truth for power: Informational strategy and regulatory policy making*. Center for

Business and Government, John F. Kennedy School of Government, Harvard University.

Cohen, Mark A. 1999. Monitoring and enforcement of environmental policy. In *International yearbook of environmental and resource economics*, 3, edited by Tom Tietenberg and Henk Folmer. Cheltenham, U.K.: Edward Elger.

——. 2001. Information as a policy instrument in protecting the environment: What have we learned? *Environmental Law Reporter* 31: 10425.

Cohen, Mark A., and V. Santhakumar. 2002. *Information disclosure as environmental regulation: A theoretical analysis.* Working paper, Vanderbilt University.

Cohen, Mark, Scott A. Fenn, and Shameek Konar. 1997. *Environmental and financial performance: Are they related?* Working paper, Vanderbilt University.

Cole, Luke W. 1992. Empowerment as the key to environmental protection: The need for environmental poverty law. *Ecology Law Quarterly* 19 (4): 619–83.

Commission for Environmental Cooperation of North America. 2003. *Taking stock 2000: North American pollutant releases and transfers.* Montreal: Commission for Environmental Cooperation.

Commission for Racial Justice. 1987. *Toxic wastes and race in the United States: A national report on the racial and socio-economic characteristics of communities with hazardous waste sites.* New York: Commission for Racial Justice, United Church of Christ.

Cormier, Denis, and Michel Magnan. 1999. Corporate environmental disclosure strategies: Determinants, costs and benefits. *Journal of Accounting, Auditing and Finance* 14 (4): 429–51.

Corporate Technology Information Services. 1991. *Corporate technology directory, 1991.* Wellesley Hills, Mass.: Corporate Technology Information Services.

Council on Economic Priorities. 1998. *The corporate report card.* New York: Dutton.

Coyne, Marty. 2003. EPA refuses to define trace metals under toxics reporting. *Environment and Energy Daily*, 10 (9), 26 September.

——. 2004. Regulations: Paperwork burden for key EPA programs increased in 2003. *Greenwire*, 10 (9), 3 May.

Crandall, Robert W. 1983. *Controlling industrial pollution: The economics and politics of clean air.* Washington, D.C.: The Brookings Institution.

Cropper, Maureen L., William N. Evans, Stephen J. Berardi, Maria M. Dulca-Soares, and Paul R. Portney. 1992. The determinants of pesticide regulation: A statistical analysis of EPA decision making. *Journal of Political Economy* 100: 175–97.

Crow, Patrick. 1988. SARA in perspective. *Oil & Gas Journal*, 20 June, 21.

Cushman, John H., Jr. 1995. Efficient pollution rule under attack. *New York Times*, 28 June, A16.

——. 1996. Court backs EPA authority on disclosure of toxic agents. *New York Times*, 2 May, A20.

——. 1997. EPA is pressing plan to publicize pollution data. *New York Times*, 12 August, A1.

Cutter, Susan L., Danika Holm, and Lloyd Clark. 1996. The role of geographic scale in monitoring environmental justice. *Risk Analysis* 16 (4): 517–26.

Cutter, Susan L., Michael S. Scott, and Arleen A. Hill. 2002. Spatial variability in toxicity indicators used to rank chemical risks. *American Journal of Public Health* 92 (3): 420–22.

Cutter, Susan L., and William D. Solecki. 1996. Setting environmental justice in space and place: Acute and chronic airborne toxic releases in the Southeastern United States. *Urban Geography* 17 (5): 380–99.

Daniels, Glynis, and Samantha Friedman. 1999. Spatial inequality and the distribution of industrial toxic releases: Evidence from the 1990 TRI. *Social Science Quarterly* 80 (2): 244–62.

Davis, Joseph A. 1985. Some in chemical industry endorse regulation: Bills on toxic pollutants picking up support. *CQ Weekly*, 30 March.

Davis, Joseph A., and Nancy Green. 1984. Bhopal tragedy prompts scrutiny by Congress, *CQ Weekly*, 22 December.

Davis, Phillip A. 1992. RCRA bill slogs along, faces troubled waters. *CQ Weekly*, 2 May.

Deily, Mary E., and Wayne B. Gray. 1991. Enforcement of pollution regulations in a declining industry. *Journal of Environmental Economics and Management* 21: 260–74.

de Marchi, Scott, and James T. Hamilton. 2004. *Trust, but verify: Assessing the accuracy of self-reported pollution data in the Toxics Release Inventory*. Working paper, Department of Political Science, Duke University.

Denzau, Arthur T., and Michael C. Munger. 1986. Legislators and interest groups: How unorganized interests get represented. *American Political Science Review* 80: 89–106.

Dewees, Donald N. 1983. Instrument choice in environmental policy. *Economic Inquiry* 21: 53–71.

Diamond, Stuart. 1985. Carbide asserts string of errors caused gas leak. *New York Times*, 24 August, section 1, 1.

Dingell, John. 1985. Representative Dingell speaking against the Edgar Superfund Amendment to the House. 99th Cong., 1st sess. *Congressional Record*, 9 December, vol. 131, no. 169.

Dodd, Peter, and Jerold B. Warner. 1983. On corporate governance: A study of proxy contests. *Journal of Financial Economics* 11 (1–4): 401–38.

Downs, Anthony. 1957. *An Economic Theory of Democracy*. New York: Harper and Row.

———. 1972. Up and down with ecology: The "issue-attention cycle." *Public Interest* 28 (Summer): 38–50.

Dranove, David, Daniel P. Kessler, Mark B. McClellan, and Mark Satterthwaite. 2002. *Is more information better? The effects of "report cards" on health care providers*. NBER Working Paper No. w8697, National Bureau of Economic Research.

Dudley, Susan E. 1999a. *Comments on the EPA's lead and lead compounds; lowering of reporting thresholds; community right-to-know toxic chemical release reporting; proposed rule*. Regulatory Studies Program, Mercatus Center, George Mason University.

———. 1999b. *Comments on the EPA's proposed amendments to the Toxic Release Inventory (TRI) persistent bioaccumulative toxic (PBT) chemicals*. Regulatory Studies Program, Mercatus Center, George Mason University.

———. 2002. *It is time to reevaluate the Toxics Release Inventory*. Written testimony prepared for Subcommittee on Regulatory Reform and Oversight, Committee on Small Business, U.S. House of Representatives, "The TRI lead rule: Costs, compliance, and science," 13 June.

Dun and Bradstreet. 1991a. *Dun's industrial guide: The metalworking directory, 1989*. New York: Dun and Bradstreet.

———. 1991b. *Million dollar directory: America's leading public and private companies*. New York: Dun and Bradstreet.

Durden, Garey C., Jason F. Shogren, and Jonathan I. Silberman. 1991. The effects of interest group pressure on coal strip-mining legislation. *Social Science Quarterly* (June): 239–50.

Durham-Hammer, Kathryn E. 2004. Left to wonder: Reevaluating, reforming, and implementing the Emergency Planning and Community Right-to-Know Act of 1986. *Columbia Journal of Environmental Law* 29: 323–57.

Echeverria, John D., and Julie B. Kaplan. 2002. *Poisonous procedural "reform": In defense of environmental right to know*. Georgetown Environmental Law and Policy Institute, Georgetown University Law Center.

Elliott, E. Donald. 1994. TQM-ing OMB: Or why regulatory review under Executive Order 12,291 works poorly and what President Clinton should do about it. *Law and Contemporary Problems* 57 (1& 2): 167–84.

———. 2003. Science in the regulatory process: Strengthening science's voice at EPA. *Law and Contemporary Problems* 66: 45–62.

Entman, Robert M. 1993. Toward clarification of a fractured paradigm. *Journal of Communication* 43 (Autumn): 51–59.

———. 2004. *Projections of power: Framing news, public opinion, and U.S. foreign policy*. Chicago: University of Chicago Press.

Environmental Health Center. 1989. *Chemicals, the press, and the public: A journalist's guide to reporting on chemicals in the community*. Washington, D.C.: Environmental Health Center, National Safety Council.

Environmental Integrity Project and the Galveston-Houston Association for Smog Prevention. 2004. *Who's counting? The systematic underreporting of toxic air emissions*. Available from http://www.ghasp.org/publications/trireport/trireport.html.

Environmental Laboratory Washington Report. 2000. General Electric facility named among worst for airborne cancer risk. *Environmental Laboratory Washington Report*, 11 (3), 17 February.

———. 2003. Court ruling allows mining industry to avoid TRI reporting. *Environmental Laboratory Washington Report*, 14 (12), 20 June.

Epstein, David, and Sharyn O'Halloran. 1999a. *Delegating powers: A transaction cost politics approach to policy making under separate powers*. Cambridge: Cambridge University Press.

———. 1999b. Asymmetric information, delegation, and the structure of policy-making. *Journal of Theoretical Politics* 11 (1): 37–56.

Eskridge, William N., Jr. 1988. Politics without romance: Implications of public choice theory for statutory interpretation. *Virginia Law Review,* 74 (2): 275–338.

Esterling, Kevin M. 2004. *The political economy of expertise: Information and efficiency in American national politics.* Ann Arbor, Mich.: University of Michigan Press.

Esty, Daniel C. 2004. Environmental protection in the information age. *New York University Law Review* 79: 115.

Fairley, Peter. 1995. Compromise limits EPA budget cut, removes House riders. *Chemical Week,* 22 November, 17.

――――. 1996. TRI: Growing pains. *Chemical Week,* 12 June, 18.

――――. 1997a. EPA's Internet leaves industry feeling exposed. *Chemical Week,* 2 April, 43.

――――. 1997b. CMA trounced again in TRI expansion lawsuit. *Chemical Week,* 13 August, 13.

――――. 1997c. EPA, OMB deadlock on expansion. *Chemical Week,* 26 March, 38.

――――. 1997d. Clinton breaks deadlock, ending wholesalers' bid to avoid TRI reporting. *Chemical Week,* 30 April, 17.

Fairley, Peter, Rick Mullin, and Andrea Foster. 1998. Scorecard hits home. *Chemical Week,* 3 June, 24.

Farber, Daniel A. 1992. Politics and procedure in environmental law. *Journal of Law, Economics, and Organization* 8 (1): 59–81.

――――. 1999. *Eco-pragmatism: Making sensible environmental decisions in an uncertain world.* Chicago: University of Chicago Press.

――――. 2003. Probabilities behaving badly: Complexity theory and environmental uncertainty. *Environs: Environmental Law and Policy Journal* 27 (1): 145–73.

Farrell, Joseph. 1987. Information and Coase Theorem. *Journal of Economic Perspectives* 1 (2): 113–29.

Feinstein, Jonathan S. 1989. The safety regulation of U.S. nuclear power plants: Violations, inspections, and abnormal occurrences. *Journal of Political Economy* 97: 115–54.

――――. 1990. Detection controlled estimation. *Journal of Law and Economics* 33: 233–76.

Ferejohn, John A. 1987. The structure of agency decision process. In *Congress: Structure and Policy,* edited by Matthew D. McCubbins and Terry Sullivan. New York: Cambridge University Press.

Fiorino, Daniel J. 1995. *Making environmental policy.* Berkeley, Calif.: University of California Press.

Firestone, Jeremy M. 2002. Agency governance and enforcement: The influence of mission on environmental decisionmaking. *Journal of Policy Analysis and Management* 21 (3): 409–26.

Flavin, Dick. 1989. Talking about toxic waste is chic. *USA Today,* 21 June, final edition, 8A.

Foreman, Christopher H., Jr. 1998. *The promise and peril of environmental justice.* Washington, D.C.: Brookings Institution Press.

Fort, Rodney, William Hallagan, Cyril Morong, and Tesa Stegner. 1993. The ideological component of Senate voting: Different principles or different principals? *Public Choice* 76 (1&2): 39–57.

Foster, Andrea. 1998. TRI expansion options shift. *Chemical Week*, 6 May, 33.

Frank, Robert H., and Cass R. Sunstein. 2001. Cost-benefit analysis and relative position. *University of Chicago Law Review* 68: 323.

Franz, Damon. 2002. Subcommittee to scope EPA lead reporting rule. *Environment and Energy Daily*, 10 (9), 10 June.

Fricker, Ronald D., and Nicolas W. Hengartner. 2001. Environmental equity and the distribution of toxic release inventory and other environmentally undesirable sites in metropolitan New York City. *Environmental and Ecological Statistics* 8: 33–52.

Friedman, Sharon M., Sharon M. Dunwoody, and Carol L. Rogers, eds. 1999. *Communicating uncertainty: Media coverage of new and controversial science.* Mahwah, N.J.: Lawrence Erlbaum Associates.

Friends of the Earth. 1999. *The geographic relation between household income and polluting factories.* Available from http://www.foe.co.uk/resource/ reports/income_pollution.html.

———. 2001. *Pollution and poverty – breaking the link.* London: Friends of the Earth, Policy and Research Unit.

Fung, Archon, Mary Graham, and David Weil. 2002. *The political economy of transparency: Foundations of continuous improvement in information-based regulation.* Transparency Policy Project, John F. Kennedy School of Government, Harvard University.

———. 2003. *The political economy of transparency: What makes disclosure policies sustainable?* Faculty Research Working Paper Series, John F. Kennedy School of Government, Harvard University.

Fung, Archon, Mary Graham, David Weil, and Elena Fagotto. 2004. *The political economy of transparency: What makes disclosure policies sustainable?* Faculty Research Working Paper Series, John F. Kennedy School of Government, Harvard University.

Fung, Archon, and Dara O'Rourke. 2000. Reinventing environmental regulation from the grassroots up: Explaining and expanding the success of the Toxics Release Inventory. *Environmental Management* 25 (2): 115–27.

Furlong, Scott R. 1997. Interest group influence on rule making. *Administration and Society* 29 (3).

Gamper-Rabindran, Shanti. 2004. *Did the EPA's Voluntary Industrial Toxics Program reduce emissions? A GIS analysis of distributional impacts and by-media analysis of substitution.* Working paper, University of North Carolina, Chapel Hill.

Garvie, Devon A., and Barton L. Lipman. 2000. Regulatory rule-making with legal challenges. *Journal of Environmental Economics and Management* 40: 87–110.

Gayer, Ted, James T. Hamilton, and W. Kip Viscusi. 2000. Private values of risk tradeoffs at Superfund sites: Housing market evidence on learning about risk. *Review of Economics and Statistics* 83 (3): 439–51.

———. 2002. The market value of reducing cancer risk: Hedonic housing prices with changing information. *Southern Economic Journal* 69 (2): 266–89.

General Sciences Corporation. 1990. *Riskpro: Environmental pollution modeling system.* Laurel, Md.: GSC.

Glickman, Theodore S. 1994. Measuring environmental equity with geographical information systems. *Resources* (Summer): 2–6.

Goff, Brian L., and Kevin B. Grier. 1993. On the (mis)measurement of legislator ideology and shirking. *Public Choice* 76 (1&2): 5–20.

Goldman, Benjamin A. 1994. *Not just prosperity: Achieving sustainability with environmental justice.* Washington, D.C.: National Wildlife Federation.

Gormley, William T., Jr. 2000. *Environmental performance measures in a federal system.* Research Paper Number 13, National Academy of Public Administration, Washington, D.C.

Gormley, William T., Jr., and Steven J. Balla. 2004. *Bureaucracy and democracy: Accountability and performance.* Washington, D.C.: CQ Press.

Gormley, William T., Jr., and David L. Weimer. 1999. *Organizational report cards.* Cambridge, Mass.: Harvard University Press.

Graham, John D. 2002. Letter to Kim T. Nelson, 4 March. Available from http://www.whitehouse.gov/omb/inforeg/epa_tri3_prompt030402.html.

Graham, John D., Nancy Dean Beaulieu, Dana Sussman, March Sadowitz, and Yi-Ching Li. 1999. Who lives near coke plants and oil refineries? An exploration of the environmental inequity hypothesis. *Risk Analysis* 19 (2): 171–86.

Graham, John D., and Jonathan Baert Wiener, eds. 1995. *Risk versus risk: Tradeoffs in protecting health and the environment.* Cambridge, Mass.: Harvard University Press.

Graham, Mary. 2001. *Information as risk regulation: Lessons from experience.* Institute for Government Innovation, John F. Kennedy School of Government, Harvard University.

———. 2002. *Democracy by disclosure: The rise of technopopulism.* Washington, D.C.: Governance Institute, Brookings Institution Press.

Graham, Mary, and Catherine Miller. 2001. Disclosure of toxic releases in the United States. *Environment* 43 (8): 9–20.

Grant, Don Sherman II. 1997. Allowing citizen participation in environmental regulation: An empirical analysis of the effects of right-to-sue and right-to-know provisions on industry's toxic emissions. *Social Science Quarterly* 78 (4): 859–73.

Grant, Don Sherman II, and Liam Downey. 1995/1996. Regulation through information: An empirical analysis of the effects of state-sponsored right-to-know programs on industrial toxic pollution. *Policy Studies Review* 14 (3/4): 339–52.

Grant, Don Sherman II, and Andrew Jones. 2003. Are subsidiaries more prone to pollute? New evidence from the EPA's Toxics Release Inventory. *Social Sciences Quarterly* 84 (1): 162–73.

Gray, Wayne B., and Carol Adaire Jones. 1991. Longitudinal patterns of compliance with OSHA health and safety regulations in the manufacturing sector. *The Journal of Human Resources* 26: 623–52.

Gray, Wayne B., and Ronald J. Shadbegian. 2002. *"Optimal" pollution abatement – Whose benefits matter, and how much?* NBER Working Paper 9125, National Bureau of Economic Research.

Green, Krista. 1999. Comment: An analysis of the Supreme Court's resolution of the Emergency Planning and Community Right-to-Know Act citizen suit debate. *Boston College Environmental Affairs Law Review*, 26 (Winter): 387–434.

Greenwire. 1991. Interview: Using carrots and sticks to prevent pollution. *Greenwire*, 18 June.

———. 1993. Monsanto: Firm announces reduction of toxic emissions. *Greenwire*, 20 July.

———. 1996. Regulation: Conservative climate slows flow of Fed rules. *Greenwire*, 20 February.

Grier, Kevin B., ed. 1993. Empirical studies of ideology and representation in American politics. *Public Choice* 76 (1&2): 1–173.

Grier, Kevin B., and Michael C. Munger. 1991. Committee assignments, constituent preferences, and campaign contributions. *Economic Inquiry* 29 (1): 24–43.

Grier, Kevin B., Michael C. Munger, and Brian E. Roberts. 1994. The determinants of industry political activity, 1978–1986. *American Political Science Review* 88 (4): 911–26.

Hadden, Susan G. 1989. *A citizen's right to know: Risk communication and public policy*. Boulder, Colo.: Westview Press.

Hahn, Robert W. 1987. Jobs and environmental quality: Some implications for instrument choice. *Policy Sciences* 20 (4): 289–306.

———. 1990. The political economy of environmental regulation: Towards a unifying framework. *Public Choice* 65 (1): 21–47.

———. 1994. United States environmental policy: Past, present, and future. *Natural Resources Journal* 34: 305–48.

Hahn, Robert W., and Robert E. Litan. 2002a. *An analysis of the fifth government report on the costs and benefits of federal regulations*. Joint Center AEI-Brookings Joint Center for Regulatory Studies, May.

———. 2002b. *Recommendations for improving federal regulation: Testimony before the Subcommittee on Regulatory Reform and Oversight House Committee on Small Business*. Joint Center AEI-Brookings Joint Center for Regulatory Studies, June.

Hahn, Robert W., Sheila M. Olmstead, and Robert N. Stavins. 2003. Environmental regulation during the 1990s: A retrospective analysis. *Harvard Environmental Law Review*, 27 (2): 377–415.

Hahn, Robert W., and Cass R. Sunstein. 2002. A new executive order for improving federal regulation? Deeper and wider cost-benefit analysis. *University of Pennsylvania Law Review* 150: 1489.

Hall, Bob, and Mary Lee Kerr. 1991. *1991–1992 Green Index*. Washington, D.C.: Island Press.

Hall, Richard L., and Frank W. Wayman. 1990. Buying time: Moneyed interests and the mobilization of bias in Congressional committees. *American Political Science Review* 84: 797–820.

Hamilton, James T. 1991. Lower pay for analysis: Greater rewards are offered those writing economics from human interest and political viewpoints. *Nieman Reports, The Nieman Foundation at Harvard University*, 45 (3): 19–22.

————. 1993. Politics and social costs: Estimating the impact of collective action on hazardous waste facilities. *RAND Journal of Economics* 24: 101–25.

————. 1995a. Pollution as news: Media and stock market reactions to the Toxics Release Inventory data. *Journal of Environmental Economics and Management* 28: 98–113.

————. 1995b. Testing for environmental racism: Prejudice, profits, political power? *Journal of Policy Analysis and Management* 14: 107–32.

————. 1996a. Going by the (informal) book: The EPA's use of informal rules in enforcing hazardous waste laws. In *Reinventing Government and the problem of bureaucracy*, edited by Gary Libecap. Greenwich, Conn.: JAI Press.

————. 1996b. Private interests in "public interest" programming: An economic assessment of broadcaster incentives. *Duke Law Journal* 45 (6): 1177–92.

————. 1997. Taxes, torts, and the Toxics Release Inventory: Congressional voting on instruments to control pollution. *Economic Inquiry* 35: 745–62.

————. 1999. Exercising property rights to pollute: Do cancer risks and politics affect plant emission reductions? *Journal of Risk and Uncertainty* 18 (2): 105–24.

————. 2004. *All the news that's fit to sell: How the market transforms information into news*. Princeton, N.J.: Princeton University Press.

————. 2005. Environmental equity and the siting of hazardous waste facilities in OECD countries: Evidence and policies. In *International Yearbook of Environmental and Resource Economics 2005/2006*, edited by Tom Tietenberg and Henk Folmer. Northampton, Mass: Edward Elger.

Hamilton, James T., and Christopher H. Schroeder. 1994. Strategic regulators and the choice of rulemaking procedures: The selection of formal vs. informal rules in regulating hazardous waste. *Law and Contemporary Problems* 57 (1&2): 111–60.

Hamilton, James T., and W. Kip Viscusi. 1999. *Calculating risks?: The spatial and political dimensions of hazardous waste policy*. Cambridge, Mass: MIT Press.

Harden, Blaine. 2004. Pollsters doubt fish rules will move votes. *Washington Post*, 7 May, A04.

Hardin, John W. 1998. Advocacy versus certainty: The dynamics of committee jurisdiction concentration. *The Journal of Politics* 60 (2): 374–97.

Harford, Jon D. 1978. Firm behavior under imperfectly enforceable pollution standards and taxes. *Journal of Environmental Economics and Management* 5: 26–43.

————. 1997. Firm ownership patterns and motives for voluntary pollution control. *Managerial and Decision Economics* 18: 421–31.

Harpaz, Beth J. 1999. *Gore attacks Bush's environmental record*. Associated Press, New York dateline, 8 October.

Harrington, Winston, Richard D. Morgenstern, and Peter Nelson. 1999. *On the accuracy of regulatory cost estimates*. Discussion paper, Resources for the Future, Washington, D.C.

Harris, Michael Ray. 1996. Promoting corporate self-compliance: An examination of the debate over legal protection for environmental audits. *Ecology Law Quarterly* 23 (4): 663–722.

Harrison, Kathryn, and Werner Antweiler. 2003. Incentives for pollution abatement: Regulation, regulatory threats, and non-governmental pressures. *Journal of Policy Analysis* 22 (3): 361–82.

Hazardous Waste Litigation Reporter. 1997a. DC Circuit strikes addition of bronopol, DMP to Toxic Inventory. *Hazardous Waste Litigation Reporter*, 18 August, 32650.

————. 1997b. DE judge rejects challenge to EPAs placement of 'nitrate compounds' on TRI. *Hazardous Waste Litigation Reporter*, 15 September, 32688.

Hebert, H. Josef. 1996. *Judge rules EPA acted properly in expanding list of toxic chemical.* Associated Press, 2 May.

Hecker, Jim. 1998. EPCRA citizen suits after Steel Co. v. Citizens for a Better Environment. *Environmental Law Reporter*, 28: 10306.

Heilprin, John. 2001. *Bush upholds new lead reporting requirements on 10,000 businesses.* Associated Press, Business News, 17 April.

————. 2003. Government exploring ways to ease reporting requirements of toxic chemical release. *Washington Post*, 25 September.

Heinzerling, Lisa. 1998. Regulatory costs of mythic proportions. *Yale Law Journal* 107: 1981–2070.

————. 2002. Markets for arsenic. *Georgetown Law Journal* 90: 2311–39.

Heinzerling, Lisa, and Cameron Powers Hoffman. 2001. Tortious toxics. *William and Mary Environmental Law and Policy Review* 26: 67–91.

Helland, Eric. 1998. The enforcement of pollution control laws: Inspections, violations, and self-reporting. *Review of Economics and Statistics* 80: 141–53.

Helland, Eric, and Andrew B. Whitford. 2003. Pollution incidence and political jurisdiction: Evidence from the TRI. *Journal of Environmental Economics and Management* 46: 403–24.

Heller, Karen. 1992. Toxics use reduction, the future battleground. *Chemical Week*, special report, 19 August, 52.

Henriquez, Blas Perez. 2004. Information technology: The unsung hero of market-based environmental policies. *Resources* (Fall/Winter): 9–12.

Henry, Gary T., and Craig S. Gordon. 2001. Tracking issue attention: Specifying the dynamics of the public agenda. *Public Opinion Quarterly*, 65: 157–77.

Hess, Glenn. 2000. US Senator, CMA fault EPA on nitrate fines, procedures. *Chemical News and Intelligence*, 26 May.

Hill, Jeffrey S., and James E. Brazier. 1991. Constraining administrative decisions: A critical examination of the structure and process hypothesis. *Journal of Law, Economics, and Organization* 7 (2): 373–400.

Hird, John A. 1993. Congressional voting on Superfund: Self-interest or ideology? *Public Choice* 77 (2): 333–57.

Hockman, Elaine M., and Charles M. Morris. 1998. Progress towards environmental justice: A five-year perspective of toxicity, race and poverty in Michigan, 1990–1995. *Journal of Environmental Planning and Management* 41 (2): 157–76.

Hodges, Hart. 1997. *Falling prices: Cost of complying with environmental regulations almost always less than advertised.* Economic Policy Institute Briefing Paper.

Hulse, Carl. 2001. A reversal on public access to chemical data. *New York Times*, 27 March, A18.

Iceland, John, and Erika Steinmetz. 2003. *The effects of using census block groups instead of census tracts when examining residential housing patterns.* Working paper Available at http://www.census.gov/hhes/www/housing/resseg/pdf/unit_of_analysis.pdf.

International Right to Know Campaign. 2003. *You have a right to know.* Washington, D.C.: International Right to Know Campaign.

Irwin, Douglas A., and Randall S. Kroszner. 1996. Log rolling and economic interests in the passage of the Hawley-Smoot Tariff. *Carnegie-Rochester Conference Series on Public Policy* 45 (December): 173–200.

Iyengar, Shanto, and Donald Kinder. 1987. *News that matters: Television and American opinion.* Chicago: University of Chicago Press.

Jehl, Douglas. 1989. 1 chemical skews data listing state first in toxics, officials explain. *Los Angeles Times*, 20 June.

Jerrett, Mike, John Eyles, Donald Cole, and S. Reader. 1997. Environmental equity in Canada: An empirical investigation into the income distribution of pollution in Ontario. *Environment and Planning A* 29: 1777–800.

Jin, Ginger Zhe, and Phillip Leslie. 2003. The effect of information on product quality: Evidence from restaurant hygiene grade cards. *Quarterly Journal of Economics* (May): 409–51.

Jobe, Margaret M. 1999. The power of information: The example of the U.S. Toxics Release Inventory. *Journal of Government Information* 26 (3): 287–95.

Jones, Jonathan D., Christopher L. Jones, and Fred Phillips-Patrick. 1994. Estimating the costs of the Exxon Valdez oil spill. *Research in Law and Economics* 16: 109–49.

Kagan, Elena. 2001. Presidential administration. *Harvard Law Review* 114: 2245.

Kahn, Matthew E., and John Matsusaka. 1997. Demand for environmental goods: Evidence from voting patterns on California initiatives. *Journal of Law and Economics* 40: 137–73.

Kalette, Denise. 1989. Toxic disaster is possible; lax rules drawing attention. *USA Today*, 2 August, 7A.

Kalt, Joseph, and Zupan, Mark. 1984. Capture and ideology in the economic theory of politics. *American Economic Review* 74 (3): 279–300.

———. 1990. The apparent ideological behavior of legislators: Testing for principal-agent slack in political institutions. *Journal of Law and Economics* 33 (1): 103–31.

Karey, Gerald. 1995. House will not press its effort to gut MACT rules. *Platt's Oilgram News*, 73 (212): 1.

Karkkainen, Bradley C. 2001. Information as environmental regulation: TRI and performance benchmarking, precursor to a new paradigm? *Georgetown Law Journal* 89: 257.

Karpoff, Jonathan, John R. Lott Jr., and Eric W. Wehrly. 2004. *The reputational penalties for environmental violations: Empirical evidence.* Working paper, University of Washington School of Business.

Keohane, Nathaniel O., Richard L. Revesz, and Robert N. Stavins. 1998. The choice of regulatory instruments in environmental policy. *Harvard Environmental Law Review* 22: 313–67.

Kenworthy, Tom. 1996. At issue: Differences on environment are often a matter of degree. *Washington Post*, 8 October, A01.

Kenworthy, Tom, and Gary Lee. 1995. Divided GOP falters on environmental agenda. *Washington Post*, 24 November, A01.

Kerwin, Cornelius M. 2003. *Rulemaking: How government agencies write law and make policy*. Washington, D.C.: CQ Press.

Khanna, Madhu. 2001. Non-mandatory approaches to environmental protection. *Journal of Economics Surveys* 15 (3): 291–324.

Khanna, Madhu, and Wilma Rose Q. Anton. 2002. Corporate environmental management: Regulatory and market-based incentives. *Land Economics* 78 (4): 539–58.

Khanna, Madhu, and Lisa A. Damon. 1999. EPA's voluntary 33/50 Program: Impact on toxics releases and economic performance of firms. *Journal of Environmental Economics and Management* 37: 1–25.

Khanna, Madhu, Surender Kumar, and Wilma Rose Q. Anton. 2002. *Environmental self-regulation: Implications for environmental efficiency and profitability*. Working paper, Dept. of Agricultural and Consumer Economics, University of Illinois at Urbana-Champaign.

Khanna, Madhu, Wilma Rose H. Quimio, and Dora Bojilova. 1998. Toxics release information: A policy tool for environmental protection. *Journal of Environmental Economics and Management* 36: 243–66.

Kiewiet, D. Roderick, and Mathew D. McCubbins. 1991. *The logic of delegation: Congressional parties and the appropriations process*. Chicago: The University of Chicago Press.

King, Andrew, and Michael Lenox. 2000. Industry self-regulation without sanctions: The chemical industry's Responsible Care Program. *Academy of Management Journal* 43 (4): 698–716.

———. 2002. *Sustaining industry self-regulation in the face of free-riding*. Working paper, Stern School of Business, New York University.

Kirschner, Elisabeth. 1993. Monsanto cuts air toxics 92% worldwide, 85% in U.S. *Chemical Week*, 28 July, 7.

Kleindorfer, Paul R., and Eric W. Orts. 1998. Informational regulation of environmental risks. *Risk Analysis* 18 (2): 155–70.

Knight, Peter P. 1999. Encouraging regulated entities to comply with federal environmental mandates: The need for a federal environmental audit protection statute. *New York University School of Law Journal of Legislation and Public Policy* 3 (1): 125–96.

Kohlhase, Janet E. 1991. The impact of toxic waste sites on housing values. *Journal of Urban Economics* 30: 1–26.

Koman, Karen L. 1989. Monsanto on list of possible cancer-causing pollution. *St. Louis Post-Dispatch*, 20 June.

Konar, Shameek, and Mark A. Cohen. 1997. Information as regulation: The effect of community right to know laws on toxic emissions. *Journal of Environmental Economics and Management* 32 (1): 109–24.

———. 2001. Does the market value environmental performance? *Review of Economics and Statistics* 83 (2): 281–9.

Kraft, Michael E., Troy D. Abel, and Mark Stephan. 2004. *Information disclosure and risk reduction: The sources of varying state performance in control of toxic chemical emissions.* Conference on Corporate Environmental Behavior and the Effectiveness of Government Interventions, U.S. EPA National Center for Environmental Economics, Washington, D.C., April 26–27.

Krehbiel, Keith. 1993. Constituency characteristics and legislative preferences. *Public Choice* 76 (1&2): 21–38.

Kriesel, Warren, Terence J. Centner, and Andrew G. Keeler. 1996. Neighborhood exposure to toxic releases: Are there racial inequalities? *Growth and Change* 27 (4): 479–99.

Lambrecht, Bill. 1991. Polluters ranked, environmental advocacy group puts Monsanto No. 2 in U.S. *St. Louis Post-Dispatch*, 12 July, 1B.

Lancaster, John. 1989. 42 companies fined after EPA check. *The Washington Post*, 27 June.

Laplante, Benoit, and Paul Lanoie. 1994. The market response to environmental incidents in Canada: A theoretical and empirical analysis. *Southern Economic Journal* 60 (3): 657–72.

Lavelle, Marianne. 1993. Environment vise: Law, compliance. *The National Law Journal*, 30 August, S1–S9.

Lazarus, Richard J. 2000/2001. Highways and bi-ways for environmental justice. *Cumberland Law Review* 31: 569–97.

League of Conservation Voters. 1994. *National environmental scorecard, 103rd Congress, second session.* Washington, D.C.: League of Conservation Voters.

———. 1996. *National environmental scorecard, 104th Congress, first session.* Washington, D.C.: League of Conservation Voters.

Lenox, Michael, and Jennifer Nash. 2001. Adverse selection and industry self-regulation. *Journal of Law, Economics, and Organization.* Working paper, Stern School of Business, New York University.

Lester, James P., and Ann O'Meara Bowman, eds. 1983. *The politics of hazardous waste management.* Durham, N.C.: Duke University Press.

Lester, Will. 2000. *RNC $3.7 million ad campaign criticizes Gore on environment.* Associated Press, Political News, 7 August.

Lewis, Christopher J. 2000. When is a trade secret not so secret? The deficiencies of 40 C.F.R. Part 2, Subpart B. *Environmental Law Northwestern School of Law of Lewis & Clark College* 30 (1): 143–76.

Lewis, Tracy R. 1996. Protecting the environment when costs and benefits are privately known. *RAND Journal of Economics* 27: 819–47.

List, John A., and Daniel M. Sturm. 2004. *How elections matter: Theory and evidence from environmental policy.* NBER Working Paper 10609, National Bureau of Economic Research.

Livernois, John, and C. J. McKenna. 1999. Truth or consequences: Enforcing pollution standards with self-reporting. *Journal of Public Economics* 71: 415–40.

Lowenstein, Laura J., and Richard L. Revesz. 2004. Anti-regulation under the guise of rational regulation: The Bush administration's approaches to valuing human lives in environmental cost-benefit analyses. *Environmental Law Reporter* 34: 10954.

Lupia, Arthur, and Mathew D. McCubbins. (Forthcoming). Lost in translation: Social choice theory is misapplied against legislative intent. *Journal of Contemporary Legal Issues.*

Lynn, Francis M., and Jack D. Kartez. 1994. Environmental democracy in action: The Toxics Release Inventory. *Environmental Management* 18 (4): 511–21.

Lyon, Thomas P., and John W. Maxwell. 1999. 'Voluntary' approaches to environmental regulation: A survey. Forthcoming in *Environmental economics: Past, present and future*, edited by Maurizio Franzini and Antonio Nicita. Aldershot, Hampshire, U.K.: Ashgate Publishing Ltd.

Macauley, Molly K., Michael D. Bowes, and Karen L. Palmer. 1992. *Using economic incentives to regulate toxic substances.* Washington, D.C.: Resources for the Future.

MacKerron, Conrad B. and Laurie A. Rich. 1987. Superfund's Title III: Not easy to digest. *Chemical Week*, 27 May, 20.

———. 1988a. Title III compliance; CPI managers hustle to meet the deadline. *Chemical Week*, 22 June, 22.

———. 1988b. Industry prepares for Title III. *Chemical Week*, 2 March, 40.

MacLean, Alair. 1995. *The right stuff: Information in the public interest.* Washington, D.C.: The Right to Know Network, OMB Watch and Center for Public Data Access.

MacLean, Alair, and Paul Orum. 1992. *Progress report: Community right-to-know.* Washington, D.C.: Working Group on Community Right-to-Know.

Magat, Wesley A., Alan J. Krupnick, and Winston Harrington. 1986. *Rules in the making: A statistical analysis of regulatory agency behavior.* Washington, D.C.: Resources for the Future.

Magat, Wesley A. and W. Kip Viscusi. 1990. Effectiveness of the EPA's regulatory enforcement: The case of industrial effluent standards. *Journal of Law and Economics* 23: 331–60.

———. 1992. *Informational approaches to regulation.* Cambridge, Mass.: MIT Press.

Marks, Peter. 1999. The ad campaign: Attacking Bush's environmental record. *New York Times*, 1 December, 20.

Maxwell, John W., Thomas P. Lyon, and Steven C. Hackett. 2000. Self-regulation and social welfare: The political economy of corporate environmentalism. *Journal of Law and Economics* 43: 583.

McCombs, Maxwell E., Donald Lewis Shaw, and David H. Weaver, eds. 1997. *Communication and democracy: Exploring the intellectual frontiers in agenda-setting theory.* Mahwah, N.J.: Lawrence Erlbaum Associates.

McCubbins, Mathew D. 1985. The legislative design of regulatory structure. *American Journal of Political Science* 29: 721–48.

McCubbins, Mathew D., and Thomas Schwartz. 1984. Congressional oversight overlooked: Police patrols versus fire alarms. *American Journal of Political Science* 28: 165–79.

McCurdy, Patrick P. 1987. Title III: How about a preemptive strike? *Chemical Week*, 18 November, 3.

McGarity, Thomas O. 1991. The internal structure of EPA rulemaking. *Law and Contemporary Problems* 54 (4): 57–111.

McLeod, H., I. H. Langford, Andy Jones, J. R. Stedman, R. J. Day, Irene Lorenzoni, and Ian J. Bateman. 2000. The relationship between socio-economic indicators and air pollution in England and Wales: Implications for environmental justice. *Regional Environmental Change* 1 (2): 78–85.

McNollgast. 1987. Administrative procedures as instruments of political control. *Journal of Law, Economics, and Organization* 3: 243–77.

————. 1989. Structure and process, politics and policy: Administrative arrangements and the political control of agencies. *Virginia Law Review* 75: 431–82.

————. 1994. Legislative intent: The use of positive political theory in statutory interpretation. *Law and Contemporary Problems* 57 (1&2): 3–38.

————. 1995. Politics and the courts: A positive theory of judicial doctrine and the rule of law. *Southern California Law Review* 68: 1631–83.

Melamed, Dennis. 1988. EPA's right-to-know net widens. *Chemical Week*, 17 February, 16.

Mendeloff, John M. 1988. *The dilemma of toxic substance regulation: How overregulation causes underregulation at OSHA.* Cambridge, Mass.: MIT Press.

Mennis, Jeremy. 2002. Using geographic information systems to create and analyze statistical surfaces of population and risk for environmental justice analysis. *Social Science Quarterly* 83 (1): 281–97.

Merrill, Mike. 2002. The Internet helps us keep an eye on the industries next door. *Buffalo News*, 20 January, H1.

Milgrom, Paul, and John Roberts. 1986. Relying on the information of interested parties. *RAND Journal of Economics* 17 (1): 18–32.

Millimet, Daniel M., and Daniel Slottje. 1999. *The distribution of pollution in the United States: An environmental Gini approach.* Departmental Working Paper No. 9902, Department of Economics, Southern Methodist University.

Minnesota Emergency Response Commission. 1992. *Toxic release inventory data quality assurance project.* St. Paul, Minn.: Minnesota Emergency Response Commission.

Moe, Terry M. 1985. Control and feedback in economic regulation: The case of the NLRB. *American Political Science Review* 79 (4): 1094–116.

————. 1987. An assessment of the positive theory of "Congressional Dominance." *Legislative Studies Quarterly* 12 (4): 475–520.

Montgomery, Christian. 1986. Reducing the risk of chemical accidents: The post-Bhopal era. *Environmental Law Reporter* 16 (October): 10300.

Moriarty, Jo-Ann. 1986. Dateline: Washington. *States News Service*, 16 October.

Muoghalu, Michael I., H. David Robinson, and John L. Glascock. 1990. Hazardous waste lawsuits, stockholder returns, and deterrence. *Southern Economic Journal* 57 (2): 357–70.

Nakamura, Robert T., and Thomas W. Church. 2003. *Taming regulation: Superfund and the challenge of regulatory reform.* Washington, D.C.: Brookings Institution Press.

Natan, Thomas E., Jr., and Catherine G. Miller. 1998. Are Toxics Release Inventory reductions real? *Environmental Science and Technology* 32 (15): 368A–74A.

National Academy of Sciences. 1990. *Tracking toxic substances at industrial facilities; engineering mass materials accounting.* Washington, D.C.: National Academy Press.

Natural Resources Defense Council (NRDC). 1989. *A who's who of American toxic air polluters.* New York: Natural Resources Defense Council, June.

Naysnerski, Wendy, and Tom Tietenberg. 1992. Private enforcement of environmental law. *Land Economics* 68 (1): 28–48.

Nelson, Douglas, and Eugene Silberberg. 1987. Ideology and legislator shirking. *Economic Inquiry* (January): 15–25.

Nelson, Kim T. 2002. Letter in reply to John D. Graham, Ph.D., 28 March. Available from http://www.whitehouse.gov/omb/inforeg/.

Nieman Foundation. 2002. Environment reporting. *Nieman Reports, The Nieman Foundation for Journalism at Harvard University*, 56 (4).

Noble, Kenneth B. 1986. Union Carbide faces fine of $1.4 million on safety violations. *New York Times*, 2 April, A1.

Nye, Joseph S. 2004. *Soft power: The means to success in world politics.* New York: Public Affairs.

Oberholzer-Gee, Felix, and Miki Mitsunari. 2003. *Information regulation: Do the victims of externalities pay attention?* Working paper. Weidenbaum Center, Washington University.

OECD. 2003. *Voluntary approaches for environmental policy: Effectiveness, efficiency and usage in policy mixes.* Paris: Organisation for Economic Co-operation and Development.

———. 2004. *Environment and distributional issues: Analysis, evidence and policy implications.* Paris: Organisation for Economic Co-operation and Development.

Office of Management and Budget. 2001. *Making sense of regulation: 2001 report to Congress on the costs and benefits of regulations and unfunded mandates on state, local, and tribal entities.* Washington, D.C.

———. 2002. Office of Information and Regulatory Affairs. *OIRA Q & A's.* Available from http://www.whitehouse.gov/omb/inforeg/qa_2-25-02.pdf.

———. 2004. *Terms of clearance for TRI form.* OMB No.: 2070-0093, 01/09/2004. Washington, D.C.

O'Leary, Rosemary, Robert F. Durant, Daniel J. Fiorino, and Paul S. Weiland. 1999. *Managing for the environment: Understanding the legal, organizational, and policy challenges.* San Francisco: Jossey-Bass.

Olewiler, Nancy, and Kelli Dawson. 1998. *Analysis of national pollutant release inventory data on toxic emissions by industry.* Working Paper 97–16, Technical Committee on Business Taxation.

Olson, Mancur. 1971. *The logic of collective action: Public goods and the theory of groups.* Rev. ed. New York: Schocken Books.

Olson, Mary. 1996. Substitution in regulatory agencies: FDA enforcement alternatives. *Journal of Law, Economics and Organization* 12 (2): 376–407.

OMB Watch. 2001. *A citizen's platform for our environmental right-to-know.* Washington, D.C.: OMB Watch.

Orum, Paul. 1994. Reports using Toxics Release Inventory (TRI) data. *Working Notes on Community Right-to-Know*, July–August, 1–11.

――――. 1996. Toxics Release Inventory status reports. *Newsletter of the Science and Environmental Health Network, Right-to-Know,* 1 (5), July.

O'Toole, Laurence J., Jr., Chilik Yu, James Cooley, Gail Cowie, Susan Crow, Terry DeMeo, and Stephanie Herbert. 1997. Reducing toxic chemical releases and transfers: Explaining outcomes for a voluntary program. *Policy Studies Journal* 25 (1): 11–26.

Palmer, Karen, Wallace E. Oates, and Paul R. Portney. 1995. Tightening environmental standards: The benefit-cost or the no-cost paradigm? *The Journal of Economic Perspectives* 9 (4): 119–32.

Pargal, Sheoli, and David Wheeler. 1996. Informal regulation of industrial pollution in developing countries: Evidence from Indonesia. *Journal of Political Economy* 104 (6): 1314–27.

Pashigian, B. Peter. 1985. Environmental regulation: Whose self-interests are being protected? *Economic Inquiry* (October): 551–84.

Patten, Dennis M. 2002. Media exposure, public policy pressure, and environmental disclosure: An examination of the impact of TRI data availability. *Accounting Forum,* 26 (2): 152–71.

Pedersen, William F. 2001. Regulation and information disclosure: Parallel universes and beyond. *Harvard Environmental Law Review* 25: 151.

Peters, B. Guy, and Brian W. Hogwood. 1985. In search of the issue-attention cycle. *Journal of Politics* 47: 238–53.

Pfaff, Alexander S. P., and Chris William Sanchirico. 1999. *Environmental self-auditing: Setting the proper incentives for discovery and correction of environmental harm.* Working Paper no. 4, Columbia University School of International and Public Affairs.

Pianin, Eric. 2001. Bush scrambles to block Clinton rush orders. *Washington Post,* 21 January, A18.

Poje, Gerald V., and Daniel M. Horowitz. 1990. *Phantom reductions: Tracking toxic trends.* Washington, D.C.: National Wildlife Federation.

Porter, Michael E., and Claas van der Linde. 1995. Toward a new conception of the environment-competitiveness relationship. *The Journal of Economic Perspectives* 9 (4): 97–118.

Portney, Paul R. 1981. Housing prices, health effects, and valuing reductions in risk of death. *Journal of Environmental Economics and Management* 8: 72–78.

Posner, Eric A. 2001. Controlling agencies with cost-benefit analysis: A positive political theory perspective. *University of Chicago Law Review* 68 (4): 1137–200.

Potoski, Matthew, and Aseem Prakash. Forthcoming. Green clubs and voluntary governance: ISO 14001 and firm's regulatory compliance. *American Journal of Political Science.*

Prewitt, Edward, and Richard H. K. Vietor. 1992. *Allied Signal: Managing the hazardous waste liability risk.* Boston: Harvard Business School.

PR Newswire. 1988. Monsanto announces program to reduce air emissions by 90%. *PR Newswire,* 30 June.

――――. 1990. EPA proposes $566,000 in fines under right-to-know law. *PR Newswire,* 22 October.

_____. 1991a. Four New Jersey firms agree to improve facility operation to benefit environment; EPA collects $45,000 for right-to-know violations. *PR Newswire*, 24 January.

_____. 1991b. Six New York firms agree to improve facility operations to benefit the environment: EPA also collects $34,275 in penalties. *PR Newswire*, 24 January.

_____. 1991c. Dow announces commitment to exceed EPA request for emission reductions. *PR Newswire*, 1 May.

_____. 1991d. DuPont subscribes to EPA emissions program. *PR Newswire*, 1 May.

_____. 1991e. Kodak will participate in new EPA initiative to cut target emissions in half. *PR Newswire*, 10 May.

_____. 1991f. 200 companies participate in voluntary national pollution control program – eight companies located in Connecticut. *PR Newswire*, 19 July.

_____. 1996. U.S. EPA White House wants more public access to toxics data; newest stats. *PR Newswire*, 26 June.

_____. 1999. Court removes phosphoric acid from TRI list. *PR Newswire*, 20 April.

_____. 2000a. EPA: Clinton/Gore administration announces first-ever data on toxic emissions from seven major industrial sectors. *PR Newswire*, 11 May.

_____. 2000b. New Sierra Club ad clears up Bush's Texas record asks people to urge Bush to clean up Texas' air and water. *PR Newswire*, 11 August.

Radian Corporation. 1991. *Site visit program to assess 1988 Toxic Release Inventory data quality*. Report to EPA Office of Toxic Substances, Herndon, Va.

Rasinski, Mike. 2000. EPA fines Kirkhill for skipping report. *Rubber & Plastics News*, 19 June, 3.

Real Estate/Environmental Liability News. 2000. EPA guidance for metal mining industry subject to judicial review. *Real Estate/Environmental Liability News*, 11 (19).

Reitze, Arnold W., Jr., and Steven D. Schell. 1999. Self-monitoring and self-reporting of routine air pollution releases. *Columbia Journal of Environmental Law* 24 (1): 63–135.

Richardson, Lilliard E., Jr., and Michael C. Munger. 1990. Shirking, representation, and Congressional behavior: Voting on the 1983 amendments to the Social Security Act. *Public Choice* 67: 11–33.

Riker, William H. 1986. *The art of political manipulation*. New Haven: Yale University Press.

Ringleb, Al H., and Steven N. Wiggins. 1990. Liability and large-scale, long-term hazards. *Journal of Political Economy* 98: 547–95.

Ringquist, Evan J. 1997. Equity and the distribution of environmental risk: The case of TRI facilities. *Social Science Quarterly* 78 (4): 811–29.

Robins, G. Stephen. 1997. President G. S. Robins and Company speaking on behalf of the National Association of Chemical Distributors. U.S. House of Representatives, Committee on Small Business, 17 April.

Roe, David. 2000. *Starting blocks for environmental information policy*. Working paper, Environmental Defense Fund.

———. 2002. Ready or not: The coming wave of toxic chemicals. *Ecology Law Quarterly* 29: 623.

Romer, Thomas, and James M. Snyder Jr. 1994. An empirical investigation of the dynamics of PAC contributions. *American Journal of Political Science* 38 (3): 745–69.

Rosegrant, Susan. 1992. *The Toxics Release Inventory: Sharing government information with the public.* Harvard University, Kennedy School of Government Case Program.

Rothenberg, Lawrence S. 2002. *Environmental choices: Policy responses to green demands.* Washington, D.C.: CQ Press.

Rotman, David. 1989. A new EPA database details the sources of toxics releases. *Chemical Week*, 28 June, 8.

Rotman, David, with Ronald Begley. 1991. Producers report progress on 1990 Toxics Release. *Chemical Week*, 24 June, 15.

Roy, Manik. 1992. EDF defends TUR. *Chemical Week*, 11 November, 6.

Russell, Clifford S., Winston Harrington, and William J. Vaughan. 1986. *Enforcing pollution control laws.* Washington, D.C.: Resources for the Future.

Ryan, William, and Richard Schrader. 1991. *An ounce of toxic pollution prevention: Rating states' toxics use reduction laws.* Boston, Mass.: National Environmental Law Center, January.

Sadd, James L., Manuel Pastor Jr., J. Thomas Boer, and Lori D. Snyder. 1999. "Every breath you take...": The demographics of toxic air releases in southern California. *Economic Development Quarterly* 13 (2): 107–23.

Samuelsohn, Darren. 2002. Budget: Bush proposes $300 million in EPA cuts. *Greenwire Environment and Energy Daily*, 10 (9).

———. 2003. Inhofe's chemical security bill passes out of EPW panel. *Environment and Energy Daily*, 10 (9).

———. 2004. Leavitt's first Hill testimony as EPA chief to focus on $7.76 billion budget. *Environment and Energy Daily* 10 (9), 1 March.

Sand, Peter H. 2004. *Cross-cutting theme: Information disclosure.* Revised version of paper presented to 2nd Transatlantic Dialogue on "The reality of precaution: Comparing approaches to risk and regulation," June 15, 2002, Warrenton, Va.

Santos, Susan L., Vincent T. Covello, and David B. McCallum. 1996. Industry response to SARA Title III: Pollution prevention, risk reduction, and risk communication. *Risk Analysis* 16 (1): 57–66.

Sarokin, David, and Jay Schulkin. 1991. Environmentalism and the right-to-know: Expanding the practice of democracy. *Ecological Economics* 4: 175–89.

Schierow, Linda-Jo. 1997. *Toxics Release Inventory: Do communities have a right to know more?* CRS Report for Congress, at National Library for the Environment.

Schneider, Keith. 1991. Toxic pollution shows drop in '89. *New York Times*, 17 May, A32.

Scholz, John T. 1991. Cooperative regulatory enforcement and the politics of administrative effectiveness. *American Political Science Review* 85: 115–36.

Scholz, John T., and Wayne B. Gray. 1990. OSHA enforcement and workplace injuries: A behavioral approach to risk assessment. *Journal of Risk and Uncertainty* 3: 283–305.

Scholz, John T., and Neil Pinney. 1995. Duty, fear, and tax compliance: The heuristic basis of citizenship behavior. *American Journal of Political Science* 39: 490–512.

Scholz, John T., Jim Twombly, and Barbara Headrick. 1991. Street-level political controls over federal bureaucracy. *American Political Science Review* 85: 829–50.

Scholz, John T., and Feng Heng Wei. 1986. Regulatory enforcement in a federalist system. *American Political Science Review* 80: 1249–70.

Schroeder, Christopher H. 1998. The political origins of modern environmental law: Rational choice versus Republican moment- explanations for environmental laws, 1969–73. *Duke Environmental Law & Policy Forum* 9 (1): 29–60.

———. 2000. Third way environmentalism. *University of Kansas Law Review* 48: 801.

Schroeder, Christopher H., and Robert L. Glicksman. 2001. Chevron, State Farm, and the EPA in the Courts of Appeals during the 1990s. *Environmental Law Reporter* 31: 10371, April.

Scorse, Jason. 2004. *Do pollution rankings affect facility emissions? Evidence from the U.S. Toxic Release Inventory.* Working paper, Department of Agricultural and Resource Economics, University of California, Berkeley.

Segerson, Kathleen, and Thomas J. Miceli. 1998. Voluntary environmental agreements: Good or bad news for environmental protection? *Journal of Environmental Economics and Management* 36: 109–30.

Settina, Nita, and Paul Orum. 1991. *Making the difference, Part II: More uses of right-to-know in the fight against toxics.* Washington, D.C.: Center for Policy Alternatives and Working Group on Community Right-to-Know, October.

Shapiro, Marc D. 2003. *Equity and information: Information regulation, environmental justice, and risks from toxic chemicals.* Forthcoming in *Journal of Policy Analysis and Management.*

Sheiman, Deborah A. 1991. *The right to know more.* Washington, D.C.: Natural Resources Defense Council, May.

Sheiman, Deborah A., David D. Doniger, and Lisa L. Dator. 1990. *A who's who of American ozone depleters: A guide to 3,014 factories emitting three ozone-depleting chemicals.* Washington, D.C.: Natural Resources Defense Council, January.

Shepsle, Kenneth A. 1992. Congress is a "they," not an "it": Legislative intent as oxymoron. *International Review of Law and Economics* 12: 239–56.

Sheridan, John H. 1992. Deadline dilemma: Tardy EPA forms put industry in a bind. *Industry Week*, 15 June, 69.

Shogren, Elizabeth. 2001. EPA to keep Clinton rule to curb lead. *Los Angeles Times*, 18 April, A1.

Shover, Neal, Donald A. Clelland, and John Lynxwiler. 1986. *Enforcement or negotiation: Constructing a regulatory bureaucracy.* Albany, N.Y.: State University of New York Press.

Sigler, Jay A., and Joseph E. Murphy. 1988. *Interactive corporate compliance: An alternative regulatory compulsion.* New York: Quorum Books.

Sigman, Hilary. 1996a. The effect of hazardous waste taxes on waste generation and disposal. *Journal of Environmental Economics and Management* 30 (2): 199–217.

―――. 1996b. Cross-media pollution: Responses to restrictions on chlorinated solvent releases. *Land Economics* 72 (3): 298–312.

―――. 2003. *Letting states do the dirty work: State responsibility for federal environmental regulation.* NBER Working Paper 9451, National Bureau of Economic Research, January.

Sissell, Kara. 1998. Industry outreach enters the information age. *Chemical Week*, 21 October, 51.

―――. 1999. Court upholds petition to delist phosphoric acid; Toxics Release Inventory. *Chemical Week*, 28 April, 16.

Skrzycki, Cindy. 1995. With more toxic waste on the line, an industry erupts. *Washington Post*, 8 September, B01.

―――. 2003. EPA seeks middle ground in toxic-release reporting. *Washington Post*, 18 November, E01.

Smith, Matthew J. 1993. "Thou shalt not violate!": Emergency Planning and Community Right-to-Know Act authorizes citizen suits for wholly past violations – Atlantic States Legal Foundation, Inc. v. Whiting Roll-Up Door Manufacturing Corp. *Pace Environmental Law Review*, 10 (Spring): 1051.

Snyder, Lori D. 2003. *Are management-based regulations effective?: Evidence from state pollution prevention programs.* Regulatory Policy Program, John F. Kennedy School of Government, Harvard University.

―――. 2004. *The effect of reporting thresholds on the validity of TRI data as measures of environmental performance: Evidence from Massachusetts.* John F. Kennedy School of Government, Harvard University.

Spence, David B. 1997. Administrative law and agency policy making: Rethinking the positive theory of political control. *Yale Journal on Regulation* 14: 407–50.

―――. 2001. The shadow of the rational polluter: Rethinking the role of rational actor models in environmental law. *California Law Review* 89: 917–98.

―――. 2002. A public choice progressivism, continued. *Cornell Law Review* 87 (2): 397.

Spence David B., and Frank Cross. 2000. A public choice case for the administrative state. *Georgetown Law Journal* 89: 97.

Spiller, Pablo T. 1996. A positive political theory of regulatory instruments: Contracts, administrative law or regulatory specificity. *Southern California Law Review* 69: 477–515.

Stafford, Sarah L. 2002. The effect of punishment on firm compliance with hazardous waste regulations. *Journal of Environmental Economics and Management* 44 (2): 290–308.

―――. 2003. Assessing the effectiveness of state regulation and enforcement of hazardous waste. *Journal of Regulatory Economics* 23 (1): 27–41.

Standard and Poor's Corporation. 1989. *Daily stock price record, 1989.* Palo Alto, Calif.: Investment Statistics Laboratory.

Stavins, Robert, ed. 2000. *Economics of the environment: Selected readings.* New York: W. W. Norton and Company.

Stephan, Mark. 2002. Environmental information disclosure programs: They work, but why? *Social Science Quarterly* 83: 190–205.

Steyer, Robert. 1991. Monsanto cuts air pollution by 58 [%], emissions cutbacks fail to keep pace overseas. *St. Louis Post-Dispatch*, 12 July, 1B.

Stiglitz, Joseph. 2000. The contributions of the economics of information to twentieth century economics. *The Quarterly Journal of Economics* 115 (4): 1441–78.

Stoll, Richard G. 2001. Court forces EPA to comply with due process standards. *Hazardous Waste Litigation Reporter* 21 (4): 10.

Stratmann, Thomas. 1991. What do campaign contributions buy? Deciphering causal effects of money and votes. *Southern Economic Journal* 57 (3): 606–20.

———. 1992. The effects of logrolling on congressional voting. *American Economic Review* 82 (5): 1162–76.

Streitwieser, Mary L. 1994. *Cross sectional variation in toxic waste releases from the U.S. chemical industry*. Center for Economic Studies, U.S. Bureau of the Census, August.

Stringer, Judy. 1995. EPA faults industry on TRI limit, reform. *Chemical Week*, 18 October, 14.

Sunstein, Cass R. 1999. Informational regulation and informational standing: *Akins* and beyond. *University of Pennsylvania Law Review* 147: 613–75.

———. 2000. Cognition and cost-benefit analysis. *Journal of Legal Studies* 29: 1059.

———. 2003. Preferences and rational choice: New perspectives and legal implications beyond the precautionary principle. *University of Pennsylvania Law Review* 151: 1003.

———. 2004. Lives, life-years, and willingness to pay. *Columbia Law Review* 104: 205.

Szasz, Andrew, and Michael Meuser. 2000. Unintended, inexorable: The production of environmental inequalities in Santa Clara. *American Behavioral Scientist* 43 (4): 602–32.

Templet, Paul H. 1995. The positive relationship between jobs, environment and the economy: An empirical analysis. *Spectrum* (Spring): 37–49.

Terry, Jeffrey C., and Bruce Yandle. 1997. EPA's Toxic Release Inventory: Stimulus and response. *Managerial and Decision Economics* 18: 433–41.

Thomas, John K., Joseph S. Kodamanchaly, and Patricia M. Harveson. 1998. Toxic chemical wastes and the coincidence of carcinogenic mortality in Texas. *Society and Natural Resources* 11 (8): 845–66.

Tietenberg, Tom. 1998. Disclosure strategies for pollution control. *Environmental and Resource Economics* 11 (3–4): 587–602.

———. 1999. Disclosure strategies for pollution control. In *The market and the environment: The effectiveness of market-based policy instruments for environmental reform*, edited by Thomas Sterner. Northampton, Mass.: Edward Elgar.

———. 2002. *Environmental and Natural Resource Economics*. Boston: Addison-Wesley

Tietenberg, Tom, and David Wheeler. 1998. *Empowering the community: Information strategies for pollution control*. Frontiers of Environmental Economics Conference, Airlie House, Virginia, October 23–25.

Toxic Chemicals Litigation Reporter. 1996. DC District Court upholds EPA rulemaking for toxic chemicals. *Toxic Chemicals Litigation Reporter*, 4 June, 23212.

———. 1997. DC Circuit strikes addition of bronopol, DMP to Toxic Inventory. *Toxic Chemicals Litigation Reporter*, 11 August, 25304.

———. 1999. EPA can require toxic emission reports from electric plants, says DC Circuit. *Toxic Chemicals Litigation Reporter*, 16 (23): 6, 3 May.

Tyson, Rae, and Julie Morris. 1989. Exclusive report: The chemicals next door, a first peek "behind the plant gates." *USA Today*, 31 July.

USA Today. 1989. Where you can get data. *USA Today*, 2 August, 7A.

———. 1991. Reilly gives his views on other environmental issues. *USA Today*, 3 April, 13A.

U.S. Census Bureau. 1995. *Statistical Abstract of the United States*. Washington, D.C.

U.S. Environmental Protection Agency. Office of Policy Analysis. 1987. *Unfinished business: A comparative assessment of environmental problems (overview report)*. Washington, D.C.

———. 1988. 40 CFR Part 372 Toxic chemical release reporting: Community right-to-know, final rule. Washington, D.C.

———. Office of Pesticides and Toxic Substances. 1989. *The Toxics-Release Inventory: A national perspective*. Washington, D.C.

———. Office of Pesticides and Toxic Substances. 1990. *Toxics in the community: National and local perspectives (the 1988 Toxics Release Inventory National Report)*. Washington, D.C.

———. Office of Pesticides and Toxic Substances. 1991. *Toxics in the community: National and local perspectives (the 1989 Toxics Release Inventory National Report)*. Washington, D.C.

———. 1992a. *Environmental equity: Reducing risk for all communities. Volume 1: Workgroup report to the Administrator*. Washington, D.C.

———. 1992b. *Environmental equity: Reducing risk for all communities. Volume 2: Supporting document*. Washington, D.C.

———. Office of Pollution Prevention and Toxics. 1993a. *1991 Toxics Release Inventory*. Washington, D.C.

———. Office of Pollution Prevention and Toxics. 1993b. *Toxics Release Inventory (TRI) Data Use Conference*. Washington, D.C.

———. Office of Pollution Prevention and Toxics. 1994. *1992 Toxics Release Inventory public data release*. Washington, D.C.

———. Office of Pollution Prevention and Toxics. 1995. *1993 Toxics Release Inventory public data release*. Washington, D.C.

———. Office of Pollution Prevention and Toxics. 1996. *1994 Toxics Release Inventory public data release*. Washington, D.C.

———. Office of Pollution Prevention and Toxics. 1998a. *1994 and 1995 Toxic Release Inventory data quality report*. Washington, D.C.

———. Office of Pollution Prevention and Toxics. 1998b. *1996 Toxic Release Inventory data quality report*. Washington, D.C.

———. 1998c. *Final guidance for incorporating environmental justice concerns in EPA's NEPA compliance analyses*. Washington, D.C.

———. Office of Pollution Prevention and Toxics. 1999a. *33/50 Program: The final record*. Washington, D.C.

———. Office of Enforcement and Compliance Assurance. 1999b. *Sector Facility Indexing Project evaluation*. Washington, D.C.

———. Office of Regulatory Enforcement, Office of Enforcement and Compliance Assurance. 1999c. *Enforcement Response Policy for Sections 304, 311 and 312 of the Emergency Planning and Community Right-to-Know Act and Section 103 of the Comprehensive Environmental Response, Compensation and Liability Act*. Washington, D.C.

———. Office of Enforcement and Compliance Assurance. 2000a. *Annual report on enforcement and compliance assurance accomplishments in 1999*. Washington, D.C.

———. Office of Environmental Justice. 2000b. *Environmental justice in the permitting process: A report from the National Environmental Justice Advisory Council's Public Meeting on Environmental Permitting*. Arlington, Va, November 30–December 2.

———. Office of Compliance Monitoring of the Office of Prevention, Pesticides and Toxic Substances. 2001. *Enforcement response policy for Section 313 of the Emergency Planning Community Right-to-Know Act (1986) and Section 6607 of the Pollution Prevention Act (1990) [Amended]*. Washington, D.C.

———. Office of Environmental Information. 2002a. *2000 Toxics Release Inventory public data release*. Washington, D.C.

———. Office of Enforcement and Compliance Assurance. 2002b. *The National Nitrate Compliance Initiative*. Washington, D.C.

———. 2003a. *Phase II Stakeholder Dialogue – burden reduction options*. Working paper. Washington, D.C.

———. Office of Environmental Information, Office of Information Analysis and Access. 2003b. *How are the Toxics Release Inventory data used? – government, business, academic and citizen uses*. Washington, D.C.

———. Office of Environmental Information. 2003c. *2001 Toxics Release Inventory public data release report*. Washington, D.C.

———. Office of Environmental Information. 2003d. 2001 *Toxics Release Inventory state fact sheets*. Washington, D.C.

———. 2004a. Toxics Release Inventory Program Division. *Summary of Ad Hoc Metals Coalition vs Christie Todd Whitman and US EPA*. Washington, D.C.

———. 2004b. *Summary of the EPA's Budget, FY 2005*. Available from http://www.epa.gov/ocfopage/budget/budget.htm.

———. Office of Inspector General. 2004c. *EPA should take steps to improve industrial reporting to the Toxics Release Inventory system*. Report no. 2004-p-00004. Washington, D.C.

———. 2004d. International PRTR, April 12. Washington, D.C.

———. Office of Inspector General. 2004e. *EPA needs to consistently implement the intent of the Executive Order on Environmental Justice*. Report no. 2004-p-00007. Washington, D.C.

———. Office of Policy, Economics, and Innovation. 2004f. *International experiences with economic incentives for protecting the environment*. EPA-236-R-04-001, November. Washington, D.C.

————. 2004g. *2002 Toxics Release Inventory (TRI) public data release report.* EPA-260-R-04-003, June. Washington, D.C.

U.S. General Accounting Office. 1991. *Toxic Chemicals: EPA's Toxics Release Inventory is useful, but can be improved.* Washington, D.C.

————. 2000. *Regulatory Flexibility Act: Implementation in EPA program offices and proposed lead rule.* Washington, D.C.

————. 2002. *Information on the Environmental Protection Agency's actual and proposed funding for enforcement activities for fiscal years 2001–2003.* Washington, D.C.

U.S. House of Representatives. 1985a. Committee on Public Works and Transportation. Subcommittee on Water Resources. *Reauthorization of Superfund: Hearings before the Subcommittee on Water Resources of the Committee on Public Works and Transportation.* 99th Cong., 1st sess. 26, 27, and 28 March; 1 May; 24 and 25 July.

————. 1985b. Committee on Energy and Commerce. Subcommittee on Health and the Environment. *Hearings on H.R. 2576: A bill to control toxic releases into the air, and for other purposes.* 99th Cong., 1st sess. 11 and 19 June.

————. 1985c. Committee on Energy and Commerce. Subcommittee on Commerce, Transportation, and Tourism. *Hearing on Superfund provisions: Community right-to-know and cleanup of abandoned hazardous wastesites located at federal facilities.* 99th Cong., 1st sess. 20 December.

————. 1989a. Committee on Energy and Commerce. Subcommittee on Transportation and Hazardous Materials. *Hazardous Waste Reduction Act: Hearing on H.R. 1457, a bill to improve Environmental Protection Agency data collection and dissemination regarding reduction of toxic chemical emissions across all media.* 101st Cong., 1st sess. 25 May.

————. 1989b. Committee on Government Operations. Subcommittee on Government Information, Justice, and Agriculture. *Hearings on Federal Information Dissemination Policies and Practices.* 101st Cong., 1st sess. 18 April; 23 May; 11 July.

————. 1990. Committee on Energy and Commerce. Subcommittee on Transportation and Hazardous Materials. *Hearing on pollution prevention and hazardous waste reduction.* 101st Cong., 2nd sess. 31 May.

————. 1999a. Committee on Commerce. Subcommittee on Health and Environment and Subcommittee on Oversight and Investigations. *Joint Hearing on internet posting of chemical "worst case" scenarios: A roadmap for terrorists.* 106th Cong., 1st sess. 10 February.

————. 1999b. Committee on Commerce. Subcommittee on Health and Environment. *The Chemical Safety Information and Site Security Act of 1999.* 106th Cong., 1st sess. 19 and 26 May.

————. 2001. Committee on Small Business. Subcommittee on Regulatory Reform and Oversight. *EPA rulemaking: Do bad analyses lead to irrational rules?* 107th Cong., 1st sess. 8 November.

————. 2002. Committee on Small Business. Subcommittee on Regulatory Reform and Oversight. *The TRI lead rule: Costs, compliance and science.* 107th Cong., 2nd sess. 13 June.

———. 2003. Committee on Resources. Subcommittee on Energy and Mineral Resources. *Toxic Release Inventory impact on federal minerals and energy.* 108th Cong. 25 September.

U.S. PIRG. 1998. *Trust us, don't track us: An investigation of the chemical industry's Responsible Care Program.* United States Public Interest Research Group. Available from http://www.pirg.org/reports/enviro/track98/index.htm.

U.S. Senate. 1985. Committee on Small Business. *Community right-to-know legislation and its regulatory and paperwork impact on small business.* 99th Cong., 1st sess. 18 June.

———. 1988. Committee on Environment and Public Works. Subcommittee on Superfund and Environmental Oversight. *Oversight of the Emergency Planning and Community Right To Know Act of 1986: Hearing on the implementation of the Emergency Planning and Community Right To Know Act of 1986 (Title III of Public Law 99–499, the Superfund Amendments and Reauthorization Act of 1986).* 100th Cong., 2d sess. 26 May.

———. 1989. Committee on Environment and Public Works. Subcommittee on Superfund, Ocean, and Water Protection. *Hearing on oversight of right-to-know pollution data.* 101st Cong., 1st sess. 10 May.

———. 1990a. Committee on Environment and Public Works. *A legislative history of the Superfund Amendments and Reauthorization Act of 1986, vol. 1.* Report prepared by The Environment and Natural Resources Policy Division of the Congressional Research Service of the Library of Congress. 101st Cong., 2d sess. Committee Print.

———. 1990b. Committee on Environment and Public Works. *A legislative history of the Superfund Amendments and Reauthorization Act of 1986, vol. 2* Report prepared by The Environment and Natural Resources Policy Division of the Congressional Research Service of the Library of Congress. 101st Cong., 2d sess. Committee Print.

———. 1990c. Committee on Environment and Public Works. *A legislative history of the Superfund Amendments and Reauthorization Act of 1986, vol. 5.* Report prepared by The Environment and Natural Resources Policy Division of the Congressional Research Service of the Library of Congress. 101st Cong., 2d sess. Committee Print.

———. 1990d. Committee on Environment and Public Works. *A legislative history of the Superfund Amendments and Reauthorization Act of 1986, vol. 6.* Report prepared by The Environment and Natural Resources Policy Division of the Congressional Research Service of the Library of Congress. 101st Cong., 2d sess. Committee Print.

———. 1991. Committee on Environment and Public Works. Subcommittee on Superfund, Ocean, and Water Protection. *Hearing on expansion of the right to know program.* 102nd Cong., 1st sess. 27 June.

Utility Environment Report. 1992. House panel rejects bid to require utilities to report toxic releases. *Utility Environment Report,* 3 April, 1.

VanDoren, Peter M. 1990. Can we learn the causes of Congressional decisions from roll-call data? *Legislative Studies Quarterly* (August): 311–40.

———. 1999. *Chemicals, cancer, and choices: Risk reduction through markets.* Washington, D.C.: Cato Institute.

Van Houtven, George L., and Maureen L. Cropper. 1993. *When is a life too costly to save? The evidence from environmental regulations.* Washington, D.C.: Resources for the Future.

Videras, Julio. 2003. *Political values and the supply of environmental regulation: The case of state voluntary disclosure laws.* Working paper, Hamilton College, May 14.

Videras, Julio, and Anna Alberini. 2000. The appeal of voluntary environmental programs: Which firms participate and why? *Contemporary Economic Policy* 18 (4): 449–61.

Vidovic, Martina, and Neha Khanna. 2003a. *Can voluntary pollution prevention programs fulfill their promises? Evidence from the EPA's 33/50 program.* Economics Department Working Paper WP0315, Binghamton University.

———. 2003b. *Reducing toxic releases through voluntary efforts: Incentives for participation in the 33/50 program and implications for the distribution of pollution.* Paper prepared for Western Economic Association International 78th Annual Conference, Denver, Colo., July 11–15.

Villamana, Molly. 2003. Toxics: Mining industry exempt from reporting releases of some; metals. *Greenwire,* 4 June.

Viscusi, W. Kip. 1986. The impact of occupational safety and health regulations, 1973–1983. *RAND Journal of Economics* 17 (4): 567–80.

Viscusi, W. Kip, and James T. Hamilton. 1999. Are risk regulators rational? Evidence from hazardous waste cleanup decisions. *American Economic Review* 89 (4): 1010–27.

Vise, David A. 2000. EPA to limit web information; officials fear terrorists use of data on toxic waste, chemicals. *Washington Post,* 27 April, A25.

Volokh, Alexander, Kenneth Green, and Lynn Scarlett. 1998. *Environmental information: The Toxics Release Inventory, stakeholder participation, and the right-to-know.* Reason Public Policy Institute, policy study no. 246, December 1998.

Waterman, Richard W., and B. Dan Wood. 1993. Policy monitoring and policy analysis. *Journal of Policy Analysis and Management* 12: 685–99.

Weingast, Barry R., and Mark J. Moran. 1983. Bureaucratic discretion or congressional control? Regulatory policymaking by the Federal Trade Commission. *Journal of Political Economy* 91 (5): 765–800.

Weisman, Jonathan, and Mimi Hall. 2001. Arsenic fouls review of new rules, uproar marks turning point for president. *USA Today,* 20 April, 8A.

Weiss, Janet A. 2002. Public information. In *The tools of government: A guide to the new governance,* edited by Lester M. Salamon. New York: Oxford University Press.

Weisskopf, Michael. 1992. Minorities' pollution risk debated: Some activists link exposure to racism. *Washington Post,* 16 January, A25.

Wiener, Jonathan Baert. 1999. Global environmental regulation: Instrument choice in legal context. *Yale Law Journal* 108: 677.

Williamson, Oliver E. 1979. Transaction-cost economics: the governance of contractual relations. *Journal of Law and Economics* 22: 233–61.

Winter, Soren C., and Peter J. May. 2001. Motivation for compliance with environmental regulations. *Journal of Policy Analysis and Management* 20 (4): 675–98.

Wold, Amy. 2003. DEQ reports drop in toxic matter in state's air, soil, water in 2001. *Advocate (Baton Rouge)*, 21 May.

Wolf, Sidney M. 1996. Fear and loathing about the public right to know: The surprising success of the Emergency Planning and Community Right-to-Know. *Journal of Land Use and Environmental Law* 11 (2): 217–324.

Wolverton, Ann. 2002. *Does race matter? An examination of a polluting plant's location decision.* National Center for Environmental Economics, USEPA. Washington, D.C.

Wood, B. Dan. 1988. Principals, bureaucrats, and responsiveness in clean air enforcements. *American Political Science Review* 82: 213–34.

_____. 1992. Modeling federal implementation as a system: The clean air case. *American Journal of Political Science* 36: 40–67.

Wood, B. Dan., and Richard W. Waterman. 1991. The dynamics of political control of the bureaucracy. *American Political Science Review* 85: 801–28.

_____. 1994. *Bureaucratic dynamics: The role of bureaucracy in a democracy.* Boulder, Colo.: Westview Press.

Working Group on Community Right-to-Know. 1991. *The "recycling" loophole in the Toxics-Release Inventory: Out of site, out of mind.* March.

_____. 1994. Reports using Toxics Release Inventory (TRI) data. *Working Notes on Community Right-to-Know*, August.

_____. 1995. Know nothing movement emerges. *Working Notes on Community Right-to-Know*, September–October.

Wu, JunJie, and Bruce A. Babcock. 1999. The relative efficiency of voluntary vs. mandatory environmental regulations. *Journal of Environmental Economics and Management* 38: 158–75.

Yandle, Bruce. 1989. *The political limits on environmental regulation: Tracking the unicorn.* New York: Quorum Books.

Yu, Chilik, Laurence J. O'Toole Jr., James Cooley, Gail Cowie, Susan Crow, and Stephanie Herbert. 1998. Policy instruments for reducing toxic releases: The effectiveness of state information and enforcement actions. *Evaluation Review* 22 (5): 571–89.

Zimmerman, Rae. 1994. Issues of classification in environmental equity: How we manage is how we measure. *Fordham Urban Law Journal* 21: 633–69.

Index

election-of-friends strategy, 23, 260
feedstock tax, 23
influence-legislators strategy, 23, 32, 260
legislator ideology and, 32
by PAC type (table), 43
petroleum and chemical firms, 23
targeted taxes and, 26
Tobit models of (table), 31
See also congressional voting
paper industries, 68–69, 150, 173, 273
paperwork burdens, 35, 119, 128
Paperwork Reduction Act, 50, 117, 120, 132, 141
partisanship politics, 149, 154
PBTs. *See* persistent bioaccumulative toxic chemicals
penalty policies, 195. *See also* supplemental environmental project
Pence, Rep. Mike, 155, 156
Pennsylvania, Butler County, 226
persistent bioaccumulative toxic (PBTs) chemicals, 132, 140–141, 157, 162–163, 202, 204
personal injury suits. *See also* Frank amendment
pesticides, 99
petitions
to add chemicals, 132
deckstacking and, 36
to delist chemicals, 121–127
environmental damage criteria, 36
by governors. *See* governors
health criteria for, 36
petroleum bulk stations – wholesale, 138–140
Phantom Reductions: Tracking the Toxic Trends (1990), 221
Phelps Dodge, 76
phosphoric acid, 169
plant behaviors
internally generated information and legal exposure, 39
responses to frequent regulator visits, 100
responses to regular inspections, 100
trade secrets. *See* trade secrets
voluntary pollution audits, 39
plant decisions
residents and, 8
plant management
certification of TRI form by. *See* certification requirement

plant ownership information, 47
plant shutdowns, 173
plant technical representatives, 48
plastics pipe industry, 2
Poisons in Our Neighborhoods: Toxic Pollution in the United States (Citizens Fund 1990), 77
Poje, Gerald, 56, 221
police patrol policies, 254–255, 274
policy instrument selection theories, 20–21
policy instruments
political support for, 13
political entrepreneurs, 252
Pollutant Release and Transfer Registers (PRTRs), 9
polluter costs concentrated
resident benefits dsipersed, 18
pollution and ownership, 62
pollution cases, 62
pollution control
economies of scale in, 61
pollution control and abatement expenditures, 58–59
pollution control instrument selection, 11
pollution data. *See also* trade secrets
pollution liability litigation, 58–59
pollution pathways, 59, 66–68
by type of company ownership (table), 63
pollution prevention, 5, 145–146, 149
Pollution Prevention Act of 1990 (PPA), 2, 77, 117, 143, 145–146
production index of, 146
Pollution Prevention . . . or Public Relations?, 173
pollution reduction modeling
air carcinogen toxicity and, 112
air carcinogens, 108, 110
air emission quantities, 103
chemicals in, 103
collective action, 105, 107, 112, 113
command and control regulation, 112
community characteristics and, 100–101
dispersion, regional air/wind data and, 103
environmental program support, 105
EPA regions, 102
home values, 105
human health risks, 107
information provisioning effects, 106–107
measures of reduction, 101
pathway level analysis, 101–102